JUVENILE DELINQUENCY

JUVENILE DELINQUENCY

Donald J. Shoemaker

ROWMAN & LITTLEFIELD PUBLISHERS, INC.
Lanham • Boulder • New York • Toronto • Plymouth, UK

ROWMAN & LITTLEFIELD PUBLISHERS, INC.

Published in the United States of America
by Rowman & Littlefield Publishers, Inc.
A wholly owned subsidary of The Rowman & Littlefield Publishing Group, Inc.
4501 Forbes Boulevard, Suite 200, Lanham, Maryland 20706
www.rowmanlittlefield.com

Estover Road, Plymouth PL6 7PY, United Kingdom

British Library Cataloguing in Publication Information Available

Library of Congress Cataloging-in-Publication Data

Shoemaker, Donald J.
    Juvenile delinquency / Donald Shoemaker.
        p. cm.
    Includes bibliographical references and index.
    ISBN-13: 978-0-7425-4706-3 (hardcover : alk. paper)
    ISBN-10: 0-7425-4706-X (hardcover : alk. paper)
    ISBN-13: 978-0-7425-4707-0 (pbk. : alk. paper)
    ISBN-10: 0-7425-4707-8 (pbk. : alk. paper)
    eISBN-13: 978-0-7425-6580-7
    eISBN-10: 0-7425-6580-7
    1. Juvenile delinquency. I. Title.
HV9069.S524 2009
364.36—dc22   2008019281

Printed in the United States of America

⊚™ The paper used in this publication meets the minimum requirements of
American National Standard for Information Sciences—Permanence of Paper for
Printed Library Materials, ANSI/NISO Z39.48-1992.

To Beth, Neslie, Nestor, Nesvie-Ann, and Neileen

CONTENTS

ACKNOWLEDGMENTS

ALL BOOKS require attention to detail, commitment, and a lot of support and encouragement from family, friends, and colleagues. I would like to thank many people for their support and assistance in the preparation of this book. Of course, over the many times I have taught the subject of this book and discussed its topics, I have received invaluable comments and suggestions from students and colleagues that eventually made their way into the contents of the book, in one way or another. In addition, I want to express my gratitude for the support of Alan McClare, executive editor at Rowman & Littlefield, for his encouragement and continued support in the initial and continuing phases of this book's completion. I would also like to express my appreciation to the staff at Rowman & Littlefield for their professional and encouraging support in the production stages of the book. Also, I would like to thank my research assistants, Danielle McDonald and Laura Boutwell, for their invaluable contributions to the collection and display of essential components of the book, especially with tables and figures. Danielle has also contributed most of the information in chapter 11, Female Delinquency, as well as supplementary materials for the book. Most of all, I want to acknowledge the continued love and support of my family for their understanding and patience during the past four years as the demands of research, writing, and meeting production schedules often took much of my free time from them. Thank you, Elizabeth, Neslie, Nestor, Nesvie-Ann, and Neileen, for your love and encouragement through the entire process of completing this work.

INTRODUCTION

EVERY DAY we read or hear of crimes committed by juveniles. From all of the press we see and hear concerning juvenile crime, one might wonder if all of our nation's youth are into crime—whether or not they have been arrested. We read about school shootings and crimes committed by youths who are then tried in adult courts. In fact, it is not appropriate to think our youth are going to pot, so to speak. While it is true that many young people are using and/or selling drugs and committing serious crimes, most are basically law-abiding kids who are sometimes enticed into committing law violations but who will mature out of illegalities before they reach 18.

However, there are cases of juveniles committing serious crimes. In many of these situations, the case is waived, or transferred, to the adult criminal justice system. One of the more recent and celebrated cases of juveniles committing "adult" crimes is that of Lee Boyd Malvo, who was convicted of first-degree murder in a Virginia court in December 2003 and sentenced to life in prison without parole in March 2004 (Roanoke Times 2004). Malvo was 17 years old when he committed the crimes for which he was convicted. The crimes included murder and attempted murder and were committed in several states, as well as in Washington, D.C. In situations such as this, that is, when crimes are committed in more than one state and/or in federal areas, the decision of whom will prosecute often rests with where the defendant was caught. In the case of Lee Boyd Malvo, the arrest was made in

Maryland, but the federal authorities had the priority of prosecution because some of the crimes occurred in federal areas. Ultimately, the authorities in the other jurisdictions allowed Virginia prosecutors to prosecute Malvo and his accomplice, John Allen Muhammed, an adult who was convicted and given the death penalty for his roles in the crimes. One reason this decision was made was because Virginia allows the death penalty for juveniles (16–17 years of age), while other jurisdictions, such as Maryland and the federal government, do not.

The case of Lee Boyd Malvo is only one of many situations in which young people are charged with serious crimes and transferred to the adult criminal justice system. For example, there is the case of a 14-year-old in Miami accused of murdering another classmate in the school restroom, an attack which involved more than 40 stab wounds to the victim. The 14-year-old in this case is charged with first-degree murder and is being processed in the adult court system in Florida. He faces a possible sentence of life in prison if convicted. However, most juvenile offender cases are processed within the juvenile justice system. The juvenile justice system is thought to have begun in the United States, when the first juvenile delinquency law was established in Chicago in 1899. In the next chapter, we will see that there were many developments concerning the handling of youthful offenders before the passage of the Illinois delinquency law. However, the formal system of court procedures we now see for youthful offenders was created at that time.

Before the laws concerning delinquency were passed, societies tended to deal with youthful offenders as if they were adults. Wiley Sanders (1970) provides considerable evidence that youngsters were very much involved in criminal activity even though there were no delinquency laws specifically designed to handle the crimes of young people. Sometimes preteen children were sentenced to death for their criminal behavior. In one case, for example, a nine-year-old girl was sentenced to death by a jury in 18th-century London for stealing (p. 34). Today, offenders tried in juvenile court in the United States cannot be subjected to the death penalty, no matter what offense they have committed.

The development of laws and courts to handle juvenile offenders and those who have violated rules and procedures occurred over hundreds of years. Many of these developments occurred as a result of social changes, such as industrialization and urbanization. Others were the result of technological changes that developed over hundreds of years. Neil Postman (1982), for example, contends that the concept of "childhood" in Western society began to emerge after the development of the printing press in the

15th century. The historical development of the contemporary juvenile justice system will be discussed in the next chapter.

Definition of Juvenile Delinquency

From the preceding discussion, it might seem as if juvenile delinquency included only serious criminal activity. While delinquency does include crimes, it also includes a variety of other behaviors that are not criminal. Examples of such offenses include running away from home, truancy from school, and disobeying the lawful commands of parents or legal guardians. These acts are often referred to as *status offenses*, which refers to the condition of the person's age at the time the offense was committed (Teitelbaum 2002). Usually the maximum age for juvenile court jurisdiction is 18, but, as we shall see later in this book, some states have lowered the age limit. This upper age limit is usually referred to as the age of majority—the age at which a person is considered an adult, at least in terms of voting privileges and civil status in society. Accordingly, anyone under the age of majority technically can be charged with a status offense because of the legal status of childhood. The term *childhood* is used here because young people under the age of majority, whatever that age may be in a given state, are legally considered minors, or children. Thus, *childhood* is not meant in any demeaning or pejorative sense, but, rather, it is used as a legal term, one commonly found within the records of the juvenile justice system.

Actually, the legal meaning of *child* or *childhood* is not consistent with developmental views of growth and maturity, biologically, psychologically, or socially. Policy makers and lawmakers seem to consider a bifurcated system of development—either child or adult—with shades of development often lost in legal parlance (Scott 2002). For example, the legal definition of adulthood usually starts at age 18, but why was this age selected as opposed to, say, age 16 (which is the maximum age of juvenile court jurisdiction in some states, such as Georgia)? In addition, selecting any particular age for the definition of adulthood presumes that all juveniles mature at the same rate, which few, if any, would accept. Yet that is what is assumed by selecting an age limit for childhood or adulthood and organizing laws and policies around that age limit.

The upper age limit of delinquency jurisdiction is not an idle, academic exercise. The age limit has specific implications for the venue of jurisdiction. All states contain provisions in their delinquency laws for the *transfer*, or *waiver*, of juveniles from juvenile court jurisdiction to adult court jurisdiction.

Usually, transfers or waivers of cases to the adult criminal justice system are petitioned to the juvenile court judge presiding over the case, but in many states, recent changes in the laws have allowed prosecutors to make this decision, and in some cases, there are laws known as presumptive laws, which mean that cases meeting certain conditions are automatically assigned to the adult court.

Typically, two conditions must be met before a case can be waived from juvenile court to adult court jurisdiction: the age of the offender at the time the alleged offense was committed and the nature of the offense. Most states define the "age of transfer" as well below the age of majority. For example, in Virginia, the age at which a case may be waived is 14. Some states do not specify a lower age limit. In these situations, it is presumed the age of transfer must be at least seven, to conform to common law tradition. In the past few years, the national trend has been toward a decrease in the age of transfer, which is reflective of a "get tough" attitude on juvenile offenders that has been evident in many states since the 1980s.

In addition to the age of the offender, the type of offense is also a consideration in the decision to waive a case from juvenile to adult court. In general, the offense must be a serious felony, such as murder or forcible rape, although the crime does not necessarily have to be a capital offense, that is, one that may be punished by the death penalty. Despite the "get tough" orientation that seems to have fueled interest in waivers, the number of transfer cases across the nation seems to have peaked in 1994, although a few states, such as Florida, still use the process more often than other states (Young and Gainsborough 2000:5). The conditions and specifications concerning waiver will be discussed again in chapter 13, when the contemporary American juvenile justice system is described in more detail.

Besides upper-age definitions and parameters, the definition of delinquency is framed by lower-age parameters. According to common law tradition, which most states follow, a person under the age of *seven* cannot be charged with a crime. However, the juvenile justice system is able to handle cases of very young children accused of criminal activities because it is not bound by the strict guidelines of the adult system. Thus, if a child under the age of seven were charged with aggravated assault, the likely response would be assignment to the juvenile system, where he or she might be put into some kind of treatment program, along with increased supervision at home, or perhaps removal from the home altogether.

When all of these conditions and parameters are considered, the definition of delinquency involves the following: (1) any offense that is considered a crime in the legal codes of a community or state and that is committed by a juvenile under the age of majority (usually 18); and (2) any offense that is in the juvenile codes and is committed by one under the age of majority.

Under this specific definition of delinquency, during the past few years the number of juvenile arrests has decreased. In 2004, for example, there were 2.2 million juveniles arrested for one of 29 offenses listed in the FBI's Uniform Crime Reports. However, the number of juveniles arrested for serious violent and property crimes, such as burglary, larceny, homicide, robbery, and aggravated assault, peaked in the early to mid-1990s and has been dropping steadily since (Snyder 2006). In 2006, there were 1.626 million arrests of juveniles (see chapter 3). Despite the decline in juvenile arrests, the "problem" of delinquency remains an important issue in society. Teenage drinking and smoking behaviors, juvenile gangs, bullying, and many other forms of juvenile crime and delinquency are still prevalent and of concern in society.

Besides these two important criteria for defining delinquency, juvenile courts also frequently handle cases of juveniles that fall outside illegal behavior, cases such as child abuse or child abandonment, and these cases were included in the original juvenile court law passed in Illinois in 1899 (Tanenhaus 2002). In these situations, children may be given to foster-home care, or they may be ordered into treatment. Thus, while youths in these kinds of situations may not be technically delinquent, their cases are found within the arenas of juvenile courts. One of the consequences of such reactions to abuse or neglect is that the child victim is now part of the juvenile justice system and may be under court supervision even though he or she has not committed an offense.

Brief History of "Delinquency"

Earlier, it was mentioned that, throughout most of the world, juvenile offending has been recognized for hundreds of years. It would be logical to wonder exactly how juvenile offenders in historical times were handled. For one thing, as indicated earlier, there were no formalized juvenile courts until 1899. There were, however, juvenile institutions and other procedures for handling juveniles that were created in America during the 19th century (Rosenheim et al. 2002). Historical accounts of the development of the juvenile justice systems throughout the world indicate that before separate institutions and proceedings for juveniles were established in the 19th century, juveniles were often treated as if they were small adults. Even children of royal families in England, for example, were exposed to adult situations, such as sexual activity among adults, and were thought to be ready for adult roles in society if they were exposed to hardships and adult behaviors as youngsters.

In American society, and this may be the case throughout the world as well, citizens and leaders were concerned *for* children as much as they were concerned *with* children, or as Grossberg puts it, "a fear for children and a fear of children" (2002:3). This kind of tension between wanting to help juvenile offenders and wanting to punish them has always existed in society, it seems, and it still influences the structures and operations of juvenile courts and other parts of the juvenile justice system today (Shoemaker 1988).

In the 1800s, several events occurred that helped to shape the development of the juvenile justice system as we know it today. These events will be discussed in the next chapter. For the present, however, it is important to note that the first law that specifically identified delinquency was the result of a long series of efforts on the part of reformers and other "child savers" (Platt 1977). Many of these reformers were the wives and daughters of influential industrialists who became important philanthropists in their own right throughout the 19th century. Their continued vigilance and reformist efforts resulted in the eventual passage of the delinquency law in Chicago, followed soon after by a similar law in Colorado, and, ultimately, throughout the United States within the next 30 years.

Juvenile Delinquency Law in Illinois

The delinquency law passed in Illinois was named "An Act for the Treatment and Control of Dependent, Neglected and Delinquent Children" (Tanenhaus 2002:42). It is clear from the title of this act that not only were dependent and neglected children to be included within the jurisdiction of the juvenile court but also juvenile courts in Illinois were to be concerned with treatment as well as control, or punishment, of juvenile offenders or children considered in need of the court's attention.

A significant feature of this new law was the creation of a separate category of offending, reserved for youth only: the status offense, which was explained earlier. Before this legislation, laws permitted authorities (not parents) to punish children for things such as disobeying parents, and, in colonial times, governments, such as the Massachusetts Bay Colony, permitted the death penalty for any child over 16 who was "stubborn or rebellious"

(Teitelbaum 2002:160). However, the 1899 delinquency law in Illinois expanded this authority and created specific laws that focused on youth.

The practice of removing children from the homes of their parents or guardians and placing them into institutions or homes of strangers was justified through a legal doctrine known as *parens patriae*, which has been interpreted as "the king as father of the country." It was often used by royalty in England to justify removing children and other members of their families from their homes and property in the name of the king.

In America, *parens patriae* has been used by judges and other figures of authority to justify removing delinquent, wayward, homeless, and other youths thought to be trouble or be in trouble from their homes and placing them in institutions, foster homes, or whatever the "state" authorities deem as proper placements for these youths. However, the courts take a dim view of such practices, especially when children are removed from their homes and placed in institutions without due process, that is, usually without legal representation or parental consent and without specific legislation permitting this practice.

Plan of This Book

The purpose of this book is to present the reader with an overview of the important concepts related to delinquency, along with discussions of the historical roots of delinquency laws, the extent of delinquency and its sociological parameters, and important theoretical explanations of delinquency. In addition, this book provides detailed discussions of female delinquency, drug use and related behavior, and juvenile gangs. The concluding chapters present information on the juvenile justice system in contemporary terms, including separate discussions of the police, the courts, and institutions. Throughout these discussions, information on relevant treatment or prevention programs will be provided.

For the most part, the context of the information and discussions in this book will pertain to the United States. However, no system of juvenile justice stands alone. As indicated in succeeding chapters, the systems of juvenile justice in the United States and Great Britain share some common threads. Some current practices in juvenile justice in the United States, such as restorative justice, have conceptual traditions stemming from other societies, such as Australia and New Zealand, and from Native American traditions. In addition, in the modern world of global technologies, such as cell phones and the Internet, events that happen in one country are almost instantly communicated to people all over the world. Thus, knowledge concerning delinquency and societal responses to it are shared among societies throughout the world, and juvenile justice systems considered unique to one particular country are becoming less common. However, some readers may be interested in reading or studying broader, more global contexts of delinquency and juvenile justice. Examinations of juvenile offending and juvenile justice systems throughout the world may be found in anthologies, such as *International Handbook on Juvenile Justice* (Shoemaker 1996) and *Delinquency and Juvenile Justice in the Non-Western World* (Friday and Ren 2006).

In the end, of course, no text is able to provide all of the answers to questions that students may have. It is hoped, however, that the reader will have received some useful information from having read this book and will be more appreciative of the complexities and dynamics of the topic than before.

References

Friday, Paul C., and Xen Ren, eds.
    2006   Delinquency and Juvenile Justice in the Non-Western World. Monsey, NY: Criminal Justice Press.
Grossberg, Michael
    2002   Changing Conceptions of Child Welfare in the United States, 1820–1935. *In* A Century of Juvenile Justice. Margaret K. Rosenheim, Franklin E. Zimring, David S. Tanenhaus, and Bernardine Dohrn, eds. Pp. 23–41. Chicago: University of Chicago Press.
Platt, Anthony M.
    1977   The Child Savers: The Invention of Delinquency. 2nd edition, enlarged. Chicago: University of Chicago Press.
Postman, Neil
    1982   The Disappearance of Childhood. New York: Delacorte Press.
Roanoke Times
    2004   Malvo Gets Life Sentence for Role in Sniper Spree. Roanoke Times, March 11: 1-A.
Rosenheim, Margaret K., Franklin E. Zimring, David S. Tanenhaus, and Bernardine Dohrn, eds.
    2002   A Century of Juvenile Justice. Chicago: University of Chicago Press.
Sanders, Wiley B.
    1970   Juvenile Offenders for a Thousand Years: Selected Readings from Anglo-Saxon Times to 1900. Chapel Hill: University of North Carolina Press.

Scott, Elizabeth S.
    2002   The Legal Construction of Childhood. *In* A Century of Juvenile Justice. Margaret K. Rosenheim, Franklin E. Zimring, David S. Tanenhaus, and Bernardine Dohrn, eds. Pp. 113–142. Chicago: University of Chicago Press.

Shoemaker, Donald J.
    1988   The Duality of Juvenile Justice in the United States: History, Trends, and Prospects. Sociological Spectrum 8:1–17.

Shoemaker, Donald J., ed.
    1996   International Handbook on Juvenile Justice. Westport, CT: Greenwood Press.

Snyder, Howard N.
    2006   Juvenile Arrests 2004. Juvenile Justice Bulletin, December. Washington, DC: U.S. Department of Justice, Office of Justice Programs.

Tanenhaus, David S.
    2002   The Evolution of Juvenile Courts in the Early Twentieth Century: Beyond the Myth of the Immaculate Construction. *In* A Century of Juvenile Justice. Margaret K. Rosenheim, Franklin E. Zimring, David S. Tanenhaus, and Bernardine Dohrn, eds. Pp. 42–73. Chicago: University of Chicago Press.

Teitelbaum, Lee
    2002   Status Offenses and Status Offenders. *In* A Century of Juvenile Justice. Margaret K. Rosenheim, Franklin E. Zimring, David S. Tanenhaus, and Bernardine Dohrn, eds. Pp. 158–175. Chicago: University of Chicago Press.

Young, Malcolm C., and Jenni Gainsborough
    2000   Prosecuting Juveniles in Adult Court: An Assessment of Trends and Consequences. Washington, DC: The Sentencing Project.

THE HISTORY OF JUVENILE JUSTICE IN AMERICA

A S A LEGAL TERM, *juvenile delinquency* is a recent concept. The notion that children should be treated differently than adults is only a couple of hundred years old. Before the middle of the 18th century, young people were treated as if they were small versions of adults. As Robert Mennel suggests, the term *juvenile delinquency* was first seen during the 18th century (1973:xvii). Not until the end of the 19th century did the legal meaning of delinquency become established in Illinois.

These introductory comments do not assume that before the 18th or 19th centuries children were not committing criminal acts. As Wiley Sanders's informative book *Juvenile Offenders for a Thousand Years* (1970) clearly indicates, juveniles were substantially involved in criminal activity long before the word *delinquency* was used to describe it. Sanders traces the history of juvenile offending back to the seventh century, at least as far as European history is concerned. For example, English laws in the seventh and eighth centuries clearly identified criminal penalties for crimes committed by children as young as 10 or 11. As mentioned in chapter 1, English common law stipulated that youngsters as young as seven could be held accountable for their actions.

Some, such as Neil Postman, argue that age seven was selected as the age of criminal responsibility because during the Middle Ages, reading and written instruction were not available to the people. Thus, seven was the age "at which children have command of speech" (Postman 1982:13).

John Sutton (1988) presents interesting and persuasive data indicating that in the American colonies, deviant children were thought of as "stubborn." According to Sutton's analysis, the first stubborn-child law was passed in Massachusetts in 1646, and laws such as this one were heavily influenced by Puritan religious concepts (chapter 1). For one thing, Puritan values stressed the importance of the family and the requirement that children (usually those under age 16) follow the orders and commands of their parents. Thus, one of the provisions of the first stubborn-child law was that disobedient children could be put to death and that such a penalty came directly from the book of Deuteronomy in the Bible (pp. 10–11). One interesting facet of this law was that the parents who were disobeyed were not the ones to exact the death penalty themselves but, instead, were to bring the recalcitrant child directly to court officials, who would then carry out the death penalty (although it is not clear how this process was to be carried out and how long it might take to be accomplished). As a footnote to this law, although it is extremely harsh in its provisions, there are no records that confirm that the death penalty was ever used for disobedient, or stubborn, children in colonial times.

The indiscriminate treatment of juveniles was not reserved for the American colonies. As Philippe Aries (1962) indicates, youngsters in Europe during medieval times were subjected to adult humor in the forms of play and games and were dressed like small adults until the 17th century (chapters III, IV).

Dancing by children, for example, was not considered sinful in medieval times, and even members of royalty were involved in dances that were often provocative. According to Aries, for example, in some paintings of those times, "There is scarcely any difference between the children's dance and that of the adults" (p. 80). In fact, Aries contends that to medieval Europeans, sex and sexuality were considered neither important nor particularly exciting to prepubescent youngsters, so sexually suggestive behavior and game playing were not perceived as things that should be separated from children (p. 106). Playing with the private parts of children was widespread in society during the Middle Ages (Postman 1982:17).

Infants were often wrapped tightly in cloth, a practice known as swaddling, and were then dressed in the same manner as adults as soon as possible. As Aries puts it, "Nothing in medieval dress distinguished the child from the adult" (p. 50). But by the 17th century, paintings and writings clearly indicated that children were to be dressed differently from adults. This change in clothing style for youngsters is one clear sign that children were being viewed as different from adults, although, as observed earlier, young people in those days were still subject to adult penalties for criminal, or even merely disobedient, behavior.

By the 17th century, however, societal views, especially in Europe, were changing with respect to children. Now, instead of being viewed as miniature adults, so to speak, children were beginning to be seen as young innocents, and their moral and spiritual development became matters of concern and importance to adults and leaders. Off-color jokes and displays of sexual body parts were considered immoral and were to be avoided in European countries. Sexual modesty was becoming the norm for juveniles. Children were considered weak and in need of guidance and adult supervision.

Neil Postman suggests that childhood, as an age of innocence and lack of criminal responsibility, ended with the assumption of criminal responsibility at the age of seven. However, with the invention of the printing press, in the mid-15th century, the practice of teaching and instructing youth with the written word began to spread. Over time, one result of this new method of learning and communication was to extend the age of childhood beyond seven and into what is now known as adolescence (Postman 1982:20–64).

Several principles concerning children seemed to be emerging, and often these principles were enunciated by religious authorities. First, children were not to be left unattended but always to be under adult supervision. Second, children were not to be pampered or spoiled but were to be subjected to strong discipline (in what would seem to be a holdover from previous views of young people). Third, children were to be treated with modesty and not subjected to nudity and lewd behavior, including foul language, especially from adults. Fourth, proper language and dress and everyday manners were to be instilled in youth, and adults, especially parents, were to be continually treated with respect (Aries 1962:114–117).

Early in the 17th century, England and France passed what are now known as poor laws. Essentially, these laws governed the education of children from poor and destitute families, which became another means of controlling these populations (Aries 1962:303). As Aries states in reference to the scope and focus of these laws, "In this way it was hoped to make pious, serious workers out of what had been depraved adventurers" (p. 303). For example, the Elizabethan Poor Law in England, passed in 1601, provided that parents take care of their children and vice versa when parents became old, but it also established a welfare system that sought to take care of poor children, albeit at the expense of parental control (Grossberg 2002:6–7).

19th-Century Reform Efforts and Practices

While European authorities and leaders were changing their minds about what constituted proper behavior of and toward children, their ideas gradually changed attitudes toward juveniles in the American colonies and states. For example, some historians contend that English poor laws, along with other traditional English legal concepts, particularly the doctrine of *parens patriae*, were adopted almost wholly by the American colonies (Grossberg 2002:7). Thus, as mentioned in chapter 1, youth in early United States history were handled by laws and practices that came from England, including *parens patriae*, the legal policy that the state is the final authority in matters concerning children and youth.

Gradually, the notion that children were to be considered in need of nurturance and special care and supervision began to appear in Europe and in the newly established country of the United States. One specific illustration of this emerging concept was the establishment of a special "house of refuge" in New York City in 1825. Within the next three years, similar houses of refuge were established in Boston and Philadelphia. According to one social historian, these three houses of refuge dominated juvenile corrections and treatment for 25 years in the United States (Mennel 1973:3–4).

Houses of refuge were urban establishments, to be sure, and their purpose was to reclaim the lives of youngsters who were roaming the streets of metropolitan cities or who had been referred by the courts (note that these would not have been juvenile courts at that time). Interestingly, these institutions often did not accept convicted offenders, but rather those on the verge of falling into a life of crime because of their social circumstances. The youths who were sent to these facilities were typically not from middle-class or upper-class families. Rather, the residents of houses of refuge in the 19th century were most often the sons and daughters of the poor and the immigrant families who populated the urban landscape. The minority youths who populated these institutions were thus not migrants from rural areas but immigrants from other countries. Black youths, for example, were typically kept out of the first houses of refuge. As an example of the racial policies of early houses of refuge, in 1849 Philadelphia established a "House of Refuge for Colored Juvenile Delinquents" (Mennel 1973:17).

Houses of refuge were designed to prevent youth from becoming involved in criminal activity, or more likely, from becoming more criminal in their behavior. Many, if not most, of the youths placed in these facilities were not actually criminals but kids who were displaying what were thought to be signs of criminal development—signs such as idleness, vagrancy, and disruptive public behaviors. Thus, prevention became a key watchword for the administrators and supporters of these institutions.

Because so many of the policies and practices of houses of refuge were based on the notion of prevention, many of the youngsters sent there were not seen as threats to the community. In addition, because of *parens patriae*, many of the parents and guardians of these youth were not fully involved in their placements. It should be no surprise, therefore, to learn that significant challenges to the legality of some placements began to work their way though the court system by the middle of the 19th century.

One of the more far-reaching cases involving houses of refuge was *Ex Parte Crouse*, heard by the Pennsylvania Supreme Court in 1838. In this case, the father of Mary Ann Crouse, who was sent to the Philadelphia House of Refuge at the request of her mother, complained that his daughter was unfairly confined because she was committed without his consent. The Pennsylvania Supreme Court denied the father's petition on the grounds that the state has a right to remove children from the home, even over parental objections, because of *parens patriae* (Mennel 1973:14; Grossberg 2002:18*)*. The following quotation from the decision reflects not only this opinion but also some of the guiding philosophies and goals of houses of refuge:

> The object of the charity is reformation, by training its inmates to industry; by imbuing their minds with principles of morality and religion; by furnishing them with a means to make a living; and, above all, by separating them from the corrupting influence of improper associates. To this end, may not the natural parents, when unequal to the task of education, or unworthy of it, be superseded by the *parens patriae*, or common guardian of the community? (Mennel 1973:14)

According to this decision and others similar to it, "failed parents lost their rights" (Grossberg 2002:18) to raise their offspring as they saw fit. Rather, through the power of *parens patriae*, these "failed" parents were forced to give up their natural parental rights to authorities selected or appointed by, and representative of, the state.

These passages and examples indicate the power of court and other governmental authorities to control child rearing in the early 19th century United States. The examples are historical in nature, but they should not be considered historically dead, so to speak. *Parens patriae* is alive and well in modern society. Contemporary examples of the power of the state will be introduced in chapter 13, when the contemporary juvenile justice system is discussed in detail.

Houses of refuge were not the only institutions that were able to separate children and youth from their parents. In the 1840s and 1850s, children's aid societies and other philanthropic organizations began to develop and flourish in the country's major cities, such as Boston, Chicago, New York, and Philadelphia. Perhaps the most far-reaching of these organizations in terms of programs affecting juvenile welfare was the Children's Aid Society, formed in New York City in 1853 by Charles Loring Brace (Mennel 1973:32). While Brace was a social reformer who publicly displayed a philanthropic interest in the welfare of poor and homeless youth and professed a deep faith in Christianity and the potential salvation of mankind in general, he also demonstrated a disdainful attitude toward some children as well as toward the parents of poor and destitute children. For example, Brace is credited with first using the term *dangerous classes* to refer to street children in New York, children who were described as "vicious" and "reckless," among other terms, and who were thought to be outside the control of their parents. As Grossberg aptly puts it, Brace was as much in fear *of* these children as he was in fear *for* them (Grossberg 2002:19).

A concrete illustration of Brace's attitudes toward vagrant and ungoverned children and their parents was his idea of "orphan trains" and the general practice of "placing out," which he initiated in the mid-1850s through the auspices of the New York City Children's Aid Society (Mennel 1973:35; Grossberg 2002:19–21). Placing out was a concept that emphasized placing children from the streets of New York into families in the Midwest, often farm families, which were thought to be virtuous, intact, and religious, much like the families that caught Brace's attention when he visited Germany in the early 1850s. Over time, such placements became so common that "orphan trains" were used to ferry the children to these homes. Children were taken from the streets and placed on westward-bound trains, where they would be dropped off with deserving farm families along the way at the discretion of the organization. According to Mennel, this practice was "informal," which means it might have been done with the knowledge of the courts but not at the direction and order of judges. By what legal right placing out was practiced is uncertain, but probably again through the doctrine of *parens patriae* was such a practice permitted. That placing out was an important feature of handling juvenile offenders and others considered at risk, using a more contemporary term, is illustrated by the contention that between 1854 and 1879, Charles Loring Brace and his Children's Aid Society alone accounted for shipments of more than 150,000 youths from the streets of New York to rural families in the West (Grossberg 2002:20). Although Brace apparently felt that placing out would work only in the United States because of its vast farmlands, in the 1860s the practice was also introduced in some English colonies, such as Canada and Australia (Mennel 1973:40–41).

Long-Term Juvenile Institutions

By the end of the 19th century, Brace's practice of placing out disadvantaged youth to midwestern farms was becoming unacceptable. Among other challenges, leaders of the Catholic Church began putting pressure on Brace and other leaders of the Children's Aid Society to cease their practices of identifying children from city streets for assignment to orphan trains. Presumably, many of these children were from Catholic families, and such practices were undermining the strength of the Catholic religion in these families, again presumably because many of the "farm families" were headed by men and women influenced by Protestant religions (Grossberg 2002:21).

In the middle of the 1850s, juvenile justice reformers developed yet another approach to the management and, ideally, prevention of criminal and other offensive behaviors committed by juveniles. These new types of institutions were called by many names, but mostly, they were known as reformatories, training schools, or industrial schools.

The earliest reformatories were developed using private and public funds. Often, they were promoted by private philanthropists and supported with public money. For example, in the early 1850s, a group of businessmen in Portland, Maine, bought a large farm and house to give to the state so that it could be turned into a reformatory for young offenders (Mennel 1973:50).

The first reformatory was established in Massachusetts in 1846 at a facility named the Lyman School for Boys. The first public female reformatory was established in 1855, also in Massachusetts. This first female institution also introduced the *cottage system*, which soon became a popular model for juvenile reformatories in the United States. The cottage system is still evident today, although it is now only one of several types of juvenile institutional designs and models. The cottage system is based on the notion that institutions can assume the form and function of a family. Cottage systems usually consist of residential buildings housing around 30 youths. There may be three or four cottages on the grounds of an institution. Ideally, each cottage is supervised by a set of cottage "parents," again, ideally a husband-and-wife team, who live in the same facility with the youths. The residential components of the cottage are typically separated by what may be called a "day room," or a central gathering place for the inmates, the supervisors, other institutional workers, such as counselors and teachers, and visitors. In practice, however, cottages may be headed by single adults, especially during holidays and vacation times or when there is a temporary shortage of full-time parents to supervise the youth.

The cottage system was a reflection of correctional thinking in the middle of the 19th century, thinking that placed the strength of the family at the center of troubled youths' lives. It was assumed by many that by reinserting a strong family presence in the lives of these youngsters, their attitudes and habits may be turned from criminal pursuits to conventional thinking and behaviors. In those days, little, if any, evaluations of programs and practices were conducted, so no one really knows whether this system worked to reduce what today we would call delinquent behavior, criminal or otherwise. Even today, we do not know how truly effective this system may be in terms of changing delinquents' attitudes and/or behavior. It should be remembered that cottage "parents" are supervisors and often counselors to the juveniles with whom they live, but they are not their parents, so any kinds of bonds or levels of affection established by these adults and the youth they supervise are, by definition, artificial. More discussion about the role of cottage parents will be presented in chapter 15, when contemporary institutions are discussed.

Despite the lack of evidence concerning the effectiveness of these new models of juvenile corrections, the popularity of reformatories seemed to grow throughout the rest of the 19th century. Census accounts of institutional populations did not begin until 1880. However, Commissioner of Education reports indicated that in 1868, there were 30 facilities with 7,463 residents, but by the late 1870s, there were 51 reformatories, 23 of which were operated by states, 12 by local governments, 12 privately run, and three operated by both state and local governments (Cahalan 1986:108; Mennel 1973:49). By 1880, the Office of Education reported 68 institutions with 11,921 inmates, while the census indicated 53 institutions with 11,468 inmates. According to the census, by 1890, the number of institutions increased to 58, and the number of inmates grew to 14,486. Comparable figures for 1904 were 93 institutions and 23,034 residents (Cahalan 1986:104, 108). Historical accounts indicate that by 1890, almost all states outside the South had at least one juvenile reformatory plus at least one reformatory for juvenile females (Mennel 1973:49), but by 1904, even most southern states had established juvenile institutions.

According to the figures mentioned above, the average number of inmates in these early juvenile reformatories was from about 175 to around 250. However, these statistical head counts do not differentiate among types of facilities. Some of the earlier juvenile institutions, not based on the cottage system model, were truly imposing places, with high, granite walls and fortresslike features (Barnes and Teeters 1959:424–433). Although most administrators felt their institutions were family-style facilities (Mennel 1973:52), only cottage or "family" systems seemed designed to recreate the family model within the institution. But, as indicated earlier, even the cottage system can be questioned as to how closely it approximates a "family" within the walls of a reformatory.

While juvenile reformatories handled all kinds of juvenile offenders, John Sutton (1988:92–102) makes the case that lawmakers in the 19th century definitely intended juvenile institutions to handle incorrigible youth, that is, juveniles who were considered "beyond control." For example, all but three New England states expanded their incorrigible laws after institutions were built or at the same time as reformatories were opened.

Often the architectural structure of an institution indicates its intended purpose. For example, if a facility is built with strong walls and plenty of secure locks, a secure facility, then it can be assumed that the intended purpose of such a place is to prevent inmates from leaving. In addition, if these facilities have large populations, it can be assumed that individualized attention is not a primary focus. From the physical descriptions of the earlier juvenile reformatories, it can be assumed that their intended purpose was not to rehabilitate but, rather, to maintain custody and control among the inmates. Historical accounts and biographies, however, suggest that administrators of juvenile reformatories felt they were "saving" their charges from a life of crime and destitution. The feeling seemed to be that the workers at these places could somehow turn around the attitudes and lives of the young inmates who were sent there, not only by separating the youngsters from the criminogenic environments from which they came, that is, the urban streets, but also by employing a family-like environment within the institutions, even if these situations were not natural but bureaucratic in nature.

Since these reformatories were large institutions, they had to be run on strict schedules, similar to the operations of their forerunners, the houses of refuge. Inmates were guided by a rigid schedule of events from rising to rest and were subject to constant supervision during waking hours. Such bureaucratic procedures often diminish individual attention and treatment in favor of adherence to rigid rules and policies. Rule violations were often met with swift and sometimes severe punishments. Even more enlightened administrators, such as Zebulon Brockway, the first warden of the Elmira, New York, Reformatory in the 1870s eventually resorted to physical punishment, including beatings with nailed boards, to control the inmates (Barnes and Teeters 1959:426–431).

Nonetheless, almost all reformatories and juvenile institutions established in the 19th century, including houses of refuge, were thought to have treatment and educational functions, despite their imposing structures and the presence of rigid schedules and sometimes harsh discipline and punishment given to their inmates. Some argue that one reason the Crouse case was decided on the grounds of *parens patriae* was because the Philadelphia House of Refuge was considered a school rather than a prison (Sutton 1988:95).

It should be remembered that throughout this time, the legal category of juvenile delinquent had not been established and recognized throughout the country. No juvenile courts had been created, and what we now call status offenses were just being developed. During the Civil War, juvenile institutions were receiving more youth, partly as a result of so many adult males being sent off to war, so several institutions released their older inmates to make room for new ones (Mennel 1973:57–59). Despite this influx of youngsters into juvenile reformatories and houses of refuge, however, major reforms in matters pertaining to juveniles seemed to be put on hold during the Civil War.

Late 19th-Century Developments

After the Civil War, events regarding juvenile justice reform continued to occur. Settlement houses in large cities had been established long before the Civil War, but now many of the supporters and leaders of these establishments began to approach reforms in the handling of juveniles with more urgency. For example, Hull House was established in 1889 on Chicago's Near West Side as a place for poor and immigrant children and their families to establish social and economic ties to the community as well as to become exposed to the teachings of Protestant Christianity (Addams 1910). Its founder, Jane Addams, and its earliest officers, such as Louise Bowen, helped create many welfare programs aimed at combating illiteracy and poverty among immigrant youth (Addams 1910; Platt 1977:83–98).

These reform efforts at Hull House and similar settlements throughout large urban areas were important efforts for juvenile development and juvenile justice reform. However, post–Civil War events seemed to focus the attention and energy of many others toward significant and lasting juvenile justice reform. For example, in 1869, Massachusetts formally introduced probation into its court system for juveniles (Tanenhaus 2002:46–47). Even before 1869, courts in Massachusetts were using probation as an element in handling juvenile offenders. After all, probation started in the 1840s in Boston through the efforts of a shoemaker named John Augustus (Mennel 1973:43).

In 1870, however, the Illinois Supreme Court issued a ruling that would have lasting effects on juvenile justice and the reform of then-current juvenile justice practices for decades to come. The case is *People ex rel. O'Connell v. Turner* or simply *O'Connell v. Turner*. It involved a boy of 14, Daniel O'Connell, who had been placed in the Chicago Reform School for vagrancy. His father offered a writ of *habeus corpus*, a legal demand to know why one has been imprisoned. O'Connell had been sent to the reform school for noncriminal reasons. "Simple misfortune" was the term often used in those days, a term that covered a multitude of noncriminal offenses, including perceived lack of parental supervision, homelessness, and a general lack of adult guidance. Parental rights for these youths were minimal. Some, perhaps like Daniel, were spirited away by police or other authorities and sent to the reform school without parental permission or sometimes, it can be assumed, without parental knowledge. Youngsters were kept in this "school" until they were 21 years old or had become "good boys." Parents were not allowed to visit their children without the consent of the school's authorities, again under the doctrine of *parens patriae* (Dohrn 2002:299–300; Mennel 1973:125).

Upon hearing the petition of O'Connell's father, the Illinois Supreme Court decided that Daniel's confinement for vagrancy or misfortune was unconstitutional and that youngsters charged with noncriminal offenses should not be imprisoned without due process. This decision set aside the earlier Pennsylvania Supreme Court ruling in *Crouse* and generally sealed the doom of many existing institutions and the procedures and policies that placed children in their care. Essentially, the court ruled that institutions were not schools and that thus its charges were subject more to legal rights than to the practices of social correction in the name of educational pursuits. Other court decisions ruled in favor of the state's power to confine juveniles without criminal charges and without due process in the name of *parens patriae*, such as *Ex parte Ah Peen* in California, in 1876. For the most part, however, the die had been cast, and the ability of local and/or state authorities to throw juveniles into reform schools or other institutions for noncriminal charges and without due process was coming to an end. Largely because of the *O'Connell* decision, the Chicago Reform School was later closed, and the state of Illinois was essentially out of the reform school business by 1890 (Dohrn 2002:299–300; Mennel 1972; 1973:125–128).

Some refer to these post–Civil War programs and policies as the "child-saving movement" and those who supported them as "child savers" (Platt 1977). Principally, these reforms were spearheaded by numerous philanthropic women, almost all of whom were connected to positions of wealth and influence in the cities and states where they lived. Included among these influential "child savers" were Julia Lathrop and Lucy Flowers, who were close friends as well as collaborators on many child-saving projects (Platt 1977:chapter 4; Tanenhaus 2002:42–50). Platt and others suggest that the motives of these child savers may have been less philanthropic than the title indicates. Platt, for example, charges that, among other things, the child savers of the 19th century were more interested in "the inculcation of middle-class values and lower-class skills" (1977:176) than they were in promoting the social welfare of disadvantaged children. In addition, as already observed, the policies and programs of the child savers, particularly within institutions, were often supported by physical punishment and force.

This radical view on the motives of the 19th-century child savers is echoed by a study of the early juvenile justice system in Memphis, Tennessee (Shelden and Osborne 1989). In Memphis, for example, most of the promoters of the fledging juvenile court movement and of training schools and other juvenile institutions in the county and throughout the state "were among the most wealthy and prominent people in Memphis" (p. 762). In addition, most of the young people confined to these institutions were charged with "status offenses and very minor offenses, which were class based" (p. 762). It is also clear that juvenile institutions were heavily used to accommodate these new offenders. The Tennessee Industrial School, for example, opened in 1888 with 74 inmates. In 1902, the institution received 615 juveniles (p. 762).

Not all accounts of the child-saving movement criticized the upper-middle class for the promotion of its class interests. A study of the development of the juvenile justice system in Wilmington, Delaware, for example, concluded that ulterior motives were not prominent in the creation of the juvenile court (Salerno 1991). Salerno concludes that the child savers in Wilmington were motivated by altruistic reasons, fueled by a long history of private organizational support for poor and needy children and their families in that city and state. Even the primary juvenile institution in Delaware, the Home for Friendless and Destitute Children, was created in 1864 primarily, according to Salerno, to offset the effects of the Civil War on families and children.

Most social commentators suggest that a combination of several socioeconomic factors contributed to the development of the juvenile justice system in the 19th century. In particular, three conditions are often identified: *industrialization, urbanization,* and *immigration* (Feld 1999:24–28). As the country industrialized, its system of work shifted from agricultural products to more mechanized and manufacturing jobs, which, in turn, led to greater population movements to the cities. This population shift was augmented by immigration movements, again, most often into the larger cities of the country. All of theses factors were thought to have also contributed to the breakdown of the supervision and control that families, particularly parents, had on children. Thus, it is no accident that most social reformers of that day looked to the breakdown of the family and the criminogenic characteristics of the large city as major contributors to delinquency or juvenile offending (Salerno 1991). Of course, these conditions were present in the early part of the 19th century, but they seemed to be even more pronounced in the aftermath of the Civil War and well into the rest of that century.

Given these social conditions, it is not surprising that some commentators would feel that social reformers, such as the child savers, were interested in protecting their way of life, which to many of them had become the idealized lifestyle to which all should aspire. It is equally possible, however, that some, perhaps most, of these child savers were interested in protecting the health and welfare of children who were not in school or were left wandering the streets while their parents were at work or out of the home (Grossberg 2002). As with most such debates, the truth probably lies somewhere between the extremes of these arguments.

The First Delinquency Law and the Establishment of the Juvenile Court

Despite the true motives of the child savers, events from 1870 to 1900 seemed to be moving more in the direction of separate procedures for handling juvenile offenders. In addition, one of the goals of the child savers was to create a separate set of laws governing youthful offenders.

Since the O'Connell decision was rendered in Illinois, it is not surprising that while child savers were working in different parts of the country, many of them came from that state, particularly from Chicago (Platt 1977:chapters 4 and 5).

An instrumental organization that led the way to new legislation and the first juvenile court was the aforementioned Hull House. In particular, the efforts of Lucy Flower and Julia Lathrop are often mentioned in connection with Hull House's activities in this area. For example, one of the residents of Hull House toward the end of the 19th century was John Dewey, one of the country's leaders in the field of education at that time. Through the efforts of Dewey, Lathrop, and others, the value of educating children, delinquent or not, became a primary concern of child savers and the new institutions and policies they were advocating (Grossberg 2002; Tanenhaus 2002; Dohrn 2002).

Eventually, the efforts of the child savers resulted in the creation of the first delinquency law and its corresponding juvenile court on July 1, 1899, in Cook County, Illinois. This first delinquency law, known as "An Act for the Treatment and Control of Dependent, Neglected, and Delinquent Children" (Tanenhaus 2002:42), established the age of 16 as the jurisdictional age of the juvenile court, but that age was later raised to 17 for boys and 18 for girls (Dohrn 2002:271). This meant that youths under these ages were referred to the juvenile court for handling. It should be noted that Denver, Colorado, also had a functioning juvenile court at this time, led by the efforts of Judge Ben Lindsey, but there was not a specific law establishing it as a separate juvenile court until after the passage of the juvenile delinquency law in Illinois (Dohrn 2002:272–273). It is interesting to note, however, that this new law did not allow jury trials for juveniles whose cases were heard in juvenile court settings.

The popularity of this law is reflected in the fact that by 1925, all but two states, Maine and Wyoming, had some kind of delinquency law, and juvenile courts were present in all cities of 100,000 people or more (Tanenhaus 2002:45). The very title of this new law in Illinois indicates that the scope of its jurisdiction was to extend beyond delinquency to include neglect and dependent cases. Furthermore, the jurisdiction of this court, and virtually all of those founded on its example, included what we now term status offenses. While Illinois and Colorado recognized truancy as a "delinquent" act before 1899, this new law and its imitators clearly extended the stretch of these supervisory concerns beyond the doors of schools and into families, as well as the streets, by defining incorrigibility, recalcitrance, running away, and similar acts as delinquent, including the sexual activity of young females (Dohrn 2002:272; Teitelbaum 2002), a jurisdiction that seems to be what the Illinois Supreme Court was advocating in the O'Connell case decades earlier.

The educational function of the newly formed juvenile court was clearly identified in Chicago by the creation of "parental schools" used in connection with the court. A parental school was a place where truants were sent to be educated. The parental school established for males in Chicago in 1902 was created by the Parental School Law, which "provided that any truant officer, any agent of the Board of Education, or any reputable citizen could petition the juvenile court to inquire into the conditions of children aged seven to fourteen who were not attending school, were habitually truant, or were in persistent violation of school rules" (Dohrn 2002:273–274). In addition, the first chief probation officer in Chicago was Henry Thurston, a noted educator at that time (Dohrn 2002:273). In Denver, probation officers were also truant officers, and children were considered either working or in school (Dohrn 2002:292). Thus, despite the conclusions of court decisions, such as the O'Connell case, that juvenile reformatories and similar institutions were *not* primarily places of education, one of the functions of the first juvenile courts was to force truants and other "recalcitrant" juveniles into some kind of educational program. However, in the latter part of the 19th century, industrial schools were created, and in 1882, in yet another challenge to the authority of such institutions to house "unfortunate children," the Illinois Supreme Court ruled that industrial schools were more schools than prisons (Dohrn 2002:300). Perhaps this kind of reasoning encouraged reformers to continue with the notion that the juvenile justice system should be focused on education as opposed to punishment.

Another feature of the new delinquency law in Chicago was an emphasis on psychological and/or psychiatric treatment. This concern probably reflects the growing popularity of psychoanalysis and the notion that delinquency was symptomatic of underlying or at least individualized conditions, a kind of illness, so to speak. This approach to understanding delinquency is discussed in chapter 4. In 1909, for example, the Juvenile Psychopathic Institute was founded, and similar clinics were established in other cities (Tanenhaus 2002:66). As can be imagined, it was not long before the medical, the legal, and the social welfare/education positions relative to juvenile offending were in conflict, and these conflicts still exist today. However, the focus of the first juvenile courts on education and psychological treatment clearly signaled that the court was to be an institution that went far beyond assigning punishment to criminal offending among juveniles.

It is interesting that while the negative influences of urban life and the inability of parents and the family in general to handle juveniles were still important features of the emerging juvenile court system, now the focus of attention was more and more on the individual delinquent and his or her personal problems, particularly from a psychological viewpoint. Again, the significance of these theoretical ideas will be explored in more detail in other chapters of this book.

Early 20th-Century Developments

Despite the popularity of juvenile courts throughout the United States in the early 20th century, these institutions were not without their problems and detractors. Racial issues were present in many of the courts, especially with respect to probation. Black youth were often assigned to black probation officers or to "volunteers," such as in New Orleans. In addition, few courts were actually using psychiatric clinics, and many were placing juveniles in local jails, contrary to the spirit of the delinquency laws (Tanenhaus 2002:54, 67).

Often, these first courts were not funded by public monies, and many did not have separate juvenile court buildings until well into the 20th century. The first juvenile court in Chicago, for example, was guided by the efforts of Lucy Flower and the members of the Chicago Women's Club, who helped create funds for the operation of the court and the payment of its officers, such as probation officers. This was accomplished by an oversight committee called the Juvenile Court Committee (Tanenhaus 2002:50). Later, in 1912, the U.S. Children's Bureau was established as an oversight organization to collect data and investigate charges of abuse and mismanagement among the nation's juvenile courts and institutions (Grossberg 2002:27–29), even though the federal government had little to do with the prosecution and handling of youthful offenders. Interestingly, the first chief of the Children's Bureau was Julia Lathrop, one of the early leaders of the child savers in Chicago (Tanenhaus 2002:42).

With the oversights offered by the courts and the Children's Bureau, the newly emerging system of juvenile justice, particularly the courts and their attendant schools and clinics, were left to map out their paths and directions for much of the first half of the 20th century. Another challenge to the new laws and the court system established by these laws was presented to the Pennsylvania Supreme Court in 1905, the *Commonwealth v. Fisher* case. The court ruled in favor of the delinquency laws in that state and, in effect, reaffirmed the doctrine of *parens patriae* as a guiding legal principle for matters concerning juvenile justice (Mennel 1973:144–145). As the members of the U.S. Children's Bureau continued to write reports and conduct investigations into operations of juvenile courts, clinics, and institutions throughout the land, the new system of juvenile justice was becoming firmly established in the country, and its basic authority was not seriously challenged for several decades.

Summary

The contemporary juvenile justice system in the United States has historical roots that go back several hundred years. Some of the practices that even today guide the philosophy and practices of juvenile justice in the United States can be traced to England. One such principle is the legal concept of *parens patriae*, which gives a government, usually the state, legal control and authority concerning the rearing of children, authority that exceeds that of parents.

Specific juvenile and youth institutions, however, began to appear in the early part of the 19th century with the creation of houses of refuge. Around the middle of the 19th century, many urban homeless, destitute, and/or vagrant children were placed out of their homes with families located in what today we call the Midwest, some without the knowledge or permission of their parents. Around that same time, larger institutions, first called reform schools and training schools and then later called industrial schools, were established to handle even more youth, often for long periods of time. While public and private institutions were established to handle juvenile offenders in the first half of the 19th century, more and more private philanthropic organizations such as Hull House and the Chicago Women's Club became involved in the call for reforms in juvenile justice. These people are often referred to as child savers, and their concerted effort is called the child-saving movement.

The authority of public officers and organization leaders to remove young people from their families and to place them with other families or into institutions was often defended and legally protected via the doctrine of *parens patriae. Parens patriae* is an English legal doctrine that establishes the state as the legal authority in matters dealing with minors.

The efforts of these social reformers became more focused after the Civil War and after state supreme court cases, such as *O'Connell v. Turner*, were decided in favor of parental rights over the doctrine of *parens patriae*. Juveniles could no longer be incarcerated or imprisoned without due process or for things such as misfortune or vagrancy without specific laws defining such acts as illegal. These legal decisions, along with changes in social thinking, eventually led to the creation of a separate set of delinquency laws and the establishment of juvenile courts. The first of these was created in Chicago, Illinois, in 1899, but by the end of the first quarter of the 20th century, all but a couple of states had established similar laws, and juvenile courts had become part of the legal scene in all large cities.

The first juvenile courts were not unanimously welcomed, and many of them were not even funded by the laws that created them. In cities such as Chicago, oversight committees were established to supervise and raise private donations and money for the operations of these courts. Eventually, in 1912, the U.S. Children's Bureau was created to serve as a sort of watchdog and overseer of the nation's newly emerging juvenile court system and institutions designed to serve the functions of these new courts.

After these developments, this new system of juvenile justice seemed to receive a honeymoon of sorts, in that few legal challenges and major policy changes occurred before the 1960s. These challenges and policy shifts will be examined in more detail in chapter 13, where the contemporary juvenile justice system is discussed.

References

Addams, Jane
    1910   Twenty Years at Hull House. New York: Macmillan.
Aries, Philippe
    1962   Centuries of Childhood: A Social History of Family Life. Robert Baldick, trans. New York: Alfred A. Knopf.
Barnes, Harry Elmer and Negley K. Teeters
    1959   New Horizons in Criminology. 3rd edition. New York: Prentice-Hall.
Cahalan, Margaret Werner, with the assistance of Lee Anne Parsons
    1986   Historical Corrections Statistics in the United States, 1850–1984. Washington, DC: U.S. Department of Justice, Bureau of Justice Statistics.

Dohrn, Bernardine

    2002   The School, the Child, and the Court. *In* A Century of Juvenile Justice. Margaret K. Rosenheim, Franklin E. Zimring, David S. Tanenhaus, and Bernardine Dohrn, eds. Pp. 267–309. Chicago: University of Chicago Press.

Feld, Barry C.

    1999   Bad Kids: Race and the Transformation of the Juvenile Court. New York: Oxford University Press.

Grossberg, Michael

    2002   Changing Conceptions of Child Welfare in the United States, 1820–1935. *In* A Century of Juvenile Justice. Margaret K. Rosenheim, Franklin E. Zimring, David S. Tanenhaus, and Bernardine Dohrn, eds. Pp. 3–41. Chicago: University of Chicago Press.

Mennel, Robert M.

    1972   Origins of the Juvenile Court—Changing Perspectives on the Legal Rights of Juvenile Delinquents. Crime and Delinquency 18:68–78.

    1973   Thorns & Thistles: Juvenile Delinquents in the United States, 1825–1940. Hanover, NH: University Press of New England.

Platt, Anthony M.

    1977   The Child Savers: The Invention of Delinquency. 2nd edition, enlarged. Chicago: University of Chicago Press.

Postman, Neil

    1982   The Disappearance of Childhood. New York: Delacorte Press.

Salerno, Anthony W.

    1991   The Child-Saving Movement: Altruism or a Conspiracy? Juvenile & Family Court Journal 42: 37–49.

Sanders, Wiley B.

    1970   Juvenile Offenders for a Thousand Years: Selected Readings from Anglo-Saxon Times to 1900. Chapel Hill: University of North Carolina Press.

Shelden, Randall G., and Lynn T. Osborne

    1989   "For Their Own Good": Class Interests and the Child Saving Movement in Memphis, Tennessee, 1900–1917. Criminology 27:747–767.

Sutton, John R.

    1988   Stubborn Children: Controlling Delinquency in the United States, 1640–1841. Berkeley: University of California Press.

Tanenhaus, David S.

    2002   The Evolution of Juvenile Courts in the Early Twentieth Century: Beyond the Myth of the Immaculate Construction. *In* A Century of

Juvenile Justice. Margaret K. Rosenheim, Franklin E. Zimring, David S. Tanenhaus, and Bernardine Dohrn, eds. Pp. 42–73. Chicago: University of Chicago Press.

Teitelbaum, Lee

2002   Status Offenses and Status Offenders. *In* A Century of Juvenile Justice. Margaret K. Rosenheim, Franklin E. Zimring, David S. Tanenhaus, and Bernardine Dohrn, eds. Pp. 158–175. Chicago: University of Chicago Press.

THE MEASUREMENT OF DELINQUENCY

S TORIES OF gangs, school shootings, drug use among juveniles, and other instances of delinquency provide some insight and understanding of the extent and nature of juvenile delinquency. Often, these events provide what some call anecdotal evidence about delinquency. Anecdotal evidence is usually not representative of the total picture of a subject. This is not to say that such information is incorrect but, rather, that anecdotal evidence is incomplete. That is, data are collected or presented on one or two instances, which may or may not be representative of all such behavior.

However, to get a clearer and more objective picture of what is happening among youth today and the extent of delinquency, it is important to consult several sources of information, most of which attempt to gather data on a large number of youth, often throughout the country. Using these multiple sources of data, the measurement of delinquency can be divided into several categories: official, self-report and victimization surveys, and qualitative studies, such as observations and analyses of accounts of delinquency obtained from published stories, newspaper articles, and similar documents. The purpose of this chapter is to acquaint the reader with specific information regarding delinquency from each of these sources of data and to develop indications of the extent and distribution of delinquent behavior from this information.

Before discussing these measures of delinquency, it is important to distinguish two similar yet separate concepts relating to statistical data. First, there is a concept known as a measure of *incidence*. Incidence data tell us how much of a behavior is occurring. For example, if we were told that there were four million arrests of juveniles in the United States in a given year, that would be an incidence measure or statistic. We also see statistics that tell us what proportion of a population is involved in an activity. This is referred to as a *prevalence* measure. Using the example above, if we were told that 35 percent of youth in America were arrested in a given year, this would be an example of prevalence. Both measures of behavior are important, yet they each have their own uses and limitations. Measures of incidence are useful for determining how many young people are involved in delinquency or the magnitude of delinquent behavior in a city or country, as illustrated by arrest totals. However, saying that there have been four million arrests or that there have been 400,000 incidences of delinquency reported in a country or community does not tell us how many different youths have been involved. That information is better obtained from prevalence measures. It often happens in matters of delinquency, for example, that a few youngsters are responsible for the majority or a significant proportion of delinquency in a community. So briefly, if you want to know how much delinquency behavior is occurring, go to measures of incidence. If you want to know more about what percentage of youth in a population are committing acts of delinquency, use prevalence measures.

Arrest Data

Probably the best source of information on arrest figures in the United States is a publication titled *Crime in the United States*, also known as the Uniform Crime Reports or the UCR. The UCR was originally published in 1930 by the FBI. Today, this document is published annually by the FBI and is based on information provided by local police departments throughout the country. Even though the FBI uses a standard form for reporting purposes, in many states the reporting is done on a voluntary basis, so the information is not always complete.

The UCR contains a lot of information about crime that can be used for different purposes. The list of crimes included in these publications is divided into two broad categories: index offenses and nonindex offenses. There are eight index offenses subdivided into two sections, violent and property (or nonviolent). The violent index offenses include murder and non-negligible manslaughter, forcible rape, robbery, and aggravated assault. The property offenses include burglary, automobile theft, larceny theft, and arson. The FBI maintains that these eight crimes should be considered index offenses because they are serious offenses and because they are reliably reported. While many may quarrel with these assumptions, all of these index offenses were included in the first publications of the UCR in the 1930s with the exception of arson, which was added to the list in 1980.

In addition to the index offenses, the UCR also includes information on 21 other offenses, which include some status offenses. However, it is only with the index offenses that we receive detailed information on crimes reported to the police. For the index crimes and for all other offenses, the UCR reports detailed information on arrests, which is of important concern to students of delinquency.

With these caveats taken into consideration, it is useful to examine arrest data as one measure of the extent of delinquency in the United States today. Arrest figures show that 1.626 million juveniles were arrested in 2006 (Federal Bureau of Investigation 2006:table 38). The definition of juveniles in this figure is anyone under 18. The number of juveniles arrested in 2006 was about 24 percent lower than the number of juveniles arrested in 1997, so the incidence of juvenile arrests is declining, compared with the trend for adults, which is steady (Federal Bureau of Investigation 2002:table 32). However, from 2002 to 2006, the decline in juvenile arrests is less dramatic, 3.1 percent (Federal Bureau of Investigation 2006:table 34). The decline in juvenile arrests has been evident from the mid-1990s until now. This trend is reversed for drug abuse arrests, which increased dramatically from the late 1980s until 1997 and then declined steadily between 1997 and 2004. However, drug abuse arrests increased for females between 1997 and 2004 (Snyder 2006).

In addition, the number of juveniles arrested is significantly lower than the number of adults arrested. Juveniles account for only about 16 percent of all arrests (Snyder 2006). However, as will be discussed below, the peak age of arrest among juveniles is fairly young, well below age 21, and many crimes, especially property offenses, are committed by juveniles. One reason juveniles comprise only 16 percent of all arrests, compared with adults, is that there are many more adults than juveniles in the country.

Since juveniles under the age of 10 are rarely arrested, it would be better to look at the arrests of youths 10–18 to get a better idea of the size of the incidence of arrests for juveniles. In 2006, there were 1,626,523 arrests of juveniles reported in the UCR. However, there were only 13,420 arrests of youths under the age of 10, none for murder, but mostly for the crimes of other assaults, larceny-theft, vandalism, and disorderly conduct (Federal Bureau of Investigation 2006:table 38).

Arrest Patterns

Gender

Arrest patterns of juveniles vary by gender. For every offense except prostitution and running away, a status offense, there were more arrests for males than for females. For example, in 2006, there were 1,156,871 arrests of juvenile males and 469,652 arrests of female juveniles. The numbers of juvenile male and female arrests *decreased* from the past five and ten years, but the declines have slowed over the past five years (Federal Bureau of Investigation 2006:tables 33, 35, 39, and 40). The offense for which both males and females were arrested most often was larceny-theft, which includes shoplifting. The difference in arrests for males is most apparent for violent crimes. In 2006, for the *index violent* crimes, there were 49,274 arrests of juvenile males and only 10,411 arrests of juvenile females, a ratio of more than 4:1. For the *index property* crimes, there were 171,449 male arrests, compared with 83,112 female arrests, a ratio of about 2:1 (Federal Bureau of Investigation 2006:table 35).

The higher number of arrests of juvenile females for prostitution is understandable. However, it should not be overlooked that there are many juvenile males who are arrested for prostitution every year. In 2006, for example, there were 317 arrests of juvenile males for prostitution and commercialized vice (Federal Bureau of Investigation 2006:table 39; see also Finkelhor and Ormrod 2004). The higher number of arrests of juvenile females, compared with males, for the offense of running away, however, is not so easily explained. In 2006, there were 47,472 arrests of *female* juveniles for running away, compared with 36,402 arrests of *males* for this offense (Federal Bureau of Investigation 2006:tables 39 and 40). Perhaps juvenile females simply run away more than their male counterparts. Official data, such as those found in the UCR, do not offer information that can be used to test this explanation. After all, the data being discussed at this point are arrest data, which reflect not only behavior but also reactions to this behavior by the police and the members of the community.

It is possible that females actually do not run away more than males but that the community and the police react differently to such behavior when committed by females. There may be a kind of *paternalistic* attitude toward females who run away, such that it is thought by members of the community that runaway girls need to be arrested and put into the care of the juvenile justice system to protect them from the consequences of running away, such as being enticed into a life of drugs and prostitution. This issue will be addressed again when self-report measures of delinquency are examined.

Race

Arrests of juveniles are also patterned by race, with whites being arrested more often than blacks, American Indians, or Asian Americans. In 2006, for example, there were 1,088,376 arrests of whites for all 29 offenses recorded in the UCR, 490,838 for blacks, 18,579 for American Indians and Alaskan Natives, and 23,361 for Asian Americans and Pacific Islanders (Federal Bureau of Investigation 2006:table 43). However, when considering the percentage of black youth in the population, there is a considerable disproportionate arrest bias against blacks. In 2005, for example, black youth (those under age 18) represented 14 percent of the population (Puzzanchera et al. 2006). The 490,838 arrests of black youth in 2006 represented 30.3 percent of all arrests of youth that year, which is more than twice the estimated percentage of black youth in the population.

The disproportionate arrests of black youth are greater for some crimes than for others. For example, in 2006, 51 percent of arrests for index violent crimes were of black youth, and more than half of arrests for murder and robbery were of black youth. However, only 30.9 percent of arrests for index property crimes were of black youth, and within this category, only 18.3 percent of arrests for arson were of black juveniles (Federal Bureau of Investigation 2006:table 43).

Separate analyses of UCR arrest data suggest that the difference in the rate of arrests for black versus white youth is declining. In 1980, for example, black youth were 6.3 times more likely to be arrested than white youth for an index violent crime. By 2004, this difference had declined to 4.1 times (Snyder 2006).

Similar to the arguments raised earlier with regard to females arrested for the offense of running away, the disproportionate arrests of black youth for index crimes, especially murder and robbery, may be a result of greater numbers of black youth committing these offenses. Or these unusually high arrest figures may reflect prejudice and bias against black youth, most likely black males. Examinations of other measures of delinquency, particularly self-report figures, should shed more light on this issue.

Age

As was mentioned earlier, arrests of juveniles rarely occur for youth under the age of ten. However, between ages 10 and 18, there are differences in arrests by specific ages. Among juvenile males, the peak age of arrest for all crimes is 17–18, 13–14 for index property crimes and 18 for index violent crimes (Federal Bureau of Investigation 2006:table 39). Among juvenile females, the peak age of arrest for all crimes and property and violent index offenses is 13–14 (Federal Bureau of Investigation 2006:table 40). However, these estimates are based on percentages of age categories represented among all age categories, so they are not clearly indicative of the rate of juveniles in each category who are arrested.

A more accurate way to assess the age–crime pattern is to compare rates of arrest by the numbers of people in a certain age category. This type of comparison is presented in figure 3.1. In this figure, the arrest rates by age are presented for all people from age 10 to age 24 and then separately for males and females. In addition, the data are presented for index violent crimes and index property crimes. As the lines in figure 3.1 indicate, the peak age of arrest for violent crimes and property crimes is the same, about age 18. The patterns differ slightly by gender. For males, the peak age of arrest is 18 for violent and property crimes. The comparable peak ages for females are 17 for property crimes and virtually no differences from age 16–24 for violent offenses.

Some refer to this trend or pattern of declining arrest rates with age as the *maturation* or *desistance effect*, which means that by a certain age, usually at or before 18, most juvenile offenders desist from committing more crimes, or mature out of crime, so to speak. Other estimates of crime and delinquency report similar age–crime patterns, so there must be something to this effect. Accordingly, it is important for students of delinquency to understand that explanations of delinquency must be able to provide insight into not only why juveniles start committing crimes but also why they *stop* committing crimes. This concept will be raised again when explanations of crime and delinquency are discussed in more detail.

The peak age figures for arrests also suggest something else, that is, property crimes are much more common among youth than are violent crimes. Earlier, it was mentioned that the most common crime for which juveniles are arrested is larceny-theft. This crime includes many kinds of theft, including shoplifting, and it is easy to see where it may be common among youth. But the peak age of arrest estimates, especially for females, also suggest that crime is a youthful endeavor, particularly property crime.

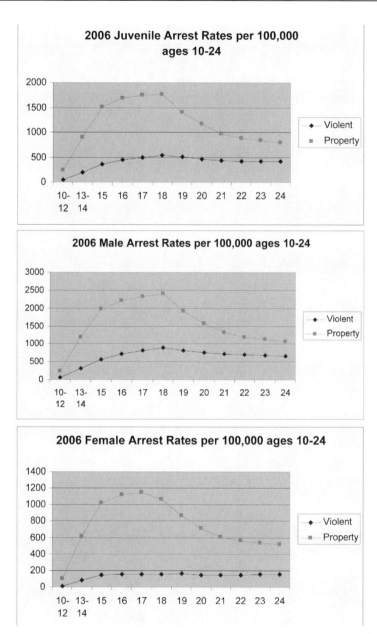

FIGURE 3.1 Arrest Rates by Age for Index Property and Violent Crimes
Source: Crime in The United States, 2006 Uniform Crime Reports, Federal Bureau of Investigation, Tables 38, 39, and 40 and U.S. Census Bureau, 2006, National Population Estimates.

In addition, separate analyses of arrests by age indicate that violent crimes are not the domain of juveniles. For example, in 2004, for every 100,000 juveniles in the population, only 269, or less than 1 percent, were arrested for a violent index crime (Snyder 2006).

Arrest data from sources such as the UCR are useful in what they can offer to the student of delinquency. However, it should be stressed again that these data are not complete. In addition to not covering all jurisdictions, the UCR data typically report only the most serious crimes in any incident. If a person were charged with murder and arson, for example, only the charge of murder would be recorded in the UCR. In addition, the arrest figures mentioned above do not tell us how many individual people were involved in a criminal incident, only the number of arrests made (see also Snyder 2006). For this reason, with a few exceptions, most of the arrest figures discussed above concern incident data, not prevalence information. In order to get additional information on delinquency, other sources of data must be used. The following sections offer a brief look at some of these additional sources of data on delinquency, starting with juvenile court data.

National Incident-Based Reporting System (NIBRS)

In the late 1970s, law enforcement agents and administrators began to call for a more comprehensive system of collecting information on crimes in the United States. The result of these efforts was the creation of an incident-based reporting system that is being implemented in several states, with the goal of full implementation in all 50 states. As of 2004, over 5,200 law enforcement agencies were using this system and the FBI had approved 26 states for NIBRS participation.

An important feature of this new reporting system is the collection of information on *all* crimes committed in a criminal event. Traditionally, crime-reported data typically include only the most serious crime if more than one crime occurs in a criminal event. This new system classifies crimes into two categories: group A, which includes 22 offense categories and 46 particular crimes, and group B, which includes 11 offense categories. Information for group A crimes will include crime-reported data as well as arrest data. Group A crimes include all eight of the current list of index offenses plus several other crime categories, such as drug offenses, fraud, kidnapping, and pornography offenses. Only arrest data will be reported for group B crimes. Thus, the NIBRS system is greatly expanded, compared with the traditional system of collecting crime information (http://www.fbi.gov/ucr/faqs.htm, accessed October 9, 2007).

Juvenile Court Data

There are hundreds of juvenile courts in the United States, one for nearly every city and jurisdiction in the country. However, there are currently no national comprehensive statistics on juvenile courts, as we have for arrest data. The UCR present some information on what happens to cases coming to the attention of the police—for instance, what happens to cases of arrests— but again, this information is incomplete and not detailed. Juvenile court offices are not required to report their data to any particular agency, so the information we do have is primarily voluntary. Nonetheless, the National Center for Juvenile Justice, located at the University of Pittsburgh, in connection with the Office of Juvenile Justice and Delinquency Prevention, issues regular reports on juvenile court cases based on data provided by juvenile court jurisdictions in the country.

To begin, most cases of arrest are forwarded on to the juvenile courts. In 2006, the UCR reported that of those juveniles taken into custody (the juvenile justice term for arrested), 69.3 percent were referred to a juvenile court for further processing. In 20.8 percent of arrests, the case was handled within the police department, which means that it was probably dealt with as a warning or in some similar semi-official or informal manner. In 8.2 percent of these arrests, the case was referred to the adult criminal court in the area. The remaining cases were either referred to welfare agencies or handled by other police units (Federal Bureau of Investigation 2006:table 68). Referral is called a *waiver*, or *transfer*, to the adult system. The process of waiver will be discussed in later chapters, when the system of juvenile justice is discussed in more detail.

Referrals of arrests to the juvenile court are increasing. In 1980, for example, 58 percent of juvenile arrests were referred to the juvenile court. In addition, the practice of referring arrest cases to juvenile court is not affected by type of jurisdiction. The numbers are similar for city, suburban, and rural locations (Snyder 2006; Federal Bureau of Investigation 2006:table 68).

In 2004, there were 1,660,700 delinquency cases handled within 2,100 juvenile courts in the United States, which represented almost 75 percent of the population. Most (81 percent) of the referrals to juvenile court come from the police. Other sources of referrals to juvenile court include schools, social service agencies, probation officers, parents or guardians, and victims of crime. In terms of the most serious charge in a case, the most common criminal offense referred to juvenile courts was larceny-theft, but the referrals for larceny-theft were much smaller in 2004 compared with 1985. Overall, referrals to juvenile court increased between 1985 and 1997 but decreased between 1997 and 2004 (Snyder and Sickmund 2006:156-158; Stahl et al. 2007:chapter 2).

Overall, juvenile court caseloads tend to increase with age of offender. In 2004, the case rate for 17-year-olds was 112.0 per 1,000, compared with 4.0 per 1,000 for 10-year-olds and 62.1 per 1,000 for 14-year-old youth. The case rate increased with each specific age category between 10 and 17. However, over half (57 percent) of all delinquency cases handled by juvenile courts in 2004 involved youth under the age of 16 at the time they were referred to the courts. One reason juvenile courts tend to handle more cases of youth under age 16 is because 13 states consider age 16 or 17 as the age of majority, and cases involving youth of these ages are referred to the adult criminal justice system. Thus, while older youth represent *proportionately* more of the juvenile court caseload, overall, courts tend to deal with younger children (Snyder and Sickmund 2006:166; Stahl et al. 2007:chapter 2).

Offense *patterns* tend to vary by age. In 2004, cases for younger juveniles, those aged 15 or less, more often involved property and person offenses, while cases for older youth more often involved property and public order offenses, such as obstruction of justice and disorderly conduct (Stahl et al. 2007:chapter 2). In 2002, among juveniles under age 12, 34 percent of the referrals were for person, or violent, offenses, compared with those age 13 or older, among whom only 22 percent were charged with a violent offense. In addition, 48 percent of referrals for younger children were for property crimes, compared with 38 percent of older youth. On the other hand, 27 percent of the offense referrals for older youth were for public order offenses, compared with 16 percent for younger kids (Snyder and Sickmund 2006:167).

Most of the juvenile court cases in 2004 involved males, 73 percent. However, between 1985 and 2004, cases for females increased by 104 percent, compared with an increase of 30 percent for males. Offense patterns are similar for males and females. Property offenses were most common for both, again largely because of larceny-theft, and public order offenses were nearly equally distributed (27 percent for males and 29 percent for females). Cases for males were more likely to be for drug offenses (13 percent compared with 9 percent), while females were *more* likely to be in juvenile court for violent offenses (26 percent) compared with males (23 percent) (Stahl et al. 2007:chapter 2).

In 2004, the majority (two-thirds) of all delinquency cases and 57 percent of violent offenses in juvenile courts involved whites, while blacks represented 31 percent of court cases. However, juvenile court figures demonstrate disproportionate involvement among blacks, compared with whites. In 2004, the overall delinquency case rate for blacks was 99.7 per 1,000 youth, compared to a rate of 44.6 for whites. For person offenses, the rate per 1,000 for blacks was 30.1, compared with 9.6 for whites (Stahl 2007:chapter 2). Case rates for both white and black youth are declining, but the proportionate disparity still exists. Issues of racial disparity in the juvenile justice system will be discussed again in chapter 13, "The Contemporary Juvenile Justice System."

Self-Report Data

The previous discussions have presented information on measurements of delinquency that are considered official data sources. However, UCR data and juvenile court data do not offer a complete picture of delinquency. In addition to being incomplete, these sources of data do not include much information on the circumstances of delinquent acts, nor of the social and attitudinal correlates of offenders. One way to supplement these insufficiencies is to turn to other sources of information on delinquency that are often considered unofficial. One of the more popular unofficial sources of data on delinquency is a method of inquiry called self-reported delinquency. Self-report measures ask juveniles whether they have committed one or more of a list of delinquent behaviors, usually within a certain period of time, such as the past year.

Self-report studies have been around a long time. They were first used in the 1940s on college and adult populations (Porterfield 1943). The first use of self-report measures on juvenile populations was in the 1950s, when James F. Short, Jr., and the late F. Ivan Nye administered self-report questionnaires concerning delinquency and a variety of other questions to high school and institutional populations in Washington State (Short and Nye 1958).

Reliability and Validity Issues or Concerns

Despite the fact that self-report studies have been around for over 50 years, critics of this method point out that asking juveniles to tell on themselves, so to speak, is not an accurate way to discover the truth about delinquency. For example, some contend that juveniles will not divulge their deviant behaviors to strangers for fear they may be caught and punished. This concern seems greater for those juveniles who are already in institutions. However, from the earliest uses of self-report studies, researchers have shown that incarcerated youth admit to having committed more delinquent acts than comparative samples of high-school students. They have usually simply not been caught for the vast majority of these acts. In fact, some research shows that institutionalized youth are more delinquent than even the most delinquent high-school youngster who has not been caught and put into the juvenile justice system (Cernkovich et al. 1985).

A detailed analysis and discussion of the reliability and validity of self-report measures of delinquency concluded that these measures are reliable and valid enough to use, especially when analyzing correlates of delinquency (Hindelang et al. 1981). After looking at a number of examples of reliability and validity, such as comparing self-report measures to official measures, examining test results, looking at various sources of self-reports besides respondents, and reviewing statistical reliability measures, Hindelang et al. conclude that self-report measures are not "fundamentally flawed" and are useful tools for measuring delinquency (p. 114).

Another factor to remember is that today, almost all research on humans, especially youth and more especially incarcerated youth, is protected by government restrictions on abuse of human subjects. It would be a rare event if a researcher were to use such instruments without granting anonymity, confidentiality, and assurances that subjects could opt out of answering any question at any time. In addition, most studies of youth today must permit parental approval before a juvenile is allowed to answer questions that may put him or her at risk of sanctions.

Another criticism of self-report studies is that they typically do not tap the serious delinquent youths in a community because they do not include the most violent cases of crime, such as murder and forcible rape. To some extent, this criticism is true, especially in the earlier studies. However, many current self-report studies do attempt to measure the more violent and serious kinds of offenses, but still typically not homicide and rape.

Conclusions of Self-Report Studies

Gender and Race

Many researchers have developed and used a self-report measure of delinquency. However, for the past 20 years, an annual collection of self-report data on high-school students, particularly seniors, has provided us a wealth of information on the unrecorded deviant behaviors of our nation's youth. This study is called Monitoring the Future (MTF), and it is administered by researchers with the Institute for Social Research at the University of Michigan. Every year, this study surveys a random sample of high-school students. The earlier studies included only seniors but currently include seniors, eighth graders, and tenth graders as well. Respondents are asked questions on a variety of subjects, including drug use and delinquency. We will return to this study in chapter 9 about drug use.

One of the advantages of the MTF research is that it provides longitudinal data on a lot of issues. This advantage reflects another value of self-report studies. That is, they can be used to correlate a number of social and attitudinal factors to admitted delinquency and deviance. Table 3.1 displays answers among seniors to questions on delinquency by gender of respondent for the years 1990 and 2003. Respondents were asked to indicate how often they had committed a listed offense within the past year. The data in table 3.1 indicate that for all but one offense listed, males admit to being more delinquent than do females. That is, a higher percentage of males admit to having committed the offense at least once (a prevalence measure) compared with females. The only offense that does not reflect this trend is "argued or had a fight with either of your parents." Some offense categories show marked differences between males and females, such as "hurting someone badly enough to need bandages or a doctor," "taken part of a car without permission of its owner," and "damaged property at work on purpose."

In table 3.2, the same offenses are listed by race of respondent. These data show that in several instances, white youth admit to having committed an offense at least once more often than do black youth. In some cases, such as "taken something not belonging to you worth over $50," "hit an instructor or supervisor," and "taken a car that didn't belong to someone in your family without permission," the prevalence rates are nearly the same. Collectively, the data in table 3.2 do not uniformly support the arrest figures for race. Blacks do not admit to having committed offenses in the same proportion in which they are arrested, including violent offenses. Interestingly, in 2003, white and black students admitted to being arrested for an offense in equal proportions (these data were not available in 1990). This finding clearly contrasts with the disproportionate arrest rates for nonwhites reported in the UCR.

Besides the MTF surveys, there are numerous self-report studies that shed additional light on the extent of unrecorded delinquency. Several years

TABLE 3.1 Self-Reported Delinquency by Gender (in percentages)

	Class of 1991			Class of 2003		
Delinquent Activity (within the past year)	Males (N = 1,280)	Females (N = 1,205)	All High School Seniors (N = 2,569)	Males (N = 1,164)	Females (N = 1,246)	All High School Seniors (N = 2,517)
Argued or had a fight with either of your parents						
Not at all	12.2	7.0	10.0	6.9	7.6	10.3
At least once	87.8	93.0	90.0	93.1	92.4	89.7
Hit an instructor or supervisor						
Not at all	95.3	98.9	97.0	97.5	99.1	96.8
At least once	4.7	1.1	3.0	2.5	0.9	3.2
Gotten into a serious fight in school or at work						
Not at all	76.6	88.1	82.1	87.9	91.2	85.7
At least once	23.4	11.9	17.9	12.1	8.8	14.3
Taken part in a fight where a group of your friends were against another group						
Not at all	73.8	86.4	79.6	82.2	85.1	80.2
At least once	26.2	13.6	20.4	17.8	14.9	19.8
Hurt someone badly enough to need bandages or a doctor						
Not at all	79.1	96.0	87.1	89.8	94.9	88.0
At least once	20.9	4.0	12.9	10.2	5.1	12.0

Used a knife
or gun
or some
other thing
(like a club)
to get something
from a person

Not at all	94.7	98.8	96.6	97.6	99.1	96.1
At least once	5.3	1.2	3.4	2.4	0.9	3.9

Taken something
not belonging to
you worth
under $50

Not at all	58.2	78.3	68.1	73.1	78.9	72.3
At least once	41.8	21.7	31.9	26.9	21.1	27.7

Taken something
not belonging to
you worth
over $50

Not at all	85.0	95.6	89.9	91.6	94.9	90.4
At least once	15.0	4.4	10.1	8.4	5.1	9.6

Taken something
from a store
without paying
for it

Not at all	60.4	78.0	68.9	76.6	77.2	73.2
At least once	39.6	22.0	31.1	23.4	22.8	26.8

Taken a car
that didn't
belong to
someone in
your family
without
permission

Not at all	91.7	96.1	93.8	96.0	97.6	94.7
At least once	8.3	3.9	6.2	4.0	2.4	5.3

(Continued)

TABLE 3.1 Self-Reported Delinquency by Gender (in percentages) (Continued)

	Class of 1991			Class of 2003		
Delinquent Activity (within the past year)	Males (N = 1,280)	Females (N = 1,205)	All High School Seniors (N = 2,569)	Males (N = 1,164)	Females (N = 1,246)	All High School Seniors (N = 2,517)
Taken part of a car without permission of the owner						
Not at all	89.4	98.3	93.7	95.7	97.9	94.5
At least once	10.6	1.7	6.3	4.3	2.1	5.5
Gone into some house or building when you weren't supposed to be there						
Not at all	69.3	82.7	75.7	77.1	82.7	77.0
At least once	30.7	17.3	24.3	22.9	17.3	23.0
Set fire to someone's property on purpose						
Not at all	96.4	99.4	97.9	96.6	99.1	96.2
At least once	3.6	0.6	2.1	3.4	0.9	3.8
Damaged school property on purpose						
Not at all	81.2	93.5	87.2	87.4	93.6	86.8
At least once	18.8	6.5	12.8	12.6	6.4	13.2
Damaged property at work on purpose						
Not at all	89.2	98.2	93.4	93.3	97.4	93.2
At least once	10.8	1.8	6.6	6.7	2.6	6.8

Been arrested or
taken to a police
station

Not at all	X	X	X	92.9	95.4	92.0
At least once	X	X	X	7.1	4.6	8.0

Note: X = not included.

Source: Adapted from Monitoring the Future Surveys, 1991 and 2003, *Sourcebook of Criminal Justice Statistics Online*, http://www.albany.edu/sourcebook/wk1/t344.wk1.

TABLE 3.2 Self-Reported Delinquency by Race (in percentages)

	Class of 1991			Class of 2003		
Delinquent Activity (within the past year)	*White (N = 1,818)*	*Black (N = 289)*	*All High School Seniors (N = 2,569)*	*White (N = 1,631)*	*Black (N = 273)*	*All High School Seniors (N = 2,517)*
Argued or had a fight with either of your parents						
Not at all	6.8	22.4	10.0	6.9	24.3	10.3
At least once	93.2	77.6	90.0	93.1	75.7	89.7
Hit an instructor or supervisor						
Not at all	97.3	95.9	97.0	97.5	98.5	96.8
At least once	2.7	4.1	3.0	2.5	1.5	3.2
Gotten into a serious fight in school or at work						
Not at all	83.1	76.8	82.1	87.9	81.6	85.7
At least once	16.9	23.2	17.9	12.1	18.4	14.3
Taken part in a fight where a group of your friends were against another group						
Not at all	80.8	76.5	79.6	82.2	78.6	80.2
At least once	19.2	23.5	20.4	17.8	21.4	19.8

(Continued)

TABLE 3.2 Self-Reported Delinquency by Race (in percentages) (Continued)

	Class of 1991			Class of 2003		
Delinquent Activity (within the past year)	White (N = 1,818)	Black (N = 289)	All High School Seniors (N = 2,569)	White (N = 1,631)	Black (N = 273)	All High School Seniors (N = 2,517)
Hurt someone badly enough to need bandages or a doctor						
Not at all	88.2	84.4	87.1	89.8	85.6	88.0
At least once	11.8	15.6	12.9	10.2	14.4	12.0
Used a knife or gun or some other thing (like a club) to get something from a person						
Not at all	97.4	94.1	96.6	97.6	97.2	96.1
At least once	2.6	5.9	3.4	2.4	2.8	3.9
Taken something not belonging to you worth under $50						
Not at all	67.2	74.9	68.1	73.1	78.8	72.3
At least once	32.8	25.1	31.9	26.9	21.2	27.7
Taken something not belonging to you worth over $50						
Not at all	90.5	93.2	89.9	91.6	93.0	90.4
At least once	9.5	6.8	10.1	8.4	7.0	9.6

Taken something from a store without paying for it						
Not at all	68.3	74.5	68.9	76.6	69.7	73.2
At least once	31.7	25.5	31.1	23.4	30.3	26.8
Taken a car that didn't belong to someone in your family without permission						
Not at all	94.4	92.2	93.8	96.0	95.0	94.7
At least once	5.6	7.8	6.2	4.0	5.0	5.3
Taken part of a car without permission of the owner						
Not at all	94.6	91.8	93.7	95.7	94.8	94.5
At least once	5.4	8.2	6.3	4.3	5.2	5.5
Gone into some house or building when you weren't supposed to be there						
Not at all	75.0	78.6	75.7	77.1	80.4	77.0
At least once	25.0	21.4	24.3	22.9	19.6	23.0
Set fire to someone's property on purpose						
Not at all	98.1	98.3	97.9	96.6	97.3	96.2
At least once	1.9	1.7	2.1	3.4	2.7	3.8
Damaged school property on purpose						
Not at all	87.4	88.0	87.2	87.4	90.8	86.8
At least once	12.6	12.0	12.8	12.6	9.2	13.2

(Continued)

TABLE 3.2 Self-Reported Delinquency by Race (in percentages) (Continued)

	Class of 1991			Class of 2003		
Delinquent Activity (within the past year)	White (N = 1,818)	Black (N = 289)	All High School Seniors (N = 2,569)	White (N = 1,631)	Black (N = 273)	All High School Seniors (N = 2,517)
Damaged property at work on purpose						
Not at all	93.4	95.7	93.4	93.3	95.3	93.2
At least once	6.6	4.3	6.6	6.7	4.7	6.8
Been arrested or taken to a police station						
Not at all	X	X	X	92.9	91.4	92.0
At least once	X	X	X	7.1	8.6	8.0

Note: X = not included.

Source: Adapted from Monitoring the Future Surveys, 1991 and 2003, *Sourcebook of Criminal Justice Statistics Online,* http://www.albany.edu/sourcebook/wk1/t348.wk1.

ago, for example, the National Youth Survey was conducted on a sample of over 1,700 youth throughout the country. Analyses of these data have provided considerable insight into the extent and correlates of self-reported delinquency. Rachelle Canter's (1982) analysis, for instance, concludes that the patterns of male and female delinquency are similar, despite the preponderance of male delinquency over female delinquency. Moreover, in this study, males were more involved in serious and violent crimes than were females, but not so for status offenses. In fact, the prevalence ratio of male to female self-reported offending for running away and other status offenses was 1.6:1 or even closer, which means the proportion of males and females admitting these offenses was nearly equal (pp. 377–383).

Earlier, the issue of running away was discussed in connection with arrest rates. It was observed that females are arrested for running away more than are males. Now, it is seen that males and females admit to running away in equal proportions. This finding suggests that females are arrested more often for running away than males at least in part because of discrimination against females. This discrimination is not always done out of malice or evil intentions. Perhaps girls are picked up on the street to keep them from being victimized, that is, to protect them. This motive may be based on an attitude of *paternalism* directed toward girls. Paternalism means acting toward someone as if they were children and in need of supervision and protection. This attitude may be offensive to some (perhaps most) girls, but it helps explain why they are so often arrested for being beyond the supervision of their parents or guardians. This issue of paternalism will be discussed again, when the juvenile justice system is discussed in more detail.

Social Class

While the official data on delinquency discussed above provide little in the way of information on the social class status of youth who are arrested or referred to juvenile court, some self-report studies conclude that *incidence* measures of delinquency reveal significant social class differences but fewer differences relative to *prevalence* measures. That is, if you measured delinquency by counting the number of acts committed, there would be significant differences by social class, with working- and lower-class youth having the higher numbers of delinquency, especially for the more serious, or index, offenses. However, if delinquency were measured by the proportion of youth who admitted to committing crime and delinquency, then the rates would be similar for youth of different social class backgrounds (Elliott and Huizinga 1983).

Other self-report studies of delinquency, however, conclude that there is little, if any, relationship between social class, or SES (socioeconomic status), and delinquency, no matter how delinquency is measured. In fact, these studies suggest that where differences occur, it is sometimes the middle-class youth who are more delinquent than lower-class youngsters (Hindelang et al. 1981:181–198). Other studies, such as those conducted in the Philippines, conclude that middle-class youth are more delinquent than lower-class youth (Shoemaker 1994). Other research concludes that maybe one reason researchers cannot find consistent differences between social class background and delinquency is that working- and lower-class youth are involved in more serious forms of crime and delinquency while middle-class youth are more involved in less serious crimes and status offending, so there appears to be no difference between the social classes and overall measures of delinquency (Wright et al. 1999).

The topic of social class and delinquency is also discussed in the next section of this chapter and throughout this book, in connection with theoretical explanations of delinquency, gang delinquency, and the juvenile justice system. For the moment, it is clear from the results of self-report studies that delinquency is not a province of poor and minority youth but is often committed by the more well-to-do youth in our communities (Vaz 1967; Wooden and Blazak 2001).

Cohort Studies

Another way to measure and study delinquency is to use what is known as a *cohort study*. Cohort studies usually examine a sample of youth, often within a particular city or metropolitan area, and then observe patterns of delinquency and correlates among this sample over a period of time. For this reason, most cohort studies are longitudinal in nature. That is, they follow a sample of youth over an extended period of time rather than examine them at one point in time. While there are several examples of cohort studies, the ones chosen to discuss here are the Philadelphia cohort studies.

There were two Philadelphia cohort studies, informally named Cohort I and Cohort II. The first one examined a sample of 9,945 males who were born in 1945 and who lived in Philadelphia from their 10th to their 18th birthday. The second study included 13,160 males and 14,000 females who were born in 1958 and lived in Philadelphia between their 10th and 18th birthday. In both studies, census and school data were used to identify the youth to be included in the sample. Detailed police records were obtained so that the researchers could examine who was involved in an arrest, the specifics of the case, and the particular demographic information of the juveniles involved, including where they lived. Detailed census information was also used to assign youth to social class positions, based on the socioeconomic characteristics of the areas where they lived (Tracy et al. 1990:14–30). With regard to police records, the researchers found that in most instances, the data were reported as "contacts," not only arrests.

The results of the Cohort I study concluded that 3,475 males, or 34.9 percent of the sample, had at least one contact with the police by their 18th birthday. In the Cohort II study, this figure dropped to 32.8 percent among the males (corresponding figures for females were not given in this report). In the Cohort I study, only 18.7 percent of the total sample were recidivists, that is, contacted more than once. However, only a small percentage of the sample, 6.3 percent, were considered *chronic recidivists*, which meant they were contacted by the police more than four times. In the Cohort II study, the recidivists represented 19.1 percent of the sample, and the chronic offenders represented 7.5 percent of the sample. Thus, comparing the two cohorts and time periods, it seems as if the newer sample was contacted less often than the earlier sample of males, but their cohort included more chronic recidivists (Tracy et al. 1990:38–39, 294).

A significant feature of the chronic recidivists, however, was not only that they represented a majority of all contacts recorded, but that they also were contacted more for the serious, index types of offenses. For example, in Cohort I, the chronic recidivists represented 63.3 percent of all contacts for index crimes among the sample. In Cohort II, chronic recidivists represented 68.4 percent of all index crime contacts among the sample (Tracy et al. 1990:90).

Another characteristic of the chronic offenders is that they tended to be overrepresented by minority and low SES youth. However, detailed examinations of police records and handling procedures led the authors to conclude that in both cohorts, there was evidence to suggest discriminatory handling of nonwhite youth and lower-class youth, despite the offenses for which they were contacted, although these discriminatory practices seemed to lessen in the 1958 cohort (Tracy et al. 1990:chapters 7, 12, and 13).

Another feature of the cohort studies is their detailed analysis of age and delinquency. One finding was that age of onset of delinquency, or police contact, was strongly related to more involvement in delinquency. For example, youth first contacted by the police at the age of 10 or 11 had higher mean scores of delinquency than those youth first contacted by the police when they were 14–17 years of age (Tracy et al. 1990:176–179). However, the researchers found little connection between age of onset and severity of delinquency. As they put it, "The assumption that a delinquency career started early will produce severe delinquency was not confirmed" (Tracy et al. 1990:211).

Another age-related characteristic of delinquency found in the cohort studies is the relationship between age of offense and delinquency. Earlier, it was concluded that the peak age of arrest is around 17. The cohort studies conclude the same thing. Specifically, in both Cohorts I and II, the mean number of offenses peaks at age 16. This relationship is particularly true for nonwhites, but for whites in the 1958 cohort, the peak age is 17. In addition, the apex of delinquency for age 16 holds for index and nonindex crimes. For violent crimes, however, the peak age is higher, 17, particularly among whites and in the 1958 study (Tracy et al. 1990:chapter 11). Overall, the analysis of these two cohort studies concluded that the age–crime relationship changed somewhat between Cohorts I and II, with the latter sample showing longer periods of delinquency involvement than the first sample.

However, it is again shown that rates of crime and delinquency tend to peak in latter adolescence and then fall off. Could it be that juveniles simply get smarter at these ages and avoid detection? Or do they seem to fear the stronger penalties associated with the criminal justice system? Or do juveniles get more mature as they age? In part, the reasons for this "maturation effect" will be addressed in the following chapters, as explanations for delinquency are considered. For the moment, however, it is appropriate to caution anyone trying to understand the causes of delinquency that explanations of why juveniles *start* committing acts of crime and delinquency should also try to explain why they *stop* committing delinquent acts.

Victimization Studies

Delinquency can also be measured by looking at the victims of crime. In this case, researchers are looking for patterns of who gets involved in criminal behavior. Most victimization surveys look at the circumstances surrounding the act or acts of crime rather than the personal motivations of the offender. Consequently, some students of delinquency discount victimization surveys as not very useful toward understanding why juveniles commit crimes. However, sometimes knowing who a victim is can give a clue as to why a person commits criminal behavior.

Most of our information on victims of crime comes from a national survey named the National Crime Victimization Survey, or NCVS. The NCVS has been conducted annually since the early 1970s, so a lot of experience and information is available on victims of crime across the country. Currently, the NCVS interviews a random sample of household members of age 12 and over, usually starting with the head of the household. In 2005, the Bureau of Justice Statistics conducted these interviews with 72,200 households and 134,000 people (Catalano 2006:11).

The crimes surveyed in the NCVS are divided into personal and property crimes. Personal crimes include the violent crimes found in the Index Crimes of the UCR, with the exception of murder. Personal crimes, however, also include simple assault and personal theft. Property crimes include household burglary, motor vehicle theft, and theft in general (larceny).

The results of this survey indicated that there were nearly 23 million crime victimizations in 2005. The numbers of victimizations have been declining, much as the crimes reported in the UCR have been declining, over the past several years. The number of violent crimes reported in the NCVS declined 58 percent from 1993 to 2005, and the number of reported victimizations of property crimes declined 52 percent in the same period. In fact, crimes of theft declined steadily from 1973 to 2005 (Catalano 2006:5).

In terms of age, the victimization studies almost always indicate that the most common victims are young people, while elderly people, those age 65 and older, have the lowest rates of victimization. In 2004–2005, for example, the rate of violent crime victimization was highest for the age groups 16–19 and 20–24, 45.0 per 1,000, and the group with the lowest victimization was 65 years of age and older, with a rate of 2.3 per 1,000 (Catalano 2006:4). One likely reason for this finding is that young people are out and about more so than the elderly. Separate analyses of victimization studies conclude that young people, particularly ages 18–24, tend to have the highest rates of violent crime victimization, not including murder (Klaus and Rennison 2002).

An extended study of the relationship between juvenile offending and victimization is also found in a national survey of more than 5,000 youthful offenders and victims called the National Longitudinal Study of Adolescent Health, or the ADD Health Study. According to analyses of these data, violent juvenile offenders are often victims of violent crimes and they share similar characteristics, such as being male, minority status, and more physically developed (Shaffer and Ruback 2002:1–5). These results suggest that victims of violent crimes are likely to be violent crime offenders one or two years later and vice versa (p. 4). While it may be logical to presume that a victim might become an offender, because of the trauma and psychological effects of the victimization, there seems to be an interaction between both victimization and offending. This goes back to a point raised earlier, although with more data, that one reason young people are more likely to be victims of crime more than the elderly is that they are more often outside their homes and among other people.

Because the NCVS studies ask heads of households about victims of crime in their families, it is possible that some of the victimizations that occur to juveniles are not captured in the surveys. Furthermore, it is likely that the identities of offenders are not known to victims, especially if the crime is a property crime. Even with personal crimes, knowledge of the ages of offenders may be guesswork on the part of victims, unless victim and offender know each other well. Of particular interest in this situation is the crime of murder. Since victimization surveys do not include murder, it is difficult to use these studies to learn much about the chances and circumstances of juvenile murder victims. However, for several years, the FBI has conducted separate analyses of murder in its UCR publications. Analyses of these data indicate that victims of murder tend to be young and mostly minority, that is, African American and Hispanic. Homicide rates for adults are much higher than for juveniles, but that is likely because the victimization rates are highest for young adults, ages 18–24. Despite the high murder rates for young adults, researchers conclude that the rate of juvenile victimization for murder in America is higher than for any other developed country (Finklehor and Ormrod 2001:2–3).

A Note on Hate Crimes

A hate crime is defined by the FBI as a crime motivated by bias against any one of several characteristics. Characteristics of victims that qualify a crime as a hate crime vary but usually include race, ethnicity, religion, and sexual orientation. The federal law does not include women as victims of hate crimes because of the Violence Against Women Act of 1994, which places female victimizations of all violent crimes under federal legislation, despite Supreme Court challenges to some parts of the law. However, in many states, violent crimes against women are included in hate crime laws (Gerstenfeld 2004:29). In 1990, Congress passed the Hate Crime Statistics Law, and since 1991, the FBI has collected data on hate crimes. Since 1994, these data have also included disability as a characteristic of hate crime victimization, although federal law does not recognize sexual orientation or disability as a target of hate crime acts.

In 2005, the Hate Crime Statistics report recorded a total of 7,163 hate crime incidences and 8,804 victims. By far, the victim category most often reported in connection with hate crimes has been that of race, and this was true in 2005. Of the 7,163 hate crimes that year, over half, 4,895, were of race, and this was mostly because of African American status of the victim (Hate Crime Statistics 2005:table 1).

Although the Hate Crime Statistics publication does not include ages of offenders or victims, studies of hate crimes often conclude that hate crime offenders are young people, acting in a group context rather than alone. In addition, few reported hate crimes are committed as a result of membership in large organizations, such as Skinheads or other organized hate groups (Gerstenfeld 2004:chapter 4, especially pp. 72–73). The influence on young people to commit hate crimes seems to stem more from group dynamics and the influence of peers in a social setting than ingrained indoctrination from organized extremist groups. Hate crimes are of interest in this textbook because they represent another example of criminal behavior committed by young people.

A much-publicized hate crime situation occurred in Jena, Louisiana, in December 2006. The case involved six African American high-school students and one white student and has become known as the "Jena Six" case. The African American youth have been charged with the beating of the white youth over the hanging of a noose on school grounds. According to news reports, the case started when a freshman African American student at the high school in Jena asked the principal, in an assembly of students, whether he and his friends could sit under a tree used by white students as a hangout. They were allowed to do so, but soon after, three nooses were found hanging from the tree (which could be classified as a hate crime). Racial tensions at the school flared, and the white youth was beaten by the African American youths. One youth, thought to be the main attacker, was first tried and convicted in adult court, but that conviction was overturned, and the youth is now facing a hearing on the charges in juvenile court. Subsequent to this case, officials have noted several instances of noose hangings in the country. These additional incidents, along with the lack of charges filed in connection with the noose hangings in Jena, have led social commentators to argue that the charges levied against the African American youth indicate racial bias in the handling of this hate crime as well as in other instances of hate crimes in the country (Sniffen 2007).

Other Methods

In some cases, such as the study of gangs, researchers have to use other methods than the ones described in this chapter. Studies of gangs, for example, often use observations and interviews with gang members as a basis for their information. Sometimes, *participant observation* is used in the study of gangs or otherwise hard-to-reach populations, such as runaways or street children. Participant observation means actually participating in the group's activities while studying their behavior patterns (see some of the studies of gangs discussed in chapter 10, on juvenile gangs).

Another method of studying delinquency is the *experimental method*. In this case, people are studied in a confined setting, perhaps even a laboratory, and their behavior is observed, recorded, and analyzed. Most often, when researchers use this method to study behavior, they are looking for specific behaviors in response to particular causes. For example, studies of the effects of television or other stimuli on behavior can be conducted in an experimental fashion. The researcher would look for specific effects when exposed to certain kinds and/or amounts of violence, such as aggressive behavior exhibited after watching a violent program or scene on television.

Sometimes researchers are able to conduct an experiment in a "natural" setting, which means where youth live and congregate. In this case, such as a study about the effects of a curfew on young people's behavior, the study is organized around the conditions and situations of the natural setting. For example, observers may post themselves at a shopping mall or popular cruising site and observe while tabulating and recording the movements of young people who visit these locales at particular times.

In addition, some researchers use *content analyses* of published reports and newspaper accounts of delinquency activity, including gangs, to get a better idea of delinquency in a particular population. In this case, the goal is to organize and categorize concepts, themes, patterns, and so on from the material read or seen in an effort to get a better understanding of the kinds of delinquent acts discovered and their characteristics.

Summary

There are several methods of measuring and studying delinquency. Each has its advantages and disadvantages, and no single method is so superior to the others that it can always be used or used exclusively. The wise approach to a fuller or more complete understanding of delinquency is to use as many methods as possible or practical.

Despite the differences found in various measures of delinquency, several common results seem to stand out. Students of delinquency should keep these conclusions in mind when assessing information concerning theories of delinquency, which will be presented later in this book.

- Rates of delinquency in the United States have been falling since the mid 1990s except for females arrested for drug abuse, the rate of which has been increasing since the mid-1990s.
- Rates of delinquency are higher for males than for females except for some sex crimes, such as prostitution, and status offenses such as running away.
- Arrest and referral to court rates are disproportionately high for minorities, but some studies suggest that some of this disproportionality is because of discrimination against minorities.

- Racial and gender differences in rates of delinquency seem to be greater for official estimates of delinquency, such as arrest and court data, compared with self-report studies, but these differences remain in self-report data.
- Rates of delinquency among males peak at around the age of 18, and for females at around age 17, and then decrease over the life course for both males and females.
- A small proportion, between 5 percent and 10 percent of all juveniles, are responsible for the majority of criminal and delinquent acts in a population of juveniles, and usually, their crimes are the more serious offenses, such as violent crimes.

The findings listed above are not all of the conclusions one can reach regarding patterns of delinquency, but, again, they are consistent findings that emerge from different sources of measuring and studying delinquency. The next several chapters will present explanations of delinquency that are based on various sources of information. As the reader encounters these theories and the data often used to evaluate the theories, close attention should be paid to the source of the data being used as well as the points listed above. Does the theory make sense, so to speak, of consistent findings regarding the extent and patterns of delinquency? In addition, these facts should be considered when discussions of the juvenile justice system, the police, and the courts are presented later in the book.

References

Canter, Rachelle J.
    1982   Sex Differences in Self-Reported Delinquency. Criminology 20: 373–393.
Catalano, Shannon M.
    2006   National Crime Survey: Criminal Victimization, 2005. Washington, DC: U.S. Department of Justice, Office of Justice Programs.
Cernkovich, Stephen A., Peggy C. Giordano, and Meredith D. Pugh
    1985   Chronic Offenders: The Missing Cases in Self-Report Delinquency Research. Journal of Criminal Law and Criminology 76(3):705–732.
Elliott, Delbert S., and David Huizinga
    1983   Social Class and Delinquent Behavior in a National Youth Panel. Criminology 21:149–177.

Federal Bureau of Investigation
   2002   Crime in the United States, 2002. Electronic document, http://www
          .fbi.gov/ucr/cius_02/html/web/index.html, accessed April 21, 2008.
   2005   Hate Crime Statistics, 2005. Electronic document, http://www
          .fbi.gov/ucr/hc2005/table1.htm, accessed April 21, 2008.
   2006   Crime in the United States, 2006. Electronic document, http://www
          .fbi.gov/ucr/cius2006/index.html, accessed April 21, 2008.
Finkelhor, David, and Richard Ormrod
   2001   Homicides of Children and Youth. Juvenile Justice Bulletin, Octo-
          ber. Washington, DC: U.S. Department of Justice, Office of Justice
          Programs.
   2004   Prostitution of Juveniles: Patterns from NIBRS. Juvenile Justice Bul-
          letin, June. Washington, DC: U.S. Department of Justice, Office of
          Justice Programs.
Gerstenfeld, Phyllis B.
   2004   Hate Crimes: Causes, Controls, and Controversies. Thousand Oaks,
          CA: Sage.
Hindelang, Michael J., Travis Hirschi, and Joseph G. Weiss
   1981   Measuring Delinquency. Beverly Hills: Sage.
Klaus, Patsy, and Callie Marie Rennison
   2002   Age Patterns in Violent Victimization, 1976–2000. Bureau of Justice
          Statistics Crime Data Brief. Washington, DC: U.S. Department of
          Justice.
Porterfield, Austin L.
   1943   Delinquency and Its Outcome in Court and College. American
          Journal of Sociology 49:199–208.
Puzzanchera, C., T. Finnegan, and W. Kang
   2006   Easy Access to Juvenile Populations. Electronic document, http://
          ojjdp.ncjrs.gov/ojstatbb/ezapop, accessed April 21, 2008.
Shaffer, Jennifer N., and R. Barry Ruback
   2002   Violent Victimization as a Risk Factor for Violent Offending among
          Juveniles. Juvenile Justice Bulletin, December. Washington, DC: U.S.
          Department of Justice, Office of Justice Programs.
Shoemaker, Donald J.
   1994   Male-Female Delinquency in the Philippines: A Comparative Analy-
          sis. Youth & Society 25:299–329.
Short, James F., Jr., and F. Ivan Nye
   1958   Extent of Unrecorded Juvenile Delinquency: Tentative Conclusions.
          Journal of Criminal Law, Criminology, and Police Science 49:296–302.

Sniffen, Michael J.
    2007   The FBI Reports Hate Crimes Were Up Nearly 8 Percent in 2006. Roanoke Times, November 20: A3.

Snyder, Howard N.
    2006   Juvenile Arrests 2004. Juvenile Justice Bulletin, December. Electronic document, http://www.ncjrs.gov/html/ojjdp/214563/contents.html, accessed April 21, 2008.

Snyder, Howard N., and Melissa Sickmund
    2006   Juvenile Offenders and Victims: 2006 National Report. Washington, DC: U.S. Department of Justice, Office of Justice Programs, Office of Juvenile Justice and Delinquency Prevention.

Stahl, Anne L., Charles Puzzanchera, Sarah Livsey, Anthony Sladky, Terrence A. Finnegan, Nancy Tierney, and Howard N. Snyder
    2006   Juvenile Court Statistics 2003–2004. Electronic document, http://www.ojjdp.ncjrs.gov/ojstatbb/njcda, accessed April 21, 2008.

Tracy, Paul E., Marvin E. Wolfgang, and Robert M. Figlio
    1990   Delinquency Careers in Two Birth Cohorts. New York: Plenum.

Vaz, Edmund V.
    1967   Middle-Class Juvenile Delinquency. New York: Harper & Row.

Wooden, Wayne S., and Randy Blazak
    2001   Renegade Kids, Suburban Outlaws: From Youth Culture to Delinquency. 2nd edition. Belmont, CA: Wadsworth.

Wright, Bradley R. Entner, Avshalom Caspi, Terrie E. Moffitt, Richard A. Miech, and Phil A. Silva
    1999   Reconsidering the Relationship between SES and Delinquency: Causation but Not Correlation. Criminology 37:175–194.

The Classical School, Rational Choice, and Individualistic Explanations of Delinquency

B EFORE THE 19th century, most explanations of crime and delinquency were based on a free will conceptualization of human behavior. The basic idea was that people do what they do because they gain something from such behavior; that is, they profit in one way or another from their behavior. This logic applies to criminal activity as well as conformity. Today, criminologists often refer to this line of thinking as the *classical school* of thought concerning criminal behavior. Crime is committed because of the exercise of free will to obtain some gain or profit. Accordingly, the best way to prevent crime is to make it unprofitable, that is, to punish offenders. In addition, the classical view of behavior often did not distinguish between juveniles and adults. As was discussed in chapter 1, the concept of delinquency was not clearly formed until the latter years of the 19th century, and scholars of criminal behavior were not often thinking of human development by age in their theoretical reasoning. A modern view of the traditional classical school of thought is the idea that people exercise *rational choices* in deciding whether to commit a crime, including where the crime is committed.

The development of explanations of delinquency is characterized by a rethinking of the concept of free will. This line of thinking is usually identified with developments of the 19th century. One example of this shift in thinking about the motivations for crime is called the *positive school*. In addition, explanations of crime and delinquency influenced by the positive school and other theories are characterized by data collection and analysis, compared to logical reasoning. In fact, the term *positive* comes from the philosophical notion that empirical investigations into a subject are examples of positivistic thinking.

Earlier examples of positivistic explanations of crime and delinquency focused on those that identified individualistic factors as the major explanations of juvenile offending. These theories are what Albert Cohen calls "kinds of people theories" (Cohen 1966:42). That is, the emphasis is on what is wrong with the people committing the illegal acts. Two disciplines that have offered most of these individualistic explanations of delinquency are biology and psychology.

Biological and psychological explanations of delinquency can be divided into earlier and more modern periods, and the discussions of these theories will be presented in temporal order. While people may differ on the specifics of the break between early and modern, the break used in this chapter is pre-1950 and post-1950. This division will apply to the classical school and biological and psychological explanations of delinquency.

The Classical School

In 1764, an Italian philosopher and economist named Cesare Beccaria published a small book titled *On Crimes and Punishments*. The contents of this book were to become the basis for what is now known as the classical school in criminology. In his book, Beccaria laid out the ideas and philosophies of what he considered a just system of punishment for crimes. Beccaria saw the administration of justice in late 18th-century Europe as unjust and capricious. Judges would hand out widely different sentences for similar crimes without any apparent reason or system for doing so. The result, according to Beccaria, was not only confusion among those who worked in the system and those who were affected by it but also disrespect among criminals and those who were familiar with the haphazard manner in which crimes were punished.

To develop a fairer, more just, and, ultimately, more effective system of criminal justice, Beccaria outlined some basic principles of human behavior and its management. One of the guiding principles of this philosophy was the notion that all people act according to their free will. A second principle of this "new" school of thought was that people act according to a hedonistic philosophy, namely that we act in order to maximize our pleasure and to minimize our pain. Thus, we do what we do because it pleases us or gives us profit.

From these two basic ideas, Beccaria fashioned the framework for developing a fair system of justice for society. He argued for a system of punishment that would offset the gains made from committing crimes. In addition, the punishments for crimes were to be established by legislators, not judges. The role of judges was to be focused on deciding guilt or innocence, not on determining proper punishments for those found guilty of a crime. Moreover, punishment was not to be excessive, but, rather, only enough to negate the positive aspects of committing a crime. Capital punishment, for example, was not advocated by Beccaria (Martin et al. 1990:14–15).

The impact of this set of ideas on European governments and members of the judicial community was significant. Beccaria's book was read by many throughout Europe, and his ideas were soon incorporated into systems of criminal justice throughout the continent. In 1791, after its revolution in 1789, France incorporated many of Beccaria's ideas into a revised penal code. However, several years later, this system was again revised, at least in part because a literal translation of Beccaria's principles became impractical to implement in the real world of establishing fair and effective systems of punishment. For one thing, Beccaria did not recognize age or mental condition as conditioning factors in the use of punishment as a means to control crime. The idea that juveniles are not as fully formed in terms of cognitive awareness and judgment was not appreciated by Beccaria. Nor did he view mental abnormalities as important in the understanding of human behavior. Thus, the hard rules that Beccaria's system of justice imposed on judgers and society proved unworkable in the world of justice and punishment (Martin et al. 1990:6; Vold et al. 2002:20).

The recognition that extenuating circumstances should be considered when trying to understand the motivations for behavior is often referred to as the *neoclassical school* (Vold et al. 2002:20). An earlier example of the ideas of the neoclassical school is the English philosopher Jeremy Bentham, who wrote *An Essay on the Principles of Morals and Legislation* in 1789. Actually, this school of thought is not as clearly defined as the classical school. It is associated with the belief that free will exists but it is tempered or affected by personal and social situations. For example, Bentham made the case that an addict may not be as logical in his or her choice to use a drug as would be one who is not addicted to drugs. Therefore, to punish the addict on the grounds that he or she is thinking clearly on whether or not to use drugs would be to impose a system of logic on the addict that is not realistic.

Even in more mundane situations, the logic of the neoclassical school may apply. It is clear that in, most instances, we choose to do something, say, select a certain food to eat. However, it is also the case that that choice is often affected by a variety of factors, some internal, some external, that have a bearing on that choice. What is the lunch preference for a typical American teenager? Hamburgers and fries? What about the choice for, say, a Filipino child? Rice and fish? Cultural factors can play an important role in shaping our tastes and preferences for food, in the same way as they may play an important role in the choice to obey or disobey the law, according to the neoclassical school of thought. As some would say, our free will is "conditioned" (Fishbein 1990:30). It is even logical to assume that our whole system of juvenile justice is based on the neoclassical concept that we act according to free will but that the actions of children and youth are not as culpable as are those of adults. That is why we reserve different punishments and approaches to the control and prevention of delinquency as opposed to those for adult crime.

Rational Choice Theory and Delinquency

A modern view of the free choice argument is expressed in rational choice theory. This view of behavior suggests that people choose to act in accordance with a rational assessment of the costs and benefits of their behavior (Cornish and Clarke 1986). This notion is similar to an economic interpretation of behavior, in which acts are thought to occur in accordance with our economic interests. However, when this idea of rational, calculating thought processes is applied to juveniles, the logic seems to break down. For one thing, the whole system of juvenile justice in the United States is predicated on the assumptions that juveniles are not as rational as adults and that they cannot as clearly reason the consequences of their actions. Of course, young people do think and calculate behavior and act freely. But they, as with all people, are also influenced by social circumstances such that free will is "conditioned," as was mentioned earlier. With juveniles, however, this influence is filtered through less-developed reasoning ability—at least, that is what our judicial philosophy assumes.

Research on rational choice theory suggests that, among adults, perceived opportunities to commit crimes are more important in the explanation of self-reported criminality than are perceived punishments for committing crimes (Piliavin et al. 1986). However, this theory has not been tested very often among samples of juveniles. The research that does exist suggests that among a sample of juveniles, "rational" choices to commit acts of crime or delinquency or to stop committing such activity are not as clear as rational choice theory would suggest (Paternoster 1989).

Both rational choice theory and its foundation, classical theory, have some merit as explanations of delinquency. Clearly, many acts of delinquency are planned and carried out with specific consequences in mind. However, when we are dealing with youngsters, it is important to remember that often, youth do things with little forethought of their consequences. It seems useful, then, to explore alternative explanations of delinquency, such as the individualistic theories considered in the remainder of this chapter as well as several sociological explanations that will be discussed in succeeding chapters.

Lombroso and the Positive School

The transition from the classical idea that we all act according to free will to the notion that free will is conditioned gradually gave way to another traditional school of thought in criminology, the positive school. The positive school is associated with the idea that behavior is not only conditioned but also determined, especially by individualistic characteristics, and thus not really a product of free will (Vold et al. 2002:26–28).

The person most often associated with the positive school is an Italian physician named Cesare Lombroso. Lombroso became interested in the physical aspects of crime when he was performing autopsies on the cadavers of well-known criminals in Italy. He was influenced by the thinking of Charles Darwin and began to theorize that criminals were born to be criminal (Cohen 1966:49–50). Lombroso also used the term *atavist* or *atavism* to describe the born criminal. By this term, he meant a throwback to an earlier form of evolutionary life. Essentially, criminals were placed lower on the evolutionary chart than were other people.

Another feature of Lombroso's theory was that born criminals were characterized by numerous physical features, such as a hunched back, long forearms, low forehead, and so on, even to include tattoos (Cohen 1966:49–50). These physical features could be measured, according to Lombroso, and studied in a "scientific" manner. Interestingly, Lombroso reasoned that such features would largely be observable in advanced societies because in "savage" societies, the distance between criminal and normal was not great and the advancement of human evolution had not progressed very far (Horn 2003:43–44).

The use of measurement and careful assessment of the physical features of criminals is one reason Lombroso's work is called the positive school. Positivism involves empiricism. However, Lombroso's methods were not scientific because carefully selected subject and specific control groups were not used. Subjects were not chosen randomly, but by convenience. He did not use matching control groups in conducting research and when comparison or "normal" groups were used, they were not selected in any systematic way, such as by random lot or by characteristics similar to the criminal population he was studying (Horn 2003: chapters 2 and 3).

To summarize, the positive school contained several features:

1. It developed toward the end of the 19th century.
2. It was favored by physicians and others with biological training who lived in Italy (hence, this school is sometimes called the "Italian school").
3. It emphasized empiricism and measurement of traits, but not the use of adequate control groups.
4. It emphasized biological determinism as opposed to free will as the basis for explaining human behavior.

Early Biological Explanations of Delinquency

Inheritance and Delinquency

Toward the end of his career, Lombroso began to move away from earlier theories and ideas. For example, he classified about one-third of criminals as born, with the rest being classified as insane, epileptic, or occasional, including the criminaloid, that is, one prone to commit crime but not showing the physical "abnormalities" of the born criminal (Wolfgang 1972; Martin et al. 1990:21–44.). In addition, subsequent researchers, namely the English statistician Charles Goring (1913), collected evidence that refuted Lombroso's ideas of born criminality. Later work done by a Harvard anthropologist, Earnest Hooton, tended to support Lombroso's work, but research and conclusions were so criticized that they, too, tended to discredit Lombroso's ideas of born criminality being evidenced through physical appearance (Rafter 2004).

Nonetheless, the search for the biological roots of crime had been established in the theories of many criminologists in the late 19th and early 20th centuries. One such theory concerns the inheritance of criminal traits and/or tendencies. Lombroso was never clear about the inherited nature of crime, although the concept of the born criminal would definitely suggest such a position. However, toward the end of the 19th century, scholars and social commentators began to pursue theories of biological inheritance as the basic cause of crime and deviance in society. One of these studies was that of the Juke family in upstate New York, conducted by Richard Dugdale (1888). Dugdale used the "family tree" method to study the lineage of a family called the Jukes. Using official data and news accounts, Dugdale concluded that the Juke family had shown patterns of deviance, such as drunkenness, prostitution, and crime, for several generations. This finding led him to conclude that crime and other social problems are inherited.

Another family tree study was conducted by H. H. Goddard, also in the late 19th century. Goddard was a superintendent of a home for the feeble-minded in New Jersey. He conducted a study of the family history of one of his patients, a girl named Kallikak (1912). Goddard found that the Kallikak line was divided. On one side was the offspring of a Union soldier and a retarded woman in the family. On the other side was the progeny of the same mother but a father with a reputation for crime and deviance. The line produced by the soldier included many prominent citizens, such as a senator and a physician. The line from the criminal father produced a succession of criminals and deviants. These results led Goddard to conclude that criminal (and, by logic, politically and economically successful) behavior was biologically inherited.

Of course, these studies would be considered naïve at best by today's standards of research and measurement. A hundred years ago, however, this kind of research led to many conclusions that crime and deviance were inherited. Around the turn of the 20th century, *eugenics* was legalized and became a method of crime prevention. Eugenics was a practice of sterilization used on inmates of institutions, particularly those with low IQs. However, the practice was also used on inmates of various other types, including delinquents. The idea behind eugenics was that since deviance was inherited, if society sterilized deviants, ultimately there would be no more deviants in the population.

Involuntary sterilization sometimes led to abuses, but in 1927, in a case known as *Buck v. Bell*, the United States Supreme Court legitimized eugenics, and that decision has not been overturned. Carrie Buck was thought to be a retarded young woman who had given birth out of wedlock. For this and other reasons, she was confined to an institution in Virginia, where she was sterilized. An attorney took up her case and brought it to the U.S. Supreme Court. Speaking for the majority decision in that case, Chief Justice Oliver

Wendell Holmes, Jr., wrote, "Three generations of imbeciles is enough" (Rowe 2002:141–142). Years later, researchers concluded that Carrie Buck was not retarded, nor was her daughter, but at least for several decades, the issue had been settled in the courts. Today, the practice of eugenics is outmoded, and few, if any, cases of involuntary sterilization of inmates have been recorded in recent years (Bishop 1994; Rowe 2002:142). However, the idea that we can cure the problem of crime via medical procedures is still with us and not likely to fade anytime in the near future.

Somatotypes and Delinquency

Somatotype research is based on the assumption that people are born with certain body types and that these body types influence personalities and behavior. William Sheldon, for example, reasoned that there are three dominant body types: *ectomorph, mesomorph,* and *endomorph.* Somatotypes are determined on the basis of relative scores along each dimension of the three dominant ones, ectomorph, mesomorph, and endomorph. The range of scores is from 1 to 7. Thus, an individual receiving a score of 2, 6, 3, for example, would be classified as a mesomorph. In some cases, the scores are not distinct, so the body type is classified as mixed. In Sheldon's studies, measurements were determined by inspections of photographs (1949).

In addition, each body type is associated with a personality, according to Sheldon. Ectomorphs are characterized by a thin, frail body type. Mesomorphs are muscular and athletic, while endomorphs are soft, round, and flabby. Ectomorphs are shy and withdrawn, mesomorphs are aggressive, and endomorphs are outgoing and happy. It is not clear which factor actually causes delinquency, but it is presumed that all operate together to produce a tendency to commit juvenile crime.

Sheldon normed the body types on college students in the 1930s and 1940s. In those studies, college students seemed to be distributed fairly evenly. He later decided to study body types among delinquents, choosing the residents of an institution in Boston called the Hayden Goodwill Inn. Sheldon concluded that the typical delinquent body type was mesomorphic. Thus, one conclusion from this research was that mesomorphic, aggressive males were more likely to commit delinquency than were other males (Sheldon 1949:726–729).

Sheldon's body types and measurement techniques were adopted in a study of 500 male delinquents compared with 500 male nondelinquents living in Boston. This study was also conducted in the 1940s by Sheldon and

Eleanor Glueck and named *Unraveling Juvenile Delinquency* (1950). The Gluecks conducted several kinds of measurements: not only body types but also personality scores and social characteristics. Some of their results are discussed in other parts of this book. For the present discussion, however, their study concluded that the predominant body type among delinquents was the mesomorph, while that among nondelinquents was the ectomorph.

After further consideration, the Gluecks offered an alternative explanation of their findings as compared to the biological view that trait characteristics determined personality and behavior. This alternative view suggested that there might be some kind of *social selection* occurring such that physically strong and aggressive males might be encouraged to join gangs, where their involvement in delinquent acts would also be encouraged (Glueck and Glueck 1956).

Contemporary Biological Explanations of Delinquency

Contemporary biological explanations of delinquency continue to examine many of the earlier explanations of delinquency, but some are looking at the question of why youth commit crime in different ways than before. This section covers many of these contemporary biological approaches to understanding delinquency, some extensions of earlier lines of inquiry, and some branching off into new theories.

Inheritance and Delinquency—Newer Studies

Contemporary research investigating the impact of biological inheritance on crime is more sophisticated than earlier research. For example, new studies on this subject often include hundreds and sometimes thousands of cases of twins. Much of this research is conducted in Scandinavian societies, where social registries and birth record information are more easily accessible than in other countries, such as the United States. Moreover, these databases of twins are not biased in terms of starting with at least one twin already incarcerated. The significance of this point is that concordance rates for delinquency are purer, since it is not known before the study how many of a sample of twins are delinquent. However, there are few published studies of twins and delinquency per se from Scandinavian countries (Lyons 1996). In addition, current studies of twins are informed by more precise indications of twins' status, often based on blood analyses, compared to physical appearance alone. This point is underscored by the designation of identical, or maternal, twins as monozygotic, or MZ, compared with fraternal twins, which are designated as dizygotic, or DZ.

The contemporary studies of inheritance and delinquency using samples of twins as the basis of comparison still find that the concordance rate for delinquency is higher among MZ twins than among DZ twins, as expected, but the numbers are lower than in previous studies. In addition, some contemporary students of the topic suggest that the concordance rate among twins is higher for crime than for delinquency, although studies of youth and crime are few (Rowe 2002:30).

Some current research also examines adoptions and crime, again often coming from Scandinavian countries. One study of over 14,000 adopted males in Denmark, for example, found that adoptive sons have criminal records more similar to that of their biological fathers, compared with their adoptive fathers. Also, those adopted sons whose fathers, adoptive or biological, had no criminal record had the lowest rate of crime. However, in no comparison was the concordance rate higher than 25 percent (Mednick et al. 1987). Nonetheless, the directions of the relationships suggest some degree of biological influence in the explanation of criminality.

Altogether, the recent research and thinking on the biological connection to crime and delinquency has moved more and more into the area of interaction, or at least mutual influence between biological factors and the environment. In a study of several hundred twins in Sweden, for example, researchers found that the concordance rate of crime was greater for MZ twins than for DZ twins, an expected finding. However, when the environmental background of the MZ twins was considered, the effect of inheritance was reduced to near zero. The concordance rate of crime among both MZ and DZ twins treated similarly as children and youth was significantly higher than the rate for those twins who had been raised independently as separate individuals (Dalgard and Kringlen 1978). Also, Mednick's research on adoptees in Denmark concluded that social conditions can affect criminal behavior irrespective of genetic background (Mednick et al. 1987:86).

Somatotype Studies Continued

Somatotype research has fallen off since the studies of the 1940s and 1950s, but some attention was still paid to this subject as late as the 1970s. In a study of 100 male delinquents and 100 male nondelinquents, Cortes and Gatti concluded that the mesomorphic body type was dominant among the delinquents but not the nondelinquents, many of whom were classified as endomorphic (1972). The methods of Cortes and Gatti were an improvement over that of Sheldon and the Gluecks in that they classified body types on the basis of more careful physical measurements as opposed to observations of photographs. Still, they used official records of delinquency as their measurement of delinquency, thus cutting off a significant amount of youthful offending, as was noted in chapter 3.

In all of the research conducted on somatotypes and delinquency the consistent conclusion is that mesomorphs, no matter how measured, predominate in the population of delinquents. The theoretical notion that mesomorphs are somehow inherently inclined to be aggressive and delinquent, however, is difficult to accept because so many other possible explanations exist to explain this persistent finding. Since all of the studies done thus far have measured delinquency on the basis of official records, namely institutionalized youth, it is possible, maybe even likely, that social selection operates to produce the overabundance of mesomorphs in these institutions. This is a different explanation than the social selection view discussed earlier. In this case, the suggestion is that mesomorphic youngsters, these physically imposing youth, are selected for treatment or punishment by court officials because of their appearance, which is a type of labeling idea. Labeling theory is discussed in more detail in chapter 12 of this book.

There is also the issue of why some youngsters who are physically imposing choose sports as an outlet rather than crime or delinquency. The career paths of youngsters are not solely explained by chance or biological drives, but rather by social factors and processes. Tall boys may be encouraged to play basketball, and strong, athletic youth may be encouraged to play football in areas where these opportunities exist. Rational choices for these youth may result in sports as opposed to crime in many, probably most, situations. Why, then, do some turn to crime? The answer likely rests more with social opportunities and circumstances than with genes. As David Rowe (2002) says, after a thoughtful and detailed examination of genes and behavior, "There are no genes for specific behaviors in humans; rather, the genes usually code for proteins, and the proteins in turn can affect and interact with a host of physiological traits" (p. 105).

Learning Disabilities

The relationship of learning disabilities to delinquency has a fairly brief history, and one that has been characterized by disagreements and uncertainties.

As a concept, learning disabilities started to become well known in the 1960s (Murray 1976). While it is certain that education specialists were aware of this condition before then, people often did not know what to do with children who had learning disabilities, or how to diagnose the situation in the first place. Today, of course, there are teachers and school administrators specifically trained to recognize, diagnose, and handle youth with learning disabilities, but that has not always been the case.

A learning disability is a condition that interferes with a person's patterns of learning. It is typically not associated with hearing or sight loss, but rather with brain functions that operate differently from those of "normal" patterns of learning. A full diagnosis of a learning disability within a school setting usually involves evaluations by several specialists, including a physician, a psychologist, a social worker, and teachers and school administrators. In addition, the signature of a parent or guardian of a minor child must be secured before a school district can officially label a child learning disabled.

There are several kinds of learning disabilities, and some people have more than one. Probably the most well-known type of learning disability is *dyslexia*, a condition that affects a person's ability to read. With dyslexia, words are often jumbled, such that the word *saw*, for example, is seen as *was*. While a beginning reader will often mix up words and letters, dyslexia is a more permanent condition and one that makes it difficult to develop confident reading skills. Other learning disabilities include *aphasia*, which hinders interpretations of spoken directions and instructions, and *hyperkinesis*, which often results in excessive movement of large and small muscles (Murray 1976).

In the 1970s, researchers began to investigate the connection between learning disabilities and delinquency, thinking that these conditions would make it more likely that children would experience difficulties in the classroom and in society. Initial results indicated a substantial disagreement on the connection between the two. Estimates of learning-disabled delinquents ranged from 20 percent to over 90 percent (Murray 1976). Part of the reason for this discrepancy was that measures and diagnoses of learning disabilities were not uniform, especially 30–40 years ago. In addition, most of these studies examined youth in juvenile institutions, which might have biased the samples in terms of youth with behavioral problems.

Over the years, substantial research on learning disabilities and how to deal with them has contributed to more knowledge about how learning disabilities may contribute to delinquency. Basically, researchers suspect there are two avenues connecting delinquency with learning disabilities, a *direct* link and a *school-based* connection.

The direct link between delinquency and learning disabilities suggests that learning-disabled youngsters have a hard time getting along with others, including teachers and other adults. In addition, these youth do not seem to learn from their experiences as others do, so they are prone to repeat their mistakes and to get into further trouble with others. These difficulties can then lead these youngsters into conflicts with the police, teachers, and other legal authorities (Murray 1976; Morrison 1978).

The school-based link between learning disabilities and delinquency suggests that learning-disabled youth develop difficulties in school based in part or in whole on their disability. These negative school experiences then lead to a low self-concept and to real problems in handling academic subjects, problems that only seem to mount as the child grows older. In addition, the child receives a label that identifies him or her as a slow learner, a different kind of child, and so on, which only seems to worsen the situation (see chapter 12 on labeling theory). Eventually, these school problems and self-concept issues result in acts of delinquency, in part as a means to help alleviate the situation, at least in the child's mind (Murray 1976; Fleener 1987; C. Fink 1990).

Both of these linkages between delinquency and learning disabilities have merit. There is, for instance, a consistent correlation between learning disabilities and delinquency, although the prevalence of learning disability among delinquent youth is closer to 35 percent as opposed to 90 percent (Casey and Keilitz 1990). However, the school-based link seems more plausible at this time. As will be seen later, in chapter 8, on schools and delinquency, school failure and academic problems in general are important correlates of delinquency. Therefore, any factor that might contribute to academic problems should be carefully considered in attempts to understand delinquency.

In addition, research has demonstrated that not all learning-disabled youth become delinquent. Some are able to deal with their situation and overcome the obstacles to academic success that learning disabilities pose (Pickar and Tori 1986; Perlmutter 1987).

Terrie Moffitt's (1990) longitudinal research in New Zealand also addresses the connection between learning problems and delinquency by focusing on attention deficit disorder (ADD). Her study suggests that children with ADD do not always become delinquent. Nearly half of those classified as ADD were "nondelinquent." In addition, Moffitt's study found that social advantages, such as "strong verbal skills and/or good family circumstances" helped reduce the negative effects of ADD (pp. 905–907). Again, this research suggests that the potentially negative impacts of learning problems can be reduced by positive environmental factors and that there is by no means an automatic link between learning problems, such as ADD and learning disabilities, and delinquency.

A key factor in this relationship seems to be the kind of assistance and reception learning-disabled youth receive as they attempt to come to terms with their situation, making friends, doing well in school, and, in general, developing into adolescence. If they receive good support, lacking in invidious labels and negative stereotyping, they have a good chance to develop socially and academically with no more difficulties than other children. If they do not receive such assistance and guidance, they are more likely to develop academic problems, low self-concepts, pejorative labels, and, eventually, a lifestyle involving delinquency.

Conditionability (ANS) and Delinquency

Several decades ago, a British psychobiologist named Hans Eysenck proposed an explanation of delinquency based on the notion that some people are born with an autonomic nervous system (ANS) that is slow to react to environmental stimuli (Eysenck 1977). Essentially, such persons have a *slow reaction time* and are less able to connect their behavior with feedback they receive from others. For example, in school, a child with a slow reaction time who has been disciplined for misbehavior will not understand why he or she is being punished. One result of this situation is the slower development of "inhibitory controls," that is, the ability to control one's emotions and behaviors. In effect, one's conditionability, or ability to be socialized, is inhibited.

Another feature of this explanation of delinquency is that such children develop personality traits that are considered outgoing, or *extroverted*. In part, this expectation comes from the idea that a person with a slow reaction time often overcompensates for what is perceived to be inadequate reactions from others. He or she thinks the teacher is not paying any attention, so behavior must be louder or more disruptive for a reaction to occur. Unfortunately for the child, the reaction from a teacher may be negative—that is, punitive—but at least it is some kind of response.

This theory has been tested by Eysenck and others in different countries and settings. One fairly consistent finding is that delinquent youth have slower reaction times than do control groups (Eysenck 1977, 1989; Eysenck and Eysenck 1978; Siddle et al. 1977; Mednick et al. 1981). Reaction time is often measured in terms of "electrodermal recovery" tests, such as galvanic skin response tests or electroencephalographic tests. In addition, much of Eysenck's research concludes that prisoners and incarcerated youth are more extroverted than controls, although some research disputes this claim (Hoghughi and Forrest 1970).

However, almost always these studies rely on institutionalized samples of youth or official records as the measure of delinquency. Aside from the potential bias such a sample might present, there is the additional issue of cause and effect. Some research suggests, for example, that emotional deprivation in childhood can lead to slower reaction time among samples of psychopathic offenders (see below), particularly during stressful situations (Walsh et al. 1987). It might be assumed that being arrested, sent to court, and placed into an institution are stressful events. What can happen, then, is that stressful situations can lower or inhibit reaction times after a crime has been committed and while a person is being processed through the criminal or juvenile justice system, and this could lead to an inaccurate interpretation of the connection between crime and delinquency and slow reaction times. In addition, some studies suggest that slower reaction times are linked to delinquency mostly among those in the "lower middle and middle classes" (Mednick et al. 1977), which suggests that environmental factors affect delinquency beyond the physical factor of simply possessing a defective ANS.

Despite these methodological problems and issues, the theory of conditionability, or ANS, and delinquency has shown some promise for further research, especially longitudinal studies that can disentangle the causal connection between response time and delinquency (Magnusson et al. 1992). However, this theory seems better suited as an explanation of particular sets of delinquents, such as psychopathic offenders or middle-class delinquents, rather than most juvenile offenders. Once again, however, the research on this topic clearly suggests that biological factors interact with environmental conditions to encourage delinquency, and this recognition is an important difference between earlier and more modern biological explanations of delinquency.

Psychological Explanations of Delinquency

Psychological explanations of delinquency have often been combined with biological theories, such as Sheldon's somatotypes and personality explanation. Strictly psychological views, which focus on attitudes and mental characteristics, however, do have a history in the explanation of crime and delinquency. As with earlier biological theories, early psychological explanations tended to blend crime and delinquency.

The Psychoanalytic View

One of the earliest psychological interpretations of crime and delinquency, the psychoanalytic approach, was offered by Sigmund Freud and his followers. Freud conceptualized the human mind into three categories: the *id*, the *ego*, and the *superego*. The id is the basic part of ourselves, the part of our mind that is selfish and full of basic "instincts," such as the instinct for survival. The ego is thought to be the rational component of our psychological makeup. It is the part of ourselves that regulates and balances id impulses with social restrictions and conventions. These social conventions, sometimes called morals, are represented by the superego. This component of the mind is also referred to as the conscience (Freud 1927, 1930, 1935).

Freud's theory is also developmental in that people are seen as growing and developing in stages. Furthermore, with psychoanalysis, these stages of growth are typically viewed in terms of sexual growth. Personalities are shaped in terms of the regular, or normal, development of sexual growth or by periods in which such growth is arrested or somehow altered in abnormal ways. For example, it is normal and typical for children to be attracted to a parent of the opposite sex. However, if this attraction becomes too intense or dominant, problems in personality development can occur. If a male child comes to view his father as a rival for the affections and attention of his mother, a complex can develop, referred to as the *Oedipus complex* (Freud 1927). A similar situation involving a girl viewing her mother in the same way is called the *Electra complex.*

Another feature of psychoanalytical thinking is the notion that painful experiences, particularly those occurring before adolescence, are repressed into the *unconscious* (Freud 1927). That is, people who have had bad things happen to them tend to forget, on a conscious level, those experiences, but the deeper recesses of the mind still retain these memories. In addition, these memories, although on an unconscious level, affect one's outward behavior. Motives for behavior, then, are hidden from the individual and all around him or her. Substitute objects for true feelings and objects of emotions often develop in place of the real reasons for behaviors and attitudes. For example, a young male who urinates into his father's alcohol bottle may be expressing hostility or jealousy toward the father, but the son cannot openly admit such feelings (Aichhorn 1965). It is through intense analysis using projective techniques, such as the Rorschach test, through dream analysis, or through hypnosis or more modern drugs that the therapist can get to these hidden motives.

While Freud did not often use his theory to explain crime or delinquency, others have adopted Freudian concepts and theory to explain delinquency. An illustration of the application of Freudian concepts to an explanation of delinquency is provided in Hewitt and Jenkins' typology of 500 youth living at the Michigan Child Guidance Institute (Hewitt and Jenkins 1946). The typology consisted of (1) the "overinhibited," or Type I personality; (2) the "unsocialized aggressive," or Type II personality, and (3) the "socialized delinquent," or Type III personality. In their assessment of the personalities of these youth, Hewitt and Jenkins concluded that a faulty superego was prominent in the psychological makeup of many of the boys. In the first type, Type I, the person is said to have a strong superego, resulting in a shy, neurotic personality. Type II was described as the opposite of Type I, with a weak superego, resulting in an aggressive, impulsive personality. Type III is a hybrid personality, consisting of a normal superego, and thus, normal behavior, when interacting with members of a group or gang, but a weak superego and aggression displayed toward all out-group members (pp. 81–83; see also Cohen 1966:55). It is interesting to note that all three types combined represented less than 40 percent of all the youths examined in the study, suggesting that over 60 percent of these troubled youth had "normal" personalities.

Intelligence and Delinquency

Scholars of crime and delinquency have been interested in the connection between intelligence and crime for over a hundred years. Earlier views consistently argued that intelligence and crime are inherited, so intelligence and crime must also be connected. In the early 20th century, the popular notion was that crime was "caused" by the lack of intelligence. This view was proposed by many of the earlier biological researchers discussed earlier, such as Lombroso, Goring, and Hooton. Low intelligence was also identified as one reason for the inheritance of criminality by the authors of the studies of the Jukes and the Kallikaks. H. H. Goddard, for example, was a superintendent of a home for the feebleminded in New Jersey. It was not coincidental that he attributed, in large measure, the inheritance of crime to the inheritability of intelligence, low intelligence.

Soon after the Stanford-Binet intelligence test was developed in the early 20th century, scientists began to study the connection between delinquency and intelligence based more on empirical testing than on general observations. In a study of feeblemindedness and criminality (1914), Goddard concluded that among inmates of 16 reformatories, the average prevalence of feeblemindedness was 50 percent.

Using intelligence test figures, Goddard defined feeblemindedness as an IQ of 75 or less. Additional earlier research tended to support Goddard's general conclusion that low intelligence contributed to delinquency (A. Fink 1938).

However, after World War I, when the U.S. Army administered intelligence tests to soldiers and draftees, cutoffs for feeblemindedness and other definitions of low intelligence had to be revised. Using established figures for that time, for instance, would lead one to conclude that about one-third of the draft population was feebleminded (Zeleny 1933). While some military drill instructors might agree with this assessment, it presented a dilemma for most scholars, since, clearly, they could not accept a conclusion that about one-third of the general population was feebleminded.

Using a revised estimate of feeblemindedness, which resulted in an IQ of 50 or lower, research done on the topic in the 1920s and 1930s tended to downplay the connection between low intelligence and criminality, and some studies found delinquents to be of higher intelligence than army draftees (Murchison 1926).

After World War II, the research on intelligence and delinquency began to fade in favor of investigations of other factors, such as social class and race. In the 1960s, the topic was raised again and became somewhat of a controversy because some associated IQ with race as well as crime (Jensen 1969). Robert Gordon (1976) also implies an association of race with IQ and delinquency, but his arguments eventually drift to more sociological than biological connections. For example, Gordon reasons that parents with low IQs are not only more likely to have low-IQ children but also less able to raise their offspring in conventional ways of thinking and behaving, thus increasing the likelihood of raising delinquent children. Of course, this reasoning is flawed on numerous grounds (Sagarin 1980), but the effort demonstrates attempts to place the connection between IQ and crime in larger contexts than biological inheritance.

The indirect connection between IQ and delinquency is still being investigated, but in different ways. One emerging indirect link is through the school. It is thought that those with low IQs (but not profoundly retarded) find it more difficult to do well in academic subjects and that school failure then contributes to delinquency (Hirschi and Hindelang 1977; Denno 1985).

There is some merit to this argument, in part because the connection between academic failure and delinquency is well documented (see the discussion in chapter 8). However, this viewpoint fails to take into account the existence of "bright delinquents" (Tennent and Gath 1975) or the possibility that more intelligent youth may be better able to avoid detection or to argue their way out of legal problems such as arrests and/or court convictions (Hirschi and Hindelang 1977).

Remember, too, that the whole issue of a connection between IQ and delinquency is partly based on belief in the validity of IQ tests. Considerable discussion and debate on IQ tests, however, cast doubt on this assumption (Eysenck and Kamin 1981). There is a probable connection between IQ and criminality, but it is likely this connection is neither direct nor consistent (Denno 1985).

Personality Factors

Another aspect of a psychological connection with delinquency is what is generally known as "personality." While not all scholars agree on the definition of this term, the concept of personality is generally thought of as a relatively permanent set of attitudes and values that people exhibit in most situations. Some suggest that a personality is a set of orientations, or dispositions, to act or think in certain ways (Miller and Lynam 2001:784).

Typically, personality has been connected with delinquency in a straightforward fashion. That is, a bad or negative personality is thought to be connected with a bad behavioral outcome, such as delinquency. This kind of thinking is sometimes called "kinds of people" theorizing (Cohen 1966:42). Whatever the source of the "bad" personality, the predicted outcome is negative, and this behavior is to be expected because these "kinds of people" often act the way they do regardless of the situation. Actually, this assessment of delinquency is similar to many of the biological explanations discussed earlier, only in this case, the suspected cause is more mental than physical.

Traditional personality explanations of delinquency tend to focus on what is sometimes referred to as a "core personality." In other words, researchers have looked for a dominant or overriding personality feature that is most often associated with delinquency. In this regard, it might be expected to hear that the "typical" delinquent is aggressive, or maybe outgoing, or impulsive (Lynam et al. 2001).

Efforts to find a "delinquent" personality have not been effective. The aforementioned study of 1,000 Boston youth by the Gluecks, for example, found that delinquents were statistically more likely to exhibit suspicion, hostility, and defiance, compared with the nondelinquents. But these authors also concluded that nondelinquents were more neurotic than the delinquents and that nearly half of the delinquents had no identifiable psychological characteristics (Glueck and Glueck 1950). Note again that the detailed analyses of personalities among the youth in the previously discussed study by Hewitt and Jenkins found that nearly 60 percent of these youth had no clear psychodynamic personality pattern.

Literature reviews have also failed to consistently locate dominant personality characteristics among delinquents when compared with nondelinquents. Often when such differences do appear, they are based on responses to paper-and-pencil inventories, which are subject to reliability and validity issues (Waldo and Dinitz 1967; Tennenbaum 1977). A more recent meta-analysis, that is, an analysis of existing studies, concluded that some specific personality traits seem to distinguish antisocial youth from others, traits such as agreeableness and conscientiousness (the lack of these traits being more pronounced among antisocial youngsters). However, this review concluded that it is more likely that delinquents and criminals have a tendency to act and feel in certain ways in certain situations, as opposed to having a dominant trait that leads to negative, or delinquent, behaviors in nearly all situations (Miller and Lynam 2001).

One psychological inventory that has been studied in connection with delinquency is the Minnesota Multiphasic Personality Inventory, or the MMPI. First developed in the 1940s, the MMPI is a lengthy inventory, with over 500 items divided into ten subscales. The subscale that seems to be most strongly associated with delinquency is called the psychopathic deviant, or Pd subscale (Hathaway and Monachesi 1963; Waldo and Dinitz 1967). Since this subscale was developed and normed using troubled juveniles, some of whom were incarcerated, it is not too surprising that it would be connected with delinquency. However, some studies suggest that using the MMPI yields more differences among delinquents than between delinquents and nondelinquents (Waldo and Dinitz 1967). In addition, efforts to predict future delinquent behavior using the MMPI have not been very successful, again suggesting that there is more to the explanation of delinquency than responses to paper-and-pencil inventories.

In retrospect, it would seem logical to realize that there is not one personality type that explains delinquency. There is no one personality to explain any subset of a population. We are all influenced by our surroundings or environment, and those influences can have significant effects on the way we think and react to situations. There may be personality dimensions that tend to be associated with delinquency, such as impulsiveness and unco-operativeness. However, even these associations are limited, usually to con-fined populations of juveniles, and often related to other social factors. For example, research suggests that personality factors, such as impulsiveness, have a greater impact on delinquency in lower-income settings than in wealthier districts (Lynam et al. 2001).

The Psychopathic Personality

One aspect of personality theory as applied to crime and delinquency is the concept of the "psychopathic personality." The original term *psychopath* was introduced in the latter part of the 19th century and has often been associ-ated with violence (A. Fink 1938). However, the clinical definition of the psy-chopathic personality does not highlight violence, although violence may be a part of the behavior patterns of the psychopath. While some studies on this concept conclude that there are over 50 traits associated with a psycho-pathic personality, it is usually characterized by selfishness and disregard for the feelings of others. Behaviors are committed to satisfy the individual, not those around him or her. The individual knows right from wrong but chooses to act regardless of the harm such action causes others. There is impulsiveness to behavior and little remorse for harm(s) caused by such actions (Cleckley 1976). In addition, diagnostic manuals for psychiatrists and psychologists, such as the *Diagnostic and Statistical Manual of Mental Disorders* (1994), specify a number of specific behaviors that must be exhib-ited over a period of time in order for the label to be applied, and violence is only one of several kinds of behavior that are included.

Adding to the confusion in the literature over exactly what this term means is the use of other terms, such as *sociopathic personality* or *antisocial personality* to refer to the same condition. Additionally, in recent versions of the DSM, the phrase "conduct disorder" has been used in place of "psycho-pathic" or "sociopathic" personality. This phraseology reflects a debate in the field concerning whether juveniles can actually develop a psychopathic personality. Some, such as Eysenck and Eysenck (1978) argue that the psy-chopathic personality is more common among adolescents than adults. Oth-ers, such as Robins (1966) argue that juveniles are too young to develop this kind of personality.

We should be mindful, too, of the connection between a suggested con-stant, such as a psychopathic personality, and changes in a person's behavior over time. It is theorized that the psychopathic personality not only takes time to develop, even if it can occur in adolescence, but also stays with one for a long time, if not until death. This conclusion is supportive of Laurence Steinberg's assessment of the connection between adolescence and the psychopathic personality, in which he suggests that psychopathy is a long-term condition, while adolescence, "by definition," is not (Steinberg 2002:56).

However, some research suggests that psychopathic traits can change over time or that perhaps original diagnoses have been incorrectly applied. In her longitudinal study of sociopaths in Saint Louis, Robins (1966) concluded that around one-third of those diagnosed as sociopathic in their late adolescent and young adult years exhibited few, if any, sociopathic traits as they got older, despite little psychiatric or counseling intervention. Either the diagnoses of sociopathy were incorrect, or there is no certainty that this condition is as long-lasting as many scholars would suggest.

The implications of being labeled a psychopath, however, are potentially devastating, especially for a child. Changing the name of a diagnosis, or label, say, from psychopathic personality to conduct disorder, does little to change the prediction that one has a lifetime disorder, even if that prediction may not be true. When dealing with youngsters, such labels should be very judiciously applied. Some of the characteristics associated with conduct disorder, such as running away and truancy, are what have been termed status offenses. In addition to being expressions of confusion and reaching out to others, such behavior may be connected with experimentation and just plain growing up, not always with an underlying deviant personality trait. To apply such a potentially damning label to a juvenile may worsen an already difficult time in a child's life (see chapter 12 on labeling theory).

Summaries of traditional, or early, and modern individualistic explanations of delinquency are presented in figures 4.1 and 4.2. An important difference in these two models is the inclusion of interaction between individual traits and social or environmental conditions in the explanation of delinquency, compared with the more direct trait-delinquency model advocated in the traditional biological and psychological explanations of crime delinquency.

Summary

One of the earliest views of human nature is called the classical school of thought. The classical school emphasized behavior motivated by self-interest and reflective of free will. The notion of free will still seems embedded in

Biological Conditions
Low ANS Response
Mesomorphic Body Type   →   Crime and Delinquency
"Bad" Genes
Etc.

Psychological Characteristics
Overactive Id, Weak Superego
Aggressive Personality   →   Delinquency
Low IQ
Etc.

FIGURE 4.1 Individualistic Explanations of Delinquency: Traditional Model

Biological and Psychological Characteristics
Learning Disabilities   Poor School
Biochemical Problems   Performance
Low ANS Response   ↔ Difficult Family   ↔ Delinquency
Psychopathic   Relationships
   Personality   Attachments to
   Etc.   Delinquent Peers

FIGURE 4.2 Individualistic Explanations of Delinquency: Modern Approach

popular thinking concerning the motivation for crime and is expressed theoretically in a contemporary theory known as rational choice theory. There is
a debate among scholars relative to the ability of young people to truly think
through the consequences of their actions, which is connected to the philosophy of the juvenile justice system and to a developmental perspective of youth.
If juveniles are not able to fully appreciate the consequences of their acts, as
the philosophy of the juvenile justice system would suggest, then how can they
be credited with making clear, rational choices regarding their behavior?

In partial response to the classical school of thought was the emergence of the positive school, most often identified with the work of Cesare Lombroso. Lombroso emphasized the use of statistical measurements and the biological motivations of behavior, including criminality, and tended to reject the notion of free will. A related early biological explanation of criminality focused on inherited traits in a general way. Such explanations of crime (delinquency was rarely separated from crime in those earlier studies) gave little hope for reform and fostered, intentionally or not, programs such as sterilization, or eugenics, as a "cure" for crime.

Later biological theories have maintained the focus on scientific discovery, but such explanations of crime have moved away from inheritance and direct biological causes for crime and delinquency. Many of these more recent biological explanations have been offered in combination with psychological or sociological, (environmental) factors to give a more comprehensive explanation of criminality. For example, an analysis of early pubertal development and delinquency among a national sample of 5,700 males indicates that boys who display early physical signs of development do, indeed, admit to higher rates of self-reported delinquency. However, this relationship is more heightened by association with delinquent friends (a subject to be discussed in chapter 6) and among those who are more successful in school (Felson and Haynie 2002). Thus, a distinct biological factor, early pubertal development, is found to affect delinquency when combined with specific environmental factors, such as delinquent friends and academic success.

Psychological explanations of delinquency started to appear in the latter part of the nineteenth century. One of the earlier psychological explanations of crime and delinquency was the psychoanalytic theory, which emphasized hidden motives for behavior, motives that have been repressed into one's subconscious. Such explanations of criminality were popular until the second half of the 20th century, when psychological scales and inventories were developed.

Another early focus of psychological theories of delinquency was on intelligence. The assumption has been that those with low intelligence are more prone to commit crimes than those with higher levels of intelligence. However, considerable research on this topic casts doubt on such a direct relationship between intelligence and criminality. For one thing, there are "bright" delinquents, which casts doubt on the relationship between low IQ and delinquency. Also, current research suggests that the connection between IQ and delinquency may be indirect and likely influenced by performance in school. That is, possessing a low IQ may affect one's ability to do well in school, which would then affect self-esteem and social relationships, which, in turn, might encourage one to seek out delinquent friends and delinquent behaviors as compensation for doing poorly in school.

More current explanations of delinquency tend to continue the view that delinquency is not easily accounted for by single-cause, direct explanations. Most of the current biological and psychological explanations of delinquency tend to incorporate interactions between biological and psychological situations and delinquency. For example, it is difficult to pinpoint a "delinquent" personality. Rather, it is more likely that people have certain tendencies to react to situations in certain ways, which ultimately may nudge them into delinquent behavior patterns. Impulsiveness may be a relatively common trait among delinquents, but more so in lower-class settings. Our personality may affect how we perceive situations, but situational experiences may also affect our personality. In this sense, we are continually involved in the shaping of our thoughts and actions through experiences, both past and present.

While it is true that we all act and react to situations based on contemporary conditions, it is also true that our past experiences influence how we view present conditions and how we react to these conditions. This is another way that personal and environmental factors interact to produce behavior. Just as it would be inaccurate to say that what happened to us during our early childhood years directly affects our behavior today, regardless of current circumstances, the opposite would also be true. That is, it is inaccurate and shortsighted to argue that we are affected only by current situations, having no effects or "baggage" from our previous experiences.

We should be cautious, therefore, in applying all-encompassing terms to one's persona, especially terms such as *psychopath* or *antisocial personality*, which connote long-term, damning implications for one's state of well-being. Such terms can rarely, if ever, capture the fullness and richness of human beings, their complexities and motivations for behavior. "Kinds of people" theories have a difficult time handling known changes in criminal behavior patterns over time and/or over different social settings, changes that we know do occur. Therefore, these kinds of explanations of behavior are better understood in combination with environmental factors, which is precisely the direction in which contemporary individualistic explanations are moving.

Contemporary interest in biological and psychological influences on delinquency has also turned to developmental explanations of behavior, that is, those factors that shape one's attitudes and behaviors over time. This interest is further incorporating environmental conditions into explanations of delinquency and has further led to the understanding that delinquency is not a uniform set of behaviors or something to be explained by one set of contributive factors. Rather, the contemporary studies of delinquency are often focused on examinations of different pathways to delinquency, for example, one track for the typical, short-lived delinquency pattern, and another for the small percentage of juveniles who commit more serious acts of crime and tend to do so for longer periods of time. Developmental concepts and different pathways to delinquency will be discussed in the next chapter.

References

Aichhorn, August
  1965 Wayward Youth. New York: Viking.
  [1925]
American Psychiatric Association
  1994 Diagnostic and Statistical Manual of Mental Disorders, DSM-IV. 4th edition. Washington, DC: American Psychiatric Association.
Beccaria, Cesare
  1963 On Crimes and Punishment. Henry Paolucci, trans. New York:
  [1764] Bobbs-Merrill.
Bentham, Jeremy
  1948 An Introduction to the Principles of Morals and Legislation. New York:
  [1789] Hafner.
Bishop, Mary
  1994 An Elite Said Their Kind Wasn't Wanted: How Social Judgments of the Day Forced Sterilizations. Roanoke Times & World News, June 26: E1, E5.
Casey, Pamela, and Ingo Keilitz
  1990 Estimating the Prevalence of Learning Disabled and Mentally Retarded Juvenile Offenders: A Meta-Analysis. *In* Understanding Troubled and Troubling Youth. Peter E. Leone, ed. Pp. 82–101. Newbury Park, CA: Sage.
Cleckley, Harvey
  1976 The Mask of Sanity. 5th edition. Saint Louis: Mosby.
Cohen, Albert K.
  1966 Deviance and Control. Englewood Cliffs, NJ: Prentice-Hall.
Cornish, Derek B., and Ronald V. Clarke
  1986 The Reasoning Criminal. New York: Springer-Verlag.

Cortes, Juan B., and Florence M. Gatti
    1972   Delinquency and Crime. New York: Seminar Press.
Dalgard, Odd Steffen, and Einar Kringlen
    1978   Criminal Behavior in Twins. *In* Crime in Society. Leonard D. Savitz
            and Norman Johnston, eds. Pp. 292–307. New York: Wiley.
Denno, Deborah W.
    1985   Sociological and Human Developmental Explanations of Crime:
            Conflict or Consensus? Criminology 23:711–741.
Dugdale, Richard L.
    1888   The Jukes: A Study in Crime, Pauperism, Disease, and Heredity. 4th
            edition. New York: Putnam.
Eysenck, H. J.
    1977   Crime and Personality. 3rd edition. London: Routledge and Kegan
            Paul.
    1989   Personality and Criminality: A Dispositional Analysis. *In* Advances
            in Criminological Theory. William S. Laufer and Freda Adler, eds.
            Pp. 89–110. New Brunswick, NJ: Transaction.
Eysenck, H. J., and S. B. G. Eysenck
    1978   Psychopathy, Personality, and Genetics. *In* Psychopathic Behavior.
            R. D. Hare and D. Schilling, eds. Pp. 197–220. New York: Wiley.
Eysenck, H. J., and Leon Kamin
    1981   The Intelligence Controversy. New York: Wiley.
Felson, Richard B., and Dana L. Haynie
    2002   Pubertal Development, Social Factors, and Delinquency Among
            Adolescent Boys. Criminology 40:967–988.
Fink, Arthur
    1938   Causes of Crime. New York: A. S. Barnes.
Fink, Carolyn Molden
    1990   Special Education Students at Risk: A Comparative Study of Delin-
            quency. *In* Understanding Troubled and Troubling Youth. Peter F.
            Leone, ed. Pp. 61–81. Newbury Park, CA: Sage.
Fishbein, Diana H.
    1990   Biological Perspectives in Criminology. Criminology 28:27–72.
Fleener, Fran Trocinsky
    1987   Learning Disabilities and Other Attributes as Factors in Delinquent
            Activities among Adolescents in a Nonurban Area. Psychological
            Reports 60:327–334.
Freud, Sigmund
    1927   The Ego and the Id. Joan Riviere, trans. London: Hogarth.

1930   Civilization and Its Discontents. James Strachey, ed. and trans. New
        York: Norton.
1935   A General Introduction to Psycho-Analysis. Joan Riviere, trans. New
[1920] York: Liveright.
Glueck, Sheldon, and Eleanor Glueck
1950   Unraveling Juvenile Delinquency. New York: Commonwealth Fund.
1956   Physique and Delinquency. New York: Harper and Brothers.
Goddard, Henry H.
1912   The Kallikak Family. New York: Macmillan.
1914   Feeble-Mindedness. New York: Macmillan.
Gordon, Robert A.
1976   Prevalence: The Rare Dictum in Delinquency Measurement and Its
        Implication for the Theory of Delinquency. In The Juvenile Justice
        System. Malcolm Klein, ed. Pp. 201–284. Beverly Hills: Sage.
Goring, Charles
1913   The English Convict. London: His Majesty's Stationery Office.
Hathaway, Starke R., and Elio D. Monachesi
1963   Adolescent Personality and Behavior. Minneapolis: University of
        Minnesota Press.
Hewitt, Lester E., and Richard L. Jenkins
1946   Fundamental Patterns of Maladjustment: The Dynamics of Their
        Origin. Springfield, IL: State of Illinois.
Hirschi, Travis, and Michael J. Hindelang
1977   Intelligence and Delinquency: A Revisionist Review. American Soci-
        ological Review 42:571–587.
Hoghughi, M. S., and A. R. Forrest
1970   Eysenck's Theory of Criminality: An Examination with Approved
        School Boys. British Journal of Criminology 10:240–254.
Horn, David G.
2003   The Criminal Body: Lombroso and the Anatomy of Deviance. New
        York: Routledge.
Jensen, A. R.
1969   How Much Can We Boost IQ and Scholastic Achievement? Harvard
        Educational Review 39:1–123.
Lynam, Donald R., Avshalom Caspi, Terrie E. Moffitt, Per-Olof Wikstrom, Rolf
Loeber, and Scott P. Novak
2001   The Interaction between Impulsivity and Neighborhood Context
        on Offending: The Effects of Impulsivity Are Stronger in Poorer
        Neighborhoods. Journal of Abnormal Psychology 109:563–574.

Lyons, Michael J.
  1996 A Twin Study of Self-Reported Criminal Behaviour. *In* Genetics of
        Criminality and Deviant Behaviour. Gregory R. Bock and Jamie A.
        Goode, eds. Pp. 61–75. Chichester, England: Wiley.
Magnusson, David, Britt af Klinteberg, and Hakan Stattin
  1992 Autonomic Activity/Reactivity, Behavior, and Crime in a Longitu-
        dinal Perspective. *In* Facts, Frameworks, and Forecasts. Joan
        McCord, ed. Pp. 287–318. New Brunswick, NJ: Transaction.
Martin, Randy, Robert J. Mutchnick, and W. Timothy Austin
  1990 Criminological Thought: Pioneers Past and Present. New York:
        Macmillan.
Mednick, Sarnoff A., Lis Kirkegaard-Sorensen, Barry Hutchings, Joachim Knop,
Raben Rosenberg, and Fini Schulsinger
  1977 An Example of Bio-Social Interaction Research: The Interplay of
        Socioenvironmental and Individual Factors in the Etiology of Crim-
        inal Behavior. *In* Biological Bases of Criminal Behavior. Sarnoff A.
        Mednick and Karl O. Christiansen, eds. Pp. 9–23. New Brunswick,
        NJ: Transaction.
Mednick, Sarnoff A., Jan Voluka, William F. Gabrielli, Jr., and Turan M. Itil
  1981 EEG as a Predictor of Antisocial Behavior. Criminology 19:219–
        229.
Mednick, Sarnoff A., William F. Gabrielli, Jr., and Barry Hutchings
  1987 Genetic Factors in the Etiology of Criminal Behavior. *In* The Causes
        of Crime: New Biological Approaches. Sarnoff A. Mednick, Terrie E.
        Moffitt, and Susan S. Stack, eds. Pp. 74–91. Cambridge, England:
        Cambridge University Press.
Miller, Joshua D., and Donald Lynam
  2001 Structural Models of Personality and Their Relationship to
        Antisocial Behavior: A Meta-Analytic Review. Criminology 39:
        765–795.
Moffitt, Terrie E.
  1990 Juvenile Delinquency and Attention Deficit Disorder: Boys' Devel-
        opmental Trajectories from Age 3 to Age 15. Child Development
        61:893–910.
Morrison, Helen L.
  1978 The Asocial Child: A Destiny of Sociopath? *In* The Psychopath.
        William H. Reid, ed. Pp. 22–65. New York: Brunner/Mazel.
Murchison, Carl
  1926 Criminal Intelligence. Worcester, MA: Clark University Press.

Murray, Charles A.
    1976   The Link between Learning Disabilities and Juvenile Delinquency.
            Washington, DC: U.S. Department of Justice.
Paternoster, Raymond
    1989   Decisions to Participate in and Desist from Four Types of Common
            Delinquency: Deterrence, and the Rational Choice Perspective. Law
            & Society Review 23:7–40.
Perlmutter, Barry F.
    1987   Delinquency and Learning Disabilities: Evidence for Compensatory
            Behaviors and Adaptation. Journal of Youth and Adolescence
            16:89–95.
Pickar, Daniel B., and Christopher D. Tori
    1986   The Learning Disabled Adolescent: Eriksonian Psychosocial Devel-
            opment, Self-Concept, and Delinquent Behavior. Journal of Youth
            and Adolescence 15:429–440.
Piliavin, Irving, Rosemary Gartner, Craig Thompson, and Ross L. Matsueda
    1986   Crime, Deterrence, and Rational Choice. American Sociological
            Review 51:101–119.
Rafter, Nicole
    2004   Earnest A. Hooton and the Biological Tradition in American Crim-
            inology. Criminology 42:735–771.
Robins, Lee N.
    1966   Deviant Children Grown Up. Baltimore: Williams and Wilkins.
Rowe, David C.
    2002   Biology and Crime. Los Angeles: Roxbury.
Sagarin, Edwin
    1980   Taboo Subjects and Taboo Viewpoints in Criminology. *In* Taboos
            in Criminology. Edwin Sagarin, ed. Pp. 7–21. Beverly Hills: Sage.
Sheldon, William H.
    1949   Varieties of Delinquent Youth. New York: Harper and Brothers.
Siddle, David A. T., Sarnoff A. Mednick, A. R. Nicol, and Roger H. Foggitt
    1977   Skin Conductance Recovery in Antisocial Adolescents. In Biosocial
            Bases of Criminal Behavior. Sarnoff A. Mednick and Karl O. Chris-
            tiansen, eds. Pp. 213–216. New York: Gardner.
Steinberg, Laurence
    2002   The Juvenile Psychopath: Fads, Fictions, and Facts. *In* Perspectives
            on Crime and Justice, 2000–2001 Lecture Series, Volume V. Alfred
            Blumstein, Laurence Steinberg, Carl C. Bell, and Margaret A. Berger,
            eds. Pp. 35–64. Washington, DC: National Institute of Justice.

Tennenbaum, David J.
    1977   Personality and Criminality: A Summary and Implications of the Literature. Journal of Criminal Justice 5:225–235.

Tennent, Gavin, and Dennis Gath
    1975   Bright Delinquents: A Three-Year Follow-up Study. British Journal of Criminology 15:386–390.

Vold, George B., Thomas J. Bernard, and Jeffrey B. Snipes
    2002   Theoretical Criminology. 5th edition. New York: Oxford University Press.

Waldo, Gordon, and Simon Dinitz
    1967   Personality Attributes of the Criminal: An Analysis of Research Studies, 1950–65. Journal of Research in Crime and Delinquency 4:185–202.

Walsh, Anthony J., Arthur Beyer, and Thomas A. Petee
    1987   Violent Delinquency: An Examination of Psychopathic Typologies. Journal of Genetic Psychology 148:385–392.

Wolfgang, Marvin E.
    1972   Cesare Lombroso. *In* Pioneers in Criminology. Herman Mannheim, ed. Pp. 232–291. Montclair, NJ: Patterson Smith.

Zeleny, L. D.
    1933   Feeble-Mindedness and Criminal Conduct. American Journal of Sociology 38:564–576.

SOCIAL DEVELOPMENT AND DELINQUENCY

ODERN BIOLOGICAL and psychological explanations of delinquency are often couched within a developmental framework. That is, one's attitudes and behavior are thought to change over time, as he or she develops physically and psychologically. In addition, these current perspectives introduce a variety of social or environmental situations that can hinder or facilitate human growth and development. In this sense, the modern theories of human development are similar to those of earlier thinkers, such as Freud. Freud, however, tended to focus on abnormalities in human growth and problems generated from such abnormalities as they occurred early in one's life.

Traditional perspectives on human development, including child development, have dealt extensively with individual parameters of growth and development, such as body movements and speech. In this regard, such perspectives have been heavily influenced by biological and psychological research, which is quite appropriate. Typically, however, discussions of human growth and child development have not spent much attention on the deviant aspects of growth, such as delinquency. In addition, when such discussions are given, often the deviance is explained in terms of psychological identity problems (Schiamberg 1988).

Kohlberg's Moral
Development Model

One model of development and its relationship to criminality is that of Lawrence Kohlberg. Kohlberg argues that people grow in terms of relationships to one another and to moral ideas and values. According to Kohlberg, people grow in stages, starting with what he terms the "preconventional" level. Next, there is the "conventional" level, followed by the "postconventional" level. In each level there are two stages, for a total of six stages of growth and development.

The first stage of preconventional moral development is characterized by doing right to avoid punishment. In the second stage of this level, people (mainly children) do what is considered right in order to satisfy their own needs, although they can recognize the needs of others. In the first stage of the conventional level of growth, behaving correctly is considered a social good, that is, people do what is right because it is socially proper and expected. In the second stage of this level, correct behavior is seen as necessary for the good of the society. In the first stage of the postconventional level, people doing right is almost a kind of contractual obligation between the individual and the government and system of authority. In the second, and thus last, stage of development, good behavior is part of a belief in a global system of moral good and is in response to the feeling that a person should do good because it is simply expected of one to do good, as a member of the human race (Schiamberg 1988:575–577).

In comparison with other psychological views of human development, such as Piaget's, the stages of growth in Kohlberg's typology correspond roughly to the following ages: the preconventional level of moral development occurs from birth to age 7; the conventional level occurs between ages 8 and 12; and the postconventional level occurs from age 12 onward (Schiamberg 1988:577).

Studies using this theory of moral development suggest that delinquents typically think and reason at the preconventional level (Adler et al. 2001:89), which suggests that their moral development is that of a young child. However, moral development does not occur in a vacuum and is considered a learned behavior. Therefore, exposing youth to good models of moral development could alter their developmental path or at least the speed of their development. This kind of change may, in turn, serve to alter patterns of delinquent behavior (Adler et al. 2001:89).

Social Development Model

The social development model (SDM) of delinquency adopts a dynamic view of human behavior, similar to some of the individualistic theories discussed in chapter 4. That is, the SDM model maintains that people grow and develop in stages. However, one difference between the individualistic explanations of delinquency discussed earlier and the social development model is that the SDM assumes growth and development to be *social* in nature. These social explanations of behavior are not considered in isolation. Rather, they are viewed as intertwined or connected to form a more complete view of the factors affecting human growth and behavior. Some maintain that social development represents "a synthesis, of control theory, learning theory, and differential association theory" (Huang et al. 2001:77). According to this view, young people learn behavior from those in their social circles, such as home and school, and among playmates. Others take a more "life-course" view of development, arguing that delinquency, much like any other type of behavior, develops and changes over the course of a lifetime. The life-course perspective is also associated with different pathways or "trajectories" to delinquency (Benson 2001:80–81).

Pathways to Delinquency

Moffitt's Research

Terrie Moffitt and her colleagues have been studying the pathways to crime and delinquency among a sample of New Zealand youth for several years. The design of this research is longitudinal, and children have been selected from youth populations of preschool age through adolescence. In the course of this study, Moffitt and associates have discovered that a small sample of youth exhibited signs of antisocial behavior from preschool age and continued to exhibit antisocial and criminal behavior through adolescence and into adulthood (Moffitt 1993). Moffitt's research suggests that these *life-course persistent* (LCP) youth are significantly different from other juveniles in terms of verbal and memory abilities (Moffitt et al. 1994). In addition, this life-course persistent group is often characterized by other biopsychological characteristics, such as attention deficit disorder (ADD). However, possessing ADD does *not* automatically signal a lifetime of difficulties with authority figures and the legal system (Moffitt 1990).

Moffitt's research suggests that life-course persistent offenders tend to remain offenders over time, well into adulthood. In contrast, her research also identified a larger category of youthful offenders, which she termed *adolescence-limited* (AL) offenders (Moffitt 1993; Moffitt et al. 1994). Adolescence-limited offenders are characterized by fewer neuropsychological problems and a much less extensive history of crime and delinquency, compared with life-course persistent offenders. They usually begin their "careers" in criminality during mid to late adolescence and do not remain involved in delinquency for much over a year or two. Furthermore, their behavior is not predicted or explained by individual pathologies. Rather, AL delinquency is better explained by many of the social factors mentioned earlier, such as weakened social bonds and delinquent peer associations. Moffitt also suggests that this pattern of delinquency has emerged with modernization and industrialization, in part because such social changes have increased independence of youth from the supervision and control of the family and the need to work at an early age (Moffitt 1993:27–29).

Both the LCP and the AL patterns of delinquency are influenced by associations with delinquent peers. However, Moffitt (1993) maintains that because of their longer involvement in delinquency and their willingness to take risks and try new things, LCP youth are able to attract the interest of peers during adolescence, some of whom may be AL youth, and even be leaders among these groups. The pattern of social activity among LCP youngsters is acting alone in early years, associating with peers during adolescence, and then going it alone, so to speak, in adulthood. For AL youth, the association with peers is more of a normal characteristic of adolescence, much of their delinquency is experimental, not serious, and much of it is not likely to continue beyond a year or two (unless they become influenced by associations with LCP delinquents).

LCP youth tend to exhibit behavioral problems at an early age, sometimes in preschool years, and tend not to outgrow these behavioral problems with age, at least through adolescence. In addition, they are characterized by significant neuropsychological conditions. Interestingly, this pattern of delinquency seems to describe males more often than females. In the New Zealand study, for example, none of the characteristics of the LCP pattern of delinquency fit the females in the sample (Moffitt et al. 1994:283). However, additional studies suggest that there is no true AL pattern for girls but that delinquent females are more like the LCP group of males. One main difference between males and females in terms of this life-course pattern is what has been called a "delayed onset" pattern for girls.

That is, the serious delinquency found among LCP males is not seen among females until they reach adolescence (Silverthorn and Frick 1999). This topic needs additional study before a clearer picture emerges about delinquency pathways among males and females. The topic of female delinquency will be discussed in more detail in chapter 11, "Female Delinquency."

The dual pathway model of delinquency proposed by Moffitt and her colleagues has been examined extensively. Overall, these studies have supported the existence of these pathways and the general characteristics of those fitting into the two trajectories. Recent research by Moffitt and colleagues, however, suggests that the adolescence-limited group is not to be considered a nondelinquent category. These youth are delinquent, although not to the same extent that exists for the life-course persistent group. In addition, continued research on this topic suggests that the AL group may not be as short-term as originally thought. Follow-up studies on the AL group of offenders in the New Zealand study indicate that these young men still fit into patterns of delinquency as young adults and have not matured out of delinquency as quickly as had been supposed. However, because of their overall favorable circumstances, it is thought these men will eventually turn away from delinquency and more toward conformist lifestyles as they age (Moffitt et al. 2002).

Continued research on these patterns of delinquency has been done in the United States, again with supportive results. For example, evidence suggestive of a life-course persistent pattern of delinquency was found among a sample of young adolescent males in a longitudinal study conducted in Pittsburgh. In particular, several psychological measurements seemed to distinguish serious delinquents from minor offenders or nondelinquents. Delinquents exhibited significantly more negative emotionality than other youth. Negative emotions include anger, irritability, resentment, and similar feelings. Negative emotions, in turn, are related to lack of adult, mostly parental, control and constraint of these males when they were very young (Caspi et al. 1994).

Additional longitudinal research has concluded that personality factors alone do not explain the LCP pattern of behavior. Research on youth in Oregon and small communities in Iowa clearly indicate the existence of multiple pathways to delinquency, particularly among early and late starters. Ineffective parenting and association with deviant peers are associated with both patterns of delinquency, but weak parenting seems to be more associated with early starters (Simons et al. 1994; Patterson et al. 1991; Patterson 1992).

A General Theory of Crime—Another View
of Persistent Criminality

Much of Moffitt's view concerning the LCD pathway to delinquency is similar to the ideas of Gottfredson and Hirschi and the general theory of crime (1990). According the general theory of crime (GTC), offenders share a basic, common trait, namely, a lack of self-control, an impulsiveness related to a need for excitement. Criminal offenders are not necessarily psychopathic or full of evil, as some of the earlier individualistic theories suggested. Rather, these people cannot control their impulsive desires, which often results in their committing illegal acts. In this sense, then, criminals are basically life-course persistent offenders.

According to the GTC, delinquents and criminals are not necessarily born with impulsiveness, but this trait is "learned," so to speak, in ways in which other behaviors and attitudes are learned. More specifically, Gottfredson and Hirschi maintain that impulsiveness and low self-control are acquired from early childhood experiences, namely, poor parenting. However, once these traits are learned or developed, usually by around age ten, they tend to stay with an individual throughout his or her life and do not change significantly over the course of one's life. Life-course experiences do not eliminate this tendency to commit crime. As Gottfredson and Hirschi put it, "In summary, the life-course or situational explanation of the decline in crime with age says that a person gains sources of satisfaction inconsistent with crime as he or she grows older. If one set of satisfactions is inconsistent with another, there is good reason to conclude . . . he or she has given up something and accepted something rather different in its place. Put in bald form, the irresponsible, thoughtless offender has become the responsible, thoughtful law-abiding citizen. The data, however, do not conform to this picture" (1990:141).

Ineffective parenting in connection with delinquency is discussed in chapter 7. Research continues to document the role of ineffective parenting as a contributor to delinquency, but some studies suggest that the link between poor parenting and delinquency is affected by psychological variables, such as low self-control. That is, low self-control may be the result of inadequate parenting, but low self-control has an independent effect on delinquency. This model has been examined with African American samples, but it remains to be seen whether it applies to wider ranges of youth in future research (Simons et al. 2007). Others have noted that the often-cited relationship between poor academic performance and delinquency (see chapter 8) is explained by low self-control. That is, young people who do poorly in school *and* become involved in delinquency do so because of low self-control. Low self-control influences both low academic achievement and delinquency (Felson and Staff 2006).

Other research is less supportive of the general theory of crime. For example, some studies suggest that low self-control is only one of several individual and social variables that may contribute to crime and delinquency. Personality, physiological, neuropsychological, and social variables such as peer relationships and social bonds (see chapters 4 and 6) can also contribute to delinquent behavior (Cauffman et al. 2005; Longshore et al. 2005; Simons et al. 2007). One longitudinal study of African American adolescents concluded that social factors, including parental experiences, can change self-control, especially among youth with moderate levels of self-control (Burt et al. 2006). Other studies conclude that self-control is not unidimensional and that different components of self-control may change differently over time. For example, impulsivity decreases over time, including for youthful offenders. However, risk taking may not change for offenders, but it seems to increase over time for nonoffenders. In addition, different aspects of self-control differ by characteristics such as race. For example, African American youth report lower levels of risk taking than do white youth (Winfree et al. 2006; see also Mitchell and MacKenzie 2006).

Ultimately, almost all criminals begin to age out of crime. Gottfredson and Hirschi recognize this general trend but attribute the decline in crime with age almost solely to "aging of the organism" (1990:141). Basically, according to this idea, criminals stop committing crimes when they become physically unable to commit crimes. However, as was discussed in chapter 3, most delinquent offenders tend to age out of crime before they reach the age of adulthood, and this trend is inconsistent with the observations of Gottfredson and Hirschi. A diagram of this model of delinquency is presented in figure 5.1.

Sampson and Laub and Turning Points in Criminal Careers

Robert Sampson and John Laub offer another view of delinquency, based on a developmental perspective (1993). Sampson and Laub re-analyzed the data collected for the Gluecks' (1950) study of 500 delinquent and 500 nondelinquent males, *Unraveling Juvenile Delinquency* (see chapter 4). Using the information in the files of this study, they examined follow-up contacts with several hundred of these males and attempted to construct profiles of what

Inadequate Socialization and Weak Family Bonds → Development of Low Self-Control → Delinquency → Eventual Decline in Crime and Delinquency Because of Physical Aging, but Little or No Increase in Self-Control

FIGURE 5.1 General Theory Model of Delinquency (Gottfredson and Hirschi)

happened in the lives of the delinquents and the nondelinquents as they grew older. The 1,000 males were contacted at ages 14, 25, and 32, providing a view into their lives at adolescence and adulthood.

Sampson and Laub noted that over time, the lives and behaviors of many of these men changed, while others persisted in committing crimes throughout the period of study. Sampson and Laub conclude that the critical factor in the lives of these males was the strength of their ties to society through their families, their schools, and their jobs. In essence, they credited the strength of the social bond (see chapter 6) with affecting the criminal career patterns of these 1,000 males. The stronger these bonds, the less likely the men were to commit criminal activity. This relationship seemed to hold whether or not a person was a "true" delinquent as a youth. As they put it:

> More precisely, job stability and marital attachment in adulthood were significantly related to changes in adult crime—the stronger the adult ties to work and family, the less crime and deviance among both delinquent and nondelinquent [sic] controls. . . . We concluded that "turning points" related to work, marriage, and military service were crucial for understanding processes of continuity and change across the adult life course. [Laub and Sampson 2003:6]

An important feature of this life-course perspective is the inclusion of turning points in the lives of people as they age. Turning points are important events in one's life that help to shape decisions, attitudes, and behavior. As mentioned above, the significant turning points in the lives of those studied involved family, the military, and work. However, it is not simply that one marries that may turn him (or her) from a path of crime and delinquency, but the nature of the marriage. Similarly, it is not simply that one obtains a job that may turn his life around, but the kind of job he has and how long it lasts.

Furthermore, these life events can and often do alter one's life in different ways. People are always in a position to change as one event occurs after another. As Laub and Sampson (1993:304) put it, "That is, despite the connection between childhood events and experiences in adulthood, turning points can modify life trajectories—they can 'redirect paths.'" Most turning points are not overwhelming. Rather, events in one's life help to shape and mold future directions in small increments that occur over time. However, the more that similar events keep happening, the more likely one's trajectory, or path, tends to move in one direction. For those engaged in a lifestyle of crime and delinquency, Moffitt (1993) and others refer to this process as "knifing off" of conventional opportunities. For example, if a juvenile ends up in detention or a reformatory, there is less likelihood of his or her returning to a conventional lifestyle upon release (Laub and Sampson 2003:chapter 7). More and more, conventional opportunities are either closed to or become too difficult to obtain for those consistently engaged in a criminal lifestyle. In part, this happens because of the stigma attached with imprisonment, a subject discussed more in chapter 12 on labeling theory. It is also the case that a criminal lifestyle can become more and more appealing and that one's associates tend to be those with similar attitudes and behavior, similar to differential association theory (see chapter 6). Thus, turning to a conventional, perhaps "boring," way of life may be both difficult and unappealing, so the antisocial pathway becomes more and more a life-course pathway.

Turning points are sometimes referred to as *social capital* (Laub and Sampson 1993). Social capital involves social connections that help to establish one in the community and to lead one to a life of conformity to laws and social norms. This term was introduced by James Coleman (1988) to help understand social organization and human interactions, but it has also been utilized by life-course theorists to help explain the process of changing from criminal behavior to a conformist lifestyle. Within the life-course perspective, social capital can be gained by acquiring an education, a good job, a good family, and so on. In addition to helping one to develop a stable, conformist lifestyle, social capital can also be used to encourage conformity for fear of losing this capital. In other words, the more one has to lose, in terms of social ties and respect in the world, the less likely he or she will do something to jeopardize that capital, such as committing acts of crime and delinquency. This concept is similar to Jackson Toby's idea of "stakes of conformity," in which he argues that juveniles and adults who have built up a lot of stakes in living a conformist life will attempt to avoid losing these stakes by engaging in criminal behavior (Toby 1957). Of course, it can be argued that all people seek to obtain social capital, even if it means connecting with criminals or delinquents (Benson 2001:95–99). In that case, the capital being accumulated would not likely point one away from criminal behavior. The kind of social capital discussed within the turning points perspective, therefore, is that associated with conformist lifestyles.

Many people do not fit neatly into one delinquent pathway or another. The two discussed so far, LCP and AL, are really more end points along a continuum of possible life patterns. In a detailed follow-up examination of 52 of the original 500 delinquents in the *Unraveling* study, Laub and Sampson (2003) interviewed men who had lived to age 70. The ages of these men are far beyond the age of delinquency. However, their life histories reveal information on patterns of crime desistance or persistence. Desisters, for example, often stopped committing crimes because of the social relationships they had made earlier in life, relationships involving jobs and families. Having a good job and a good family life seemed to increase the investments in conformity for these males, so they felt they had more to lose by committing crimes. In effect, although a few men made conscious decisions to quit their life of crime and delinquency, some would say by free will or "agency," most desisters stopped doing wrong because it became less and less attractive to do so. However, many of these men did not completely desist from deviance. They might have desisted from crime but not from drinking or ignoring family responsibilities. Their life "careers" resembled a "zigzag" pattern, whereby they moved into and out of patterns of crime and deviance (see chapter 8).

A related aspect of the turning points view of crime and delinquency is the idea that one event can trigger another event, even to the point of affecting a causal relationship. For example, it is often maintained that broken homes can "cause" delinquency, a theory discussed in chapter 7, "The Family and Delinquency." To the extent that a broken home actually does contribute to crime and delinquency, the causal connection may be reversed. For example, a difficult, antisocial child may cause so much stress and strife within a home that the parents may separate and perhaps divorce over disagreements concerning proper discipline techniques and who caused what with a child's behavior. A schematic presentation of this life-course view of delinquency is presented in figure 5.2.

Examinations of turning points and focusing on a dynamic perspective can accommodate this fluid view of behavior and its causes and consequences. This perspective of delinquency is specifically adopted by Terence

Individual Traits (psychopathic personality, low response time, learning disability, etc.) and/or Negative Social Conditions (delinquent companions, weakened social bonds, low self-concept, etc.) → Delinquency *but* Turning Points in Life (graduation, good job, good marriage) → Improved Social Conditions and Lessened Influence of Individual Traits ↔ Reduction in Delinquency

FIGURE 5.2 Life-Course Model of Delinquency (Sampson and Laub)

Thornberry and his associates in their longitudinal studies of delinquency in New York (Thornberry 1987; Thornberry et al. 1991; Thornberry et al. 1994). In proposing what has been termed *interactional theory*, Thornberry and colleagues have developed an interesting model of delinquency that incorporates sociological theories of delinquency, especially social bond and differential association theories, to give a good account of how pathways and traditional theories of delinquency can be integrated or combined to provide stronger explanations (see also Shoemaker 2005 and chapter 12).

Broadly, Thornberry and others propose that the connections between social factors and delinquency are reciprocal. That is, delinquency may be affected by certain social factors, such as a weak social bond or associations with delinquent peers, but then the result, delinquency, can also further weaken social bonds and promote further associations with delinquent peers, thus producing an interactive, spiraling effect in which cause and effect are mutually connected. The spiral toward a life of crime is assumed to be more pronounced among those living in lower-class areas as opposed to middle-class neighborhoods, but this assumption is not a necessary aspect of the theory. Two important points about interactional theory are that it is realistic and that it is able to address many of the points raised in developmental perspectives as well as in more traditional explanations of delinquency.

Summary

Developmental views on delinquency and associated pathways are becoming increasingly accepted among students in the field. As Benson (2001:80) puts it, "The fact that different offending trajectories exist is no longer seriously debated." Indeed, developmental views, life-course analysis, and examinations of turning points in the lives of gang members are now appearing in the literature (Thornberry et al. 2002). The connection between gangs and the life-course approach to understanding delinquency will be visited again in chapter 10, where juvenile gangs are discussed in more detail.

There is a lot of merit in the social development models discussed in this chapter. In particular, the view that there are several pathways, or trajectories, to crime and delinquency is appealing and seems to make sense of much that is known about patterns of delinquency. It remains to be seen how all of the models and competing theoretical explanations will fare over time, but the view that there are several paths toward crime and delinquency seems to be valid at this point.

While there are several pathways to delinquency, just as there are several avenues toward conformist behavior and successful careers in business or professional life, the view that there are at least two dominant pathways, life-course persistent and adolescence-limited, is persuasive, given current information and theoretical developments concerning delinquency. Life-course persistent offenders begin committing acts of crime and delinquency at an early age and persist in this behavior throughout most of their life. They exhibit signs of behavior and emotional problems early in life and often commit a range of behaviors from minor offenses to serious crimes. Their behavior is thought to be affected by biological and psychological factors as well as by peer relationships. Adolescent-limited delinquents usually start committing acts of delinquency at around adolescence and stop before reaching adulthood. They usually commit more minor forms of delinquency and are influenced by social factors more so than by biological and psychological variables.

Other developmental perspectives focus on a supposed general trait that influences criminal and delinquent behavior throughout a lifetime. This view is known as the general theory of crime, proposed by Gottfredson and Hirschi. According to the general theory of crime, the paramount, if not sole, factor in crime and delinquency causation is a trait called low self-control. Low self-control is thought to be learned early in life, by age ten, and is resistant to change throughout life. A contrasting view is the turning points explanation of crime and delinquency proposed by Sampson and Laub. According to this perspective, people can and do change their criminal behavior patterns over the course of a lifetime, especially if they experience significant turning points, such as successful marriage and employment. Considerable research has been conducted on both of these perspectives, with some support being reported for each view. However, the weight of the evidence thus far seems to favor the turning points view of delinquency over the tenets of the general theory of crime.

References

Adler, Freda, Gerhard O. W. Mueller, and William S. Laufer
   2001   Criminology and the Criminal Justice System. 4th edition. New York: McGraw-Hill.
Benson, Michael L.
   2001   Crime and the Life Course: An Introduction. Los Angeles: Roxbury.
Burt, Callie Harbin, Ronald L. Simons, and Leslie G. Simons
   2006   A Longitudinal Test of the Effects of Parenting and the Stability of Self-Control: Negative Evidence for the General Theory of Crime. Criminology 44:353–396.
Caspi, Avshalom, Terrie E. Moffitt, Phil A. Silva, Magda Stouthamer-Loeber, Robert F. Krueger, and Pamela S. Schmutte
   1994   Are Some Crime-Prone? Replications of the Personality-Crime Relationship Across Countries, Genders, Races, and Methods. Criminology 32:163–195.
Cauffman, Elizabeth, Laurence Steinberg, and Alex R. Piquero
   2005   Psychological, Neuropsychological and Physiological Correlates of Serious Antisocial Behavior in Adolescence: The Role of Self-Control. Criminology 43:133–175.
Coleman, James S.
   1988   Social Capital and the Creation of Human Capital. American Journal of Sociology 94 (Supplement):S95–S120.
Felson, Richard B., and Jeremy Staff
   2006   "Explaining the Academic Performance-Delinquency Relationship. Criminology 44:299–319.
Glueck, Sheldon, and Eleanor Glueck
   1950   Unraveling Juvenile Delinquency. New York: Commonwealth Fund.
Gottfredson, Michael R., and Travis Hirschi
   1990   A General Theory of Crime. Stanford, CA: Stanford University Press.
Huang, Bu, Rick Kosterman, Richard F. Catalano, J. David Hawkins, and Robert D. Abbott
   2001   Modeling Mediation in the Etiology of Violent Behavior in Adolescence: A Test of the Social Development Model. Criminology 39:75–107.

Laub, John H., and Robert J. Sampson
    1993   Turning Points in the Life Course: Why Change Matters to the Study of Crime. Criminology 31:301–325.
    2003   Shared Beginnings, Divergent Lives: Delinquent Boys to Age 70. Cambridge, MA: Harvard University Press.
Longshore, Douglas, Eunice Chang, and Nena Messina
    2005   Self-Control and Social Bonds: A Combined Control Perspective on Juvenile Offending. Journal of Quantitative Criminology 21:419–437.
Mitchell, Ojmarrh, and Doris Layton MacKenzie
    2006   The Stability and Resiliency of Self-Control in a Sample of Incarcerated Offenders. Crime & Delinquency 52:432–449.
Moffitt, Terrie E.
    1990   Juvenile Delinquency and Attention Deficit Disorder: Boys' Developmental Trajectories from Age 3 to Age 15. Child Development 61:893–910.
    1993   "Adolescent-Limited" and "Life-Course Persistent" Antisocial Behavior: A Developmental Taxonomy. Psychological Review 100:674–701.
Moffitt, Terrie E., Donald R. Lynam, and Phil A. Silva
    1994   Neuropsychological Tests: Predicting Persistent Male Delinquency. Criminology 32:277–300.
Moffitt, Terrie E., Avshalom Caspi, Honalee Harrington, and Barry J. Milne
    2002   Males on the Life-Course Persistent and Adolescence-Limited Antisocial Pathways: Follow-Up at Age 26 Years. Development and Psychopathology 14:179–207.
Patterson, Gerald R.
    1992   Developmental Changes in Antisocial Behavior. In Aggression and Violence Throughout the Life Course. Ray De V. Peters, Robert J. McMahon, and Vernon L. Quinsey, eds. Pp. 52–82. Newbury Park, CA: Sage.
Patterson, Gerald R., Deborah Capaldi, and Lou Bank
    1991   An Early Starter Model for Predicting Delinquency. In The Development and Treatment of Childhood Aggression. Debra J. Pepler and Kenneth H. Rubin, eds. Pp. 139–168. Hillsdale, NJ: Erlbaum.
Sampson, Robert J., and John H. Laub
    1993   Crime in the Making: Pathways and Turning Points through Life. Cambridge, MA: Harvard University Press.
Schiamberg, Lawrence
    1988   Child and Adolescent Development. New York: Macmillan.

Shoemaker, Donald J.

2005 Theories of Delinquency: An Examination of Explanations of Delinquent Behavior. 5th edition. New York: Oxford University Press.

Silverthorn, Persephanie, and Paul J. Frick

1999 Developmental Pathways to Antisocial Behavior: The Delayed-Onset Pathway in Girls. Development and Psychopathology 11:101–126.

Simons, Ronald L., Chyi-In Wu, Rand D. Conger, and Frederick O. Lorenz

1994 Two Routes to Delinquency: Differences between Early and Late Starters in the Impact of Parenting and Deviant Peers. Criminology 32:247–276.

Simons, Ronald L., Leslie Gordon Simons, Yi-Fu Chen, Gene H. Brody, and Kuei-Hsiu Lin

2007 Identifying the Psychological Factors that Mediate the Association between Parenting Practices and Delinquency. Criminology 45:481–517.

Thornberry, Terence P.

1987 Toward an Interactional Theory of Delinquency. Criminology 25:863–891.

Thornberry, Terence P., Alan J. Lizotte, Marvin D. Krohn, Margaret Farnsworth, and Sung Joon Jang

1991 Testing Interactional Theory: An Examination of Reciprocal Causal Relationships among Family, School, and Delinquency. Journal of Criminal Law and Criminology 82:3–35.

1994 Delinquent Peers, Beliefs, and Delinquent Behavior: A Longitudinal Test of Interactional Theory. Criminology 32:47–83.

Thornberry, Terence P., Marvin D. Krohn, Alan J. Lizotte, Carolyn A. Smith, and Kimberly Tobin

2002 Gangs and Delinquency in Developmental Perspective. Cambridge, England: Cambridge University Press.

Toby, Jackson

1957 Social Disorganization and Stake in Conformity: Complementary Factors in the Predatory Behavior of Hoodlums. Journal of Criminal Law, Criminology, and Police Science 48:12–17.

Winfree, L. Thomas, Jr., Terrance J. Taylor, Ni He, and Finn-Aage Esbensen

2006 Self-Control and Variability Over Time: Multivariate Results Using a 5-Year, Multisite Panel of Youths. Crime & Delinquency 52: 253–286.

SOCIAL PROCESS THEORIES

SOCIAL PROCESS theories examine the interpersonal actors in a person's life who have an influence on his or her attitudes and behavior. These theories of delinquency are sometimes called "micro" explanations because they focus on smaller social settings and situations rather than on larger, structural, "macro" variables. They differ from the individualistic theories mentioned earlier in that the suggested causes of crime are not sought from within the individual. That is, social process theories are not "kinds of people" explanations of behavior.

Social process explanations of delinquency hold certain assumptions that tend to separate them from other theories of delinquency.

1. *Behavior is learned, not biologically inherited.* Learning crime and delinquency can occur through the same mechanisms that apply to the learning of other behavior.
2. *Behavior is learned in social settings.* The learning of attitudes and behaviors occurs *more* through interactions with others in close, interpersonal settings than through impersonal, mass media connections. It is not maintained that the mass media, for example, do not exert any influence on behavior. Clearly, they do. However, social process theories assume that people tend to learn more from others in their immediate social circles than they do from television, movies, or similar forms of mass communication.

3. *Attention should be focused on what a person does, not on what a person "is."* Again, "kinds of people" explanations of delinquency are focused on the internal characteristics of the delinquent, while more attention should be paid to the social and environmental situations in which children or youth are located.

Social process theories are dynamic in their approach to an understanding of delinquent behavior. By "dynamic," it is meant that these explanations view behavior in terms of actions and reactions. Behaviors and attitudes change according to environmental and social settings. For example, a social process theory would be able to incorporate changes in behavior over time, as a person aged, changed associations, or changed positions in society. Thus, compared with the individualistic theories discussed in chapter 4, social process explanations of delinquency can more easily incorporate the "maturation effect."

The examples of social process theories discussed in this chapter include differential association theory, drift theory, and social control theory, which is separated into containment and social bond theory. There are other kinds of social process theories, most notably labeling theory. However, labeling theory is covered in a separate chapter, chapter 12, along with conflict theories. While it is accurate to describe labeling theory as a social process explanation, it is more focused on societal reactions to behavior rather than on the primary causes of behavior, and, as such, it is more connected with juvenile justice system concepts and processes.

Differential Association Theory

Differential association theory was developed by Edwin H. Sutherland several decades ago (Sutherland 1939). In the field of delinquency, it is sometimes referred to as a "peer relations" or "peer group" explanation because it focuses on peer relationships and friendship patterns as a basic causal nexus for delinquency. Sutherland developed this theory over several decades and tried to come up with an explanatory scheme that identified individual as well as social explanations for crime and delinquency.

In its final version (Sutherland and Cressey 1978:80–83), the theory listed nine propositions. These are listed below, in their original wording:

1. Crime is learned.
2. Criminal behavior is learned in interaction with other persons in a process of communication.

3. The principal part of the learning of criminal behavior occurs within intimate personal groups.
4. When criminal behavior is learned, the learning includes (a) techniques of committing the crime, which are sometimes very complicated, sometimes very simple, and (b) the specific direction of motives, drives, rationalizations, and attitudes.
5. The specific direction of motives and drives is learned from definitions of the legal codes as favorable or unfavorable.
6. A person becomes delinquent because of an excess of definitions favorable to violation of law over definitions unfavorable to violation of law.
7. Differential associations may vary in frequency, duration, priority, and intensity.
8. The process of learning criminal behavior by associations with criminal and anticriminal patterns involves all of the mechanisms that are involved in any other learning.
9. While criminal behavior is an expression of general needs and values, it is not explained by those general needs and values, since noncriminal behavior is an expression of the same needs and values.

The first two propositions clearly identify this theory as a learning theory. Propositions three and four outline the social context in which learning occurs. Important in these two propositions is the notion that crime and delinquency are learned in association with others in close, personal group contexts. This idea also helps differential association theory to explain gang behavior, since many juvenile gangs are considered close, personal groups (see chapter 10, "Juvenile Gangs"). Close, personal groups are sometimes called *primary groups*, that is, groups that are considered small in size, characterized by close, personal forms of communication and informal rules of interaction (Hughes and Kroehler 2005:104-105).

The fifth and sixth propositions get at another important feature of this theory. The learning of crime is based upon *definitions* of the law as *favorable* or *unfavorable*, whether the law is to be accepted and obeyed or not. Proposition 6 places the learning in a kind of ratio perspective rather than something that is "either/or." That is, behavior is responsive to a definition of legal codes or norms as appropriate or inappropriate. We have both favorable and unfavorable images of laws, either in general or, more likely, in terms of specific laws. At any given period of time in our lives, we tend to generally accept or deny the legitimacy of laws, and this balance is what shapes our behavior *vis-à-vis* the law during this time. This proposition is one reason why differential association is considered a social process theory.

That is, behavior and the motivations that produce behavior are conceptualized as part of an ongoing, fluid *process* that is changing and changeable over time because of social contacts and influences.

Propositions seven and eight specify certain conditions and characteristics of the basic notion that delinquency is learned in group contexts and in terms of definitions of the law. In particular, proposition seven indicates that group contexts vary according to their influence on our values and behavior. Frequency and duration of associations mean what they suggest, that is, the number and length of contacts we have with others. Priority is a temporal concept and indicates that associations formed earlier in life are stronger than associations formed later, an assumption that is compatible with psychoanalytic theory but that is not always true. Intensity suggests that some associations are more prestigious, and thus more attractive, in our lives than are others, such as the sway a youth gang holds over its members as opposed to, say, the influence a teacher may have on a youth gang member.

Proposition nine of this theory identifies common motivators for behavior, such as hunger, but then indicates that such needs cannot be considered true causes of crime because noncriminals have the same needs and values. In other words, if we all need to eat, why do some turn to crime to get what they need to eat while others do not? It is not only the need to eat that drives our criminal behavior but also a *definition* in our minds that stealing is an acceptable way to obtain what we need to eat.

Discussion of the Theory

A description of this theory and its relationship to delinquency is presented in figure 6.1. Differential association theory is an interesting explanation of delinquency, and it seems to make sense of some characteristics of delinquency. For example, researchers generally conclude that most acts of delinquency are committed in group or gang contexts (Sarnecki 1986; Warr 2002; Shoemaker 2005:151–152). In addition, the theory can explain why many youth "mature" out of delinquency as they age, that is, the maturation effect (Warr 2002:chapter 5). In addition, this theory shifts the focus of attention away from the problems of individuals to specific behaviors and associations. In this way, differential association differs from "kinds of people" explanations by focusing on responses to situations that might lead one to commit acts of delinquency. In other words, you can use this theory as a basis for responding to the *behavior* of a child rather than to the child as a whole entity. Thus, you can be unhappy with a child's behavior but still not reject the child.

> Exposure to Delinquent Attitudes and Behavior Patterns →
> Adoption of Delinquency Orientation → Association with Delin-
> quent Peers ↔ Delinquency

FIGURE 6.1 Differential Association and Delinquency

A similar feature of differential association theory is its focus on the *social* aspects of learning rather than on the psychological and/or biological details of the learning process. In this way, differential association theory is an extension of general learning principles established by earlier psychologists, such as Pavlov and Skinner (Vold et al. 2002:156–157), and more recent learning theorists, such as Bandura (1969, 1973). In addition, the theory is an extension of Gabriel Tarde's laws of imitation (1912). Differential association was reconceptualized into a more specific social learning theory, using the ideas of punishment and reinforcement, by Burgess and Akers (1966), and Akers has extended this reasoning into the development of a more general learning explanation of crime and delinquency (Akers 1985, 1998; Akers and Sellers 2004:chapter 5).

Many efforts to examine differential association theory focus on *peer relations*, such as associations and attitudes toward peers, as these are related to behavior. This situation is one reason why the theory has become known as a "peer relations" theory (Warr 2002:chapter 4). Most of the efforts to test the theory using measures of peer relations have tended to support its basic notion that peer influence is important in the explanation of delinquency. In fact, Mark Warr categorically states that, "No characteristic of individuals known to criminologists is a better predictor of criminal behavior than the number of delinquent friends an individual has" (Warr 2002:40). Friends are important in influencing our behaviors and attitudes, especially during adolescence (Warr 1993; 2002:chapters 3 and 4; Shoemaker 2005:150–156). This influence is, again, more important in the explanation of some kinds of behaviors (such as gang behaviors) than in others. Peer relations are also important in the explanation of drug use among adolescents (Dembo et al. 1986; Johnson et al. 1987).

Much of the current literature examining peer relationships and delinquency, or differential association theory in these terms, focuses on the nature and characteristics of friendship patterns as these influence delinquency. For example, it is generally concluded that delinquent friends do influence delinquent behavior, but it is not clear how the causal connection occurs. That is, do delinquent friends seek out other delinquents, or do delinquent associates encourage and otherwise "teach" one another how to commit delinquent acts? The answer is that both processes seem to be in operation, although most evidence suggests that delinquent companions encourage delinquency. That is, sometimes youngsters who are already "into" delinquency seek out others who are also delinquent. More often, however, youth who are not fully involved with delinquency seem to be more involved with delinquent acts once they become involved with delinquent groups, such as gangs (Warr 1993; Warr 2002:chapters 3, 4, and 6, esp. pp. 133–138 ; Haynie 2001; Liu 2003; Chesney-Lind and Shelden 2004:74; Shoemaker 2005: 152–156).

Despite the many advantages and positive features of differential association theory, there are aspects of the theory that either make it difficult to examine or seem to omit situations and conditions that make the explanation incomplete. Before discussing some of these characteristics, it should be stressed that the theory does not propose to explain all acts of delinquency. In fact, no one theory can do that, at least not with any legitimacy. For example, differential association is a good explanation of gang delinquency, for example, but probably not psychopathic deviance as this concept was discussed in chapter 4.

Although there have been many efforts to test differential association theory (Shoemaker 2005:150–156), it has never been completely examined, in part because some of its propositions are difficult to operationalize, that is, to put into specific variables that can be measured and analyzed. In particular, proposition six, the "ratio" proposition, seems elusive in terms of measurement. This is such a fluid concept that it becomes difficult to assess. For example, how can it be determined just *when* there is an excess of any kind of definitions or attitudes favorable to law violation, save the fact that a crime has been committed? If we choose to use crime as an example of its existence, the whole relationship becomes tautological and thus nonexplanatory. Still, researchers have made efforts to examine this proposition. Approximations of attitudes toward crime can be measured retrospectively, that is, from remembrance, and that is helpful to know, but still, it does not get to the specific instance of thought and behavior.

In addition, the theory has been challenged on the grounds that not all associations with criminals produce criminality. That is true, but it is also true of other explanations of delinquency. That is, no theory explains all acts of crime and delinquency but only a tendency to commit them, or, in more general terms, a greater or lesser influence than is seen for other factors. In part, this criticism of differential association theory is handled by what Daniel Glaser (1956) refers to as "differential identification." This term suggests that we use "reference groups" (Haskell 1960) to guide our thoughts and actions. Sometimes we are not actually members of these groups, again, such as juvenile gangs, but we wish to become involved with them, that is, to become a member of a group. So even though someone is not a member of a juvenile gang, he or she may well be influenced to commit acts of crime and delinquency as part of an identification with that group.

Another difficulty with differential association theory is that it cannot explain why we have the associations we have. In part, the answer to that kind of question must come from structural conditions, such as social disorganization. This is a concept that will be discussed in chapter 10, "Juvenile Gangs." Sutherland introduced a term known as *differential social organization* to explain why some are more exposed to criminal associations than are others. Differential social organization means that all communities are organized, sometimes for good behavior, sometimes for criminal or delinquent behavior. Thus, where a person lives may have an important influence on his or her associations and attitudes and, thus, on behavior (Shoemaker 2005:146–147).

The kinds of social bonds or connections we have to others in our lives, especially as teens and children to our families and schools, can also affect the nature of our peer associations. Social bond theory is discussed later in this chapter. Also, family and school factors are treated separately in chapters 7 and 8.

Overall, differential association theory remains a strong explanation of delinquency, especially delinquency that occurs in group settings. However, it is not the only kind of social process theory. Beside social control theories, including containment and social bond explanations, there is drift, or neutralization, theory.

A Note on Exposure to Media Violence and Delinquency

One of the propositions of differential association theory is that the learning of delinquency comes primarily from contacts or associations with others in a primary group setting. This idea is in contrast to the view that watching violence on television or in the movies encourages or "causes" violence among children.

Youth exposure to violence through the mass media is definitely a legitimate topic of concern in America today. American children watch an average of 28 hours of television every week, and some estimate that before a young person reaches middle school, he or she will have seen more than 8,000 homicides on television (Reiman 2003:163). In addition, major professional societies such as the American Medical Association, the American Academy of Pediatrics, and the American Academy of Child and Adolescent Psychiatry have all gone on record as suggesting a "causal connection between media violence and aggressive behavior in some children" (cited in Reiman 2003:163). When one adds to this set of figures the exposure of youth to violence through video games, computers, and movies, the amount of violence youth are seeing through mass media outlets is alarming.

The connection between witnessing violent behavior and actually committing violence has been documented from the early efforts of Albert Bandura and his "Bobo doll" experiments to more recent research. Bandura observed that children who see adults commit acts of violence on large dolls are more likely to commit such violent acts themselves (1963). Also, some research has shown that boys seem to be more influenced by seeing aggression than are girls, although recent longitudinal research concludes that media impact, particularly watching violence on television, has similar effects on subsequent violence among males and females (Huesmann et al. 2003).

Although earlier studies, including experimental research such as that conducted by Bandura and colleagues, have been criticized as being too artificial and producing only short-lived effects, more contemporary, longitudinal studies, based on self-reports of television watching and behavioral patterns, suggest the violence-producing effects of television watching are not only real but also can last from childhood into adulthood (Huesmann et al. 2003).

Despite the ample evidence that watching violence can contribute to violence, the strength and consistency of this connection are still uncertain. Part of this doubt stems from the string of rebuttals to the scientific research offered by members of the entertainment industry. Media executives typically suggest that the often-cited impact of watching violence on television or in the movies on violence committed by youth is overstated or based on faulty research designs (Bushman and Anderson 2001). In addition, even the scientific evidence is not uniform. One of the more often-cited recent studies linking media violence and youth violence is the aforementioned longitudinal study by Huesmann et al. (2003). Even the authors of this study suggest that watching violence in the media is only one of several possible factors in the causation of youth violence (p. 201). In addition, they conclude that "The effect sizes for media violence on aggression revealed in this longitudinal study are modest" (p. 218).

One possible contributing factor that calls into question the direction of this relationship is the option that children exposed to violence early in their lives, such as in the home, are attracted to violence in the media. These children are, in effect, "violence prone," and their violent tendencies are further manifested by their interest in watching violence on television or through other impersonal media. In addition, parenting attitudes and values may also interfere with the relationship between watching violence on television or video games and violent behavior among youth. Parents can inhibit or encourage youths' viewing habits as well as influence their reactions to viewing violence (Huesmann et al. 2003:218; Siegel and Welsh 2005:72–73). Some research has found, for example, that children from families where alternatives to violence and aggression are taught are less influenced by media violence than children reared in families that do not stress such alternatives (Kratcoski and Kratcoski 2004:65).

Overall, the relationship between witnessing violent acts in the mass media and committing violent behavior among youth is real and at least moderately strong. However, it should not be forgotten that adult, especially parental, supervision patterns and controls over youth can also affect this relationship. Parental controls over youth in general seem to have important effects on youth behavior, as will be discussed later in this chapter and in chapter 7. Thus, Sutherland's emphasis on the learning of crime and delinquency in primary, interpersonal groups is still worth considering, despite the real and legitimate concerns of the negative impacts of mass media portrayals of violence on youth.

Drift Theory

Drift theory, developed by David Matza and Gresham Sykes (Sykes and Matza 1957; Matza 1964), posits that juveniles *drift* into and out of delinquency during adolescence, depending on social circumstances and moods. Drift theory is considered a process theory because it does not view delinquency as an either/or situation. That is, according to this theory, juveniles move from delinquency to conformity and back, depending on circumstances. Another feature of drift theory is the notion that juveniles use free will in deciding whether to engage in delinquency, although this *free* will is influenced by peers.

An important assumption of drift theory is the idea that juvenile delin-quents are basically good kids who want to conform to rules and laws. How-ever, they have experienced injustices, or perceived injustices, in their lives, such as wrongful actions from police, teachers, or parents. This unjust treat-ment triggers feelings of anger and resentment, which can then lead to acts of crime or delinquency. An important concept in this causal chain is the concept of *neutralization*. Neutralization refers to efforts to explain away the negative or condemning consequences of committing criminal or delinquent acts. It is important to consider that neutralizations of delinquency would not be necessary if individuals did not care about the consequences of their behavior, such as psychopaths. Thus, although the juvenile is angry and hurt, he is not totally blind to the feelings of others. Neutralization, then, helps to make acceptable or right what would otherwise be considered a wrongful act on the part of the juvenile.

According to Sykes and Matza (1957), there are five *techniques of neutralization*:

1. Denial of responsibility
2. Denial of injury
3. Denial of a victim
4. Condemnation of condemners
5. Appeal to higher loyalties

Denial of responsibility suggests that one was not to blame for the act. This denial can be attributed to personal problems, such as having a bad temper, or to social circumstances, such as living in a bad neighborhood or having abusive parents, and so on.

Denial of injury means that while the act did occur and you were responsible, no one was really hurt or injured because of what you did. Denial of a victim argues that while there was a victim in the act, that vic-tim deserved what he or she received. Maybe the "victim" was a bad shop owner, a mean teacher or parent, or someone who tried to cheat others.

Condemnation of condemners reflects the sense of injury and/or injus-tice youth have received from others, particularly adults. This technique allows a juvenile to justify, or neutralize, delinquent actions by labeling those who would criticize or judge delinquent acts as hypocrites. These condem-ners are sometimes criminal or deviant themselves, so why should their judgments be important? A situation where this kind of neutralization might be used would be a juvenile caught using marijuana and lectured by parents who are regular consumers of alcohol or cigarettes.

The last technique, appeal to higher loyalties, illustrates another feature of drift theory. It also focuses on the influence of one's peers in shaping opinions and behavior, much as does differential association theory. One difference between drift theory and differential association theory, however, is the view in drift theory that delinquents have a grudge or sense of anger about them, which is not the case with differential association theory. This group nature of delinquency and the influence of others that it implies is highlighted by another concept, *situation of company* (Matza 1964). By situation of company, Matza means that youth, especially in group or gang contexts, are always being asked to show their loyalty to the group and to go along with the thinking of the members of their group. Thus, while it may be that deep down, a juvenile may not want to commit this or that act of crime, when pressed by others to go along or support the behavior, he or she follows or does as asked. In this context, then, it is easy to understand how the technique of appeal to higher loyalties could be used to neutralize negative feelings over the consequences of a crime. These ideas are summarized in figure 6.2.

Drift theory has received some support in the literature. For example, a study of delinquents in the Netherlands found that delinquents tended to see their criminal acts as acceptable except for *violent* offenses, which were not considered permissible even though the juveniles committed these acts (Landsheer et al. 1994; see also Agnew 1994). Others, however, offer little support for the theory (Hindelang 1974; Giordano 1976). Hamlin (1988) suggests that the concept of neutralization is insightful but might occur after

---

Negative (embarrassing, harassing, etc.) Experiences with Public Adult Authority Figures (police, teachers, etc.) → Receptivity to Negative Attitudes toward Laws and Law Enforcers ↔ Associations with Other "Disaffected" Youth (situation of company) → Neutralizations of Moral Constraints against Delinquency ↔ Delinquency

---

FIGURE 6.2 Drift and Delinquency

acts have been committed, not before, as Sykes and Matza presume. In addition, continued research on neutralization suggests that over the years, subcultures have evolved that tend to accept, perhaps even reward, criminal behavior and that "being bad" in these subcultures may be a good thing. Life in the streets and the "street code" (Anderson 1999) reduce the need to justify criminal behavior among peers. In this situation, criminal behavior, including violence in general, does not need to be justified. Injustice, wrongs, slights, and so on are met with violent response, and there is no need to justify such responses within the street subculture or to neutralize conventional attitudes that may not exist. If anything, in this setting, being good needs to be neutralized more than being bad. Violence and criminality may not occur in these situations because of appeals from friends or relatives or because of situational circumstances, but not because one is responding to conventional values and norms (Topalli 2005).

Overall, drift theory presents a reasonable but incomplete picture of juvenile offending. On one hand, it correctly addresses the maturation effect and the group properties of delinquency. It also considers one possible consequence of unfairly labeling juveniles (see chapter 12). On the other hand, however, several attempts to examine the theory have given it limited support. The notion of neutralization is difficult to test, especially in terms of rationalizations developed before acts occur (Topalli 2005:825–826). In addition, the theory seems incomplete because it provides little understanding of how neutralization or justification for deviance becomes accepted. Certainly, differential association theory seems able to handle that question. In addition, control theories, especially social bond theory, appear well equipped to address the issue of why some kids become more easily persuaded by their peers than other juveniles. The topic of control theories is discussed next.

Control Theories

Unlike other explanations of crime and delinquency, control theories assume that the cause of delinquent behavior is actually the absence of something internal or external to the individual. That something is a constraining or controlling factor. Thus, control theories do not assume that delinquents are driven or forced to commit crimes. Rather, deviant tendencies are not held in check, or controlled. Behind the assumption that it is the absence of something that contributes to deviance is the assumption that people, including juveniles, are prone to commit acts of crime or delinquency. This idea comes close to the Hobbesian view of the nature of man, that is, that man is basically mean and evil. Acceptance of the basic assumption of control theories, however, especially for juveniles, does not necessarily mean accepting the view of mankind as naturally mean-spirited or evil. For example, juveniles may be seen as curious or inquisitive, and that curiosity can lead to experiments with "exciting" or "dangerous" behaviors, behaviors that may be illegal or criminal. In the absence of strong internal or external controls concerning breaking rules or laws, these tendencies to test rules or live dangerously, so to speak, can sometimes lead to actual rule or law breaking, especially when circumstances such as temptations and opportunities are present.

Internal Controls

Internal controls are individualistic and consist of some of the factors discussed previously. Psychoanalytic theory is, in part, a type of internal control theory. The superego, for example, is the part of the personality that acts as a barrier against the deviant tendencies of the id. However, another theory is also considered an internal control explanation of crime and delinquency: *containment theory.*

As proposed by Walter Reckless (1961, 1967), containment theory is composed of several pushes and pulls toward crime and delinquency as well as containments or constraints against delinquency. These pushes, pulls, and containments are described as outer and inner. Outer pulls toward crime, for example, include delinquent peers (differential association) and media images and temptations. External pressures include poverty or difficult economic circumstances, discrimination and segregation (of minorities), and other social problems. Inner pushes are exemplified by drives, such as with the id, frustrations, biological and personality problems, and rebellious attitudes.

Outer containments involve strong social institutions, such as the family and school, feelings of acceptance and membership in groups and society, and, generally, social situations that encourage inclusion and supervision, a kind of joint caring and cooperation that includes controlling youth in a community or neighborhood.

Inner containments include conformist goal orientation, frustration tolerance, and commitment to prosocial norms. The most important inner constraint, however, is a strong, positive self-concept, and this is especially true in urbanized, modern, industrialized societies, where external constraints are thought to be weak. The importance of the self-concept is one reason this theory is often identified as a self-concept theory. Reckless researched the relationship between self-concept and delinquency before developing the containment theory model (Reckless et al. 1956, 1957), and the centrality of self-concept in containment remained despite the broadness of containment theory. See figure 6.3 for a schematic presentation of containment theory and delinquency.

The research of Reckless and others generally supports the connection between a positive self-concept and reduced chances of delinquency. Developing a good self-image does tend to reduce one's chances of becoming involved in delinquency. However, a number of issues question the acceptance of self-concept as a major barrier to delinquency. For one thing, Reckless's own research indicates it is difficult to change self-concepts of youth using artificial, school-based curricula (Reckless and Dinitz 1972). Even if developing a strong self-concept could significantly reduce the chances of becoming involved in delinquency, this should be initiated early in a child's life, and that may be difficult to do without concentrated community effort. In fact, current research on self-esteem indicates that, as measured on most scales, self-esteem is a dynamic concept that can and does change, especially in high-school years, not according to preplanned and artificial settings, but according to real-life experiences (Baldwin and Hoffman 2002).

Even if self-concepts in children could be easily manipulated, that is, developed in a consistent, positive fashion, there are still a number of other issues to consider. For example, self-concept scales usually ask one to compare himself or herself with others. However, some research suggests that "good boys," that is, youth who are predicted by teachers and school officials to be good students and less involved with delinquency, tend to identify with teachers, whereas "bad boys," those who are predicted not to be good students, tend to identify with their mothers (Schwartz and Stryker 1970). The lesson here is that we do not always know with whom one is comparing an

---

External Pressures and Pulls (delinquent companions, media violence, moral inconsistencies, etc.) → Weakened Social Institutions *Along with* Weakened Personal Controls (especially a low self-concept) → Delinquency

FIGURE 6.3 Containment and Delinquency (Modern Society)

image of self when constructing a self-concept measure, and such comparisons could have important impacts on behavior.

In addition, some research reports an *increase* in self-concept among delinquents (Kaplan 1978). Some suggest this unexpected relationship may occur among minorities who identify with a racial or ethnic group and take pride in that identification, even if they also commit acts of crime or delinquency (Ross 1992, 1994). Others suggest that the increase in self-esteem with increased delinquency occurs primarily among those with initial lower levels of self-concept (Kaplan 1980; Mason 2001).

Perhaps a better approach to this issue is to consider that self-concept has more of an *indirect* effect on delinquency rather than a consistent, direct impact on behavior. That is, self-concept may produce attitudes conducive to associating with others who are delinquent (differential association), or they may affect our relationships with people in our families or in school (social bond). These factors, in turn, may have a more direct effect on behavior than self-concept. It is also possible that a low self-concept makes one "disposed" to deviance in general, by affecting associations with peers and with adults in a negative way, which could lead to delinquency (Kaplan et al. 1986).

The theory of differential association has already been discussed. The impact of another kind of control, social control, or the social bond, will be discussed next.

Social Control Theory—The Social Bond

As developed by Travis Hirschi (1969), social control theory, also known as social bond theory, proposes that juveniles develop attachments to various parts of their social world, and these attachments, or bonds, help deter them from committing acts of crime and delinquency. Over the past 30 years or so, social bond theory has become one of the more researched explanations of delinquency, although it has often been combined with other explanations to accommodate new ideas and information concerning delinquency.

Hirschi described the social bond as having four essential elements, or components: *attachment, belief, commitment,* and *involvement.* Attachment is conceptualized as an emotional component of the social bond. It is usually measured as attachment to a particular representative of a social institution, such as a parent, a teacher, or a minister. Belief corresponds to an acceptance of a conventional value system in society and/or its legal systems. Commitment is associated with investments in time or energy in the policies and programs of an institution, such as trying to do well in school. It represents a more rational, cost–benefit approach to associations in society. Involvement is identified with conformist participation within an institution, such as participating in extracurricular activities in school or in church-related programs.

The prediction of social bond theory is that the stronger the attachments, beliefs, commitments, and involvements of a child to society, the less the chance of that person becoming involved in delinquent behavior. The diagrammatic depiction of the theory is presented in figure 6.4.

Hirschi theoretically envisioned all four components of the social bond as having equal weight in the prevention of delinquency. In addition, all four were thought to be positively associated with one another. That is, if a person had strong attachments, he or she would also have a conventional belief system, good commitment to social institutions, and regular involvement in various activities in the family, school, church, and so on. However, it is possible that having high degrees of participation may take time away from studying or that too much activity at school may detract from attachment, commitments, and involvements in other institutions, such as the family and religious activities. In addition, social bond theory predicts that strong attachments or bonds to peers reduce delinquency, but this prediction is opposite that of differential association theory. One resolution of this apparent contradiction is to argue that association with delinquent peers fosters delinquency, while relationships with conformist peers is associated with less delinquency (Gardner and Shoemaker 1989; Warr 2002).

Research on social bond theory, however, does not consistently support Hirschi's predictions. For example, involvement is sometimes negatively associated with delinquency, as predicted (Huebner and Betts 2002). Other studies, however, suggest that involvement is either weakly or *positively* connected with delinquency (Gardner and Shoemaker 1989). In addition, there are often gender differences (Huebner and Betts 2002) and geographic effects on the impact of the bond on delinquency. For example, Gardner and Shoemaker (1989) reported that the negative association of the social bond

> Weakened Attachments, Beliefs, Commitments, and Involvements with Conventional Figures and Institutions in Society → Delinquency

FIGURE 6.4 Social Bond and Delinquency

on delinquency was stronger in rural high-school students than among a sample of urban youth.

In addition, international research sometimes supports social bond theory and sometimes calls its value into question. In the Philippines, for example, studies of delinquency generally support the negative influences of a strong social bond on delinquency among males but not among females, in part because social controls of females are much stronger than for males in the Philippines (Shoemaker 1994). The reduced power of social bond as an explanation of delinquency among females has also been observed in Japan (Tanioka and Glaser 1991) and India (Hartjen and Kethineni 1993). Also, studies of delinquency in France do not support the strength of social bonds as preventives of delinquency, especially when compared with other factors, such as peer relations (Hartjen and Priyadarsini 2003).

Despite the qualifiers mentioned above, social bond theory provides a reasonable explanation of delinquency, but again, it is better to apply the theory in connection with other explanations, such as differential association theory. Social bond theory also provides an explanation for the influences of peers and the impact of low self-concept on delinquency. For example, weakened connections, or social bonds, to the family, the school, or religious institutions may negatively affect one's self-esteem and render that person more susceptible to the negative influences of delinquent peers. Research continues to document the connections among child–parent bonds, delinquent peer associations, and delinquency (Warr 2005).

In addition, social bond theory can address the issue of maturation. If a young person's attachments and bonds strengthen over time, it would be expected that delinquency would lessen. If one is less attached to the family or school, then changing those associations and becoming more connected with an occupation and creating your own family may well lessen the frustrations and pressures generated from old associations. Such changes could then lead to stronger bonds and less likelihood of committing crime and delinquency.

Institutional Connections and Delinquency

Another approach to an analysis of social bond theory is the examination of social institutions and delinquency. Social institutions are collective norms and values focused on important components of society. The school system and the whole context of marriage and family represent two illustrations of institutions in society. The relationship between delinquency and the family and the school will be discussed in chapters 7 and 8. For the present, the relationship between religion and delinquency will be discussed in connection with the social bond theory.

Religion and Delinquency

According to social bond theory, the stronger the connection one has with religious factors, the less delinquent one will be. For example, the more one attends religious services, the less there will be of delinquency involvement. This hypothesis has been tested many times over the past several decades. Most of this research has focused on church attendance (as a primary indicator of religion) and official records of delinquency. In general, three findings have emerged from these studies: (1) there is a *negative* association between church attendance and delinquency; (2) there is a *positive* association between the two, meaning that the more one attends church, the more delinquency is committed; and (3) there is *no significant association* between church attendance and delinquency (Shoemaker 2005:177).

The first conclusion is consistent with social bond theory. The conclusion that there is a positive connection between church attendance and delinquency is counterintuitive. One explanation for this finding is that kids who are forced to go to church by their parents may feel resentful and rebellious over this kind of control and resort to acts of crime and delinquency in response to this frustration. In this situation, the relations between youth and parent(s) may become strained or weakened, thus further increasing the chances of youth committing delinquent acts. It is also possible, however, that youth can be living in homes where educational methods and subjects used in the school system are incompatible with the religious beliefs of parents. Even though parents and children may be strongly bonded, in these homes the youth are subject to conflicts and perhaps even penalties levied by the state for attending schools unapproved or not accredited by state standards. In a technical sense, they would be delinquent by default. Although this situation is not common, it can occur, and it may be another reason for the positive association between delinquency and church attendance.

The finding that there is no relationship between church attendance and delinquency is represented by a study of over 4,000 high-school youth living in California in the 1960s, the "Hellfire and Delinquency" study (Hirschi and Stark 1969). This study examined self-report and official records of delinquency compared to self-admitted patterns of church attendance and religious attitudes. The authors concluded that those who attend church regularly are no less delinquent that those who attend church rarely, if at all.

Church attendance was also not connected with other measures of religion, such as acceptance of moral values and respect for law and authority. However, church attendance was related to belief in supernatural powers, but this belief was not associated with delinquency.

The conclusion that church attendance and other measures of religiosity have no connection with delinquency is not universally accepted among scholars. The "Hellfire" study generated several follow-up studies, many of which did not agree with the conclusions of the original research. For example, some studies conclude that church attendance, as one measure of religiosity, is inversely connected with some kinds of delinquency, such as status offenses and alcohol and drug use (such as marijuana). In addition, some research indicates that church attendance is inversely related to delinquency in geographic areas considered strongly influenced by religion, such as the "Bible Belt" (Burkett and White 1974; Higgins and Albrecht 1977; Stark et al. 1982; Jensen and Rojek 1992; Baier and Wright 2001). In addition, some research shows that church attendance is significantly related to lower rates of delinquency among African American youth (Johnson et al. 2000).

An ongoing national study of youth and religion provides further support for an important inverse effect of church attendance and religious values on delinquency. In this self-report survey of over 3,000 seniors in high schools throughout the United States, an early conclusion is that "religious" seniors, those who attend church regularly and express religious values, report significantly less involvement with delinquency, especially alcohol and drug use and "risky" behaviors, than do those youth who do not attend church or hold religious values (Smith and Faris 2002).

Overall, continuing research on this subject finds consistent negative effects of church attendance, religious values, and delinquency, despite some results to the contrary. In particular, church attendance seems to inhibit drug and alcohol use and status offending. At this point, it seems more and more evident that religion does play a small but steady inhibiting role with respect to delinquency, either in areas where religion is more dominant, in inner cities, or in national samples of youth. In addition, a meta-analysis of 60 published studies of religion and delinquency confirms a consistent negative effect of church attendance on delinquency. According to this study, going to church and/or having religious values has an overall correlation of -0.12 with delinquency (Baier and Wright 2001). While there is still some evidence that church attendance is uncorrelated with delinquent behavior or in some instances seems to promote delinquency, the rather consistent negative relationship between religion and delinquency supports social bond theory. Religion is only one of the contexts within which social bond theory can be evaluated. This explanation of delinquency will be discussed again in chapters 7 and 8, when family and school factors will be considered.

A Note on General Strain Theory

Another example of a social process theory is a recent version of anomie theory, which was proposed as a structural explanation of crime and deviance by Robert Merton (1957). Anomie theory, or strain theory, is based on the idea that society is composed of social goals for success, such as economic success, and structured means for achieving that success legally. Strain theory further assumes that sections of society, namely the lower class and the poor, do not have equal access to the legitimate means of achieving economic success, so they turn to illegal means for reaching success, such as theft. This explanation of crime and delinquency will be discussed again in connection with youth gangs in chapter 10.

For the present, however, it is important to discuss a more personalized variant of strain theory, general strain theory, or GST. As developed by Robert Agnew (1985, 1992), GST assumes that young people experience strains in their lives that are more personal and more general than the structural sources of frustration proposed by Merton. For example, GST assumes that a youngster might experience strain or frustration over such things as schoolwork, bad peer relationships, or family problems. In many ways, these sources of strain are similar to breakdowns in the social bond or in peer associations. But GST goes beyond social bond theory by arguing that young people, by virtue of their dependent status in society, cannot use acceptable societal means for relieving strains and frustrations in their lives. For example, if a child is having problems with a sibling or a parent, he or she cannot easily move out, as might be the case if he or she were an adult. Similarly, if a juvenile is having trouble in school with academics or peers, a solution such as moving or not going to school is either not easy or illegal, since truancy is a status offense. Others may attempt to run away, disobey parents, violate curfews, or commit other status offenses. Furthermore, these frustrations and limited responses can happen to all children, not only those in minority or poor circumstances. It might be true that a wealthy child would have more options than a poor one, but still, the status of youth or child limits what one can do, especially when compared with adults.

Sometimes, a youth might react to pressures and frustrations in more violent ways, such as assault or murder. One example of a violent reaction to school and peer problems is a school shooting, a topic that has been in the news the past few years. This subject will be discussed again in chapter 8, but some research suggests that school shootings are in part reactions to bullying at school (Newman et al. 2004:63–64; Lawrence 2007:160–161). To this explanation might be added the gist of GST, which is that not only does the child experience these negative events, but he or she sees little or no acceptable way out, so more extreme outlets become reasonable, such as shooting one's tormentors and others generally connected with the presumed source of the problem, that is, the school setting.

Summary

Social process theories assume that delinquency is learned, especially through human interaction in group contexts, and that juveniles are not bad to the core, but rather respond to environmental pressures, incentives, and opportunities that may be at odds with conventional aspects of society. These views of delinquent conduct also assume that it is more proper to evaluate the behavior of a young person and the environmental context within which behavior occurs rather than the individual faults or problems that the person may possess.

There are several varieties of social process theories: differential association, drift or neutralization, containment, and social bond. Each explanation has its strengths and weaknesses. Differential association, for example, is a good explanation of how crime and delinquency can continue, but it is not a good explanation of how patterns and attitudes favoring criminality develop in the first place. Likewise, social control theory offers a good explanation of how youth may get involved with delinquent youth, but it is weaker in describing how delinquency values and attitudes are transmitted within group contexts.

In general, social process theories are able to address the issue of delinquency reduction with age or maturation. In addition, they tend to offer good explanations of general patterns of delinquency and, as such, provide a good complement or extension to the individualistic explanations discussed earlier. All four examples of social process theories discussed in this chapter can also apply to juvenile gangs, although differential association theory clearly connects with that pattern of delinquency.

A recent example of social process theory is a revision of strain theory, named general strain theory, or GST. GST offers a good explanation of status offending and some violence among youth who experience painful frustrations or even humiliations in their personal lives, yet are unable to do much about those frustrations in any legal sense because of their legal status as minors in society. Thus, they may resort to illegal, again perhaps violent, means to solve their problems. The spate of school shootings over the past several years may in part be explained by GST, particularly in light of the view of some research that suggests many school shooters have been the victims of bullying in their school.

As with any explanation of delinquency or set of explanations, the strengths and weaknesses need to be considered and somehow integrated or combined in ways that complement and strengthen each theory. No one explanation of behavior, delinquent or conformist, can expect to explain all such behavior. In the next chapter, developmental ideas will be discussed, and suggestions for combining existing explanations of delinquency will be offered as part of that discussion. In addition, many of the explanations discussed in this chapter and others will be used to help understand specific examples of youth crime and delinquency, including the institutional contexts of the family and schools, as well as drug use and juvenile gangs.

References

Agnew, Robert
    1985   A Revised Strain Theory of Delinquency. Social Forces 64:151–167.
    1992   Foundation for a General Strain Theory of Crime and Delinquency. Criminology 30:47–87.
    1994   The Techniques of Neutralization and Violence. Criminology 32:555–580.
Akers, Ronald L.
    1985   Deviant Behavior: A Social Learning Approach. 3rd edition. Belmont, CA: Wadsworth.
    1998   Social Learning and Social Structure: A General Theory of Crime and Deviance. Boston: Northeastern University Press.
Akers, Ronald L., and Christine S. Sellers
    2004   Criminological Theories: Introduction, Evaluation, and Application. 4th edition. Los Angeles: Roxbury.
Anderson, Elijah
    1999   Code of the Streets. Chicago: University of Chicago Press.
Baier, Colin J., and Bradley E. R. Wright
    2001   If You Love Me, Keep My Commandments: A Meta-Analysis of the Effect of Religion on Crime. Journal of Research on Crime and Delinquency 38:3–21.

Baldwin, Scott A., and John P. Hoffman
    2002   The Dynamics of Self-Esteem: A Growth-Curve Analysis. Journal of Youth and Adolescence 31:101–113.

Bandura, Albert
    1963   What TV Violence Can Do to Your Child. Look, October 22: 48.
    1969   Principles of Behavior Modification. New York: Holt, Rinehart & Winston.
    1973   Aggression: A Social Learning Analysis. Englewood Cliffs, NJ: Prentice-Hall.

Burgess, Anthony, and Ronald L. Akers
    1966   A Differential Association Reinforcement Theory of Criminal Behavior. Social Problems 14:128–147.

Burkett, Steven R., and Mervin White
    1974   Hellfire and Delinquency: Another Look. Journal for the Scientific Study of Religion 13:455–462.

Bushman, Brad J., and Craig A. Anderson
    2001   Media Violence and the American Public: Scientific Facts Versus Media Misinformation. American Psychologist 56:477–489.

Chesney-Lind, Meda, and Randall G. Shelden
    2004   Girls, Delinquency, and Juvenile Justice. 3rd edition. Belmont, CA: Wadsworth.

Dembo, Richard, Gary Grandon, Lawrence La Voie, James Schmeidler, and William Burgos
    1986   Parents and Drugs Revisited: Some Further Evidence in Support of Social Learning Theory. Criminology 24:85–104.

Gardner, LeGrande, and Donald J. Shoemaker
    1989   Social Bonding and Delinquency: A Comparative Analysis. Sociological Quarterly 30:481–500.

Giordano, Peggy C.
    1976   The Sense of Injustice? An Analysis of Juveniles' Reactions to the Justice System. Criminology 14:93–112.

Glaser, Daniel
    1956   Criminality, Theories, and Behavioral Images. American Journal of Sociology 61:433–444.

Hamlin, John E.
    1988   The Misplaced Role of Rational Choice in Neutralization Theory. Criminology 26:425–438.

Hartjen, Clayton A., and Sesharajani Kethineni
    1993   Culture, Gender, and Delinquency: A Study of Youths in the United States and India. Women & Criminal Justice 5:37–69.

Hartjen, Clayton A., and S. Priyadarsini
    2003   Gender, Peers, and Delinquency: A Study of Boys and Girls in
            France. Youth & Society 34:387–414.
Haskell, Martin R.
    1960   Toward a Reference Group Theory of Juvenile Delinquency. Social
            Problems 8: 220–230.
Haynie, Dana L.
    2001   Delinquent Peers Revisited: Does Network Structure Matter? Amer-
            ican Journal of Sociology 106:1013–1057.
Higgins, Paul C., and Gary L. Albrecht
    1977   Hellfire and Delinquency Revisited. Social Forces 55:952–958.
Hindelang, Michael J.
    1974   Moral Evaluations of Illegal Behaviors. Social Problems 21:471–487.
Hirschi, Travis
    1969   Causes of Delinquency. Berkeley: University of California Press.
Hirschi, Travis, and Rodney Stark
    1969   Hellfire and Delinquency. Social Problems 17:202–213.
Huebner, Angela, and Sherry C. Betts
    2002   Exploring the Utility of Social Control Theory for Youth Develop-
            ment. Youth & Society 34:123–145.
Huesmann, L. Rowell, Jessica Moise-Titus, Cheryl-Lynn Podolski, and Leonard D.
Eron
    2003   Longitudinal Relations Between Children's Exposure to TV Violence
            and Their Aggressive and Violent Behavior in Young Adulthood:
            1977–1992. Developmental Psychology 39:201–222.
Hughes, Michael, and Carolyn J. Kroehler
    2005   Sociology: The Core. 7th edition. New York: McGraw-Hill.
Jensen, Gary F., and Dean G. Rojek
    1992   Delinquency and Youth Crime. 2nd edition. Prospects Heights, IL:
            Waveland.
Johnson, Byron, David B. Larson, Spencer de Li, and Sung Joon Yang
    2000   Escaping from the Crime of Inner Cities: Church Attendance and
            Religious Salience among Disadvantaged Youth. Justice Quarterly
            17:377–391.
Johnson, Richard E., Anastasios C. Marcos, and Stephen J. Bahr
    1987   The Role of Peers in the Complex Etiology of Adolescent Drug Use.
            Criminology 25:323–340.
Kaplan, Howard B.
    1978   Deviant Behavior and Self-Enhancement in Adolescence. Journal of
            Youth and Adolescence 7:253–277.

1980   Deviant Behavior in Defense of Self. New York: Academic Press.

Kaplan, Howard B., Steven S. Martin, and Robert J. Johnson

1986   Self-Rejection and the Explanation of Deviance: Specification of the Structure among Latent Constructs. American Journal of Sociology 92:384–411.

Kratcoski, Peter C., and Lucille Dunn Kratcoski

2004   Juvenile Delinquency. 5th edition. Upper Saddle River, NJ: Pearson/ Prentice Hall.

Landsheer, J. A., H't Hart, and W. Kox

1994   Delinquent Values and Victim Damage: Exploring the Limits of Neutralization Theory. British Journal of Criminology 34:44–53.

Lawrence, Richard

2007   School Crime and Juvenile Justice. 2nd edition. New York: Oxford University Press.

Liu, Ruth X.

2003   The Moderating Effects of Internal and Perceived Sanction Threats on the Relationship between Deviant Peer Associations and Criminal Offending. Western Criminology Review 4(3):191–202. http:// wcr.sonoma.edu/v4n3/liu.pdf.

Mason, W. Alex

2001   Self-Esteem and Delinquency Revisited (Again): A Test of Kaplan's Self-Derogation Theory of Delinquency Using Latent Growth Curve Modeling. Journal of Youth and Adolescence 30:83–102.

Matza, David

1964   Delinquency and Drift. New York: Wiley.

Merton, Robert

1957   Social Theory and Social Structure. Rev. edition. New York: Free Press of Glencoe.

Newman, Katherine S., Cybelle Fox, David J. Harding, Jal Metha, and Wendy Roth

2004   Rampage: The Social Roots of School Shootings. New York: Basic Books.

Reckless, Walter C.

1961   A New Theory of Delinquency and Crime. Federal Probation 25:42–46.

1967   The Crime Problem. 4th edition. New York: Appleton-Century-Crofts.

Reckleess, Walter C., and Simon Dinitz

1972   The Prevention of Juvenile Delinquency. Columbus: Ohio State University Press.

Reckless, Walter C., Simon Dinitz, and Barbara Kay
    1957   The Self Component in Potential Delinquency and Potential Non-
            delinquency. American Sociological Review 22:566–570.
Reckless, Walter C., Simon Dinitz, and Ellen Murray
    1956   Self-Concept as an Insulator against Delinquency. American Soci-
            ological Review 21:744–746.
Reiman, Jeffrey
    2003   The Rich Get Richer and the Poor Get Prison: Ideology, Class, and
            Criminal Justice. 7th edition. Boston: Allyn & Bacon.
Ross, Lee E.
    1992   Blacks, Self-Esteem, and Delinquency: It's Time for a New
            Approach. Justice Quarterly 9:609–624.
    1994   The Impact of Race Esteem and Self-Esteem on Delinquency. Soci-
            ological Focus 27:111–129.
Sarnecki, Jerzy
    1986   Delinquent Networks. Stockholm, Sweden: The National Council
            for Crime Prevention, Sweden.
Schwartz, Michael, and Sheldon Stryker
    1970   Deviance, Selves, and Others. Washington, DC: American Sociolog-
            ical Association.
Shoemaker, Donald J.
    1994   Male-Female Delinquency in the Philippines: A Comparative Analy-
            sis. Youth & Society 25:299–329.
    2005   Theories of Delinquency: An Examination of Explanations of
            Delinquent Behavior. 5th edition. New York: Oxford University
            Press.
Smith, Christian, and Robert Faris
    2002   Religion and American Adolescent Delinquency, Risk Behavior and
            Constructive Social Activities: A Research Report of the National
            Study of Youth and Religion, Number 1. Electronic document,
            http://www.youthandreligion.org/publications/docs/RiskReport1.pdf.
Stark, Rodney, Lori Kent, and Daniel P. Doyle
    1982   Religion and Delinquency: The Ecology of a "Lost" Relationship.
            Journal of Research in Crime and Delinquency 19:4–24.
Sykes, Gresham M., And David Matza
    1988   Techniques of Neutralization: A Theory of Delinquency. American
            Journal of Sociology 22:664–670.
Sutherland, Edwin H.
    1939   Principles of Criminology. 3rd edition. Philadelphia: Lippincott.

Sutherland, Edwin H., and Donald R. Cressey
    1978   Principles of Criminology. 10th edition. New York: Lippincott.

Sykes, Gresham M., and David Matza
    1957   Techniques of Neutralization: A Theory of Delinquency. American Journal of Sociology 22:664–670.

Tanioka, Ichiro, and Daniel Glaser
    1991   School Uniforms, Routine Activities, and the Social Control of Delinquency in Japan. Youth & Society 23:50–75.

Tarde, Gabriel
    1912   Penal Philosophy. R. Howell, trans. Boston: Little, Brown.

Topalli, Volkan
    2005   When Being Good Is Bad; An Expansion of Neutralization Theory. Criminology 43:797–835.

Vold, George B., Thomas J. Bernard, and Jeffrey B. Snipes
    2002   Theoretical Criminology. 5th edition. New York: Oxford University Press.

Warr, Mark
    1993   Age, Peers, and Delinquency. Criminology 31:17–40.
    2002   Companions in Crime: The Social Aspects of Criminal Conduct. Cambridge, England: Cambridge University Press.
    2005   Making Delinquent Friends: Adult Supervision and Children's Affiliations. Criminology 43:77–105.

THE FAMILY AND DELINQUENCY

THE CONNECTION between family factors and delinquency has been suspected for as long as there has been a societal response to youthful offending. As indicated in the discussion of the historical development of the juvenile justice system in the United States, suspected parental indifference, neglect, or incompetence in the rearing of children lay behind many of the practices and institutional reforms in the handling of juvenile offenders in the nineteenth century. Historical research into the conditions of early institutions for juveniles indicated that many of the inmates or wards of these facilities were children from homes where one or both natural parents were missing and "could provide them neither a good example nor close supervision" (Ferdinand 1989:95).

One of the implicit (and sometimes explicit) assumptions of earlier reasoning concerning the role of the family in producing or preventing delinquency was the notion that the "typical" family consisted of both parents. This typical construct of the family is often referred to as a *nuclear* family, which consists of both parents and children. Before the effects of industrialism on the post–Revolutionary War era in America and increased urbanization in major cities, the typical family consisted of parents, children, and extended familial relationships, such as grandparents and possibly aunts or uncles. This kind of family context is referred to as an *extended* family. Both nuclear and extended families were given a primary role in the education, discipline, and supervision of juveniles in the 17th and early 18th centuries in the United States (Ferdinand 1989:840). As populations grew and American society became more formalized and complex, however, the influence of the family began to give way to the systems of local and state government in matters relating to child care and education, as suggested by the use of the doctrine of *parens patriae* in court decisions granting governments the right to remove juveniles from their homes without parental permission, in the "best interests" of the child.

Still, the role of the family in the rearing and care of children has remained an important institutional value in American society. However, the nature of the typical family constellation has changed over the years. Instead of a nuclear or extended family, the modern American family now encompasses several arrangements other than "both parents and their children." In 1960, for example, 44 percent of American families fit this father-mother-children, nuclear family description, but by 2000, this figure had dropped to 25 percent (Simons et al. 2004:77).

In contemporary society, divorce occurs in half of all marriages (Wright and Wright 1995:14), and families are often characterized by stepparents or single parents. Blended families may consist of children from two or more parental unions. As one review of family contributions to crime and delinquency put it, "The middle-class, nuclear family living in a single-family home is only one form of family" (Wright and Wright 1995:11). In 2005, 32 percent of children (over 21 million children) lived in single-parent homes, up from 31 percent in 2000. Almost two-thirds (65 percent) of African American children lived in single-parent families in 2005, compared with 49 percent for American Indian children, 36 percent for Hispanic youth, and 23 percent for non-Hispanic white youth (Kids Count 2007:54).

In addition, many children are born to young or unwed parents. In 2002, for example, there were over 850,000 mothers under the age of 20, and the percentage of births to unmarried women compared to the total number of births increased from 28 in 1990 to 34 in 2002 (Kids Count 2004:11, 45).

"Broken Homes" and Delinquency

Probably the most popular family-related explanation of delinquency is the "broken" home. A home is considered "broken" if one or both natural parents is absent for a long or permanent time, such as through divorce, separation, or death). However, the term *broken home* can be considered judgmental in that, as indicated earlier, there are many types of family structures in American society, and the one containing father, mother, and biologically related children represents only about one-fourth of all families.

Studies of the connection between broken homes and delinquency have existed since the early 1900s. A detailed analysis of research on this subject concluded that there are distinct collections of findings according to historical time periods: extensive research between 1900 and 1932; a period of disinterest in the subject from 1933 to 1950; and a new period of interest from 1950 to the 1970s, which continues up through the present (Wilkinson 1974).

Research on the topic usually concludes that juveniles in correctional institutions are twice as likely to come from a broken home as other youth (Shoemaker 2005:183). One study of 1,000 males, 500 delinquents (although not necessarily institutionalized), and 500 nondelinquents found that 60 percent of the delinquents came from a broken home, compared with 30 percent of the nondelinquents (Glueck and Glueck 1950).

Not all of the earlier research on this topic concluded that broken homes were significantly related to official measures of delinquency. A detailed series of studies of neighborhoods and delinquency in Chicago during the 1920s and 1930s, for example, found no statistical association between delinquency and broken homes (Shaw and McKay 1932).

Partly on the basis of conclusions such as those by Shaw and McKay, and partly because of the rising influence of competing explanations of delinquency, such as social class, neighborhood organization, and other structural variables, the importance of the broken home as an explanation of delinquency began to decline, as Wilkinson's analysis noted. However, in the late 1950s, social scientists began to use self-report methods of measuring delinquency (see chapter 3). One of these studies was an analysis of family factors and delinquency by F. Ivan Nye (1958). Nye's analysis led him to conclude that there was no significant statistical connection between broken homes and delinquency. Since that time, many studies using the self-report method of measuring delinquency have found little to no statistical relationship between broken homes and delinquency (Shoemaker 2005:183–185).

However, renewed interest in the subject has generated longitudinal studies indicating that there are some negative effects of a broken home on children, including long-term effects (Wallerstein et al. 2000). For example, a study of over 1 million children in Sweden concluded that children reared in two-parent families, compared with those from one-parent homes, were less likely to suffer an injury or to be found in official records of psychiatric hospitals, recorded attempts to commit suicide, and records of addiction (Weitoft et al. 2003).

Meta-analyses of research on broken homes and delinquency conclude that there is an effect of broken homes on delinquency, but the impact is modest and qualified by several other factors. A meta-analysis is an effort to analyze several independent studies in one combined analysis. In one such analysis, Free (1991) looked at over 68 publications on the relationship between broken homes and delinquency and concluded that the relationship was stronger for status offenses than for crimes such as index offenses (see also Rebellion 2002). In another meta-analysis, Wells and Rankin (1991) conclude that the measurable impact of broken homes on delinquency is about 15 percent but that the most important factor in the relationship is how delinquency is measured. The relationship is strongest when delinquency is measured with official records, especially when using youth who are in special treatment programs. However, when delinquency is measured by self-report instruments, there is no consistent relationship with broken homes.

The connection between broken homes and delinquency is weak in developing societies, such as the Philippines and India, where family and community structures are strong (Shoemaker 1992; Hartjen and Kethineni 1996:chapter 7). Either few homes are physically broken, or there are extended family connections to reduce the impact of parental loss to the extent that such family "breaks" are not as difficult for juveniles to handle as they might be in more advanced countries such as the United States.

The relatively weak connection between broken homes and delinquency in societies where family and community structures are strong may give a clue as to the structural contexts in which broken homes may or may not have a significant impact on youth in the United States. Some have argued, for example, that weak support systems for single mothers may significantly reduce the ability of a working mother to supervise and exact indirect controls over her children, that is, control and influence over children when they are not in the presence of parents (Sampson 1987; McLanahan and Booth 1989:558–560). This connection is not meant to indict working mothers, because there is little evidence to support the contention that working mothers, per se, contribute to delinquency. Rather, the point stressed here is that sometimes single mothers simply lack the financial and social support resources to provide consistent supervision while they work, and in areas where such resources are scarce, supervision and control issues become more important. In addition, single mothers may lack the respect and support of those in the legal system, such as the police and courts, and this situation may complicate their child-rearing efforts (Wright and Wright 1995:11; Morash and Rucker 1989). For instance, a single, working mother whose children are thought not to be properly supervised or controlled may run the risk of having her children declared delinquent and removed from the home.

Some have also argued that broken homes may reduce the overall level of supervision in a neighborhood, thus raising the overall risk of delinquency among youth living in these areas, regardless of their home situation (Sampson 1992). This view is consistent with numerous studies of delinquency in Chicago, beginning in the 1920s, and is connected with a social disorganization explanation of delinquency, discussed in chapter 10 (Shaw and McKay 1942; although, as indicated earlier, these studies did not find a significant connection between broken homes and delinquency).

Neighborhood context offers another connection between the family and delinquency, an indirect connection. That is, where the family lives may contribute to the risk of delinquency for youth. Youth living in high-delinquency-rate areas are at greater risk of becoming involved in delinquency than are youth living in low-delinquency-rate neighborhoods. In the mid 1990s, an experimental study named the "Moving to Opportunity," or MTO, project randomly provided economic housing vouchers to over 4,600 low-income residents with children in five cities: Baltimore, Boston, Chicago, Los Angeles, and New York. Two-thirds of the families were African American, and most of the others were Hispanic. The vouchers were used to create three options for the residents: move to a neighborhood whose poverty rate did not exceed 10 percent; move to any neighborhood of their choice; and not move but still receive social services. After several years, the study concluded that moving to higher-income (and lower-crime) neighborhoods reduced violent and property crime rates among females. However, among males, the results were mixed. Violent and property crime rates were lower for males moving to higher-income areas, but several years after the move, their arrests for property crimes were 30 percent higher than arrests among youth in the control group. These gender differences suggest that other factors in addition to neighborhood context contributed to delinquency in this study, factors including adaptation to new surroundings and willingness to take advantage of criminal opportunities wherever they may exist. Certainly, these variables do have an impact on delinquency, as would all of the other variables and explanations of delinquency discussed in this book. However, the results of this study suggest that neighborhood context can have a significant impact on delinquency, especially among females (Kling et al. 2005).

Family Relationships and Delinquency

While the connection between a physically broken home and delinquency is modest and inconsistent across different measures of delinquency, the relationship between family *relationships* and delinquency is stronger and more consistent. Family relationships represent a large constellation of interactions among family members, including discipline and supervision patterns.

One of the first studies to examine family relationships and delinquency was the *Unraveling* study by the Gluecks (1950). Although, as mentioned above, the Gluecks' study found a significant relationship between broken homes and delinquency, the authors concluded that a more important set of factors in the explanation of delinquency were what they termed "under-the-roof" variables (Glueck and Glueck 1950:260–261). These included five kinds of family relationships: discipline of the father; supervision by the mother; affection of the father for the son (this study looked only at young males); affection of the mother for the son; and cohesiveness of the family. Discipline patterns that were consistent and not too strong (not necessarily physical punishment, but abusiveness), supervision that was "suitable" and "fair," close and warm affections, and strong family cohesiveness were all related to *less* delinquency.

Nye's research, mentioned above, also concluded that family relationships were more important in the explanation of delinquency than the physical structure of the family. One of his basic conclusions was that family attachments, such as emotional bonds and happiness among all family members, including parents and children, were more strongly associated with delinquency than was a broken home. Other studies have reached similar conclusions over the years (Cernkovich and Giordano 1987; Wright and Wright 1995; Wright and Cullen 2001; Simons et al. 2004).

The nature of relationships among family members is consistently related to delinquency, regardless of how delinquency is measured. That is, how well parents and children get along and the overall harmony within the family are more important in the explanation of delinquency than whether the home is physically intact or broken. As mentioned above, it is likely that single parents, especially single mothers, will have a more difficult time providing economic resources and supervision for their children, compared with two-parent families. However, how a parent handles a divorce or the loss of another parent seems to be more critical for the behavioral patterns of children than whether one or both parents is missing.

In addition, most divorces do not seem to occur overnight, because of one traumatic event. In most cases, the decision to divorce seems to be based on the cumulative outcome of several circumstances and/or events, such as personal incompatibilities, financial stress, infidelity, and other situations. It can be assumed that in many of these cases, there has been a considerable amount of parental fighting and arguing, likely involving children, in the home before the divorce occurs. These arguments, in turn, may lead to bitterness and hard feelings between parents that can affect the attitudes and behaviors of children. Furthermore, such conflict can lead to social estrangements among family members, which is another negative component of social relationships (Wright and Wright 1995:12–14).

Parenting can also be affected by relationships with children, and vice versa. Sometimes, unhappy homes reflect difficult situations between parents and children, which can contribute to conflicts between parents. Scientists at the Oregon Social Learning Center (OSLC) proffer a "coercion model" to explain the interactions between members of a conflicting family, which can lead to a child becoming hostile, rebellious, and eventually delinquent. Many of these situations include the kinds of relationships that can lead to delinquency, as discussed earlier. However, the research at the OSLC identifies interactions among family members as a central feature of family relationships that can lead to delinquency. Parents may use discipline methods that are argumentative and ineffective in controlling the child. Sometimes, perhaps often, the parent or parents give in to the demands and wishes of the child, which teaches him or her to keep resisting whenever there are restrictions or consequences placed by the parent(s) on his or her behavior. Eventually, the child takes this learned behavior pattern outside the home, where consequences can be more severe than grounding. When the child begins to dislike peers who may disagree with the behavior, other peers are selected, peers who are more compatible with the undisciplined, rebellious style of the child (Patterson et al. 1992; Warr 2002:chapters 3 and 4; Simons et al. 2004:49–51).

Problems in the home that cross over into the public can also lead to difficulties at school because teachers and many peers will not permit children to shirk responsibilities and do as they wish. The child now faces increasing problems at school, such as bad relationships with teachers and peers, as well as academic difficulties. The situation becomes worse for the child because problems become compounded, including difficulties at home and now at school (and with conventional peers as well) (Simons et al. 2004:51), which contributes to the likelihood of becoming more involved in delinquent activity.

In some ways, the scenario described above exemplifies the life-course persistent pathway to delinquency, discussed in chapter 5, or what Patterson and others refer to as "early starters" (Simons et al. 2004:52–53). Some of these children may possess latent biological and/or psychological traits that predispose them to antisocial behavior (see chapter 4). Also, these cases may be descriptive of the lack of self-control, which is thought to be learned in early years but can contribute to a life of deviance and crime, also discussed in chapter 5 (Gottfredson and Hirschi 1990). As such, these youth might be expected to contribute to the parent–child interaction difficulties because they are prone to resistance and rebellion when confronted with supervisory and restrictive reactions to their behavior. The ineffective parenting that occurs only exacerbates the situation by teaching the child that displays of defiance and resistance can lead to "getting one's way," so to speak. However, ineffective parenting can also contribute to delinquency in any child, whether the pattern is early in starting, late in starting, limited to adolescence, or occurring over most of a youth's life. Even children who are conformist and who typically follow instructions and rules from their parents may develop behavioral problems if parenting becomes inconsistent, overly harsh, or otherwise ineffective.

The coercion model is only one way of describing the relationship between parenting behaviors and delinquency. Others, such as Simons and colleagues (2004:54), mention the ability of humans to learn vicariously, that is, by observing and learning from the experiences of others. Such vicarious learning may also help explain why some children become involved with delinquency even though they personally have not been abused or treated harshly. They have observed others getting away with bad behaviors, and so they may decide to try it themselves. This kind of learning is also included in social learning theories, such as differential association theory, discussed in chapter 6.

The "Inheritance" of Delinquency

A common question with the topic of families and delinquency is whether delinquency is "inherited," that is, whether parents pass along their delinquent and criminal genes or traits to their children. One way to answer this question is to research the relationship between crime patterns of parents and those of their children. In part, this question was addressed earlier, in chapter 4, when biological explanations of crime and delinquency were discussed. In that discussion it was observed that there is a correlation between parents and children in terms of crime and delinquency but that biological inheritance of physical traits was not the likely explanation for this correlation.

Additional information continues to support a correlation between parental, or familial, crime and delinquency. A government report in 1992, for example, concluded that over half of a sample of 2,261 juvenile inmates of correctional institutions in the United States indicated that an "immediate" family member had been confined in a jail or prison: 24 percent said their father had been confined; 9 percent said their mother had been confined; and 25 percent said a brother or sister had been put in jail or prison (Bureau of Justice Statistics 1992:7).

Biological inheritance is one explanation for this correlation between parent or familial criminality and delinquency; the learning of behavioral and attitudinal patterns is another explanation. Although there is little evidence to support the notion that criminal parents openly teach their children how to commit crimes, in the manner of differential association theory (Gottfredson and Hirschi 1990:101), the process of observing and learning can be more subtle than direct and conscious teaching. To some extent, the learning of criminal patterns of thought and behavior occurs vicariously, as children hear and see their parents committing criminal behavior or espousing sentiments favorable to criminal behavior (Simons et al. 2004:54–57). More likely, however, is the impact of bad parenting provided by criminal parents. That is, they may want their children to become conformist, productive citizens, but their lifestyles and attitudes, especially regarding child rearing, make those outcomes unlikely to occur. Hirschi (1969:94–97) and Gottfredson and Hirschi (1990:101), for example, suggest that criminal parents may have different values and ideas concerning goals in society than do conventional parents, and these values are transmitted to their children. They may not appreciate the wrongfulness of their child's acts if they themselves do not see the acts as wrong. Thus, they tacitly suggest to their children that stealing, skipping school, or other wrongful acts are not really bad (see also Wright and Wright 1995:23–24).

Also, criminal parents may lack self-control, as suggested by the general theory of crime, and may exhibit poor parenting skills, such as screaming, slapping, backing down and failing to follow through with threats or rule enforcements, and similar examples of parenting that are thought to lead to defiant, rebellious, and delinquent behaviors (Gottfredson and Hirschi

1990:101–102), as discussed earlier. Some evidence suggests, for example, that when the effects of parenting skills are controlled, the impact of criminal parents on delinquency is significantly reduced, although not all research reports this conclusion (Simons et al. 2004:55).

Another reason why children of criminal parents may themselves become involved in crime and delinquency is that institutionalized parents may be less visible and less able to supervise and otherwise effect direct controls on their children. Imprisoned parents may also be less likely to develop strong bonds with their children because of their absence from the home, and these lessened bonds may also significantly contribute to delinquency (Hirschi 1969).

Corporal Punishment and Delinquency

We often hear the question, "Is physical or corporal punishment an effective means of controlling deviant and/or oppositional behavior in children?" The debate usually focuses on the positive effects of physical punishment ("spare the rod and spoil the child") versus the presumed negative consequences of such punishment, including greater risks of a child committing violent crimes or criminal acts in general. However, the question for many parents and caregivers, temporary or permanent, is not as clear-cut as these two perspectives would suggest. While nearly 90 percent of American parents indicate they have spanked their children by the age of 5 (Simons et al. 2004:60) and spanking seems to be as common among wealthy families as poor families (Straus 1994:62; Straus and Stewart 1999), child abuse laws exist in every state, and there is no reason to believe any responsible adult in American society seriously advocates severe abuse as an effective method of discipline for misbehaving children.

Some advocate not physically touching a child in an angry manner at all. The argument here is that spanking a child, or using any physical punishment in general, teaches the child that the way to handle stressful or frustrating situations is through violence (Straus 1994). This approach has been adopted by several countries, particularly Sweden, but also Austria, Cyprus, Denmark, Finland, Germany, Italy, and Norway, all of which outlaw corporal punishment as a form of discipline (Straus 1994:179–181; Simons et al. 2004:60). Murray Straus and his colleagues (Straus 1994:esp. chapter 7; Straus 1999; Straus and Stewart 1999) present persuasive evidence that physical punishment of a child *may* lead to long-term negative consequences, including violent and delinquent behavior, even if the short-term consequences can control unwanted behavior in children (see also Hines and Malley-Morrison 2005:101–102).

Others argue that mild spanking, such as hitting on the hands or buttocks with an open hand, as opposed to the use of hitting with fists or with an object, not only fails to lead to future crime or acts of violence but also can often lead to a quick reduction of the unwanted behavior (Simons et al. 2004:66–67). One key factor here is the extent to which corporal punishment is accompanied by warm, loving parenting, a factor that is also important in cross-cultural research (Simons et al. 2000).

It would seem that an important variable in this matter is the degree to which physical discipline is incorporated into a more inclusive pattern of supervising and controlling a child in a family. If love, concern, and true parental care are behind patterns of discipline, with the exception of abuse or physical injuries (where loving purposes behind punishment are less likely to occur), then it is more likely the effect on the child's behavior will be corrective and less likely to lead to serious emotional problems for the child or long-standing breaks in relationships between parents and children.

Child Abuse and Delinquency

While spanking and other forms of corporal punishment may have short-term corrective effects on children, child *abuse* is not considered to have corrective benefits in the short or long term. In general, child abuse is a willful or intentional infliction of severe pain and/or suffering on a child, whether intended as corrective punishment or for some other reason. There are several types of abuse: *physical abuse*, which often results in bruises, burns, or broken bones; *neglect*, both *physical*, such as lack of medical or nutritional attention or care, and *emotional*, such as name calling or rejection; and *sexual* abuse or exploitation, including sexual assaults by strangers, caregivers, or relatives, that is, incest (Kempe and Kempe 1978:6–7; Simons et al. 2004:chapter 9). Emotional abuse, which is sometimes referred to as *psychological maltreatment*, may be difficult to see in terms of physical scars, but it can have lasting impacts on children, in part because it can create significant self-image problems for children and adolescents. When parents or caregivers call children names, isolate them from caring human interactions, exploit them, or terrorize them, the damages may be more harmful than if the child had been hit (Turgi and Hart 1988; Kempe and Kempe 1978:chapter 3; Wright and Wright 1995:18; Barnett et al. 2005:chapter 6).

Child abuse has been around as long as there have been caregivers to children but was largely ignored until the late 17th century and left undiagnosed until the late 19th century (Kempe and Kempe 1978:4; Holland 1988; Barnett et al. 2005:7–9). In 1641, Massachusetts passed the Body of Liberties laws, which included a provision prohibiting parental abuse, or "any unnatural severitie," of children, although this law was rarely enforced (Barnett et al. 2005:7). In 1860, a French medical professor, Ambroise Tardieu, first described what later became known as the "battered-child syndrome." Tardieu's work discussed the details of 32 children who had been beaten to death. In 1870, records in London revealed that of the deaths of 3,926 children under the age of five, 202 were murdered, 95 died of neglect, and 18 died of exposure, yet most accounts of child deaths at that time attributed the deaths and injuries to rickets (Kempe and Kempe 1978:5).

In the 1870s, the Society for the Prevention of Cruelty to Children (SPCC) was established in New York City through the efforts of its founder, Elbridge T. Gerry. The SPCC was founded and became popular throughout the country at that time partly in response to the plight of abused children, such as Mary Ellen Wilson, a case with which Mr. Gerry was involved. Interestingly, at the time of the Mary Ellen Wilson case, there were no laws against child abuse per se, so the case was developed on the basis of animal cruelty, on the grounds that Mary Ellen was part of the animal kingdom. In 1866, the first chapter of the American Society for the Prevention of Cruelty to Animals (ASPCA) was developed, so the appeal to that organization's support in the case of Mary Ellen seemed logical at that time (Kempe and Kempe 1978:5; Holland 1988; Grossberg 2002:25).

In the early 19th century, attention to the needs of youth began to materialize in the construction of special facilities for youth development, such as the House of Refuge in New York City in 1825 (see chapter 2; Kempe and Kempe 1978:4–5). However, true concern for the welfare of children was not consistently followed. Many still believed that the best way to discipline children was to punish them physically, and parental rights in these matters were considered paramount. The use of x-rays in the 1940s and 1950s helped include the medical field in the detection of child abuse and gave another perspective on its physical impact on youth, since x-rays might indicate physical damage not visible on the surface (Kempe and Kempe 1978:4–5).

In the mid 1960s, C. Henry Kempe introduced the concept of *battered-child syndrome* to the American Academy of Pediatrics and launched decades of legal, medical, and social interest in the identification, prevention, and treatment of child abuse (Kempe and Kempe 1978:5–6; Nevin and Roberts 1988:391–405; Dohrn 2002:288–290). Soon after the concept of battered-child syndrome was introduced, legislation and social service action began to develop statistical reporting databases and intervention programs designed to protect children and prevent parental discipline from developing into cases of abuse. Initial progress in this area was relatively slow. For example, officials in California reported only 4,000 cases of abuse in 1968, while in Florida and Michigan, the totals were 10 and 271, respectively. However, by 1972, the number of reported cases of abuse rose to 40,000 in California, 30,000 in Florida, and 30,000 in Michigan (Kempe and Kempe 1978:8). In terms of rates per 1,000 children, the national reported rates of child abuse and neglect increased steadily from 10.1 in 1976 to 27.3 in 1984 (Tzeng and Hanner 1988:55–56).

However, by the 1990s, the reported rates of child abuse and neglect began to decline. Based on information reported by child protective agencies in the United States, in 2003 there were an estimated 906,600 cases of child abuse and neglect and 1,500 deaths as a result of abuse and neglect in the United States. The rate of victimization was 12.4 per 1,000 children, which represented a decline from 1990, when the rate was 13.4 per 1,000 children. In addition, in 2003, most of the cases involved neglect (60 percent), while just fewer than 20 percent involved physical abuse, 10 percent sexual abuse, and 5 percent emotional maltreatment. Very young children represented the largest numbers of abuse cases. Those under age three had a victimization rate of 16.4 per 1,000 children of that age, and girls were more often victimized than boys. Also, most abusers, around 80 percent, were parents (U.S. Department of Health and Human Services, Administration on Children, Youth and Families, 2005:xiv–xviii.).

In 2005, the national rate of child victimization continued to decline, to 12.1 per 1,000. Young children were again the most victimized age group. The rate for children ages 1–3 was 16.5 per 1,000, and the rates declined for each age group from 4 through 17. In addition, most reported cases of child abuse involved neglect (62.8 percent), followed by physical abuse (16.6 percent), sexual abuse (9.3 percent), psychological maltreatment (7.3 percent), and medical neglect (2.0 percent), with 2.0 percent classified as "other." Slightly more of the victims were girls than boys, but the difference was not great (50.7 percent for girls versus 47.3 percent for boys). Most of the child victims in 2005 were abused by a parent or a parent acting with another (83.4 percent), and most often the abusing parent was the mother acting alone (U.S. Department of Health and Human Services 2007).

The figures on child abuse are estimates, based largely on reports to and from child protective agencies. Perhaps the decline in reported instances and rates of child abuse and neglect reflect increased support and treatment for distressed families in ways that reduced child abuse. This situation seems likely in view of the current laws, which mandate that suspected cases of abuse noticed by professionals who come into regular contact with children, such as teachers and physicians, be reported to child protective agencies (Barnett et al. 2005:179–182).

Gains in recognizing and reporting cases of child abuse and in methods of helping stressed families and preventing child abuse, however, should not eclipse the effects of abuse on children, both short- and long-term. Some, such as Murray Straus (1994), observe that physical punishment, and presumably abuse in general, can have long-lasting effects on children as well as society. There are, for example, *individual* effects of punishment and abuse on a child, such as an increased risk of that child's becoming more aggressive with others in his or her social setting. Probably the most extreme violent consequence of physical, sexual, or emotional abuse is when the abused child strikes back at and kills an abusive parent, or *parricide*. According to some estimates, there are between 200 and 400 homicides each year involving children who kill a parent or caregiver, although most of these cases involve abused children who have already become adults by the time the murder occurs (Heide et al. 2005:219).

Then there are *intergenerational* effects, in that abused or beaten children are at greater risk of hitting or abusing their own children or spouses (Hines and Malley-Morrison 2005:100). Intergenerational effects can also include the impact of child abuse on other members of the family, including the abusing parent (Barnett et al. 2005:209–213). In addition, there are *macro-level* effects on society because tolerance of physical punishment and abuse leads to increased use of violence to settle disputes and frustrations and less public recognition of abuse (Straus 1994:96). However, it should be remembered that there have been *fewer* cases of abuse and neglect reported in America since the 1990s, a fact that may contradict macro-level effects of abuse.

The long-term consequences of abuse often connect with behavior, violent or otherwise, that becomes delinquent or criminal (Hines and Malley-Morrison 2005:100–101, 152–153). One longitudinal study, for example, studied a group of 908 reported abused and neglected children and youth, preschool and school-age, and a matched sample of 667 control youth who had not been abused. Local, state, and federal criminal arrest records were examined for both groups for several years, into their adulthood. Results of this study indicated that abused youth had significantly higher arrest records as adults than did the matched control group; this pattern held for males and females, whites and nonwhites. In addition, the study found that abused males were significantly more likely to be arrested for crimes of violence, compared with nonabused males, but this pattern was not found for abused females (Widom 1989).

In addition, longitudinal analyses of crime and delinquency data on a sample of over 4,000 youth in Rochester, New York, the Rochester Youth Development Study, clearly indicate significant associations between child abuse/maltreatment and later delinquent and criminal activity, both self-reported and official (Smith and Thornberry 1995), but the relationships are *stronger* for youth who were *abused as adolescents* or *continually* from childhood into adolescence, compared with younger children (Ireland et al. 2002). One possible reason for this differential criminal effect of abuse on crime and delinquency by age of the abused is that older children are not as likely to accept the abuse as their fault, but rather as the consequence of uncaring or negligent parents or adults in their lives. However, in ways similar to those predicted by general strain theory (see chapter 6), these older youth may not see an immediate outlet for their sufferings other than to fight back or rebel, which can easily lead to delinquent behavior or behavior that may be interpreted as defiant or rebellious. In addition, children reared in families where abuse seems continual, if not constant, are more likely to experience poverty and mental illness in the family. Also, their involvement in delinquency may mask their abuse, since they may be seen not as victimized children, but rather as more responsible for their behavior (Ireland et al. 2002).

Despite the clear connections between abuse and later acts of crime and delinquency, there are good indications that intervention and prevention efforts can reduce this connection (Kempe and Kempe 1978:chapter 10; Kendrick 1988; Tyler and Gully 1988; Bethea 1999; Simons et al. 2004:chapter 9). While most abusive situations seem to emanate from improper parenting skills and abusive backgrounds among parents or caregivers, bad behavior patterns *can* be changed. Sometimes these patterns of abuse can be altered by getting into a loving, caring adult relationship, as suggested by the life-course perspective discussed in chapter 5 (see also Simons et al. 2004:chapter 9).

In addition, enhanced efforts by community organizations, governmental and private, can lead to greater recognition of abuse and earlier intervention, but it can also lead to increased efforts to deal constructively with the abused child so that violent or criminal consequences are less likely to occur. Zingraff and colleagues (1994), for example, indicate that positive school involvement (such as maintaining good grades and displaying regular school attendance) can mediate the crime and delinquency consequences of child abuse. That is, having a good experience in school can help offset the potentially damaging effects of abuse in the family, similar to the predictions of social bond theory (see chapter 6). These preventive and treatment strategies suggest not only that child abuse can be prevented but also that its negative effects can be lessened if it occurs.

Summary

The family plays a crucial role either in promoting, reducing, or contextualizing delinquency. There is some evidence that a broken home contributes to delinquency, but the relationship is neither strong nor consistent across all measures of delinquency. A more important family connection with delinquency is the nature of the relationships in a family between parent and child as well as among all members of the family. Uncaring parents, inconsistent, overly strict, or lax discipline and supervision, and lack of family harmony in general are good predictors of delinquency. In addition, in an indirect sense, where a family lives may have a crime-reducing or a crime-enhancing effect on children. Children living in neighborhoods characterized by high rates of crime and delinquency may be more at risk of becoming involved in delinquency than youth living in low-crime areas. The impact of neighborhood conditions on crime and delinquency, especially gang activity, is discussed in chapter 10, particularly in reference to social disorganization theory.

However, no one particular family variable may, by itself, provide a significant contribution to delinquency. Marital discord, for example, may predict delinquency, but surely not all families characterized by conflict and discord will produce delinquency among the children living in such families. Even child abuse will not automatically result in delinquency for the children in a family, including the abused child.

It is wiser to consider the impact of family factors as having a cumulative impact on delinquency. As Wright and Wright (1995) state: "The presence of any one of the family circumstances factors increases the chances of raising a delinquent child. The addition of more than one factor further enhances the odds of misbehavior" (p. 30). Thus, having cumulative family disadvantages, personal and/or environmental, can increase a child's risk of becoming involved in delinquency.

While family factors can exert a powerful effect on behavior, studies suggest the influence of the family on the attitudes and behavior of children begins to give way to the peer group as a child grows into adolescence (Wright and Wright 1995:19), although the influence of parents in adolescent decision making is still present, especially when it comes to seeking advice for long-term planning (Warr 2002:29). The influence of peers on delinquency can be very powerful, as was discussed in chapter 6. However, it is also possible that the strength of the family bond, along with a family system that consists of good child-rearing practices, can help offset the influence of peers and may help to shape the peers one chooses as an adolescent (Wright and Wright 1995:24–32; Warr 2002:28–29).

In addition, although the influence of the family in its various dimensions on delinquency is important, other institutional contexts also can have an influence on delinquency. The impact of religious factors on delinquency, for example, has already been discussed. In the next chapter, the connection between delinquency and another important institutional context, the school, will be examined.

References

Barnett, Ola, Cindy L. Miller-Perrin, and Robin D. Perrin
  2005 Family Violence Across the Lifespan: An Introduction. 2nd edition. Thousand Oaks, CA: Sage.
Bethea, Lesa
  1999 Primary Prevention of Child Abuse. American Family Physician, March 15:1–11.
Bureau of Justice Statistics
  1992 National Update. Vol. 1, No. 4. Washington, DC: Office of Justice Programs.
Cernkovich, Steven A., and Peggy C. Giordano
  1987 Family Relationships and Delinquency. Criminology 25:295–319.
Dohrn, Bernardine
  2002 The School, the Child, and the Court. In A Century of Juvenile Justice. Margaret K. Rosenheim, Franklin E. Zimring, David S. Tanenhaus, and Bernardine Dohrn, eds. Pp. 267–309. Chicago: University of Chicago Press.

Ferdinand, Theodore N.
    1989   Juvenile Delinquency or Juvenile Justice: Which Came First? Crim-
            inology 27:79–106.
Free, Marvin D., Jr.
    1991   Clarifying the Relationship between the Broken Home and Juvenile
            Delinquency: A Critique of the Current Literature. Deviant Behav-
            ior 12:109–167.
Glueck, Sheldon, and Eleanor Glueck
    1950   Unraveling Juvenile Delinquency. Cambridge, MA: Harvard Uni-
            versity Press.
Gottfredson, Michael, and Travis Hirschi
    1990   A General Theory of Crime. Stanford, CA: Stanford University
            Press.
Grossberg, Michael
    2002   Changing Conceptions of Child Welfare in the United States,
            1820–1935. *In* A Century of Juvenile Justice. Margaret K. Rosen-
            heim, Franklin E. Zimring, David S. Tanenhaus, and Bernardine
            Dohrn, eds. Pp. 3–41. Chicago: University of Chicago Press.
Hartjen, Clayton A., and Sesha Kethineni
    1996   Comparative Delinquency: India and the United States. New York:
            Garland.
Heide, Kathleen M., Denise Paquette Boots, Craig Alldredge, Brian Donerly, and
Jennifer Rebecca White
    2005   Battered Child Syndrome: An Overview of Case Law and Legisla-
            tion. Criminal Law Bulletin 41:219–239.
Hines, Denise A., and Kathleen Malley-Morrison
    2005   Family Violence in the United States: Defining, Understanding, and
            Combating Abuse. Thousand Oaks, CA: Sage.
Hirschi, Travis
    1969   Causes of Delinquency. Berkeley: University of California Press.
Holland, Ruth E.
    1988   Children in Peril: Historical Background. *In* Sourcebook for Child
            Abuse and Neglect: Intervention, Treatment, and Prevention
            Through Crisis Programs. Oliver C. S. Tzeng and Jamia Jasper
            Jacobsen, eds. Pp. 39–52. Springfield, IL: Charles C. Thomas.
Ireland, Timothy O., Carolyn Smith, and Terence P. Thornberry
    2002   Developmental Issues in the Impact of Child Maltreatment on Later
            Delinquency and Drug Use. Criminology 40:359–399.

Kempe, Ruth S., and C. Henry Kempe
   1978   Child Abuse. Cambridge, MA: Harvard University Press.
Kendrick, Judy Manning
   1988   Individual, Group and Family Treatment. *In* Sourcebook for
           Child Abuse and Neglect: Intervention, Treatment, and Preven-
           tion Through Crisis Programs. Oliver C. S. Tzeng and Jamia
           Jasper Jacobsen, eds. Pp. 261–285. Springfield, IL: Charles C.
           Thomas.
Kids Count
   2004   2004 Kids Count Data Book: State Profiles of Child Well-Being. Bal-
           timore: Annie E. Casey Foundation.
   2007   2007 Kids Count Data Book: State Profiles of Child Well-Being. Bal-
           timore: Annie E. Casey Foundation.
Kling, Jeffrey R., Jens Ludwig, and Lawrence F. Katz
   2005   Neighborhood Effects on Crime for Female and Male Youth: Evi-
           dence from a Randomized Housing Voucher Experiment. The
           Quarterly Journal of Economics 120:87–130.
McClanahan, Sara, and Karen Booth
   1989   Mother-Only Families: Problems, Prospects, and Politics. Journal of
           Marriage and Family 51:557–580.
Morash, Merry, and Lila Rucker
   1989   An Exploratory Study of the Connection of Mother's Age at Child-
           birth to Her Children's Delinquency in Four Data Sets. Crime &
           Delinquency 35:45–93.
Nevin, Robert S., and Albert R. Roberts
   1988   Establishing Cooperation with Community Agencies to Foster the
           Legal Rights of Children. *In* Sourcebook for Child Abuse and
           Neglect: Intervention, Treatment, and Prevention Through Crisis
           Programs. Oliver C. S. Tzeng and Jamia Jasper Jacobsen, eds. Pp.
           379–409. Springfield, IL: Charles C. Thomas.
Nye, F. Ivan
   1958   Family Relationships and Delinquent Behavior. New York: Wiley.
Patterson, Gerald R., J. B. Reid, and Thomas J. Dishion
   1992   Antisocial Boys: A Social Interactional Approach. Eugene, OR:
           Castalia.
Rebellion, Cesar J.
   2002   Reconsidering the Broken Homes/Delinquency Relationship and
           Exploring Its Mediating Mechanisms. Criminology 40:103–135.

Sampson, Robert J.

    1987   Urban Black Violence: The Effect of Male Joblessness and Family Disruption. American Journal of Sociology 93:348–382.

    1992   Family Management and Child Development: Insights from Social Disorganization Theory. *In* Facts, Frameworks, and Forecasts. Joan McCord, ed. Pp. 63–93. New Brunswick, NJ: Transaction.

Shaw, Clifford R., and Henry D. McKay

    1932   Are Broken Homes a Causative Factor in Juvenile Delinquency? Social Forces 10:514–524.

    1942   Juvenile Delinquency and Urban Areas. Chicago: University of Chicago Press.

Shoemaker, Donald J.

    1992   Delinquency in the Philippines: A Description. Philippine Sociological Review 40:83–103.

    2005   Theories of Delinquency: An Examination of Explanations of Delinquent Behavior. 5th edition. New York: Oxford University Press.

Simons, Ronald L., Leslie Gordon Simons, and Lora Ebert Wallace

    2004   Families, Delinquency, and Crime: Linking Society's Most Basic Institution to Antisocial Behavior. Los Angeles: Roxbury.

Simons, Ronald L., Chyi-In Wu, Kuei-Hsiu Lin, Leslie Gordon, and Rand D. Conger

    2000   A Cross-Cultural Examination of the Link Between Corporal Punishment and Adolescent Antisocial Behavior. Criminology 38:47–79.

Smith, Carolyn, and Terence P. Thornberry

    1995   The Relationship Between Childhood Maltreatment and Adolescent Involvement in Delinquency. Criminology 33:451–481.

Straus, Murray A., with Denise A. Donnelly

    1994   Beating the Devil Out of Them: Corporal Punishment in American Families. San Francisco: Jossey-Bass.

    1999   The Benefits of Avoiding Corporal Punishment: New and More Beneficial Evidence. Unpublished manuscript.

Straus, Murray A., and Julie H. Stewart

    1999   Corporal Punishment by American Parents: National Data on Prevalence, Chronicity, Severity, and Duration, in Relation to Child and Family Characteristics. Clinical Child and Family Psychology Review 2:55–70.

Turgi, Paul A., and Stuart N. Hart

    1988   Psychological Maltreatment: Meaning and Prevention. *In* Sourcebook for Child Abuse and Neglect: Intervention, Treatment, and

Prevention Through Crisis Programs. Oliver C. S. Tzeng and Jamia Jasper Jacobsen, eds. Pp. 287–317. Springfield, IL: Charles C. Thomas.

Tyler, Ann H., and Kevin J. Gully
  1988   Intervention and Treatment of Child Sexual Abuse. *In* Sourcebook for Child Abuse and Neglect: Intervention, Treatment, and Prevention Through Crisis Programs. Oliver C. S. Tzeng and Jamia Jasper Jacobsen, eds. Pp. 345–377. Springfield, IL: Charles C. Thomas.

Tzeng, Oliver C. S., and Linda J. Hanner
  1988   Abuse and Neglect: Typologies, Phenomena and Impacts. *In* Sourcebook for Child Abuse and Neglect: Intervention, Treatment, and Prevention Through Crisis Programs. Oliver C. S. Tzeng and Jamia Jasper Jacobsen, eds. Pp. 53–77. Springfield, IL: Charles C. Thomas.

U.S. Department of Health and Human Services, Administration on Children, Youth and Families
  2005   Child Maltreatment 2003. Washington, DC: U.S. Government Printing Office.

U.S. Department of Health and Human Services
  2007   Child Welfare Information Gateway. Electronic document, www.childwelfare.gov, accessed October 31, 2007.

Wallerstein, Judith, Julia Lewis, and Sandra Blakeslee
  2000   The Unexpected Legacy of Divorce: A 25-Year Landmark Study. New York: Hyperion.

Warr, Mark
  2002   Companions in Crime: The Social Aspects of Criminal Conduct. Cambridge, England: Cambridge University Press.

Weitoft, Gunilla, Anders Hjern, Bengt Haglund, and Mans Rosen
  2003   Mortality, Severe Morbidity, and Injury in Children Living with Single Parents in Sweden: A Population-Based Study. Lancet 361: 289–295.

Wells, L. Edward, and Joseph H. Rankin
  1991   Families and Delinquency: A Meta-Analysis. Social Problems 38:71–93.

Widom, Cathy Spatz
  1989   Child Abuse, Neglect, and Violent Criminal Behavior. Criminology 27:251–271.

Wilkinson, Karen
  1974   The Broken Home and Juvenile Delinquency: Scientific Explanation or Ideology? Social Problems 21:726–739.

Wright, John Paul, and Francis T. Cullen
    2001   Parental Efficacy and Delinquent Behavior: Do Control and Support Matter? Criminology 39:677–705.
Wright, Kevin N., and Karen E. Wright
    1995   Family Life, Delinquency, and Crime: A Policymaker's Guide. Washington, DC: Office of Juvenile Justice and Delinquency Prevention.
Zingraff, Matthew T., Jeffrey Leiter, Matthew C. Johnson, and Kristen A. Myers
    1994   The Mediating Effect of Good School Performance on the Maltreatment-Delinquency Relationship. Journal of Research in Crime and Delinquency 31:62–91.

SCHOOLS AND DELINQUENCY

W HILE THE family and numerous individual factors clearly have an impact on delinquency, as has been discussed in this book, the school setting provides one of the more common locations for delinquency, both in terms of victimization and the commission of delinquent acts. This situation is understandable from a couple of perspectives. For one, the influence of peers is more pronounced during adolescence than at other points in one's life, as has already been addressed. Second, with some exceptions, such as poor health, school attendance is compulsory for all youth under the age of 16 in all 50 states. While some parents may opt for homeschooling for their children, most youth attend school in congregate settings, either in public or private schools. This kind of commingling provides a fertile source for youth interactions and the formation of peer groups, which can be important in their lives both in and out of school.

The impact of the school on delinquency will be addressed in this chapter by addressing several topics: (1) school-based factors that influence delinquency; (2) the setting of the school for crime victimization; and (3) legal issues concerning the school and delinquency.

The School as a Source of Motivation for Delinquency

An important feature of the school, even in elementary years, is the aspect of evaluation, judgment, and eventual success or failure of virtually all students.

School systems are designed to evaluate, compare, and, eventually, judge student performances. Amid all of this evaluating, sorting, and judging occurs a modification of one's self-concept, which has likely already begun to form before a child enters school. Sometimes the development of a positive self-concept is a conscious goal of school-based efforts, such as the delinquency prevention project developed by Walter Reckless and associates several years ago in Columbus, Ohio (see chapter 6). At other times the effects of school on self-concept are less calculated, but the impact can be just as real for the child.

Whether school experiences have an effect on a child's self-concept, the school setting certainly has an impact on a child's activities and peer associates. The importance of peer associations to delinquency was discussed earlier, in chapter 6, in the discussion of differential association theory. One of the more important settings for the development and influence of peer groups is the school. From the first years of elementary school through high school, students are placed in classes with others of their same age and given common instructions, lessons, and experiences with these others. Over time, these classmates become a significant source of peers for students. Sometimes, these associations develop into gang affiliations, and the presence of gangs is a continuing problem for schools (see chapter 10).

Negative experiences at school can also lead to significant disaffections with school and even peers at school, which, in turn, can lead to delinquency, such as has been suggested in general strain theory (Agnew 1985, 1992), discussed in chapter 6. Sometimes these negative experiences and feelings of frustration can lead to school shootings or bullying at school (see the discussions of these topics below).

The effect of school experiences on self-concepts, peer associations, and behavior in general are also thought to have an impact on patterns of delinquency. Studies by social scientists have consistently indicated a significant relationship between *academic performance* and delinquency. Those who have low academic achievement tend to be more involved in delinquency (Berrueta-Clement et al. 1987:224–227; Shoemaker 2005:117; Felson and Staff 2006:299; Lawrence 2007:136–137). Travis Hirschi (1969:chapter 6) contends that low academic achievement is a source of frustration for students and a reason for lack of student motivation, which, in turn, can lead to greater involvement in delinquency. Others, such as Albert Cohen (1955), suggest that low academic achievement can lead to a rejection of the school as an institution as well as a rejection of the values for which the school stands (primarily middle-class values connected with the importance of academic achievement: developing written skills, being prompt for meetings, and so on), especially for youth from *lower-class* backgrounds. Cohen further argues that low-achieving youths are primary targets for gang recruitment and involvement (see chapter 10).

The association between social class and school failure, or even educational opportunities, continues to be documented (Lawrence 2007:63, 128–131). Some suggest that lower-class status presents difficulties and challenges in life that may negate the positive benefits of educational effort. That is, despite trying to do well in school, lower-class youth may still find themselves disadvantaged in the marketplace (Hannon 2003:578–579; MacLeod 1987). From a developmental or life-course perspective (see chapter 5), educational attainment among lower-class youth may not accumulate social capital in the same way as it often does for middle-class juveniles. Others contend that the lack of academic success in schools is associated with delinquency *regardless* of social class background (Polk 1969) or that school failure, rebellion, and delinquency may be more common among youth from *middle-class* homes (Stinchcombe 1964).

The views of both Cohen and Hirschi are consistent with social bond theory and connected with general strain theory (chapter 6). The weaker the bond or connection a child has with the school system, the more likely that child will become involved with delinquency. Within the context of social bond theory, the link between academic problems and delinquency is connected with *attachment*, or the emotional connection between a young person and meaningful people in his or her environment, such as a teacher or a parent. In the case of schools, social bond theory would predict that the less one is attached to the school through teachers or peers, the more likely one would be to engage in delinquency, and vice versa. In part, this prediction is supported by research suggesting that obtaining academic success in school can overcome the negative impact of child abuse, as was discussed in chapter 7 (see Zingraff et al. 1994). Hirschi also makes this point clear by arguing that good grades and positive attachment to the school setting can offset negative relationships between a child and others. As Hirschi (1969) put it, "A favorable attitude toward school protects the child from delinquency regardless of his concern for the opinion of teachers. In every comparison possible . . . the boys who do not like school are more likely to have committed delinquent acts" (p. 132). Using the terminology of social development theory (chapter 5), youth with a positive attitude toward school are more *resilient* and better able to overcome other potentially delinquency-producing factors in their lives. As has been stressed thus far, one important way to develop a positive attitude in school is to obtain and maintain good grades or successful academic achievement.

Some research suggests that the academic performance–delinquency link is real but may be spurious because both grades in school and delinquency are connected with low self-control or perhaps a neurophysiological deficiency (Felson and Staff 2006). This interpretation is consistent with the general theory of crime proposed by Gottfredson and Hirschi (see chapter 5) and/or with individual traits (see chapter 4). In this scenario, academic performance is negatively affected by individual traits that limit attention and behavioral regulation, which, in turn, contribute to both low academic performance and delinquency.

Of course, the connection between academic problems and delinquency is not perfect. Many kids who are having a hard time academically in school manage to avoid delinquency, or at least its more serious forms. Likewise, youth who do well in school are not immune from delinquency, as William Chambliss's study of the Saints and the Roughnecks illustrates (Chambliss 1973, discussed in chapter 12). In addition, it is recognized that other problems related to the school setting can lead to delinquency, many of which have already been discussed. Academic success, however, seems to help overcome, although certainly not to eliminate, these other problems.

The connection between academic failure and delinquency is not always direct or simple, but it is linked through a number of factors, many of which have already been discussed. In part, the association between academic problems and delinquency represents an example of the importance of integrating, or at least combining, different theoretical perspectives to develop a more useful explanation of delinquency. The flowchart in figure 8.1 may help illustrate this point. This figure presents several connections between low academic performance and delinquency. It depicts poor academics as preceding, or leading to, delinquency. Certainly there are situations in which delinquency may lead to low academic performance, such as a good student taking drugs and letting school matters slide. However, the evidence suggests that the more likely scenario is that low academic performance contributes to delinquency, not vice versa.

The first point in the flowchart suggests that there are many conditions or situations that can contribute to low academic achievement, including personal and social factors. Social class is included here, partly on the basis of Cohen's arguments and those of others, although, as indicated earlier, the evidence pointing to a strong social class connection with low academic performance is inconsistent. The major point in the figure is the second one, that

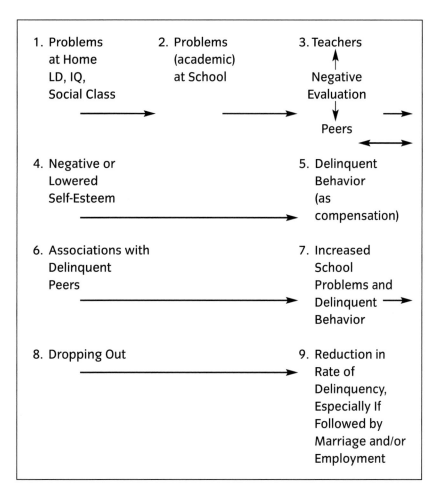

FIGURE 8.1 Academic Performance and Delinquency: An Overview

is, low academic performance. The scenario predicts negative reactions from peers and teachers alike to the school problems facing the child. This prediction is based on labeling theory, support for which, again, is inconsistent (see chapter 12). Negative reactions to school problems can contribute to a low self-concept. Low self-concept, in turn, leads to delinquency as compensation. That is, delinquency can at least temporarily alleviate the frustrations and self-concept problems engendered by low academic performance.

One way in which negative reactions to academic performance may lead to low self-esteem is through *tracking*. Tracking is the intentional placement of students in curricula designed to achieve certain goals, such as college-bound or technology-related tracks. Tracking is supposed to be based on test results, with more academically proficient students often being placed in college-bound tracks. Typically, the sorting and placing begin during middle-school grades. While the system of tracking may facilitate instructional goals, one concern of this procedure is that students placed in noncollege tracks will be labeled as less intelligent, less popular, and so on. These labels may in turn promote rebellious attitudes toward school and those placed in college-bound curricula. All of this may lead to delinquency. While this scenario is certainly plausible, longitudinal research on the consequences of tracking for student self-esteem and delinquent behavior does not support the prediction that tracking lowers self-esteem and increases delinquency, especially for high-school students (Wiatrowski et al. 1982). Perhaps the negative effects of tracking are more salient for middle-school students, or maybe these effects have been neutralized by the time students reach high school. It may also be the case that tracking helps students to bond to the school, no matter which track they are in, and this bonding inhibits delinquency. Perhaps being placed in technology or vocational tracks is not as psychologically damaging as some would think. Not everyone aspires to a college education, and some students may do well in a noncollege-track curriculum, especially if a school becomes associated with business opportunities in the community. Schools that are able to provide meaningful classes and impart important life-skills training into their curricula, even if these do not relate to college education, may be able to create stronger ties with their students and reduce the risk of truancy and/or disruption and crime in the school (Lawrence 2007:288–289). Thus, while negative labels assigned to academic performance are potentially damaging to one's self-esteem and can lead to delinquency, the system of tracking does not automatically promote this process.

Delinquency may also lead to seeking delinquent companions, although, as discussed in chapter 6, delinquent companions may contribute to delinquency, thus the double arrow between the two on the flowchart. However, delinquency and association with delinquent companions do not solve school problems over time and may contribute to more school problems, which lead to more delinquency, and so on. Ultimately, one solution to this situation is for the child to drop out of school. In some cases, especially if dropout is followed by employment or marriage, delinquency rates may fall. Using concepts from developmental theory, employment and marriage increase one's social capital, which, in turn, helps to reduce involvement in delinquency. However, remember that even though one may temporarily relieve stress and frustration in his or her life by dropping out of school and build up self-confidence and self-esteem by getting a job and marrying, the long-term results of dropping out may lead to additional problems later in life, such as layoffs from work or unemployment, marital problems, and possibly a return to crime.

School Dropout and Delinquency

Dropping out of school is not a common outcome for most students. In 2005, the percent of youth ages 16–19 who were high-school dropouts was 7. This figure dropped from 11 percent in 2000 (Kids Count 2007:168). However, geographically and socially, these numbers fluctuate widely. Dropout percentages can reach up to 50 percent in large schools in urban areas, and minorities in these schools have the highest dropout rates of all youth. Low-income youth are also at higher risks of dropping out. Ethnicity also plays a role in the decision to remain in school. Hispanic students, for example, have a school dropout rate several times greater than the rate for whites (Kids Count 2004:12–13). In 2005, for example, the percentage of white youth ages 16–19 who were considered dropouts was 6, compared with 14 percent for Hispanic youth (Kids Count 2007:46; see also Lawrence 2007:100–103).

The effects of dropping out of school can be financially difficult for those students as well as for their relatives. Dropouts on average are more often unemployed and earn less than high-school graduates (Lawrence 2007:103–104). According to Kids Count, a national report on the welfare of America's children, between 1997 and 2001, approximately one-fourth of high-school dropouts were unemployed for at least one full year, while only 11 percent of graduates were unemployed for at least one year during that same time period (Kids Count 2004:12). In addition, high-school graduates can expect to earn hundreds of thousands of dollars more than dropouts over the course of a work life (Kids Count 2004:12). Consequently, the impact of dropping out of high school, regardless of its total numbers, is important to consider, including its connection with delinquency.

The relationship between school dropout and delinquency described in figure 8.1 suggests that dropping out reduces delinquency. Actually, some studies indicate that school dropouts have a higher rate of involvement in delinquency than do graduates (Elliott and Voss 1974; Thornberry et al. 1985). However, because eventual dropouts are so involved in delinquency while they are in school, their rates of delinquency are higher than those of graduates. In a longitudinal study of over 2,600 students in California enrolled in grades 9–12, Elliott and Voss (1974:chapters 4 and 5) found that rates of delinquency, as determined by both self-report surveys and police records, *peaked just before* students dropped out of school and then declined afterward, especially if those students obtained employment or got married soon after dropping out of school. This pattern held for students in all grades but was particularly evident for male dropouts. In addition, the researchers found that low academic performance was an important cause of dropping out, consistent with the scenario depicted in figure 8.1.

However, not all studies agree with the conclusions of Elliott and Voss. Thornberry et al. (1985) conducted a longitudinal analysis of 567 males in Philadelphia (from the Philadelphia Cohort I study, discussed in chapter 3). Their analyses led to the conclusion that dropping out of school was fol-lowed by an *increase* in delinquency, as measured by arrest data, and remained high until the former students were in their twenties. Furthermore, this pattern was found *regardless* of marriage and/or employment after drop-ping out. Since these two studies were not duplicative but had several points of difference, it is not possible to say with certainty exactly which is the truer pattern of dropping out and delinquency. However, it is clear that dropping out of school has a connection with delinquency. For now, it is possible to conclude that sometimes dropping out is followed by a reduction in delin-quency, while at other times it is followed by an increase in delinquency.

In some situations, the decision to drop out of school is not made for academic reasons. Some youth may drop out for economic or health rea-sons. Some may drop out because of pregnancy (Dorn 1996). Sometimes school dropouts commit higher rates of delinquency after leaving school, and sometimes they do not. Studies do not offer consistent results on this issue (Hartnagel and Krahn 1989; Jarjoura 1993, 1996; Kaplan and Liu 1994; Lawrence 2007:104–107). Note that what is important is not always the rea-son one decides to drop out of school, but the attending attitudes toward school and maintaining a living through conformist means that accompany that decision.

Regardless of what happens after dropping out of school, the results of studies on its relationship to delinquency suggest that problems with delin-quency often precede dropping out, although dropping out does not seem to solve the problems of youth who are having problems at school, at least in the long term (Hagan 1997; Lawrence 2007:104–107). As previously noted, it is important for youth to stay in school and complete degree requirements as much as possible. However, students who are having difficulties in school to the point of dropping out should not be forced to remain in school against their will. Even if they eventually straighten things out, their forced presence in an unwelcome (for them) situation could lead to the endangerment of themselves or fellow students and others. Alternative schools are available for those who are having difficulty in school as well as in life (Lawrence 2007:287–288). The impact of alternative schooling on delinquency, however, seems to be minimal. A meta-analysis of alternative schools and delinquency concluded, "The principal negative finding was that alternative schools have been unable to affect delinquent behavior. . . . Even though alternative schools promote positive school attitudes, their effect on school performance and self-esteem is not large enough to influence delinquent behavior" (Cox et al. 1995:229; see also Lawrence 2007:287).

Overall, it seems logical to assume that staying in school is a desired goal for most youth to maintain (Lawrence 2007:107). However, things can occur that upset that goal, and, in some cases, enrollment in school is not a good thing for a child. If remedial efforts and/or involvement in school-related organizations and activities do not result in improved school performance, then placement in alternative schooling may be desirable. In all of these situations, delinquency may or may not be enhanced. There are too many variables and too many possible scenarios to say with certainty that delinquency is an inevitable outcome of dropping out of school (Lawrence 2007:107). However, we do know that poor academic performance and negative attitudes toward school are strongly associated with delinquency, so at the least there should be continued effort to help each child maximize his or her learning efforts at school and to have a rewarding experience with school as much as possible.

School Safety

The subjects of bonding with school and staying in school are important topics to consider with respect to delinquency. However, the safety of students, faculty, staff, and others in the school setting is another topic that bears discussion. In addition, students who pose a threat or danger to school safety represent another example of delinquent behavior in the school setting. Several school shootings committed by students attracted the attention of the nation in the late 1990s. In 1997–1998 alone, there were five fatal school shootings, all in small towns or suburban areas throughout the United States. Together, these five shootings resulted in the deaths of 12 fellow students and two teachers (Garbarino 2001:5). Perhaps the most discussed example of these shootings was the killing of 12 students and a teacher by two students, Eric Harris and Dylan Klebold, at Columbine High School in Littleton, Colorado, on April 20, 1999. The massacre at Columbine was the deadliest school shooting incident and stands, rightly or wrongly, as a symbol for school violence in America. Both Harris and Klebold were thought to be holders of violent and angry emotions and victims of bullying and teasing. They both committed suicide at the site of the shootings, so their specific motives can be assessed only by information obtained from their writings, such as Web site postings and family and acquaintance statements (Garbarino 2001:5; Weintraub et al. 2001).

School shootings and other violent acts are not unique to the United States (Shaw 2001; Benbenishty and Astor 2005; Lawrence 2007:24–26). In addition, while all of the school shootings identified above occurred in small towns or suburban areas and involved white offenders, a study of 37 nationwide school shootings, lethal and nonlethal, by the U.S. Secret Service in a report of the Safe School Initiative, concluded that approximately one-fourth of school shooters are nonwhite youth (United States Secret Service 2002:12–13; Moore et al. 2003:332). In addition, many, if not most, victims of youthful violence in general are African American and Hispanic youth living in inner cities (Garbarino 2001: 3–6). Thus, while the majority of the discussion to follow will focus on experiences with school violence in the United States, do not forget that shootings, murders, and other acts of violence occur among youth from different backgrounds in all parts of the country and in other countries, in and out of school.

School shootings and other acts of violence at schools often leave the impression that schools are unsafe for children. However, according to reported statistics, schools in America are becoming safer. For example, criminal victimization data indicate that in 1989, approximately 9 percent of students reported having been victimized at school, and this percentage was about the same for males and females, whites and nonwhites (Bastian and Taylor 1991:1). From 1995 to 2005, however, the percentage of students reporting having been victims of both property and violent crimes at school declined from 10 percent to 4 percent, as shown in figure 8.2. In addition, declines in victimization experiences have not been affected by grades in school or race, which suggests that the declines are not the result of age or racial effects but reflect truer reductions in crimes at school over the past decade or so (Dinkes et al. 2006:14–15).

Besides declines in victimization, both male and female students in school have also become less involved in physical fights since 1993, as shown

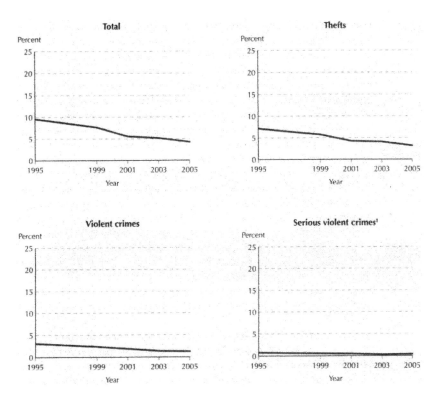

FIGURE 8.2 Percentage of students ages 12–18 who reported criminal victimization at school during the previous six months, by types of victimization: various years, 1995–2005

[1] Serious violent crimes are also included in violent crimes.

NOTE: Theft includes purse snatching, pickpocketing, all burglaries, attempted forcible entry, and all attempted and completed thefts except motor vehicle thefts. Theft does not include robbery.

Source: Dinkes et al. 2006:15, based on data from the U.S. Department of Justice, Bureau of Justice Statistics, School Crime Supplement (SCS) to the National Crime Victimization Survey, various years, 1995–2005.

in Figure 8.3. Furthermore, these declines have occurred for students in grades 9–12, again suggesting real reductions in violence, not changes attributed to students in one or two grades. There was an upward trend in physical fights away from school property between 2003 and 2005. However, this increase in fighting was not reflected on school property (Dinkes et al. 2006:40–41).

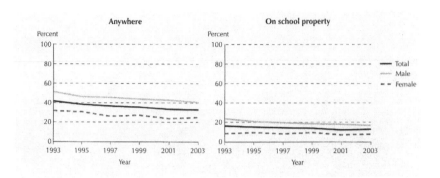

FIGURE 8.3 Percentages of students in grades 9–12 who reported having been in a physical fight during the previous twelve months, by location and sex: various years, 1993–2005

NOTE: "On school property" was not defined for survey respondents. The term "anywhere" is not used in the YRBS questionnaire; students are simply asked how many times in the last 12 months they had been in a physical fight.

Source: Dinkes et al. 2006:41, based on data from the Centers for Disease Control and Prevention, National Center for Chronic Disease Prevention and Health Promotion, Youth Risk Behavior Surveillance System (YRBSS), 1993–2005.

Teachers have also experienced reduced crime victimization at school over the past several years. As shown in figure 8.4, the percentage of teachers who were threatened at school declined from 12 percent in 1993 to 9 percent in 1999–2000 and 7 percent in 2003–2004, with the highest percentages of threats occurring in central cities. The percentage of teachers who were physically attacked also declined somewhat between 1993 and 2003–2004. Again, however, the largest percentage of attacks on teachers occurred in central cities (Dinkes et al. 2006:20–21). However, the experience of victimization among teachers varies by gender and type of school. Male teachers are more likely to report being threatened, but female teachers are more likely to report being attacked. Also, threats are more likely to be made against secondary school teachers, but attacks on teachers are more likely to come from elementary students. Threats and attacks are more likely to be made against public school teachers, compared with private school teachers (Dinkes et al. 2006:20–21).

Overall, reported data on school crime for students and teachers indicate a decline in criminal activity over the past several years. Furthermore, most crimes that do occur at schools are property crimes. Violent crimes are

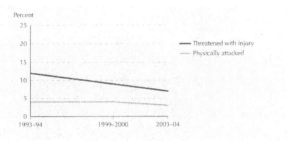

FIGURE 8.4 Percentage of public and private school teachers who reported that they were threatened with injury or that they were physically attacked by a student from school during the previous twelve months: 1993–1994, 1999–2000, and 2003–2004

NOTE: Teachers who taught only prekindergarten students are excluded. Population sizes for teachers are 2,930,000 in 1993–1994; 3,452,000 in 1999–2000; and 3,704,000 in 2003–2004. Figures were revised and may differ from previously published data.

Source: Dinkes et al. 2006: 21, based on data from the U.S. Department of Education, National Center for Education Statistics, Schools and Staffing Survey (SASS), "Public School Teacher Questionnaire," 1993–1994, 1999–2000, and 2003–2004; "Private School Teacher Questionnaire," 1993–1994, 1999–2000, and 2003–2004; "Charter School Questionnaire," 1999–2000; and "Bureau of Indian Affairs Teacher Questionnaire," 1999–2000 and 2003–2004.

far less common on school campuses throughout the country. As one report concluded, "In each school year from 1992–2000, youth ages 5–19 were 70 times more likely to be murdered away from school than at school" (DeVoe et al. 2004:1; see also Fisher and Kettl 2001 and Kimmel and Mahler 2003:1443).

The chances of criminal victimization are not uniform across all classifications of schools and jurisdictions. It has already been observed that assaults on teachers vary by gender of teacher, type of school, and size of community. Reported incidents of violent, property, and other crime also vary by size of community and size and type of school. Urban schools and schools with 1,000 or more enrolled students consistently report higher percentages of crimes at school. Some suggest that the population of a school is a major factor in school crime, with effects on crime being greater than the size of the school and with impacts on crime extending beyond the school grounds to include surrounding neighborhoods (Felson 1994:97). In addition, high schools or secondary schools have higher reported percentages of crime on campus compared with elementary and middle schools (DeVoe et al. 2004:24–27; see also Flaherty 2001:31–32).

While the data indicate that school violence is declining, a cautionary note should be raised concerning the quality of the information reported by school systems. In reaction to the provisions of the No Child Left Behind Act of 2001, some schools may be underreporting instances of violence on their campuses because such reports may lead to a school being designated as "persistently dangerous." According to a U.S. Department of Education audit of school violence, only 46 schools were designated persistently dangerous in 2006–2007 out of approximately 94,000 schools. Standards of reporting acts of violence are not uniform. For example, in Washington, DC, only serious crimes that are authenticated by the police are counted. In Virginia, a school is labeled persistently dangerous if it reports only one serious crime, such as murder or a bombing, or reports a series of other crimes beyond its enrollment "allowance" for three straight years. It is not certain that these concerns and reporting policies actually distort the true incidence of school violence, but the existence of school labels, such as persistently dangerous, and the various means of attaining that status suggest that the underreporting of acts of school violence is a distinct possibility (Hernandez 2007). Future attempts to assess the extent and nature of school violence should carefully examine the impact that the No Child Left Behind Act may have on the reporting of school violence.

Effects of School Shootings and Prevention Efforts

School shootings, such as the incident in Columbine, can affect threats of violence in the short term, even in other states. In Pennsylvania, for example, within three months of the Columbine shootings, there were 354 reports of school violence, compared with an annual average of one to two such reports before the shootings, and this increase was attributed to a "copycat" or imitation effect (Kostinsky et al. 2001; see also Sullivan and Guerette 2003). Certainly, those directly exposed to such incidents as victims or witnesses may be in need of counseling for years after the event (Lane et al. 2001; Newman et al. 2004:274–278). Effects of crime on fear, however, are less certain. A longitudinal analysis of the national criminal victimization surveys (see chapter 3), for example, found that fear of crime at school among a random sample of 12- to 18-year-old students did not significantly increase after the shootings at Columbine High School in 1999 (Addington 2003).

Regardless of how severe, long-lasting, or extensive are the effects of school shootings and other acts of violence, most would agree that this is an unacceptable behavior pattern that should be prevented as much as possible. Preventing school violence, however, is a difficult and multipronged task. It has already been shown that factors such as school size and location have a relationship to school shootings and violence, but not always in the same direction. While it may be difficult to modify significantly where a school is located and its size, schools have adopted various policies and programs designed to reduce shootings and other forms of violence on school property since the rash of school shootings in the late 1990s. Some of these practices are in response to federal laws and policies. For example, the U.S. Department of Education now has an Office of Safe and Drug-Free Schools (for a list of their programs, go to www.ed.gov/about/offices/list/osdfs/programs.html). Other programs are the result of more local initiatives and concerns. Among the various options most schools have adopted over the past few years to reduce school violence are the following:

1. Increasing suspensions for carrying weapons onto campus
2. Creating and enforcing new discipline codes
3. Establishing "drug free" and "gun free" areas in schools and on school property
4. Developing conflict resolution and multicultural sensitivity programs
5. Establishing dress codes
6. Conducting locker searches (Sheley 2000:48)

Others suggest that an effective means of preventing or reducing school violence is for school authorities, that is, teachers, counselors, and administrators, to share information on students across grade levels and schools. Communication regarding academic difficulties and discipline measures for students might lead to greater attention to students showing signs of stress. Of course, such attention may also lead to unintended consequences, such as negative labeling (see chapter 12), where the evaluations of a student's condition may be based on what someone has said or written about the youth from previous experiences (Newman et al. 2004:279–280).

Some of these efforts involve schoolwide programs, while others seem to be more focused on individual characteristics of would-be offenders and/or victims. With regard to individual characteristics of offenders, for example, research on school shooters consistently, although not always, reveals that they have been the victims of *bullying* and other forms of harassment (United States Secret Service 2002:14–15; Kimmel and Mahler 2003:1447–1149; Moore et al. 2003:316–317). Many school districts have adopted actions focused on reducing bullying at schools. Some research suggests that bullies are males and they commit violent acts, often based on sexual preferences and identities of male victims, that is, *homophobic* behavior; although school shooters are not gay, they have often been victims of gay taunts and bullying (Kimmel and Mahler 2003). Other studies suggest that bullies are typically males who wish to control others and who do not suffer from anxieties or low self-esteem (Lawrence 2007:284–285).

Females are often harassed by males as a form of sexual bullying. Female victims of female bullies tend to be more indirectly bullied, such as by gossip and exclusion from groups. In addition, studies show that bullying is more prevalent among younger students, especially those in elementary and middle schools, compared with high schools (Ma 2002; Benbenishty and Astor 2005:13–16). Moreover, bullying tends to occur more often *at* school rather than on the way to or from school (Ma 2002). Also, some studies show that bullying is more common in rural areas (Ma 2002), which may be another reason why many lethal shootings in the past few years have occurred in small towns and suburban communities.*

Developing *school climates* that encourage more parental involvement in controlling bullying and adopting "zero tolerance" for bullying, along with more tolerance for differences and diversity, seem to be effective ways to reduce school bullying (Flaherty 2001; Ma 2002; Newman et al. 2004: 285–288). Bullying and violence, however, are not so predictable that authorities can adopt policies that concentrate prevention programs on only a few schools or only a few individuals in certain sizes of cities or small-town areas. Prevention efforts can be introduced in schools no matter their location, their size, or the ages of their students. Changing school characteristics or school climates are not easy things to accomplish and often depend on outside resources in order to occur, such as financial and/or personnel resources, parental support, and so on. The important point to remember is that reducing school bullying may lead to reduced incidents of other school violence, such as school shootings. In addition, such efforts may lead to increased self-

---

* As this chapter was being finalized, a shooting at a small high school (approximately 400 students) occurred in Jokela, Finland, a small town of about 5,300 people, on November 7, 2007. The shootings resulted in nine deaths, including the shooter, who shot himself, and 12 injuries. News reports indicate the shooter was a senior at the school and was a victim of bullying. The patterns of many of the school shootings noted in the United States are repeated in this incident in Finland, namely, small-town location and the shooter as a victim of bullying.

esteem, improved school performance, and reductions in delinquency among the *victims* of bullying (Ma 2002).

Violence in schools may be also attributed to family or neighborhood contexts, again making it more difficult for schools alone to tackle the problem. The potential for family conflicts and child abuse to create violence in children has already been discussed in chapter 7. It is logical to assume that some of these family-based conditions can contribute to the violence students commit at school (Felson 1994:chapter 5; Ingoldsby et al. 2001). Some child-rearing practices may encourage violence among a family's children, violence that can translate to bullying at school. Parenting that is aloof and that downgrades love and displays of affection for male children, for example, may lead to aggressiveness and bullying at school among these children. Victims of bullies tend to come from overprotective families whose parents do not interact effectively with school officials, such as teachers and counselors, concerning their child's victimization (Benbenishty and Astor 2005:16).

Neighborhoods that have high crime rates or high instances of hate crimes or domestic violence can also contribute to violence in schools (Horton 2001; Moore et al. 2003:1–8; Benbenishty and Astor 2005:17). Youngsters reared in such areas may not be able to change their behavior patterns once in the school setting. With the assistance of federal grants and resource support, many communities have established violence- and crime-reduction programs that incorporate both schools and the communities in which they are located. The Beacon Community Center Program in New York City is one example of such projects. The "Beacons" attempts to make schools a kind of community center, offering summer programs, after-school activities, employment, and individual counseling services to families and students as well as recreational activities and other services for individuals and families in high-crime neighborhoods (McGillis 1996).

However, the kinds of resources prevalent in large cities may not be available in small towns. In small communities, gossip is a good way to exercise social control, but victims of gossip are readily known by others in the area and have few choices of avoiding the sources of gossip or others who are drawn into that circle, which may be especially troubling for young people. As Katherine Newman and her colleagues observe, "Gossip leads adolescents to hide their actions and become much more secretive" (Newman et al. 2004:121). Even telling parents of difficulties being experienced in school may be dangerous for students, because a parent might inform on the offender, which might then be relayed to the offender and lead to increased difficulties not only for the student having problems but also for the parent who informs on another's child. Although small towns are thought to be close-knit and able to supervise others' children, this expectation seems to have broken down in communities that have recently experienced school shootings. Perhaps the close social structures and sharing of common problems and identities often associated with small towns and rural areas have declined over the years for a variety of reasons, including increasingly demanding work schedules, child-centered activities, and single- or split-parent households, where the sharing of child care may become divided (Newman et al. 2004:122–125).

For whatever reason, analyses of school shootings typically reveal that school shooters had mounting problems that they did not share with others, including family and school officials, before the problems became too unbearable to take. Communication issues are a problem in many areas, not just small towns, and these concerns need to be addressed in order to identify and possibly prevent continued incidents of troubled adolescents acting out or escaping from their problems by embarking on violent episodes aimed at classmates and teachers.

Delinquency Prevention through Early Childhood Education

In addition to being mechanisms for the prevention and reduction of school violence and harassment, schools have been used as resources for reducing gang and drug involvement as well as delinquency in general. Drug prevention programs such as D.A.R.E. (Drug Abuse Resistance Education) and gang prevention efforts such as G.R.E.A.T. (Gang Resistance Education and Training) are discussed in the chapters on drugs (chapter 9) and gangs (chapter 10). Besides these programs, there have been efforts to prevent delinquency and other forms of adolescent deviance by introducing preschool-based programs aimed at developing academic and social skills that, in the long run, might lead to increased graduation rates and employment opportunities and a reduction in crime and delinquency. Although some have discounted the positive impact of preschool programs (Herrnstein and Murray 1994), some programs have produced positive results during school and post–high school (Lawrence 2007:285–287).

One of the most studied of such programs has been the High/Scope Perry Preschool Project, from 1962–1965, in Ypsilanti, Michigan. The Perry Preschool Project identified 123 African American children, mostly males, for inclusion in the program. Selection criteria were based on parental education and socioeconomic status and IQ of the children. Children with IQs in the 60–90 range and whose parents were of low socioeconomic status and low educational status (only 20 percent of the parents were high-school graduates) were eligible for the program. From the 123 children selected, 58 were randomly chosen to participate in the program, and 65 were assigned to a control group (Luster and McAdoo 1996:27–28; Bracey 2003:32).

The program focused on helping the students learn to ask questions rather than to prepare for specific tests. More specifically, the project focused on creativity, language skills, social relationships, numbers, and math concepts such as seriation (creating patterns from series) and classification, as well as music and group interaction skills. The program was for one-half day and lasted eight months. The children in 1962 received this treatment for one year, at age four, while those in subsequent years received the treatment for two years, at ages three and four. In addition, the classes were supported with 90-minute home visits every week for the eight months the treatment lasted (Bracey 2003:32–33).

The results of the project have been evaluated several times, when the children were in school and at ages 19 and 27. Testers and teachers who interacted with the youth subsequent to the treatment did not know which children were in the treatment group and which were controls (Bracey 2003:32). The results of these follow-up studies have consistently concluded that the children exposed to the treatment performed better in school and had lower incidences of crime and delinquency as adolescents and young adults. Specifically, among the 27-year-old cohort, which included 95 percent of the original 123 participants, 71 percent of the preschool (treatment) group had received a high-school diploma (including a GED), compared with 54 percent of the controls. In addition, 42 percent of the preschool group was making over $2,000 a month, compared with 6 percent of the controls. Also, the preschoolers had more stable marriages and higher rates of home ownership compared with the controls (Schweinhart and Weikart 1993:55; Luster and McAdoo 1996:28; Bracey 2003:33). In addition, the preschoolers had higher test scores "at the ages of 4–7, 14, 19, and 27" (Schweinhart and Weikart 1993:55).

With regard to criminal behavior, by age 27, the preschoolers had averaged 2.3 arrests, compared with an average of 4.6 arrests for the controls. In terms of criminal careers, 7 percent of the preschoolers had been arrested five times or more (chronic offenders), compared with 35 percent of the controls (Schweinhart and Weikart 1993:55). Self-report offense estimates also favored the preschoolers, and these differences began to show up at age 15 (Schweinhart and Weikart 1997:132).

By age 40, 70 percent of the experimental subjects had graduated from high school, compared with 60 percent of the control group. Most of this effect was attributed to the females in the study. Among the females who went through the program, 88 percent had graduated from high school by age 40, compared with 46 percent of the controls. Significantly fewer of the program participants, especially females, had received special education for mental impairment by age 40, and significantly fewer of the experimental program females were retained in a grade and/or dropped out of school, compared with controls. In addition, significantly more of the preschool subjects had jobs, higher incomes, cars, and home mortgages compared with controls. More of the program group had been married for more than 10 years by the time they were 40 years old, and more expressed satisfaction with their families, compared with the control group. Also, by age 40 the differences in crime noted in earlier years continued. Program participants had significantly fewer arrests for all types of crimes, prison sentences, school-reported misconduct, and self-reported crime, than controls. The differences in arrest and sentencing seemed more pronounced by age 40 than at age 27, suggesting that the crime-reducing impact of the program became more powerful over time (Schweinhart et al. 2005:51-119).

The results of the High/Scope Perry Preschool Project have been impressive. As the authors of a report on the study through age 40 concluded, "High quality preschool programs for young children living in poverty contribute to their intellectual and social development in childhood and their school success, economic performance, and reduced commission of crime in adulthood" (Schweinhart et al. 2005:214). In addition to the positive results for educational attainment, occupational stability, marriage stability, and reduced criminal activity, evaluations of the program have also concluded that it has saved significant financial investments as well. Evaluators have concluded that the program has provided a cost–benefit ratio of 7:1, or a $7 return for every $1 invested (Schweinhart and Weikart 1993:56; Bracey and Stellar 2003:33). Follow-up analyses to age 40 for the experimental group shows a dollar cost–benefit ratio ranging from 17:1 (Karoly et al. 2005:111) to approximately 13:1 (Schweinhart et al. 2005:152–154).

Although the High/Scope Perry Preschool Project has been the most studied preschool program, others have also been successful, such as the Chicago Child–Parent Center Program, the Abecedarian Project in North Carolina, and Head Start programs throughout the country (Schweinhart and Weikart 1993:121–122; Bracey and Stellar 2003:33–35). Reviews of these programs have also concluded that they are successful in improving reading and math skills, increasing rates of high-school graduation, reducing crime, delinquency, and behavioral problems, extending into adulthood, and providing a positive cost–benefit ratio ranging from 3:1 to 7:1 (Karoly et al. 2005:55–121). Although some have criticized the value of preschool programs for educational and delinquency prevention purposes, studies of these programs have concluded that such efforts are effective in improving the educational and occupational opportunities for youth, as well as serving to help reduce crime and delinquency, and with impressive cost–benefit ratios.

Legal Rights of Students at School

The topic of juvenile rights will be addressed in more detail in chapter 13, on the juvenile justice system. There are many issues concerning the rights of students, such as free speech and assembly, worship, dress codes, and so on. For this chapter, the rights to be discussed involve issues concerning possible criminal or deviant behavior and the rights of students with respect to searches of property and person and drug testing.

In the past several years, three important U.S. Supreme Court decisions have affected the legal rights of juveniles concerning searches at school or on school property. Briefly, these cases have challenged searches on the grounds that they violate citizens' rights against unreasonable search and seizure under the Fourth Amendment to the U.S. Constitution. School responses have in part been based on the legal concept of *in loco parentis*, in which schools are allowed to act in the place of parents regarding authority and decision making. Using this logic, it may be argued that schools have the same rights to search students for contraband items as parents have to examine their children's rooms and possessions, that is, without evidence and over any objections of youth (Sanborn and Salerno 2005:144).

The first and probably the most far-reaching case (Sanborn and Salerno 2005:144) in this matter was *New Jersey v. T.L.O.* (1985), or simply *T.L.O.* In this case, a female high-school student, T.L.O., was accused by an assistant vice-principal of smoking in the girls' lavatory, although smoking at that time and place was neither against school rules nor illegal. The vice-principal demanded that the girl open her purse for inspection to see whether there were any cigarettes in the purse. Even though T.L.O. refused to give her permission, she was forced to comply. During the inspection, the vice-principal found cigarettes, marijuana, and evidence that T.L.O. had been selling and distributing marijuana at the school. Later, she confessed to selling marijuana at school and was found delinquent by a local juvenile court judge, in part based on the evidence found in the purse. Her lawyers appealed the "conviction," arguing that the search of the purse was illegal, and the verdict was overturned by the New Jersey Supreme Court. However, the state appealed this ruling, and the case was accepted by the U.S. Supreme Court. The Supreme Court ruled in favor of the state and reinstated the conviction of T.L.O. Although the Court did affirm that students do have a right to expect privacy at school and protection from unreasonable searches, in this case, the definition of "reasonable" searches was extended to include searching private property, such as purses and similar belongings of students (Sanborn and Salerno 2005:144–146; Parry 2005:153–156).

It is important to note, however, that while the decision in *T.L.O.* may have presented the possibility for virtually any student's possessions to be searched by school authorities (Sanborn and Salerno 2005:146), it did not specify which particular possessions could be searched. Thus, future cases may be raised that will specify these possessions in more detail.

The next two cases concern the rights of students to privacy against drug testing. In the first case, *Vernonia School District 47J v. Acton* (1995), or *Vernonia*, the issue was whether students participating in athletic programs could be randomly tested for the presence of drugs in their body. School District 47J, in Vernonia, Oregon, had a policy that allowed random drug testing for student athletes. The reasoning for this policy was that athletes are public figures and, to a degree, they represent the school when they perform as athletes. As Justice Scalia, writing for the Court's majority opinion in this case, stated, "Students who voluntarily participate in school athletics have reason to expect intrusions upon normal rights and privileges, including privacy" (Parry 2005:159). In addition, drug use among juveniles is a general concern, but drug use can be particularly harmful to athletes, who may be injured while under the effects of a drug. However, the parents of some athletes objected to the random drug testing policy on the grounds that it violated the right to privacy of the student and the Fourth Amendment right to unreasonable searches. Upon reviewing the arguments of the case, the U.S. Supreme Court decided, in a 6–3 opinion, that the Vernonia policy was constitutional. Again speaking for the majority opinion, Judge Scalia wrote, "Taking into account all the factors we have considered above—the decreased expectation of privacy, the relative unobtrusiveness of the search, and the severity of the need met by the search—we conclude Vernonia's policy is reasonable and hence constitutional" (Parry 2005:160).

The issue of student drug testing was raised again in 2002, in a case titled *Board of Education of Independent School District No. 92 of Pottawatomie County et al. v. Earls et al.* In this case, the issue was not random drug testing for student athletes, but students participating in any extracurricular activity. The Tecumseh, Oklahoma, school district had adopted a drug testing policy aimed at any student participating in extracurricular activities, whether or not there was any identifiable drug problem at a school. Some parents objected to this policy, again on the grounds that it violated the privacy of their children and protections against unreasonable searches granted in the Fourth Amendment. The U.S. Supreme Court ruled that the drug testing policy at Tecumseh was reasonable and thus constitutional. In rendering the reasoning of the majority opinion of the 5–4 vote, Judge Thomas stated, "Furthermore, this Court has not required a particularized or pervasive drug problem before allowing the government to conduct suspicionless drug testing" (Parry 2005:163). In addition, Judge Thomas wrote, "*Vernonia* did not require the school to test the group of students most likely to use drugs, but rather considered the constitutionality of the program in the context of the school's custodial responsibilities. Evaluating the Policy in this context, we conclude that the drug testing of Tecumseh students who participate in extracurricular activities effectively serves the School District's interest in protecting the safety and health of its students" (Parry 2005:164; see also the Web site of the Legal Information Institute at http://www.law.cornell.edu).

A consistent theme running through all three decisions is the need for schools to protect their environment and the health and safety of the students with whose care they have been entrusted. Thus, as stated earlier, the Supreme Court has not been concerned with the existence of a drug problem in order for schools or school districts to impose drug testing for students participating in sports or in extracurricular activities. Rather, it seems the overriding issue in these cases is the authority of schools to protect their interests and those of their students. Thus, drug testing, even that which may invade students' privacy, is considered reasonable and thus constitutional.

Summary

School factors play an important role in the understanding of delinquency, from a variety of perspectives. For one, schools serve as an important setting for student interactions with peers. Schools also serve as the most important source of evaluation of student performance. In this context, schools can be sources of either positive or negative emotions and experiences for youth. Academic performance is a major factor in how students perceive themselves and in their behavior. Low or poor academic performance can lead to delinquency through a series of connections, as outlined in figure 8.1. Significant negative outcomes in school include dropping out, bullying, and school shootings.

The school setting can also aid delinquency treatment or prevention. The use of preschool programs and schools as major sources of delinquency prevention has been tried for over 40 years with demonstrable success. Most notable among these prevention projects is the High/Scope Perry Preschool Project, begun in the 1960s in Ypsilanti, Michigan, as well as national Head Start efforts.

Schools have also been involved in several court cases concerning juvenile rights. In this chapter, attention was focused on the issue of illegal search and seizure, protected by the Fourth Amendment. A series of U.S. Supreme Court decisions have ruled that local schools and school districts may impose reasonable searches of students' possessions, such as purses, and conduct suspicionless drug testing on students participating in any kind of extracurricular activity. The consistent theme running through these decisions is the need of schools to protect their environment and the health and safety of their students, as opposed to the rights of students to privacy in the school setting.

References

Addington, Lynn A.
　　2003　Students' Fear After Columbine: Findings from a Randomized Experiment. Journal of Quantitative Criminology 19:367–387.
Agnew, Robert
　　1985　A Revised Strain Theory of Delinquency. Social Forces 64:151–167.
　　1992　Foundations for a General Strain Theory of Crime and Delinquency. Criminology 30:47–87.
Bastian, Lisa D., and Bruce M. Taylor
　　1991　School Crime: A National Crime Victimization Survey Report. Washington, DC: U.S. Government Printing Office.
Benbenishty, Rami, and Avi Astor
　　2005　School Violence in Context: Culture, Neighborhood, Family, School, and Gender. New York: Oxford University Press.
Berrueta-Clement, John R., Lawrence J. Schweinhart, William Steven Barnett, and David P. Weikart
　　1987　The Effects of Early Intervention on Crime and Delinquency in Adolescence and Early Adulthood. In Prevention of Delinquent Behav-

ior: Primary Prevention of Psychopathology, Volume X. John D. Burchard and Sara N. Burchard, eds. Pp. 220–240. Beverly Hills: Sage.

Bracey, Gerald W.
2003   Investing in Preschool: Money Spent on Early Childhood Educa-
        tion is Money Well Spent. American School Board Journal 190:
        32–35.

Bracey, Gerald W., and Arthur Stellar
2003   Long-Term Studies of Preschool: Lasting Benefits Far Outweigh
        Costs. Phi Delta Kappan 84:780–783, 797.

Chambliss, William
1973   The Saints and the Roughnecks. Society 11:24–31.

Cohen, Albert
1955   Delinquent Boys: The Culture of the Gang. New York: Free Press.

Cox, Stephen M., William S. Davidson, and Timothy S. Bynum
1995   A Meta-Analytic Assessment of Delinquency-Related Outcomes of
        Alternative Education Programs. Crime and Delinquency 41:219–234.

DeVoe, Jill E., Katharine Peter, Philip Kaufman, Amanda Miller, Margaret Noo-
nan, Thomas D. Snyder, and Katrina Baum
2004   Indicators of School Crime and Safety: 2004 (NCES 2005-002/NCJ
        205290). Washington, DC: U.S. Departments of Education and Jus-
        tice.

Dinkes, Rachel, Emily Forrest Cataldi, Grace Kena, and Katrina Baum
2006   Indicators of School Crime and Safety: 2006 (NCES 2007-003
        Ncj 214262). Washington, D.C.: U.S. Departments of Education and
        Justice.

Dorn, Sherman
1996   Creating the Dropout: An Institutional and Social History of School
        Failure. Westport, CT: Praeger.

Elliott, Delbert S., and Harwin L. Voss
1974   Delinquency and Dropout. Lexington, MA: D. C. Heath.

Felson, Marcus
1994   Crime and Everyday Life: Insight and Implications for Society.
        Thousand Oaks, CA: Pine Forge Press.

Felson, Richard B., and Jeremy Staff
2006   Explaining the Academic Performance-Delinquency Relationship.
        Criminology 44:299–319.

Fisher, Kathleen M., and Paul Kettl
2001   Trends in School Violence: Are Our Schools Safe? *In* School Vio-
        lence: Assessment, Management, and Prevention. Mohammad Shafii

and Sharon Lee Shafii, eds. Pp. 73–83. Washington, DC: American Psychiatric Publishing.

Flaherty, Lois T.
    2001   School Violence and the School Environment. *In* School Violence: Assessment, Management, Prevention. Mohammad Shafii and Sharon lee Shafii, eds. Pp. 25–51. Washington, DC: American Psychiatric Publishing.

Garbarino, James
    2001   Making Sense of School Violence: Why Do Kids Kill? *In* School Violence: Assessment, Management, Prevention. Mohammad Shafii and Sharon Lee Shafii, eds. Pp. 3–24.Washington, DC: American Psychiatric Publishing.

Hagan, John
    1997   Defiance and Despair: Subcultural and Structural Linkages between Delinquency and Despair throughout the Life Course. Social Forces 76:119–134.

Hannon, Lance
    2003   Poverty, Delinquency, and Educational Attainment: Cumulative Disadvantage or Disadvantage Saturation? Sociological Inquiry 73:575–595.

Hartnagel, Timothy F., and Harvey Krahn
    1989   High School Dropouts, Labor Market Success, and Criminal Behavior. Youth and Society 20:416–444.

Hernandez, Nelson
    2007   "No Child" Data on School Violence Skewed, Audits Indicate. Roanoke Times, November 20:4A.

Herrnstein, Richard J., and Charles Murray
    1994   The Bell Curve: Intelligence and Class Structure in American Life. New York: Free Press.

Hirschi, Travis
    1969   Causes of Delinquency. Berkeley: University of California Press.

Horton, Arthur
    2001   The Prevention of School Violence: New Evidence to Consider. Journal of Human Behavior in the Social Environment 4:49–59.

Ingoldsby, Erin M., Daniel S. Shaw, and Monica M. Garcia
    2001   Intrafamily Conflict in Relation to Boys' Adjustment to School. Development and Psychopathology 13:35–52.

Jarjoura, G. Roger
    1993   Does Dropping Out of School Enhance Delinquent Involvement? Results from a Large-Scale National Probability Sample. Criminology 31:149–172.

1996   The Conditional Effect of Social Class on the Dropout Delinquency Relationship. Journal of Research in Crime and Delinquency 33:232–255.

Kaplan, Howard B., and Xiaoro Liu
1994   A Longitudinal Analysis of Mediating Variables in the Drug Use-Dropping Out Relationship. Criminology 32:415–439.

Karoly, Lynn A., M. Rebecca Kilburn, and Jill S. Cannon
2005   Early Childhood Interventions: Proven Results, Future Promise. Santa Monica, CA: Rand.

Kids Count
2004   2004 Kids Count Data Book: State Profiles of Child Well-Being. Baltimore: Annie E. Casey Foundation.
2007   2007 Kids Count Data Book: State Profiles of Child Well-Being. Baltimore: Annie E. Casey Foundation.

Kimmel, Michael S., and Matthew Mahler
2003   Adolescent Masculinity, Homophobia, and Violence: Random School Shootings, 1982–2001. American Behavioral Scientist 46:1439–1458.

Kostinsky, Spencer, Edward O. Bixler, and Paul A. Kettl
2001   Threats of School Violence in Pennsylvania After Media Coverage of the Columbine High School Massacre: Examining the Role of Imitation. Archives of Pediatrics and Adolescent Medicine 155:994–1001.

Lane, Christopher M., Robert S. Pynoos, and Jose Cardenas
2001   Wounded Adolescence: School-Based Group Psychotherapy for Adolescents Who Sustained or Witnessed Violent Injury. In School Violence: Assessment, Management, Prevention. Mohammad Shafii and Sharon Lee Shafii, eds. Pp. 163–187. Washington, DC: American Psychiatric Publishing.

Lawrence, Richard
2007   School Crime and Juvenile Justice. 2nd edition. New York: Oxford University Press.

Luster, Tom, and Harriette McAdoo
1996   Family and Child Influences on Educational Attainment: A Secondary Analysis of the High/Scope Perry Preschool Data. Developmental Psychology 32:26–39.

Ma, Zin
2002   Bullying in Middle School: Individual and School Characteristics of Victims and Offenders. School Effectiveness and School Improvement 13:63–89.

MacLeod, Jay
> 1987   Ain't No Makin' It. Boulder, CO: Westview.

McGillis, Daniel
> 1996   Beacons of Hope: New York City's School-Based Community Centers. Washington, DC: National Institute of Justice, Program Focus.

Moore, Mark H., Carol V. Petrie, Anthony A. Braga, and Brenda L. McLaughlin, eds.
> 2003   Deadly Lessons: Understanding Lethal School Violence. Washington, DC: National Academies Press.

Newman, Katherine S., Cybelle Fox, David J. Harding, Jal Mehta, and Wendy Roth
> 2004   Rampage: The Social Roots of School Shootings. New York: Basic Books.

Parry, David L., ed.
> 2005   Essential Readings in Juvenile Justice. Upper Saddle River, NJ: Pearson Prentice Hall.

Polk, Kenneth
> 1969   Class, Strain, and Rebellion among Adolescents. Social Problems 17:214–224.

Sanborn, Joseph B., Jr., and Anthony W. Salerno
> 2005   The Juvenile Justice System: Law and Process. Los Angeles: Roxbury.

Schweinhart, Lawrence J., and David P. Weikart
> 1993   Success by Empowerment: The High/Scope Perry Preschool Study Through Age 27. Young Children 49:54–58.
> 1997   The High/Scope Preschool Curriculum Comparison Study Through Age 23. Early Childhood Research Quarterly 12:117–143.

Schweinhart, Lawrence J., Jeanne Montie, Zongping Xiang, W. Steven Barnett, Clive R. Belfield, and Milagros Nores
> 2005   Lifetime Effects: The High/Scope Perry Preschool Study through Age 40. Ypsilanti, MI: High/Scope Press.

Shaw, Margaret
> 2001   Promoting Safety in Schools: International Experience and Action. Washington, DC: U.S. Department of Justice.

Sheley, Joseph F.
> 2000   Controlling Violence; What Schools Are Doing. *In* Preventing School Violence: Plenary Papers of the 1999 Conference on Criminal Justice Research and Evaluation—Enhancing Policy and Practice Through Research, Vol. 2. Sheppard G. Kellam, Ron Prinz, and Joseph F. Sheley, eds. Pp. 37–57. Washington, DC: U.S. Department of Justice.

Shoemaker, Donald J.
  2005   Theories of Delinquency: An Examination of Explanations of
         Delinquent Behavior. 5th edition. New York: Oxford University
         Press.
Stinchcombe, Arthur L.
  1964   Rebellion in a High School. Chicago: Quadrangle Books.
Sullivan, Mercer L., and Rob T. Guerette
  2003   The Copycat Factor: Mental Illness, Guns, and the Shooting Inci-
         dent at Heritage High School, Rockdale County, Georgia. *In* Deadly
         Lessons: Understanding Lethal School Violence. Mark H. Moore,
         Carol V. Petrie, Anthony A. Braga, and Brenda L. McLaughlin, eds.
         Pp. 25–69. Washington, DC: National Academies Press.
Thornberry, Terence P., Melanie Moore, and R.L. Christensen
  1985   The Effects of Dropping Out of High School on Subsequent Crim-
         inal Behavior. Criminology 23:3–18.
United States Secret Service
  2002   Preventing School Shootings: A Summary of a U.S. Secret Service
         Safe School Initiative Report. National Institute of Justice Journal
         248:11–15.
Weintraub, Philippe, Harriet L. Hall, and Robert S. Pynoos
  2001   Columbine High School Shootings: Community Response. *In*
         School Violence: Assessment, Management, Prevention. Moham-
         mad Shafii and Sharon Lee Shafii, eds. Pp. 129–161. Washington,
         DC: American Psychiatric Publishing.
Wiatrowski, Michael D., Stephen Hansell, Charles R. Massey, and David Wilson
  1982   Curriculum Tracking and Delinquency. American Sociological
         Review 47:151–160.
Zingraff, Matthew T., Jeffrey Leiter, Matthew C Johnson, and Kristen A. Myers
  1994   The Mediating Effect of Good School Performance on the Maltreat-
         ment-Delinquency Relationship. Journal of Research in Crime and
         Delinquency 31:62–91.

DRUG USE AMONG YOUTH

J UVENILE DRUG use is considered a major problem by many experts. While marijuana use seemed to peak in the late 1970s and crack cocaine use peaked in the late 1980s, illicit drug use among adolescents and preadolescents remains a significant problem in America today. This chapter addresses the extent and patterns of illegal drug use among young people. The focus of the chapter will be on criminal drug use patterns, but "status offense" types of drugs, such as alcohol and cigarettes, will also be discussed. By status offense drugs, it is meant that the use of these drugs is not illegal for adults but is restricted among minors. State laws vary, but typically, it is illegal for youth under 18 to use cigarettes and alcohol, while the restricted use of alcohol continues to age 21, again, with exceptions in some states. Generally, therefore, cigarette and alcohol use is considered illegal when committed by minors. Many other drugs are proscribed for all citizens, regardless of age. These "criminal" drugs will also be discussed in this chapter.

Drug use among adolescents is not evenly distributed by social and geographical characteristics. In addition, studies of drug use indicate that there are historical shifts in the popularity of certain drugs, such as marijuana, while "new" drugs seem to appear during every generation. While arrest and juvenile court data can reveal important insights into the extent and distribution of drug use, self-report studies have been particularly useful in gathering information on deviant drug use among juveniles. One of the longest and most extensive self-reporting inventories of juvenile drug use has been a report named "Monitoring the Future," and analyses of these types of reports are included in this chapter.

Drug use among juvenile gangs has also been common for several generations. One issue among gangs in contemporary society is the extent to which gangs are engaged in the sale and distribution of illegal drugs, and this issue is also addressed in this chapter.

Treatment of drug users is difficult because of the addictive power of many drugs. Addiction may be *physical* or *psychological.* That is, one may be physically dependent on the chemical properties of a drug. The body needs, some may say craves, more of the drug in order to prevent physical reactions or withdrawal symptoms. In addition, many drug users can become psychologically dependent on the euphoric effects of a drug and on the social setting in which drug use may occur, especially among youth. They need the social excitement and feelings associated with taking a drug. Of course, some drugs may produce both effects, and a person may be both physically and psychologically addicted to the drug. Consequently, newer treatment strategies are being developed to combat drug use that may be addictive. One of these newer strategies is the *drug court,* including juvenile drug courts, and this concept is also discussed in this chapter.

Extent and Patterns of Juvenile Drug Use

Before the 1960s, drug use among juveniles was not much researched and did not present much of a problem to society. Even earlier gang studies did not cite drug use as a problem among juvenile gangs in the first half of the 20th century. Not until the 1960s did adolescent drug use became a concern to American society, and the drugs that seemed to occupy most of the public's attention were alcohol and marijuana.

In 1975, the Institute for Social Research at the University of Michigan initiated annual surveys of high-school seniors throughout the country. This survey, named "Monitoring the Future" (MTF) is a self-report survey that addresses admitted involvement in delinquency, including drug use. In 1991, MTF was expanded to include tenth- and eighth-grade students. For the 2006 survey, approximately 50,000 students from 410 secondary schools were contacted in their classrooms: 14,800 twelfth graders, 16,600 tenth graders, and 17,000 eighth graders (Johnston et al. 2007:1–2). The results of this survey provide substantial information about the extent and distribution of drug use among American adolescents.

The 2006 MTF survey shows that illicit drug use has continued to decline for youth in all three grades since the mid-1990s. A few types of drugs have shown an increase in use since 2001: ecstasy, OxyContin, Vicodin, and inhalants (Johnston et al. 2007:5–7). Overall, however, nearly half, 48 percent, of students surveyed in 2006 indicated they had used an illegal drug by the time of high-school graduation, and 29 percent had used an illicit drug, including inhalants, by the time they were in the eighth grade. In addition, 27 percent of the students indicated they had used an illicit drug other than marijuana by the time they were seniors. Looked at in another way, 71 percent of seniors indicated they had not used another illicit drug than marijuana, and most high-school seniors disapproved of using illegal drugs (Johnston et al. 2007:10). Overall trends in drug use among youth are presented in figure 9.1, which shows the percentage of respondents reporting the use of *any* illicit drug and any illicit drug *except marijuana* during their lifetime and the past 12 months, from 1976 to 2006. The graph lines show that for seniors, overall drug use peaked in the late 1970s and 1980s, rose again in the mid- to late 1990s, and has been on a downward trajectory into the mid-2000s. The pattern is repeated for using any illegal drug except marijuana.

Additional information on use patterns for marijuana as well as perceived risk, availability, and disapproval are given in figure 9.2. For all three grades, marijuana use has been declining since the mid-1990s. These data also indicate that, among twelfth graders, or seniors, the use of marijuana peaked in 1979, but the perceived risk levels for this drug peaked several years later, in 1991. These differences suggest that the drug declined in popularity long before the perceived harmful risks were accepted among high-school seniors. However, for the past few years, perceived risk has increased while marijuana use has declined among all three age groups (with the exception of a slight decline in perceived risk among eighth graders from 2004 to 2006), which suggests that young people are allowing their knowledge of the drug's effects to guide their use patterns (see also Hawdon 2005:250–251). The declining availability of marijuana since the mid-1990s provides another reason for the decline in the admitted use of this drug over the past decade.

One concern of the authors of the MTF survey is that we may be encountering a new "generational forgetting" of the pitfalls of inhalant use, since the last major anti-inhalant campaign occurred in the mid-1990s (Johnston et al. 2007:7). At different periods of time, "new" drugs become accepted among adolescents as safe and beneficial, in terms of their presumed positive effects. In the 1970s, for example, nitrite inhalants and PCP

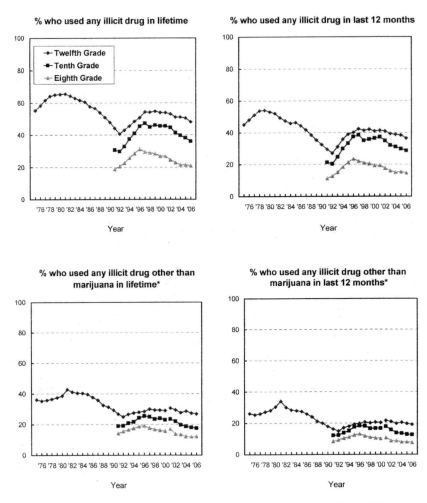

FIGURE 9.1 Trends in Illicit Drug Use: Eighth, Tenth, and Twelfth Graders

Note: *Beginning in 2001, revised sets of questions on other hallucinogen and tranquilizer use were introduced. Data for "any illicit drug other than marijuana" were affected by these changes.

Source: Johnston et al. 2007:12

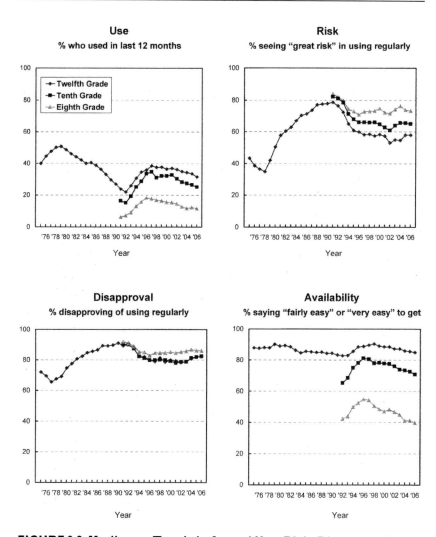

FIGURE 9.2 Marijuana: Trends in Annual Use, Risk, Disapproval, and Availability: Eighth, Tenth, and Twelfth Graders

Source: Johnston et al., 2007:14.

were the new popular drugs, while in the 1980s, crystal methamphetamine and crack cocaine became popular. In the 1990s, Rohypnol, GHB, and ecstasy became popular. In the 2000s, the new drugs so far have been inhalants, again, and OxyContin. One of the problems with the spread of drug use among adolescents is that the *supposed benefits* usually outreach the known harms of the drugs because it is easy to spread the good news through rumors and friendship groups. Now, with the availability of unsupervised Internet "blogs," these kinds of rumors can spread more quickly. As Johnston and colleagues suggest, "It usually takes longer for the evidence of adverse consequences (e.g., death, disease, overdose reactions, addictive potential) to cumulate and *then* to be disseminated" (2007:8). It takes concerted and intelligent campaigning to disseminate information on the true effects of a drug. Often there is a "grace period," during which a drug's known and *accepted* negative effects are not available and the drug becomes popular among adolescents. To counteract or reduce this grace period, objective information sharing is needed to inform the consuming public, particularly youth, of the true effects of a drug. This shortened grace-period effect seems to be occurring for the drug ecstasy. However, this kind of campaigning often has to be conducted for each particular drug because people do not transfer knowledge of one drug to another (Johnston et al. 2007:8). Sometimes, use patterns of a drug may decline before youth actually accept the negative consequences of a drug, such as has been the case with marijuana. With marijuana, for example, use patterns have not always reflected objective reasoning and consideration of known effects. A lot of information has been disseminated regarding this drug, and patterns of use among youth may have been affected by factors other than known risks associated with using the drug regularly. In addition, adolescent users may have experimented with this drug rather than taken it "regularly," so perceived harmful risks of regular marijuana use may not accurately reflect all patterns of use.

Another example of "generational forgetting" can be found with *cigarette* smoking, or what MTF calls a "licit" drug, although technically, cigarettes are prohibited to youth under a certain age, usually 18. According to the 2006 MTF survey, admitted use of cigarettes is on the decline. The MTF data indicate that cigarette smoking was high in the mid 1970s for seniors, fell off in the 1980s, and began to rise in the 1990s, peaking in 1996 (see figure 9.3). It seems that publicized efforts to highlight the dangers of nicotine and smoking in general led to a reduction in cigarette smoking throughout the 1980s. However, young people may have forgotten those lessons by the 1990s, and cigarette use began to increase in that decade. Public concern over

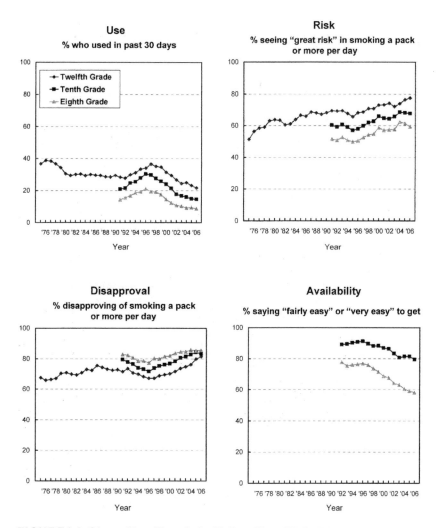

FIGURE 9.3 Cigarettes: Trends in 30-Day Use, Risk, Disapproval, and Availability: Eighth, Tenth, and Twelfth Graders
Source: Johnston et al. 2007:40.

increased adolescent use of cigarettes in the 1990s led to new efforts to publicize to young people the ill effects of tobacco, and these efforts seemed to have worked, at least for now. However, MTF is quick to caution that decreased usage of cigarettes among the young in the past few years may reflect increased cigarette prices as much as real concern for the physical effects of tobacco. The results of the 2006 survey suggest that adolescent complacency, or forgetting, may be on the rise again. The previous sharp declines in smoking began to decelerate in 2002. For eighth and tenth graders, the declines in 30-day use of cigarettes between 2004 and 2006 were negligible (Johnston et al. 2007:9, 39).

Alcohol is another licit drug whose usage patterns are troubling to the authors of the MTF surveys. In 2006, 73 percent of high-school seniors had tried alcohol by the time of graduation, 41 percent of eighth graders had consumed alcohol, and 20 percent of eighth graders reported having been drunk at least once. However, overall, alcohol use rates for seniors are on the decline and are "substantially below" the rates in the 1980s (Johnston et al. 2007:9). *Binge drinking*, defined as "having five or more drinks in a row at least once in the past two weeks," has become stable since the late 1990s. For all three grades, binge drinking has been declining since the late 1990s, although in 2006, the decline in binge drinking for eighth and tenth graders was less than that for seniors (Johnston et al. 2007:9, 37).

One reason researchers are concerned about the extent and patterns of cigarette and alcohol use among teens is because these drugs are thought to be *gateway* drugs to other, illegal drugs such as cocaine and heroin. For example, a survey sponsored by the Robert Wood Johnson Foundation concluded that cigarette use among young females was a good indicator of future drug use while early use of alcohol among males was a predictor of drug use later in life. Furthermore, 40 percent of those who began to drink before age 14 became dependent on alcohol, as opposed to 10 percent of those who started to drink at the age of 20 or later (Ericson 2001:1).

Correlates of Drug Use

Geographical

Historically, drug use and abuse have been associated with urban lifestyles. One reason is that drugs have often been associated with gangs and, as is seen in chapter 10, historically, juvenile gangs have been more common in urban areas than in suburbs or rural areas. Gangs have begun to develop in small towns and rural communities and drug use among youth has also spread outside the city environment. Surveys of juvenile drug use indicate that by the late 1980s, drug use among teenagers was as common, or more common, in rural communities as in larger cities. In 2000, the *National Household Survey on Drug Abuse* concluded that 18.2 percent of rural adolescents age 12–17 had tried drugs, compared with 18.8 percent of urban youth. Also in 2000, the Center on Addiction and Substance Abuse found that drug use among rural eighth graders was higher than among urban youngsters. Drugs included in this survey were marijuana, alcohol, and especially amphetamines, for which admitted rural eighth-grade use was *more than double* that of urban eighth graders. In 2003, a statewide survey of juvenile drug use in California found that rates of admitted use of any illegal drug at least once were 32 percent for both rural and urban youth, 34 percent among rural youth, 31 percent among urban juveniles for marijuana, and 39 percent (rural) versus 29 percent (urban) for alcohol (Ruiz et al. 2005:98).

Most of the data on adolescent drug use noted above has come from self-report surveys. Experts are not sure exactly what happened in the late 1980s to create the shift in balance of adolescent drug use from urban to rural areas, but the consistency of the conclusions from numerous national and statewide surveys suggests that the high rates of drug use among rural teens are real and must somehow be explained and understood if effective drug prevention and treatment programs are to be developed. Some studies of youth undergoing treatment for substance abuse and/or mental health problems indicate that illegal drug use is not more common among rural youth, although substance abuse is still a problem in rural areas. However, overall, it seems that drug use and abuse among juveniles should be a matter of concern for all citizens, not just parents and officials living in urban areas.

Social

In addition to geographical patterns of juvenile drug use, there are also patterns shaped by social factors such as age, gender, and race. For example, studies often show that those who begin using drugs at an *early age*, before adolescence, are at *greater risk* of continued drug use and of abusing drugs than those who first use drugs at a later age (Ericson 2001:1; Ruiz et al. 2005:100). Perhaps one reason for these age patterns is that younger users may be more likely to have other problems, such as mental health problems, or to come from environments where drugs are more available and drug use is more common. Adolescents who begin using drugs at a later age may more often only experiment with drug use, especially in a group or peer con-text. These differences are similar to developmental patterns of delinquency, such as the life-course persistent and adolescence-limited pathways discussed in chapter 5.

Besides age, there are *gender patterns* of drug use among juveniles. Research has shown that males usually report higher rates of almost all kinds of substance use (Moran et al. 2004:572). However, females more often than males experience *problems with drug use*, including mental health problems associated with drug use. Also, studies show that tobacco use among juve-nile females is a predictor of other drug use for young females, while alco-hol use among males is a predictor of other drug use for youthful males (Ericson 2001:1).

Another social variant for juvenile drug use is race. Studies often show that drug use and drug abuse are *lower among nonwhites*, especially African American youth, than among white juveniles. Moreover, African American youth are less likely to meet necessary dependence criteria for substance abuse treatment (Ruiz et al. 2005:100).

Explanations of Juvenile Drug Use

Explanations of juvenile drug use often parallel general explanations of delin-quency. However, the following discussion is about explanations specifically focused on juvenile drug use. The discussions are divided into three levels, starting with large, macro explanations, followed by social-psychological con-cepts, then personality factors.

Macro Explanations

Macro explanations of juvenile drug use maintain that the basic contribut-ing factor to such behavior lies in the large social structure or in some larger context, of which juveniles represent one part. In an excellent sociological discussion of the history and patterns of drug use in the United States, for example, James Hawdon makes a persuasive argument for the relationship between drug use and general patterns of societal development. Basically, Hawdon's argument is that with social development, or modernization, pat-terns of drug use become more similar across social categories, including age. Hawdon states, "More recently, in lesser-developed, or peripheral, nations, drug use remains highly gendered and limited to adults" (Hawdon 2005;233). Moreover, Hawdon hypothesizes that with modernization, emerging patterns of drug use are more related to *achieved statuses* than to *ascribed statuses*. That is, people are differentiated in terms of their drug use more by what they have accomplished and achieved in life, such as education, occupation, and income, than by what they were born with, such as age, race, or gender (Hawdon 2005:239–247).

Another macro-level explanation of juvenile drug use focuses on cohort size as an important contributor, especially with regard to marijuana use. For example, Mireille Jacobson (2004) argues that as the size of a birth cohort increases in number, the chances of drug use among individuals, including juveniles, in that cohort increase. Conversely, as the size of a youth cohort decreases, there are corresponding decreases in the number of youth who report using drugs, the number of youth who have been arrested for drug possession and sales, and even the street price of drugs. However, Jacobson concludes that the most important reason for the positive association between cohort size and drug use among youth is the increase of drug supplies when an age group is large. Related to the factor of supply and drug availability is the increased presence of drug users, distributors, and dealers at schools. The larger the group of drug users and sellers who appear on a school's campus, the less likely that any one person will be caught and arrested for drug use. Specifically, Jacobson states, in reference to marijuana use, "A teen's decision to use marijuana may be more directly affected by youth in the immediate vicinity" (p. 1492). This relationship between cohort size and its related effects is stronger than other important contributors, such as parental use of drugs, although part of Jacobson's argument is that large cohorts create more drug permissiveness, which is then handed down from one generation to another. This intergenerational inheritance, however, is magnified when the succeeding generation of youth is large, especially when a drug-using subculture emerges among youth (pp. 1487–1494).

Social-Psychological Factors

While macro factors help explain the availability and societal acceptance of drugs, these variables provide little explanation of how individuals or small groups of juveniles decide to use drugs and to continue using them. Another set of explanations for juvenile drug use is needed to help address this question. One such set of factors can be described as social psychological. Social-psychological variables focus on the interaction between a juvenile and his or her environment. These kinds of factors are exemplified by the social-development and social-process explanations of delinquency discussed in

chapters 5 and 6. In addition to these more general explanations of delinquency, some have suggested specific social-psychological precursors to juvenile drug use.

A common theme among social-psychological variables as contributors
to juvenile drug use is learning theory, or the idea that drug use is a learned
behavior (Triplett and Payne 2004). According to learning theory, behavior
is modeled after people we admire or with whom we associate, as discussed
in chapter 6 (see also Akers 1998). Drug use is often connected with learning
patterns among peers, friends, and associates of one's age. Learning theory
can also incorporate modeling behavior patterns as well as justifications for
behavior from any person or in any setting. One important feature of the
learning-theory approach to drug use is the inclusion of rewards and punishments as two primary factors in the decision not only to use drugs but also
to continue using drugs. Those who continue to use drugs are able to associate rewards, social and nonsocial, with using the drug rather than associating the negative consequences of such use (Triplett and Payne 2004:618–619).
Again, an important setting here is the definition of what the drug should do
and how it may enhance one's status in the community and/or among
friends. In addition, public perceptions of drugs and their effects may also
influence one's decision to use drugs (Hawdon 2005:250–259).

Consistent with a problem-solving, stress-reduction explanation of adolescent drug use is the connection between *expression of anger* and the use
of *avoidance as a method of coping* with stress and substance abuse. Studies
have shown that among incarcerated adolescents, outward expressions of
anger and the use of avoidance-coping behavior as a means to relieve or handle stress are significantly associated with substance abuse. However, both
reactions to stress are independently connected with drug use and are only
part of the overall explanation of adolescent drug use (Eftekhari et al. 2004).

Another factor related to learned patterns of drug use is the idea that
drug use is a *problem-solving* approach to difficulties in one's life. It has long
been known that people use drugs to relieve stress and pain in their lives,
but now this idea is being couched in terms of learning theory (Triplett and
Payne 2004). Problems for a juvenile can be of numerous kinds, including
the death of a family member, poor grades in school, violence and conflict
in the home, being bullied in school, early physical maturation—essentially
many of the issues raised in other chapters of this book (Triplett and Payne
2004:619–620). In many ways, this perspective is similar to Agnew's revised
or general strain theory of delinquency, discussed in chapter 6. Agnew's
argument is that youth are exposed to a variety of strains, primarily social-

psychological strains, many of which stem from their status as minors and students in society, and these strains are often handled by turning to delinquency. Although Agnew does not spend a lot of time analyzing drug use in relationship to general strains, others have, and the connection seems reasonable from both a strain and a learning perspective (Brezina 2000).

Earlier, in chapter 7, the issues of child abuse or maltreatment and its connection to general patterns of delinquency were discussed. Some have focused specifically on child abuse and its connection to drug use. One study, for example, surveyed 2,187 students in grades 10–12 in a rural county in Oregon and found significant associations among three kinds of abuse and admitted use of several types of drugs (Moran et al. 2004). Emotional, physical, and sexual abuse were all highly associated with tobacco and alcohol use as well as use of illicit drugs. Of the three kinds of abuse, emotional abuse had the lowest correlation with drug use, while a combination of physical and sexual abuse had the highest association. Although few gender differences in the patterns were observed, male youth seemed slightly more negatively affected by physical and sexual abuse, and females were more negatively affected by physical abuse (p. 572).

Personality Factors

Some feel the explanation of drug use can better be understood through analyzing the personalities of drug users. This explanation is part of the individualistic theories of delinquency discussed in chapter 4, only in this case, personality variables are being connected specifically with drug use. Investigations of drug users have typically characterized them as selfish, troubled youth who are using drugs for chemical highs. Howard Kaplan and his associates, for example, have conducted several analyses of longitudinal samples of youth to demonstrate that drug use and general patterns of delinquency among youth are, at least in part, a means to *boost low self-esteem* created by unhappy and negative experiences with peers and others (Kaplan 1978; Kaplan et al. 1986).

Others have noted that juvenile drug users tend to score higher on some personality scales than do non–drug users, such as Eysenck's scales on neuroticism and psychoticism (see chapter 4). However, often these studies use incarcerated populations of juvenile offenders (Sigurdsson and Gudjonsson 1996).

Psychological explanations of adolescent drug use are increasingly turning to a "problem-behavior" model that incorporates personal as well as social, or environmental, factors. Using a problem-behavior model, juvenile drug use is seen as part of a larger constellation of difficulties facing young people, including troubles at home, at school, and with peers, as well as individual difficulties such as learning and emotional problems (Jones and Heaven 1998; Zhang et al. 1997). Another way of expressing this approach to understanding teen drug use and delinquency is to describe youth as "at risk" of encountering behavioral, social, and legal problems as adolescents and beyond. The more problems youth have, the higher their "risk," and this includes the risk of drug use (Dryfoos 1990, 1998).

The inclusion of personal factors associated with drug use among a constellation of other problem or risk behaviors and situations is consistent with many contemporary psychological explanations of delinquency in general. However, just as with explanations of delinquency, this trend dilutes the identification of unique personality variables that clearly differentiate drug users from nonusers, especially in any kind of sequential pattern. Identifying unique personalities of youth who *will become* drug users or abusers may be difficult, just as such identification of potential delinquents in general has been difficult. Interestingly for personality explanations of substance abuse, a common conclusion in this literature is that the *most predictive factor in teen drug use is peer influence,* that is, teens tend to use drugs most with their friends. However, the selection of peers can also be influenced by the bond between parent and child, among other factors, and the kinds of values and behavior favored by parents can have important effects on the friends their children select during adolescence (Garnier and Stein 2002).

Since some researchers estimate that nearly 90 percent of juveniles have reportedly used a drug, including alcohol and tobacco (Eftekhari et al. 2004:1001), trying to establish unique personality patterns of drug users seems problematic at best. Rather, the more likely contribution of this approach to understanding juvenile drug users is to concentrate on drug abusers and those who maintain drug-using lifestyles for extended periods of time. In this sense, the approach would be similar to distinguishing between adolescence-limited and life-course persistent patterns of delinquency, as discussed in chapter 5, focusing on drug use in particular (see also Towberman 1994).

Drug Use and Delinquency

Within the problem-behavior model, drug use can be seen as either the beginning of more problems for youth later in life or as part of a larger set of deviant consequences of early entry into delinquent behavior. Juveniles in the juvenile justice system usually have a history of drug use and/or abuse. In the early 2000s, for example, of over 1.7 million juveniles adjudicated as delinquent, 60 percent were substance abusers (Watson 2004:211). In an extended analysis of risk factors for adolescents, Joy Dryfoos (1990:29–60) indicates that committing delinquent acts can have the short-term effect of drug use and a long-term impact of drug abuse, while drug use itself can lead to school dropout in the short term and criminal behavior in the long term. In other words, the relationship between drug use and delinquency is *interactional.* There is no clear, direct unidirectional path between early drug use and later delinquency, but both seem intertwined in a setting of social and personal problems. That is, early drug use predicts delinquency, and early involvement in delinquency predicts drug use later in a youth's life (Zhang et al. 1997).

Besides the relationship between general patterns of delinquency and drug use, researchers have been interested in the connection between drug use and sales and membership in *delinquent gangs* (see also chapter 10). While most studies of gangs show that gang members are frequent users of drugs, especially *marijuana* (Katz et al. 2005:60, 81), the literature is mixed. If self-report studies of gangs are used, the results often demonstrate that gang members not only use drugs but also sell them. However, studying gangs by observation methods or using arrest figures often shows little to no connection between gang membership and drug use or sales (Katz et al. 2005:59–61). Some argue that street gangs are too disorganized to set up and maintain consistent drug sales operations, at least for any extended period of time (Klein 1995:119–131; Delaney 2006:233–235). However, it is often suggested that individual gang members or cliques within gangs may be more into drug use and sales than the gang as a whole, and that is one reason why studies of gangs overall do not typically conclude that gangs, per se, are heavily into drug sales (Katz et al. 2005:59; Delaney 2006:230–231). Of course, some gangs do become more involved in drug sales than others, but the notion of "drug gangs" seems more hypothetical and stereotypical than real (Delaney 2006:229). Another hypothesis is that so-called drug gangs are typically composed of older, perhaps former gang members but not current, active members of juvenile street gangs (Klein 1995:131–135). Furthermore, drug-selling operations among *juvenile* gangs is done more for small profits needed to party and have fun than for long-term gain and increased drug sales (Delaney 2006:231). As Delaney states, "The vast majority of gangs are not drug traffickers" (p. 233).

Longitudinal studies of gangs, which are rare, suggest that gangs may attract youth who are at a high risk for drug use and dependence but that gang membership itself tends to increase the availability, justifications, and actual patterns of drug use and sales, and this effect may last a couple of years beyond gang membership (Thornberry et al. 2003:109–112; Katz et al. 2005: 64–65, 82–83). Sometimes, however, gangs will specifically force members out of the gang or deny drug users membership in the gang because of their drug use. The effects of drugs may make a gang member ineffective in terms of fighting or criminal activity, and thus unreliable (Delaney 2006:230).

Sometimes, of course, drug use, especially drug trafficking, can be tied to other crimes, especially violent criminal activity. Police reports commonly associate gang violence with drug use and sales. However, researchers suggest that gang violence is more often connected with other crimes or activities than drugs. There is little evidence to conclude that drug use or drug sales per se are associated with gang violence (Delaney 2006:236).

Treatment and Prevention of Drug Use among Juveniles

Treatment of drug users is often tailored to the individual situation of the user. Experimental drug use may well dissipate with age and new experiences. Drug use connected to gang membership would be more difficult to alter, given the circumstances of the user. Drug dependency might well be the most difficult form of use to alter because of the dependent nature of the user on the drug and the setting in which the drug use occurs. Consequently, identifying effective treatment strategies for all drug users is unrealistic, and any treatment option will have different expected outcomes for different styles and patterns of drug use (Checinski and Ghodse 2004). Overall, experts suggest that true recovery from addictive drugs is difficult to obtain. In part, the degree of success for drug treatment is affected by the type of drug used, the drug of choice. One review, for example, suggests that six months of treatment for alcoholism is effective for 40 to 70 percent of "patients," with effectiveness defined as a one-half reduction in use. In addition, six months of treatment for cocaine users is successful, or effective, for 50 to 60 percent of patients and 50 to 80 percent of opiate users (Ericson 2001).

Effectiveness of drug treatment can also be influenced by the motivation of the user, and this can be a difficult factor to overcome. The motivation of the patient can also be affected by the attitude of the therapist and the relationship developed between the therapist and the patient. The issue of motivation can be particularly difficult for those who are forced, in one way or another, to seek treatment within the criminal or juvenile justice system (Casselman 2004).

Drug Courts

Drug courts are one of the newer treatment strategies for substance abusers. Drug courts are often referred to as drug-*treatment* courts to emphasize the treatment focus of such programs. In the past, drug therapy and the criminal or juvenile justice systems were thought to be incompatible, or at least difficult to merge (Casselman 2004). In part, this view reflected the idea that treatment emphasized individual growth and change, while criminal justice concerns emphasized issues of custody and control. If a person's progress in terms of recovery from substance abuse put custody concerns at risk, there emerged serious issues of conflict with criminal justice priorities, which often made treatment difficult to continue.

In 1989, the first drug court was established in the Miami area, in part to overcome the difficulties thought to exist between treatment and criminal justice emphases, as well as to create a better system of dealing with drug offenders than simply locking them up for extended periods of time (Belenko 2001:5). In 1993, the first *juvenile* drug court was established in Key West, Florida (Belenko 2001:43). As of September 2005, there were 1,481 drug courts in all 50 states plus the District of Columbia, the Northern Mariana Islands, Puerto Rico, and Guam. Another 533 drug courts were being planned. Of the 1,481 existing drug courts, 388 were juvenile drug courts, 154 were family drug courts, and 13 were a combination of juvenile and family drug courts. Moreover, 127 juvenile, 91 family, and 2 combined drug courts were being planned as of that time (U.S. Department of Justice 2005).

Drug courts attempt to integrate treatment and judicial concerns in the effort to reduce drug use and crime as well as foster employment and stable families among their participants. While these programs may vary in some details, they all essentially operate according to ten principles:

1. Integration of drug treatment with criminal justice services and case processing
2. Use of a noncombative approach to case handling while maintaining the due process rights of participants

3. Placement of participants into the program as soon as possible in order to begin treatment
4. Provision of a range of treatments and services tailored to each participant
5. Use of random and frequent drug testing and monitoring of participants
6. Emphasis on coordination and information sharing among the members of the drug court team
7. Close judicial monitoring of each case
8. Assessments and evaluations of the effectiveness of the program
9. Provision of continuing education and updating of information for drug-court team members
10. Creation of partnerships and cooperation among treatment specialists, justice agencies, and local community agencies (National Drug Court Institute 1999:3–6)

Drug court programs essentially operate as *probation* programs with a special emphasis on close case monitoring and individualized substance abuse treatment. Participants are usually drug offenders with a record of arrests and convictions for crimes related to substance use and/or abuse. Participation is voluntary, although the alternative is a conviction and possible prison time. Participants are convicted (or found delinquent in juvenile court) of their offense by pleading guilty and then placed into the program. As indicated in the ten principles, participants are encouraged to apply for the program as soon as possible, which in practice often means within two or three weeks after they have been arrested. The programs are designed to last at least 12 months, although some extend to 18 months or longer. Successful participants—that is, those who "graduate" from the drug court—are given reduced sentences or may have their conviction dismissed entirely. Unsuccessful participants, those who leave the program or are forced out before graduation, face implementation of the sentence for the conviction, which may be imprisonment (Shoemaker and Toussaint 2003).

Drug court participation includes all of the usual rules associated with probation but includes random drug testing, regular appearances before the presiding judge, and close monitoring of all of the participant's daily activities, including family, school (for juveniles), and employment (for most). While participants are represented by an attorney before entering the drug court, defense attorneys are seldom seen at court appearances, and their role is limited while participants are in the program (National Drug Court Institute 2003).

Most drug courts operate according to phases, with decreased monitoring and supervision for each phase. For example, in phase one, participants may be required to submit to drug testing several times a week and to appear before the judge once a week. In phase three, the final phase before graduation, drug testing may decline to once a week and court appearances to once a month. Sanctions for failure to abide by the rules are usually graduated, beginning with additional urine screens or drug tests, to closer probation and/or judicial supervision, to reassignment to an earlier phase, to brief periods of incarceration, to eventual dismissal from the program (Shoemaker and Toussaint 2003).

One interesting feature of drug court programs is the development of a diverse, yet integrated team for each participant. Members include the judge, defense and prosecuting attorneys, probation officer, treatment specialists, counselors and school personnel (for juveniles), and others deemed important for a particular case. These teams meet regularly, usually before each scheduled court appearance, to discuss the particulars of the case, and they continue to meet as a whole or in selected groups until the participant finishes the program (Shoemaker and Toussaint 2003). While all members of this team are essential for a successful outcome, some argue that the *most significant member is the judge*, whose weekly or monthly presence in each case is something not usually seen in most juvenile or adult criminal cases (Marlowe et al. 2004).

Evaluations of drug courts generally find them to be successful (Belenko 2001; Gottfredson and Exum 2002; Shoemaker and McDonald 2003; Wilson et al. 2006). Most participants graduate, and those who do finish the program usually have lower rates of return to crime, or *recidivism*, fewer substance abuse problems, and higher rates of employment. In addition, evaluations of drug courts typically conclude that they are cost effective, meaning that it costs less to put an offender through a drug court than to incarcerate him or her. However, some studies show that drug courts are not effective or that the results are mixed (Miethe et al. 2000; Listwan et al. 2003).

Evaluations of juvenile drug courts are less common than those of adult drug courts, but evaluations that have been done generally conclude that these drug courts are also effective (Belenko 2001:43–47; Shoemaker and Toussaint 2003; Pitts 2006). Juvenile drug courts are somewhat more difficult to evaluate than adult courts, in part because juvenile drug courts often involve more personnel than do adult courts. As mentioned earlier, juvenile drug courts typically include counselors and school-based personnel, in contrast to adult courts. In addition, many juvenile drug courts employ multisystem therapy, or MST, as part of their treatment program, and MST usually involves inputs from different segments of the community, thus making a complete evaluation of the drug court more complicated (Randall et al. 2001).

Although most evaluations of drug courts conclude that they are effective in reducing substance abuse, crime, and unemployment, the true impact of the courts is not certain. For one thing, many studies do not use true comparison groups, involving participants and nonparticipants. In part, this lack of comparisons reflects judicial policies that do not favor randomized selection procedures for the purpose of evaluative research (Johnson and Wallace 2004). In addition, the true impact of treatment on the outcomes of participants is not clearly known (Randall et al. 2001; Shoemaker and McDonald 2003).

Another factor in evaluating drug courts is the issue of coercion. While drug courts operate on the basis of plea bargains and the maintenance of legal rights for participants, the fact remains that the alternative to a drug court experience is a conviction, likely accompanied by some period of confinement. Some maintain that *coerced treatment* is counterproductive, while others suggest that coerced treatment is not a hindrance to effective drug treatment. Satel (2000), for example, concludes that longer stays in treatment are more effective and that coerced "patients" stay in treatment programs longer than do noncoerced patients (p. 20). Others, however, argue that there is a continuum of coercion and that the impact of coercion on treatment effectiveness is dependent on a variety of circumstances, including patient motivation (Longshore et al. 2004).

Preventing Drug Use among Youth

Some argue that it is better to prevent drug use from occurring in the first place, as opposed to treating use and abuse patterns that have already been established. Some promising community-based youth drug prevention programs have been attempted in the past few years. These projects have often included parental involvement as part of the prevention effort. One such program is Preparing for the Drug Free Years (PDFY), which began in Seattle, Washington, in the late 1980s. PDFY is based on the idea that strong child–parent bonds are effective means for preventing adolescent drug use. Parental involvement is a vital and necessary part of this program. The goals of PDFY include showing parents how better to communicate with their children, reducing family conflicts, fostering better supervision and discipline patterns for children, and demonstrating clear goals and role models for children. The project in Seattle has been replicated in other communities, including rural communities, and with families of diverse backgrounds. Preliminary results indicate that the programs have been successful in reaching the goals of improving parent–child bonds and improving parent–child communication, which are praiseworthy accomplishments. In addition, children in these families have shown improved behavior patterns, although the specific impact of PDFY on drug use and/or abuse, short- or long-term, have not been established (Haggerty et al. 1999).

Another community-based juvenile drug prevention program has been implemented and tested in Baltimore. This program emphasizes drug counseling for adolescents and their parents. It focuses on African American adolescents who have been identified as being at risk of further involvement in drug and delinquency because of past deviant behaviors. Thus, one objective of the program is to reduce existing involvement with drugs rather than to prevent drug experimentation in the first place. Another feature of this program is the use of African American college students as mentors and role models, in a further effort to influence the youth away from a life of drug and crime. Preliminary results indicate the program is achieving its goals. Data analyses show lower rates of alcohol and other drug use and particularly lower rates of crime and delinquency one year after the treatment, especially for younger youth. A setback for the program, however, was the inability to significantly involve parents in the treatment sessions. Perhaps greater inclusion and participation of parents in the counseling of their children would yield more positive results, but that remains to be demonstrated (Hanlon et al. 2002).

A promising drug prevention program is Project Towards No Drug Abuse, Project TND (Sussman et al. 2004). Project TND is part of the Blueprint for Violence Prevention program located at the University of Colorado. Project TND is a drug prevention program based on the presentation of 12 sessions that include drug abuse awareness, listening and communication skills, making responsible choices in life, and thinking through the consequences of poor choices, including using drugs. Two sessions focus on tobacco and marijuana use. Each session is designed to be delivered to students in a regular classroom setting, lasting 40–50 minutes (Sussman et al. 2004:25–36). The program has been implemented and evaluated in three California school settings, including regular and alternative high schools, involving over 3,300 students, mostly from Latino and Anglo backgrounds. Results indicate that, compared with control groups, Project TND students in all three settings were less involved in "hard" drug use (including heroin, hallucinogens, and cocaine) one to two years after the program. The reduction in drug use ranged from 25 percent to 55 percent (for the two-year study). Reductions in alcohol, tobacco, and marijuana use were less consistent. In addition, experimental groups showed reductions in carrying weapons and crime victimization, compared with the control groups (Sussman et al. 2004:17, 23–45).

D.A.R.E. (Drug Abuse Resistance Education)

One of the more popular drug use prevention programs is D.A.R.E., or Drug Abuse Resistance Education. Begun in the 1980s in Los Angeles, D.A.R.E. is now offered in over 8,000 schools throughout the United States. Its budget has taken up 5 percent of the national monies allocated for the Drug Free Schools program. The basic premise of D.A.R.E. is to offer drug education classes, often through local police departments, to elementary-school students, usually fifth and sixth graders, with the goal of reducing drug use and abuse among these youth when they become adolescents. Classes are capped by the awarding of certificates and pledges by participants not to use drugs as they get older (Dryfoos 1990:158, 1998:162–3). According to D.A.R.E.'s Web site, www.dare.com/home/default.asp, each year educational programs are offered to over 26 million children in 75 percent of school districts in the United States and in 58 countries throughout the world.

Despite the consistent popularity of D.A.R.E., earlier evaluations of its success have not been very promising. The results of studies of the program often conclude that the program produces moderate positive effects, especially for alcohol and cigarette use, and more for males than for females. Analyses of several evaluations conclude that "graduates" are no less likely to become drug users or abusers than those who do not participate in the educational classes (Rosenbaum 2007). Furthermore, after the D.A.R.E. programs became popular and politically supported, reports of attempts to influence evaluations to produce more favorable results began to emerge (Dryfoos 1990:158, 1998:163; Lundman 2001:67–91).

In response to the criticisms and negative conclusions of the program's effectiveness, administrators of D.A.R.E. programs decided to revamp the curriculum. The Robert Wood Johnson Foundation awarded a five-year, $13.7 million grant to the University of Akron to assist D.A.R.E. officials with the design and evaluation of new course and educational material, highlighted by interactive and computerized instructional methods. The plan is to provide more opportunity for students to see and experience, via high-tech equipment, the impact of drugs on their health and safety. It will be interesting to see the results of this new approach to drug use prevention once they are available (www.dare.com/home/default.asp).

It is unrealistic to expect any one treatment or prevention program to have a truly significant impact on drug use and abuse among juveniles. Since drug use is often within a social setting and is affected by family and peer influences, it is reasonable to expect more significant results will be achieved with programs that focus on the social circles of juveniles and not just on the youth themselves (Dryfoos 1998:171–176). In addition, any intervention involving youth must be realistic and not judgmental or punitive. Youth who are encouraged to use drugs are already vulnerable and at risk for other harmful behavior patterns, so attempts to help them by demeaning them or using simplistic slogans are facing serious communication barriers from the start (Dryfoos 1990:168–171). Newer treatment and prevention strategies are employing these methods and ideas, which suggests the possibility for significant reductions in juvenile drug use and abuse in the future.

Summary

Juvenile drug use and abuse has been on the decline in recent years, but surveys still show that most youth admit to using drugs at least once in their lives by the time they are high-school seniors. Alcohol and cigarettes remain popular drugs among youth, but inhalants and OxyContin are becoming popular among youth today.

Research indicates that drug use among youth is primarily a social kind of behavior. Most often, youth are influenced by their peers in decisions to use drugs and in the kinds of drugs used. Of course, other factors play a role in juvenile drug use, such as parental attitudes and behavior patterns, but peer groups remain the single most important influence on juvenile drug use.

The relationship between drug use and delinquency is reciprocal, meaning that both influence each other. In one respect, drug use is illegal for juveniles in that most legal drugs, such as alcohol and tobacco, are restricted to adults and all illicit drug use is criminal, whether committed by adults or juveniles. However, using drugs is strongly correlated with overall patterns of delinquency. In addition, drug use is common among members of youth street gangs. Drug abuse and the selling of drugs, however, are not common among youth gangs. Some gangs have expelled or excluded people known to have drug problems. There are what some term "drug gangs," but these gangs are not always the same as youth gangs. Drug gangs tend to be more organized and consist of older members than typical youth gangs.

There are many explanations for juvenile drug use, but the more persuasive ones focus on patterns of social development and social connections between youth and their community, especially parents and peers. Treatment and prevention options are abundant. A newer treatment strategy that is effective is the drug court, which combines treatment and punishment in graded steps or phases. Juvenile drug courts have been in existence since 1992, and they have received positive evaluations. All juvenile drug courts incorporate team members from the juvenile justice system, the schools, and the community, which is one reason they are successful.

One of the more highly publicized juvenile drug prevention programs is D.A.R.E., or Drug Abuse Resistance Education. D.A.R.E. focuses on elementary students, usually grades five or six, and has existed for over 20 years. Evaluations of its effectiveness, however, are mixed. More recent evaluations have tended to conclude that the program does not work well in preventing drug use. However, D.A.R.E. has recently begun a new education program aimed at using modern means of instruction such as computers and high technology. D.A.R.E. supporters expect that these new methods will improve the effectiveness of the program, and evaluation research is now being conducted to determine whether this is the case.

Overall, however, truly effective drug treatment and prevention programs must be inclusive of community components and the wider social circles of youth. In addition, such programs must be realistic to youth and not appear as punitive or judgmental in order to improve effectiveness, and newer strategies appear to be incorporating these ideas into their programs.

References

Akers, Ronald
 1998   Social Learning and Social Structure: A General Theory of Crime and Deviance. Boston: Northeastern University Press.
Belenko, Steven
 2001   Research on Drug Courts: A Critical Review, 2001 Update. New York: National Center on Addiction and Substance Abuse at Columbia University.
Brezina, Timothy
 2000   Delinquent Problem-Solving: An Interpretive Framework for Criminological Theory and Research. Journal of Research in Crime and Delinquency 37:3–30.

Casselman, Joris
  2004   Motivation Enhancement in Clients Referred from the Criminal
          Justice System. *In* Drug Treatment: What Works? Philip Bean and
          Teresa Nemitz, eds. Pp. 236–241. New York: Routledge.
Checinski, Ken, and Hamid Ghodse
  2004   Types of Treatment for Types of Patients. *In* Drug Treatment: What
          Works? Philip Bean and Teresa Nemitz, eds. Pp. 31–57. New York:
          Routledge.
Delaney, Tim
  2006   American Street Gangs. Upper Saddle River, NJ: Pearson Prentice
          Hall.
Dryfoos, Joy G.
  1990   Adolescents at Risk: Prevalence and Prevention. New York: Oxford
          University Press.
  1998   Safe Passage: Making it Through Adolescence in a Risky Society.
          New York: Oxford University Press.
Eftekhari, Afsoon, Aaron P. Turner, and Mary E. Larimer
  2004   Anger Expression, Coping, and Substance Use in Adolescent
          Offenders. Addictive Behaviors 29:1001–1008.
Ericson, Nels
  2001   Substance Abuse: The Nation's Number One Health Problem.
          OJJDP Fact Sheet #17. Washington, DC: U.S. Department of Jus-
          tice, Office of Juvenile Justice and Delinquency Prevention.
Garnier, Helen E., and Judith A. Stein
  2002   An 18-Year Model of Family and Peer Effects on Adolescent Drug
          Use and Delinquency. Journal of Youth and Adolescence 31:45–56.
Gottfredson, Denise C., and M. Lyn Exum
  2002   The Baltimore City Drug Treatment Court: One-Year Results from
          a Randomized Study. Journal of Research in Crime and Delin-
          quency 39:337–356.
Haggerty, Kevin, Rick Kosterman, Richard F. Catalano, and J. David Hawkins
  1999   Preparing for the Drug Free Years. Juvenile Justice Bulletin. Wash-
          ington, DC: U.S. Department of Justice, Office of Juvenile Justice
          and Delinquency Prevention.
Hanlon, Thomas E., Richard W. Bateman, Betsy D. Simon, Kevin E. O'Grady,
and Steven B. Carswell
  2002   An Early Community-Based Intervention for the Prevention of Sub-
          stance Abuse and Other Delinquent Behavior. Journal of Youth and
          Adolescence 31:459–471.

Hawdon, James E.
    2005   Drug and Alcohol Consumption as Functions of Social Structures:
            A Cross-Cultural Sociology. Lewiston, NY: Edwin Mellen Press.
Jacobson, Mireille
    2004   Baby Booms and Drug Busts: Trends in Youth Drug Use in the
            United States, 1975–2000. The Quarterly Journal of Economics
            119:1481–1512.
Johnson, Charles Michael, and Shana Wallace
    2004   Critical Elements to Consider for Methodologically Sound Impact
            Evaluations of Drug Court Programs. National Drug Court Insti-
            tute Review 4:35–48.
Johnston, Lloyd D., Patrick M. O'Malley, Jerald G. Bachman, and John E.
Schulenberg
    2007   Monitoring the Future, National Results on Adolescent Drug Use:
            Overview of Key Findings, 2006. (NIH Publication No. 07-6202.)
            Bethesda, MD: National Institute on Drug Abuse.
Jones, Suzanne P. and Patrick C. Heaven
    1998   Psychosocial Correlates of Adolescent Drug-Taking Behaviour. Jour-
            nal of Adolescence 21:127–134.
Kaplan, Howard B.
    1978   Deviant Behavior and Self-Enhancement in Adolescence. Journal of
            Youth and Adolescence 7:253–277.
Kaplan, Howard B., Steven S. Martin, and Robert J. Johnson
    1986   Self-Rejection and the Explanation of Deviance: Specification of the
            Structure among Latent Constructs. American Journal of Sociology
            92:384–411.
Katz, Charles M., Vincent J. Webb, and Scott H. Decker
    2005   Using the Arrestee Drug Abuse Monitoring (ADAM) Program to
            Further Understand the Relationship between Drug Use and Gang
            Membership. Justice Quarterly 22:58–88.
Klein, Malcolm W.
    1995   The American Street Gang: Its Nature, Prevalence, and Control.
            New York: Oxford University Press.
Listwan, Shelley Johnson, Jody L. Sundt, Alexander M. Holsinger, and Edward
J. Latessa
    2003   The Effect of Drug Court Programming on Recidivism: The Cincin-
            nati Experience. Crime & Delinquency 49:389–411.

Longshore, Douglas, Michael L. Pendergast, and David Farabee
    2004   Coerced Treatment for Drug-Using Criminal Offenders. *In* Drug Treatment: What Works? Philip Bean and Teresa Nemitz, eds. Pp. 110–122. New York: Routledge.

Lundman, Richard J.
    2001   Prevention and Control of Juvenile Delinquency. 3rd edition. New York: Oxford University Press.

Marlowe, Douglas B., David S. Festinger, and Patricia A. Lee
    2004   The Judge Is a Key Component of Drug Court. Drug Court Review 4:1–34.

Miethe, Terance D., Hong Lu, and Erin Reese
    2000   Reintegrative Shaming and Recidivism Risks in Drug Courts: Explanations for Some Unexpected Findings. Crime & Delinquency 46:522–541.

Moran, Patricia B., Sam Vuchinich, and Nancy K. Hall
    2004   Associations between Types of Maltreatment and Substance Abuse during Adolescence. Child Abuse & Neglect 28:565–574.

National Drug Court Institute
    1999   Development and Implementation of Drug Court Systems. Alexandria, VA: National Drug Court Institute.
    2003   Critical Issues for Defense Attorneys in Drug Court. Alexandria, VA: National Drug Court Institute.

Pitts, Wayne J.
    2006   Measuring Recidivism in a Juvenile Drug Court: Systematic Outcome Study of a Juvenile Drug Court Using Historical Information. The Southwest Journal of Criminal Justice 3:17–34.

Randall, Jeff, Colleen A. Halliday-Boykins, Phillippe B. Cunningham, and Scott W. Henggeler
    2001   Integrating Evidence-Based Substance Abuse Treatment into Juvenile Drug Courts: Implications for Outcomes. National Drug Court Institute Review 3:89–115.

Rosenbaum, Dennis P.
    2007   Just Say No to D.A.R.E. Criminology & Public Policy 6:815–824.

Ruiz, Bridget S., Sally J. Stevens, Katherine McKnight, Susan H. Godley, and Patricia Shane
    2005   Treatment Issues and Outcomes for Juvenile-Justice-Involved Youth from Rural and Nonrural Areas. Prison Journal 85:97–121.

Satel, Sally L.
    2000   Drug Treatment: The Case for Coercion. National Drug Court Insti-
            tute Review 3:1–56.
Shoemaker, Donald J., and Danielle McDonald
    2003   An Evaluation of the Drug Court of the Twenty-third Judicial Cir-
            cuit Court of Virginia: A Response to the War on Drugs. Criminal
            Law Bulletin 39:569–583.
Shoemaker, Donald J., and Jeffrey Toussaint
    2003   Outcome Evaluation of the Rappahannock Regional Adult and
            Juvenile Drug Treatment Court. Blacksburg: Virginia Polytechnic
            Institute and State University.
Sigurdsson, Jon F., and Gisli H. Gudjonsson
    1996   Psychological Characteristics of Juvenile Alcohol and Drug Users.
            Journal of Adolescence 19:121–126.
Sussman, Steve, Luanne Rohrbach, and Sharon Mihalic
    2004   Blueprints for Violence Prevention: Project Towards No Drug
            Abuse. Boulder, CO: Institute of Behavioral Science, University of
            Colorado, Boulder, Colorado.
Thornberry, Terence P., Marvin D. Krohn, Alan J. Lizotte, Carolyn A. Smith, and
Kimberly Tobin
    2003   Gangs and Delinquency in Developmental Perspective. Cambridge,
            England: Cambridge University Press.
Towberman, Donna B.
    1994   Psychosocial Antecedents of Chronic Delinquency. In Young Vic-
            tims, Young Offenders. Nathaniel J. Pallone, ed. Pp. 151–164. New
            York: Haworth Press.
Triplett, Ruth and Brian Payne
    2004   Problem Solving as Reinforcement in Adolescent Drug Use: Impli-
            cations for Theory and Policy. Journal of Criminal Justice
            32:617–630.
U.S. Department of Justice
    2005   In the Spotlight: Drug Courts. Electronic document, http://www
            .ncjrs.gov/spotlight/drug_courts/Summary.html, accessed October
            17, 2005.
Watson, Donnie W.
    2004   Juvenile Offender Comprehensive Reentry Substance Abuse Treat-
            ment. Journal of Correctional Education 55:211–224.

Wilson, David B., Ojmarrh Mitchell, and Doris L. MacKenzie

    2006   A Systematic Review of Drug Court Effects on Recidivism. Journal of Experimental Criminology 2:459–487.

Zhang, Lening, William F. Wieczorek, and John W. Welte

    1997   The Impact of Age of Onset of Substance Abuse on Delinquency. Journal of Research in Crime and Delinquency 34:253–268.

JUVENILE GANGS

THE TOPIC of gangs often conjures images of street thugs or hoodlums, intent on wreaking havoc and destruction around them, with no regard for the rights and safety of others. This stereotypical image, of course, has some basis in reality, for some gangs and gang members do engage in this kind of predatory behavior. However, there are several other types of youth gangs, as will be discussed below. One objective of this chapter is to identify different kinds of juvenile gangs and their commitment to crime and delinquency. *Delinquent*, or *criminal*, gangs clearly do have an objective of making money or getting by in their communities by committing crimes of theft and/or violence. However, not all gangs are as criminal, and some may be considered *social* gangs in that their members interact with one another much like members of a social club or a clique. Some gangs may be seen as *violent* in that their behavior and criminal patterns are oriented toward violence and the ends that violence is thought to gain. In this case, violence is not just fighting or conflict over territory, but lethal, criminal violence, such as rape, assault, and murder. It is often the case, however, that no matter what the specific organization or goal of a gang may be, participation in gang life and activity increases the delinquent and criminal behavior of its members (Thornberry et al. 1993; Thornberry et al. 2003:chapter 6).

Juvenile gangs are defined differently by research investigators, law enforcement specialists, and newspaper investigators. Most often, gangs are defined according to suspected criminal behavior and organization, that is, gangs are thought of as being organized for criminal enterprises. This view is described by some as a "law enforcement perspective" of gangs (Shelden et al. 2004:20). However, as mentioned above and discussed below, not all gangs are organized for criminal behavior. Sometimes gang members may act on their own and not as a part of gang behavior to commit a crime (Shelden et al. 2004:21–22).

Sociologically, a gang is defined according to the characteristics and attitudes of its membership. One of the first sociological definitions of gangs came from Frederick Thrasher in a study of gangs in Chicago in the 1920s. Thrasher considered gangs to be conflict (although not always criminal) groups that tended to develop in *interstitial* areas of a city, that is, areas in between or near more stable, developed sections of a city. Specifically,

> The gang is an interstitial group originally formed spontaneously, and then integrated through conflict. It is characterized by the following types of behavior: meeting face to face, milling, movement through space as a unit, conflict, and planning. The result of this collective behavior is the development of tradition, unreflective internal structure, *esprit de corps*, solidarity, morale, group awareness, and attachment to a local territory. (Thrasher 1927:57)

Gangs are often defined as *peer groups*, that is, groups consisting of members who share similar social characteristics such as gender, social class, age, and ethnicity. Most gang members are male and from working- or lower-class backgrounds, although there are also all-female and mixed-gender gangs as well as middle-class gangs, as will be discussed below. In addition, gang members typically range in age from 12 or 13 to late adolescence, although, again, some gangs consist of members who are younger or older. Contemporary gangs are often composed of young people in their early twenties (McGloin 2005:608). Gang members also typically come from the same ethnic background. However, the ethnic background of gang members in the 21st century is much different from the background of gang members 100 years ago.

In addition to sharing similar socioeconomic characteristics, observers argue that gang members also *identify* with the gang and express such identifications through displays of certain styles and colors of clothing, hand gestures, and the gang name on their clothing. This kind of display is called *representing* and will be discussed later in this chapter.

Juvenile gangs have been around a long time, at least going back to the 14th and 15th centuries in Europe and the 19th century in America. The first youth gang in America is thought to be a gang called the Forty Thieves, which developed in New York City in the 1820s. Gangs began to proliferate from the 1830s to the end of the 19th century. Even before the Civil War, some cities, such as Philadelphia, claimed that they were being "plagued" by gangs. By the end of the 19th century, some of the more notorious gangs in New York City, such as the Bowery Boys, the Pug-Uglies, and the Dusters were located in the Five Points area of the city, although it is not clear just how many of these gangs were actually "youth" gangs (Shelden et al. 2004:1–2).

Today juvenile gangs exist in all parts of the country, mainly in cities but also in suburban and rural communities (Shelden et al. 2004:32–36; Howell and Egley 2005; McGloin 2005:608). There have been many studies of gangs and analyses of their behavior. The next section of this chapter discusses several of these studies, from the first one conducted in the 1920s in Chicago to the recent national surveys of gangs and gang membership.

Studies of Youth Gangs

Thrasher's Study of Gangs in Chicago

While numerous newspaper investigative stories and government reports discussed gang problems in America's cities throughout the 19th century, it was not until the 1920s that detailed sociological studies of gangs began to appear. The first of these was conducted by Frederick Thrasher, published in a 1927 book titled *The Gang: A Study of 1313 Gangs in Chicago*. Thrasher conducted a qualitative observation analysis of gangs in Chicago over a period of seven years, mostly in the 1920s. As part of his research, Thrasher observed the gangs in their natural settings, or *turfs*, and interviewed some of their members. This is an important study because it was the first to detail gang life and development, even if confined mostly to one city. Many of Thrasher's observations and conclusions can serve as a kind of baseline set of information with which to compare more contemporary studies of gangs. Thrasher's findings included the following:

1. Most gangs were relatively small in size; while the range was from 3 to 2,000 members, most gangs consisted of 20 or fewer members (p. 319).

2. While many gangs were composed of youths and adults, most were youth gangs, and the typical age range was 11–17, followed by 16–25 (pp. 72–75). Often, if population size were large enough, younger members of a neighborhood would assume names and identifications related to gangs with older members, such as "midgets," "juniors," and "seniors" (p. 76).

3. While many gangs were composed of members of mixed nationalities, most gangs were of European descent, mainly Polish, Italian, and Irish (less than 8 percent were African American) (pp. 191–193). Gang members usually came from poor immigrant backgrounds (p. 191).

4. Most gangs were all male. "Gangs composed entirely of females are exceedingly rare" (p. 28), and the usual role of females in a gang was either to be "tomboys" and act as males or to serve as sources of support, often sexual in nature, for male gang members (pp. 221–247).

5. While fighting was common among gangs, gang members were not often in possession of guns, and violence did not often result in death or serious injury. There was one report of a gang capturing a rival gang member, cutting him with a penknife, and then rubbing salt in the wounds (p. 18). However, Thrasher did record several fatalities of youth as a result of gang warfare, not only in Chicago but also in other cities, such as St. Louis and New York City.

6. Drug use was not common among gangs. In fact, there is virtually no mention of the word *drugs*, generally or specifically, in the entire volume. The only "stimulants" identified were tobacco and alcohol (pp. 100–101).

7. There was a kind of "natural history" to gang development. A gang usually began as a social clique or play group, that is, as a social gang, which had little involvement in crime or delinquency except for minor offenses; then, if the gang encountered perceived discrimination or unfair treatment and labeling at the hands of others in the neighborhood, other gang and nongang youth, school authorities, police, business owners, and so on, it developed into a delinquency-oriented gang with an *esprit de corps* among its members and a distrust of outsiders (pp. 45–57). This last point is interesting because Thrasher's study allowed for a longitudinal perspective on gang growth and development. Conflicts with others in the community often resulted in stronger group loyalty among gang members and created a kind of "outlaw" mentality within the gang. As Thrasher states, "It often happens that boys expelled either as individuals or as a group from some formal organization are drawn together to form a gang. They have become outlaws, and it is the

old story of Robin Hood against the state" (Thrasher 1927:34). In addition, he observed, "Whether the gang always fights openly as a unit or not, it usually seems to carry on warfare against its enemies. It is as a result of collective action and particularly of conflict that the gang, especially in its solidified form, develops morale" (pp. 54–55).

8. Gangs were involved extensively in racketeering and organized crime activities as well as in local politics. However, most of this involvement occurred among older or adult gang members (pp. 409–486).

Whyte's Study of Gangs in Boston

In the 1930s, William Foote Whyte conducted another detailed study of gangs, only in this research, the focus of attention was on one gang, the "Norton Street Gang," and again, in one city, Boston, or "Eastern City" (Whyte 1955). Whyte's methodology was participant observation. He not only observed the activities of the gang in its natural setting but also lived in the same neighborhood as the gang and participated with the gang in its daily activities. According to Whyte, it took nearly two years of groundwork before he actually started the study of the gang, and then only because he was able to enlist the support, and eventually friendship, of its leader, "Doc" (Whyte 1955:283–298).

Whyte's study of the Italian gang occurred in the 1930s, during the Great Depression. One consequence of this time period for gang structures was the presence of more older gang members than was typical a decade earlier. Of the 13 members of the Norton Street Gang, none was younger than 20, and Doc was 29 (pp. 13–14). In addition, Whyte revealed a rather strong gang structure, with an identifiable, although changing, power structure. This power or status structure seemed to hold up in recreational activities, such as bowling, a major pastime of the gang (pp. 13–35).

One significant feature of the Norton Street Gang was the relative absence of violence among the gang members or between them and other gangs. One reason for this lack of violence is because the gang members, in particular Doc, had established their fighting prowess as youth. Doc was the leader of a youth gang, and this leadership continued into adulthood and the eventual formation of the Norton Street Gang (p. 3–12).

Another significant feature of the gang studied by Whyte was the absence of females in the gang structure. Dating and interaction with girls, especially members of a social club named the Aphrodite Club, was common among the members of the gang, and marriage was one reason for exiting the gang, but otherwise, women had little role in the gang's activities (pp. 25–51).

The Norton Street Gang was also active in local politics and in the numbers rackets and other forms of gambling, again a feature of the gang probably related to the older ages of its members (pp. 147–252). Again, drugs, other than alcohol and tobacco, were not mentioned in this study.

Whyte's analysis of the Norton Street Gang revealed some similarities with the gangs Thrasher studied a decade earlier, such as lack of drugs and lethal violence, immigrant and low socioeconomic status, and relative absence of women in the gang structure. However, the gang members Whyte studied were older than typical youth gang members, and their gang seemed more organized and more involved in politics than the gangs Thrasher observed.

Yablonsky's Study of Violent Gangs in New York City

For some reason, the issue of gang violence became an important concern in America's large cities after World War II. In New York, for example, the mayor commissioned a study of gang violence, violence that was more vicious than heretofore seen and relatively random, that is, not aimed at rival gangs or their individual members or at enemies of gangs. The commission concluded that, indeed, the city was experiencing a growth in "bopping gangs," or gangs that committed random violence on others. One suggested solution to the reduction of these gangs was the development of a social-work position called the *detached street worker*. The detached street worker was assigned to an office in the neighborhoods of the gangs, in part to serve as a go-between or mediator among the gangs, and also to help alert authorities of impending gang conflicts and fights, or rumbles (Yablonsky 1970:166–167, 282–290). As a detached street worker, Lewis Yablonsky worked with the gangs in the streets of New York for several years. From the advantage of working with street gangs, Yablonsky conducted an analysis of street gangs, especially violent gangs, from 1953 to1958 (Yablonsky 1970:8).

Yablonsky classified gangs into three categories: social, delinquent, and violent (p. 192). *Social gangs* are composed of "tough youths" who hang out because the gang serves to further their interests in social activities. The members may engage in delinquent activities, but not often violent crimes or serious criminal activities. They tend to have a long life, and sometimes their members become lifelong friends, forming adult clubs or social gangs.

They are not typically seen as a threat to the community, and their members are emotionally stable and healthy.

Delinquent gangs are composed of youth who organize to commit crimes, albeit mostly property crimes. They also wish to have social relationships as members of the gang, but their interest in social activities is secondary to their criminal pursuits. Delinquent gangs are tightly structured around their members. They are good examples of primary groups (see chapter 6, "Social Process Theories"). They also have a degree of permanence, but they are not as long lasting as social gangs, and their memberships tend to break up when their members are arrested and/or put into jail or prison. Like members of the social gang, the members of a delinquent gang are considered emotionally stable and commit violence when it is needed for profit making, but not as an end in itself.

Violent gangs represent the most serious threat to public safety of all types of gangs. As mentioned earlier, violent gangs are relatively recent in the history of gangs in the United States. While many gangs have been involved in fighting and other types of conflicts since gangs have been observed and studied, the violent gangs that Yablonsky worked with and studied were thought to be more vicious than those in the past. The members of violent gangs are considered emotionally immature and focused on violence for violence's sake. That is, these gang members are constantly looking for fights and opportunities to engage in wanton violence. According to Yablonsky, "Violence is the theme around which all activities center" (p. 190).

A central feature of the violent gang, aside from its inclination toward violence, was the instability of its structure and leadership. According to Yablonsky, violent gang members are psychologically unstable, especially their leaders. Leadership of these gangs is based on physical prowess and assumed bravery, and any sign of weakness in these areas is a reason for the swift departure of the individual from a position of leadership. Challenges to positions of leadership are constant, fueled by members' own presumed superiorities and abilities (pp.190–195). As Yablonsky put it, "A considerable amount of the gang boys' time is spent in sounding, a pattern of needling, ridiculing, or fighting with other members; consequently a great deal of their 'social' participation is of a negative nature. . . . There is a continual verbal and sometimes physical attack and defense going on, regardless of the subject" (p. 191). In essence, the members, again especially the leaders, of a violent gang are considered to have a *sociopathic* or *psychopathic personality* (p. 200–201; see chapter 4). However, this kind of personality is considered as having a learned origin as opposed to being inborn.

The sociopathic personality characteristic of a violent gang member is thought to be created by living and growing up in a "disorganized slum," the background of the violent gang members studied by Yablonsky (p. 268).

Significantly related to the instability of the violent gang members' personalities is the structure, or lack thereof, of the gang itself. According to Yablonsky, the violent gang is better conceived as a *near group*. A near group is a pseudogroup, taking on the appearance of a group (through such items as a name and identification, specific membership, and the appearance of cohesiveness, structure, and interaction) but lacking in permanence or direction that would qualify it as a "cohesive group." In terms of structure, the near group rests midway on a continuum of organization, between a mob and other gangs, such as social and delinquent gangs. The result is a kind of "paranoid psuedocommunity" that can never assume real stability and structure because of the psychological instability of its members (pp. 265–277).

Surveys of Gangs: The 1970s to the Present

Miller's National Survey of Gangs in the 1970s

While concerns over gang violence seemed high in the late 1940s through the 1950s and early 1960s, during the early to mid-1960s not much was heard about gangs in the United States. Media accounts of gangs, especially gang violence, declined. Scholarly research on youth gangs also became negligible (W. Miller 1975:1–2; W. Miller 2001:3). Whatever the reason for this decline in attention to gangs, the notions that gangs were not a problem and that gang violence was a thing of the past were changed during the 1970s. During that decade, renewed evidence of gang development, especially violent gang activity, and renewed interest in gangs began to appear. In the mid-1970s, the government commissioned a national study of gangs conducted by Walter Miller. Miller's study represented a change in gang research methodology from conducting in-depth, often longitudinal, observational studies of gangs in local communities to embarking on large, national studies of gangs using a cross-sectional design, or looking at the subject at one point in time. While localized, in-depth studies of gangs still appear, much of the current evidence about gangs comes from national surveys.

Miller's research utilized interviews with key figures thought to be knowledgeable of gang activity in 15 cities. Most of the information came from interviews with police, government, juvenile court, and school officials in 12 cities which these respondents considered to have at least a moderate gang problem at that time. More study and detailed interviews were conducted with officials in six cities where officials were nearly unanimous in seeing gangs as a problem in their city: Chicago, Detroit, Los Angeles, New York, Philadelphia, and San Francisco (W. Miller 1975:3–19).

Among the conclusions of Miller's study were the following (pp. 21–53):

1. Most gang members were between 12 and 22 years of age, with a modal age of 16–17. However, in all six cities, satellite gangs composed of younger-aged youth were found. A common term for these younger gangs was "midgets," or "pee-wees."

2. Most gangs were all male. The most common form of gang participation for females was as an "auxiliary" for male gangs in a neighborhood. Roughly 90 percent of all gangs were all male. For example, in the Bronx and Queens areas of New York City, only six all-female gangs were found. The auxiliary status of the female gangs was partially exemplified by the names of these units, such as "Cripettes" or "Lady Disciples."

3. Most gangs were homogeneous with respect to race and ethnicity. A significant point of this characteristic of gangs was that while most gangs were composed of youth from lower- and working-class immigrant backgrounds, the specific race and/or nationality of gang members had changed significantly between the late 19th century and the 1970s. In Miller's study the majority of known gangs were composed of youth from African American and Hispanic backgrounds. As Miller stated, "The social observers of New York City in the 1880s, when the city was swarming with Irish gangs, would be incredulous had they been told that within the century the police would be hard put to locate a single Irish gang in the five boroughs of the city" (p. 27).

4. Most gang members were arrested for violent crimes at a much higher rate than the general adolescent population, but random attacks on innocent people were not becoming more common. Also, violence in the 1970s had become more *lethal* than in previous decades, in part because gang members now had access to firearms more than in the past.

5. An important change in the context of gang violence from the 1950s to the 1970s was the increased use of violence on school grounds. Previously, gangs rarely carried out gang activity on school property. But in the 1970s, Miller found that that had changed. Again, using his words, "To a degree never before reported, gang members have 'territorialized' the school buildings and their environments—making claims of 'ownership' of particular classrooms, gyms, cafeterias, sports

facilities, and the like—in some cases applying ownership claims to the entire school" (p. 52).

Klein's National Survey of Gangs in the 1990s

In the early 1990s, Malcolm Klein conducted a national survey of gangs in the United States, along with more detailed analyses of gangs in Los Angeles. Klein's methodology for the national survey consisted of phone interviews with police officials in 261 "notable gang cities." Most of the police contacts interviewed by Klein were gang officers (Klein 1995a:32).

Some of the conclusions of Klein's study are as follows:

1. As opposed to previous studies, gangs in the 1990s were composed of older youth (reminiscent of Whyte's study of gangs in the 1930s). Klein suggested calling gangs "youth gangs" or "street gangs" as opposed to juvenile gangs to highlight the increasing ages of gang members. According to Klein's data, "Nowadays, a surprising number of gang members are in their mid- and late twenties, some in their thirties, and a few in their forties" (p. 22). However, the "average" age of a gang member in this study was "probably around 20 years of age," with a typical range of 12–30 years of age.

2. As an addition to the natural history concept, Klein observed that a "tipping point" for the transformation of a social or "play" group to a street gang consists of (1) identification of the gang members with a *criminal orientation*—not necessarily a criminal way of life, but an inclination toward crime and delinquency, and (2) belief of the gang members that their *group is a gang*, set apart from others, which is in large measure a reflection of how gang members perceive that others in the community think of them (pp. 29–30).

3. Gangs tended to exist primarily in large cities. Of gang officers interviewed in cities of 100,000 people or more, 94 percent said there were street gangs in their cities. This figure is compared with another survey conducted by Klein in which officials in several small towns indicated the presence of gangs, but not to the same degree as those from large cities (pp. 31–32).

4. Gangs have increased in number during the past few decades. Of the 261 cities surveyed, 139 experienced gangs for the first time since 1985 (p. 32). The increase is somewhat related to gang "migration," but Klein observes that most migrations have occurred from gangs in Chicago or

Los Angeles, and even then, the migrations have been largely limited to nearby cities and locations. As he states, "Most cities are experiencing indigenous street gangs—homegrowns, not imports" (p. 31). Furthermore, most cities reported having a few gangs. Although metropolitan Los Angeles reported over 1,000 gangs, 60 percent of the cities surveyed indicated the presence of ten or fewer gangs (p. 33).

5. Most gangs were all male. All-female gangs were estimated to represent from 0 to 30 percent of gangs in the cities surveyed.

6. Most gangs were homogeneous with regard to race and ethnicity. Most were either Hispanic or African American, but an increase in Asian gangs was noted in some cities (p. 29). Interestingly, on this issue Klein makes the point that the predominance of specific racial or ethnic populations among gangs in a city depends largely on the patterns of immigration for that city. For example, African American gangs predominated in Chicago before Hispanic gangs, but the reverse situation occurred in Los Angeles. In Hawaii, Asian, especially Pacific Islander, gangs have been predominant for years (pp. 105–109).

7. Most gangs were loosely structured, but some had stronger organization than others. Related to this issue were the estimated sizes of gangs, which ranged from 20–40 to over 4,000, although the vast majority of police estimates placed gang sizes at under 500. Part of the reason for this wide range of gang sizes comes from the existence of satellite gangs in a neighborhood, "wannabes" and "midgets," as well as various forms of membership, including "hard-core," "fringe," "broader-core," and other types of member status (pp. 33–36, 100–104). Klein did note that large supergangs or parent gangs seemed to be on the decline, and smaller, autonomous gangs appeared to be increasing, but the evidence for this conclusion was not strong. It does appear likely, however, that reported gang sizes of 4,000 or 5,000 members are either exaggerated or atypical.

8. While most gangs and gang members used drugs, including alcohol, drug dealing and migration patterns related to drug selling and distribution were not common among the gangs. One major reason for the lack of organized drug dealing by gangs was their relative lack of structure or organization to conduct such business (pp. 36, 119–135). To be sure, some gang members deal drugs, and new drug-selling gangs have appeared in the past few decades. But to characterize the typical street gang as a drug-dealing gang seems unwarranted at this point. As Klein put it, "Drug distribution requires good organization, and most street gangs are not well organized" (p. 127).

9. Gangs not only tend to emerge in urban locations and they typically arise in areas of the city considered "underclass," lacking in educational and/or employment opportunities and characterized by "persistent poverty" (pp. 193–195). This point is also stressed in Jankowski's study of gangs in New York, Boston, and Los Angeles (Jankowski 1991:21–34).

National Youth Gang Survey, 1998

In the mid 1990s, the National Youth Gang Center began to collect data on gangs. The surveys have been based on responses to questionnaires distributed to thousands of police and sheriff's departments in (1) cities of 25,000 people or more, (2) small cities from 2,500 to 24,999 people, (3) suburban areas, and (4) rural communities (National Youth Gang Center 2000:2–3). Most of the data collected in these surveys are estimates provided by police department respondents. The results of the third survey, conducted in 1998, are as follows:

1. Large cities, those with a population of 250,000 or more, had the highest average number of gangs (83) and gang members (4,465). Small cities, with less than 10,000 people, had the smallest averages of gangs (3) and gang members (41) (p. 14).
2. The average age of gang members was in the range 18–24, which represented an increase in average age from 1996. In all four types of location, three-fourths of gang members were between 15 and 24 years old (p. 15–17).
3. Less than 2 percent of all gangs were considered female dominated. Eighty-three percent of the areas surveyed indicated no presence of female-dominated gangs. Overall, females represented 8 percent of all gang members in the nation, with the largest estimates of female gang members reported in smaller locations as opposed to large cities (pp. 18–19).
4. The largest percentage of gang members were of Hispanic background (46 percent), followed by African American background (34 percent). Caucasians (12 percent) and Asians (6 percent) were the least represented racial and ethnic backgrounds of gang members (p. 20). These differences were maintained in all types of locations except one. In small towns, with 2,500–24,999 people, Caucasians represented 30 percent of all gang members (p. 21). Similar to the point raised by Klein, racial and ethnic backgrounds of gang members also differed by region. Caucasians were much more prevalent in small towns and rural communi-

ties located in the Midwest and Northeast, while Hispanics were more dominant in any type of location in the West. Asians were most prevalent (12 percent) in large Northeastern cities and small cities in the South (11 percent) (p. 23).

5. Gang members were more involved in drug sales (24 percent) than in any other type of crime. The kind of crime gang members were least involved with was robbery (3 percent) (p. 28).

Miller's Analysis of Gang Locations, Based on Surveys and Studies, 1970–1998

Results of the first three national gang surveys have been analyzed and compared with other gang studies in a report on gang *locations* by Walter Miller (2001). Miller utilized a variety of sources to prepare his report, including youth gang surveys based largely on reports from local police and other authorities, media reports, participation in conferences on youth gangs, academic studies of gangs, and examination of "routine" police reports on gangs (p. A-1). A summary of Miller's findings includes the following (p. 2):

1. By the end of the 1990s, all 50 states reported some kind of "gang problem," compared with 19 states reporting gang problems in the 1970s.
2. By 1998, a total of 2,547 cities had reported a gang problem, compared with 270 cities in the 1970s.
3. Between the 1970s and the late 1990s, smaller cities (less than 10,000 population), especially in southern states, experienced gang problems at a greater rate of increase than larger cities.
4. The two states with the largest number of new gangs in their cities between 1970 and 1998 were California and Illinois, followed by Texas and Florida (p. 60).
5. Gang proliferation between 1970 and 1998 tended to occur in smaller communities (between 10,000 and 50,000 population) as opposed to large cities. However, this growth in gangs was not directly the result of gang member migration, although such migration did sometimes occur (pp. 44 and 65; see also Maxson 1998).

Summary of Youth Gang Surveys, 2002–2005

The National Youth Gang Center has published an analysis of the national youth gang surveys from 2002–2005. This analysis includes comparisons of data from 1996 to 2005. Some of the conclusions of this analysis are as follows (National Youth Gang Center 2007):

1. In 2004, 29 percent of those areas responding to the survey reported a youth gang "problem."
2. The average estimated number of youth gangs from 1996 to 2005 was about 25,000. However, large cities still have the majority of gangs. For example, 17.6 percent of larger cities reported having at least 30 gangs, while no rural area reported having 30 gangs or more.
3. In 2004, most jurisdictions reported that less than 25 percent of the gangs in their areas had migrated from other localities. The "homegrown" nature of youth gangs was most prevalent in large cities and rural areas.
4. The average estimate number of gang members from 1996 to 2005 was 750,000. Dividing the number of gangs into the number of gang members yields an average of 30 gang members per gang. However, 18.5 percent of large cities and 10.6 percent of suburban counties report having gangs with more than 1,000 members.
5. Large cities and suburban areas report having more adult gangs than youth gangs, but the reverse is true for smaller cities and rural communities. This distribution of gangs by age has remained constant for ten years.
6. Over 90 percent of gang members are male. However, small cities and rural communities report having higher percentages of female gang members than do larger cities and suburban areas. For example, 31.7 percent of rural areas reported that at least half of their gangs had female members, compared with 20.6 percent of large cities.
7. Nearly 80 percent of gang members are of minority status, specifically Hispanic and African American, and this figure remained unchanged from 1996 to 2005. However, newer gangs are reported to have more Caucasian and other racial compositions than older gangs. Such gang members are usually found in areas where gangs are newly formed, such as small towns and rural areas, or among new gangs in large cities.

Summary of Gang Studies

The studies and surveys of gangs reveal several common characteristics of gangs and their members:

1. Gangs tend to form in interstitial areas of cities, and urban areas are most often where gangs are found.

2. Gangs tend to be relatively small in size, typically averaging about 30 members, although some gangs, called "supergangs" (Shelden et al. 2004:45–46), claim to have over 1,000 members.

3. Street gangs with criminal orientations will often emerge from play groups or cliques because of negative reactions to their activities by members of the community.

4. Some gangs are found in small towns and rural areas, but these tend to be short lived, partly because not enough potential gang members live in rural areas for a long-standing gang culture to form (Klein 1995a:198–199; Howell and Egley 2005:1).

5. Gangs can be specialized, but drug-dealing gangs tend to be rare.

6. Often, satellite gangs will emerge in a neighborhood, composed of "midgets" or younger juveniles who are influenced by older gang members.

7. Gangs tend to be loosely organized, operating much like primary groups, but gang organization can vary.

8. Gang violence started to become a problem in the late 1940s and remains a problem for society today.

9. Most gang members are male, and the typical role of female gangs is as an auxiliary to male gangs.

10. Most gang members are 15–24 years of age, although the ages of gang members tend to increase during times of economic hardship, and in general, gang members today are older than gang members in previous decades.

11. Most gang members are from lower-income and ethnic minority backgrounds, although the specific ethnic backgrounds of gang members change over time and from region to region to reflect specific patterns of immigration;

12. Gangs became more numerous in the 1970s through the 1990s but have leveled off in the 2000s. However, gang problems are thought to be primarily rooted in local conditions as opposed to being a product of gang "migration."

MS-13—A "New" Gang Problem?

All of the more recent gang surveys address the issue of gang violence. Most conclude that violence is a major concern of communities and the youth gangs that develop in cities and other locations. Some, such as Miller, suggest that gang violence is no more common today than it was in the 1950s, but only more lethal (see the discussion of Miller's 1975 survey above). Gang violence often spurs public attention and calls for tougher gang laws, as happened in Virginia in the early 2000s. According to police reports and other accounts, a gang known as "MS-13," or Mara Salvatrucha, has spread from the West Coast to the East Coast, particularly in northern Virginia and metropolitan Washington, DC. Some maintain that an emerging center of MS-13 activity on the East Coast is Charlotte, North Carolina (Delaney 2006:178). This gang is reportedly composed of youth and young adults primarily from El Salvador. Its origin in the United States is thought to be in Los Angeles, particularly the 13th Street section of Los Angeles, during the early 1980s. Many Salvadoran refugees fled to Los Angeles from El Salvador as a result of that country's civil war in the 1970s. The Salvadoran youths living in that section of Los Angeles referred to themselves as *la mara loca*, or "the crazy neighborhood," and later became identified as *mara Salvatruchass stoners, mara Salvatrucha*, the "Salvadoran neighborhood," or MS. The name *13* came from the street location (Delaney 2006:175–176). This gang has developed a particular reputation for violence and has been connected with machete mutilations and stabbing and shooting deaths in the northern Virginia region in the mid 2000s. One death involved a teenage girl, Brenda Paz, who was reputedly an informant and federal witness against the MS-13 gang in northern Virginia. She was found stabbed to death in July 2003. According to some police investigators, MS-13 is responsible for ten murders in northern Virginia and 90 percent of the gang crimes committed in Fairfax County, Virginia. It is estimated that the greater Washington, DC, area contains 5,000–6,000 members of MS-13, with 1,500 living in Fairfax County (Roanoke Times 2004; Zimmerman 2004).

Gangs such as the MS-13 represent a "new" kind of threat to communities that have not experienced gang problems until now. In the case of this gang, its reputed violence and large size have unsettled community members even more. Another issue with this gang, and one which may portend a new view of gangs, is the reputed illegal immigrant status of its membership. As a result of the published accounts of the gang's reputed size and use of violence and the assumed illegal entry status of its membership, Virginia has established new laws that focus on gang-related violence and immigration issues. For instance, one new law allows authorities to keep a suspect in jail for up to 72 hours if he or she has been previously convicted of a felony, been deported, and returned to America illegally (Zimmerman 2004; Roanoke Times 2004).

The word *reputed* is used in this discussion because not much is really known about this gang, its membership, or its inner workings. The illustration of the MS-13 is used here to highlight the continued concern about gang violence and its spread to cities and communities that have not had much of a problem with gangs in the past. It is also used to indicate the readiness of people to turn to repressive methods, or suppression, to handle gangs and gang violence, even when not much is known about the gangs in an area or those who are really responsible for the actions attributed to the gangs.

Gang Identification

While gangs may share many common characteristics, as indicated above, gangs dominated by members from specific ethnic or racial backgrounds are thought to have certain characteristics, especially with respect to criminal behavior. Before describing gang identifications, it should be noted that these are general characteristics that may not apply to a specific gang. In addition, by discussing criminal behavior patterns of gangs, it should not be concluded that street gangs are always committing criminal acts. While it is true that being in a gang will likely increase a young person's involvement in criminal behavior, most of the studies discussed earlier suggest that criminal activity is only one part of a gang's lifestyle and occupies less of their time than just hanging out. Since crime carries a lot of public attention and concern, the criminal behavior of a gang sometimes is used to categorize all of the gang's behaviors and motivations, and this can easily become stereotypical of the gang (Klein 1995a: 28–29).

Representing

Gang members often associate membership in a gang with a sense of belonging and identification with a group, or "set," of people who are thought (by the gang member) to be respected and protective. One way to establish identification with one's group and to be set apart form all others is through open expressions of group membership. These kinds of outward presentations are called "representing" (Shelden et al. 2004:22) Representing can be manifested through the wearing of colors, such as blue for Crips and red for Bloods, wearing certain clothing, such as bandannas, floppy hats, baggy pants, and earrings, "talking smack" through street-coded language and gestures, using hand signals, and creating graffiti (Jankowski 1991:83–84; Klein 1995a: 30; Shelden et al., 2004:54).

In the late 1970s, Chicago prison gangs reportedly organized into two dominant groups or "nations," People and Folks (Shelden et al. 2004:45–46). Some contend that representations and graffiti from these two groups now constitute the majority of gang identifications in the country (New River Valley Community Services 2004).

Graffiti and Hand Gestures

Gang members commonly display their gang memberships and identifications through written messages on walls and public buildings (graffiti) and hand gestures or signals, which can be presented or flashed in any public setting. According to some police intelligence, these public displays of membership and identification can be divided into People and Folk nations. For example, People gangs are associated with the left direction and a five-pointed star, while Folk gangs are represented by the right direction and a six-pointed star. People gangs are depicted by a downward pitchfork, while the Folk nation is associated with an upward pitchfork (New River Valley Community Services 2004). A summary of these signs is presented in table 10.1.

While not all gangs can be so neatly divided into these two categories, many can be, and the presentation of two different nation's gangs in a sin-

TABLE 10.1 Gang Nation Representations

People	Folk
Left	Right
Red Color	Blue Color
Five-Pointed Star	Six-Pointed Star
Downward Pitchfork	Upward Pitchfork
Dog Paws	
Examples:	*Examples:*
Latin Kings	Gangster Disciples
Vice Lords	Black Disciples
Bloods	Crips

Sources: New River Valley Community Services 2004; Shelden et al. 2004:102.

gle area can be the sign of existing or impending trouble between and among street gangs.

Another Look at Female Gangs

It has already been mentioned that most street gangs are composed of males. Current research still depicts independent female gangs at around 10 percent of all youth gangs (Curry and Decker 2003:109; Maxson and Whitlock 2002:21; J. Miller 2002:177–180). In earlier studies of gangs, females have often been classified as peripheral members of male gangs or as members of female gangs that were auxiliary to male gangs. Some have argued that this perception of female gangs is sexist and becoming outdated (Campbell 1984). For example, in a study of gangs in St. Louis and Cleveland, Jody Miller maintains that female gang members did not primarily become involved with gangs because they had boyfriends in a gang. Most of the girls in the gangs studied by Miller were attracted to the gang because they were abused in their homes, they knew relatives who were in a gang, and/or they lived in low-income neighborhoods where the presence of gangs was a visible reminder of ways to get out of what seemed like hard economic conditions and depressing lifestyles. In many ways, the gang offered a girl a chance to "be somebody" (J. Miller 2001:35–63). The issue of physical and sexual abuse of female delinquents, including gang members, has also been discussed at length by others (Moore 1991:chapter 6; Moore and Hagedorn 2001; Chesney-Lind and Pasko 2004:chapters 2 and 3; Chesney-Lind and Shelden 2004:chapters 3 and 4).

Stereotypic assessments of female gangs and gang members may have been reinforced by earlier studies, which tended to focus on male gang members and *their* perceptions of the roles of females in gang life (Moore and Hagedorn 2001:1–2; Curry and Decker 2003:114–122). However, more recent studies of female gangs and gang members are able to present the role of females in gangs from the perspectives of the female gang members themselves. These studies tend to challenge or at least modify the traditional view that female gang members are little more than objects and targets of male gang members in a neighborhood.

However, attempts of females to "be somebody" and to be released from the threat of physical violence and abuse can sometimes drive young women to join gangs, especially mixed-sex gangs, where the relationship of female gang members to male counterparts can be one of dependence, similar to the stereotype of female gangs from years past. Often, the victimized girl will

turn to male gangs and desired membership in such gangs as a form of protection (J. Miller 2001:155–159; Curry and Decker 2003:129–135). However,
these relationships often result in further victimization of females by males,
and female gang members can become sexual tools and objects for male
gang members (J. Miller 2001:chapter 7; Chesney-Lind and Shelden
2004:86–90). A significant feature of this kind of abusive situation between
male and female gang members is the "sexing in" initiation ritual some male
gang members engage in with females who wish to join a gang. Sexing in
means the prospective female must engage in sexual relations with all or
most of the male gang members before being accepted as a member of the
gang. Sometimes, the sexing in practice is a trick, and the girl thus treated
realizes she is not a member of the gang after all. Also, other female gang
members, who might have been beaten or physically coerced into joining a
gang, might look down upon a girl who participated in sexing in as a condition of gang membership (Miller 2001:171–176). However, that the practice occurs, and never its reciprocal, where males are "sexed into" a gang by
females, exemplifies the potential for sexual abuse of females at the hands
of male gang members.

In many ways, female gang member characteristics are similar to that
of male gang members. They tend to come from impoverished and minority backgrounds and from neighborhoods where gangs exist. They also tend
to have difficulties in school and negative attitudes toward schoolwork and
the value of an education for their future (Chesney-Lind and Shelden
2004:chapter 4). Female gang members also typically have low attachments
to family members or at least difficulties in the home. However, as mentioned earlier, these family difficulties stem from abusive situations, sexual
and physical, more often than for male gang members. In addition, female
gangs tend to have structures with leadership roles, definite physical boundaries or turfs, and identifications symbolized by colors and signs (J. Miller
2001:chapters 4 and 5).

As with male gang members, being involved in gangs also increases the
delinquency of females. However, most studies of female gangs indicate that
female gang members are less violent and less involved with dealing drugs
than are male gang members, although they are much more involved in
these activities than are nongang females (J. Miller 2001:37, chapter 6; Chesney-Lind and Shelden 2004:chapter 4). For example, Miller reports that
while the majority of the female gang members she studied committed some
serious acts of crime, such as fighting, carry concealed weapons, and selling
drugs such as marijuana and crack cocaine, the most common admitted

offenses were smoking marijuana and skipping class, and gang members were much more likely to admit committing offenses than were nongang girls (pp. 124–125).

Overall, the emerging picture of a female gang in the 21st century is of a gang becoming more independent of male gangs but still connected with males for protection and identity. While some studies suggest that female gangs are increasing, many studies suggest the proportion remains around 10 percent of all youth gangs. Female gang members are definitely involved in serious crimes, including fighting and other kinds of violence, but they more often commit status and drug-using offenses. Female gang members tend to share similar characteristics with male gang members, but they come from abusive homes, especially physically and sexually abusive, more than do males. The abuse of females in mixed-sex gangs often continues, as exemplified by the practice of "sexing in" females as initiations for gang entrance. Modern studies of female gangs differ from previous ones in that female gangs are becoming more the focus of research, rather than an afterthought. Consequently, knowledge and detailed information on female gangs is becoming more available, which will help to continue sharpening our understanding of female crime and delinquency within a gang context.

Why Do Youth Join Gangs?

The question of why a gang is attractive to youth can be addressed in two parts: (1) why are there such gangs in the first place, and (2) why are youth attracted to such gangs wherever they exist? The answer to the first question is based on structural and sociological concepts.

Structural Factors

One sociological explanation for the existence of gangs is social disorganization theory, developed by Clifford Shaw and Henry McKay in the 1930s and 1940s. *Social disorganization* is the lack of effective institutional controls on the youth in a community or the inability of the leaders of a community to meet its needs and problems (Shoemaker 2005:82). According to Shaw and McKay, social disorganization occurs when a neighborhood or community undergoes rapid transition in terms of population movement, including immigration, and/or economic change (Shaw and McKay 1942; Shoemaker 2005:83). Social disorganization can create weakened social bonds for youth in a community, leaving them vulnerable to the attractions of deviant forces and groups in a neighborhood.

In their studies of gangs and delinquency in Chicago and other cities, Shaw and McKay concluded that delinquency rates were higher in the center parts, or zones, of a city than in the outlying areas. In particular, delinquency rates were highest in the central business district and the zone in transition, both of which were located in or near the central city (Shaw and McKay 1942, 1969). Gangs were also prevalent in these areas. The presence of gangs and the lack of organized activities for youth, plus weakened social bonds between youth and institutions such as the family, school, and church, made gang life more attractive to the youth living in these areas. Gangs usually develop as play groups, as Thrasher's earlier study of gangs in Chicago revealed, but they often become a substitute for the institutional bonds lacking in a youth's life, as has been discussed in this chapter. They can become oppositional and delinquent prone when community representatives, such as school officials, police officers, store owners, and adults in general, begin to label them as troublemakers and delinquent youth. However, the major impetus for gang attraction, according to social disorganization theory, is the absence of constructive forces and institutional controls in a young person's life, absences that a youth comes to feel can be occupied by the gang.

A similar structural argument for gangs is the "urban underclass" explanation. The *urban underclass* is a term coined by William Julius Wilson to describe inner-city life in Chicago (1987), but it has been adopted to explain gang development in cities throughout America (Jankowski 1991:22–23; Klein 1995a:193–197). A central feature of the urban underclass is "persistent and pervasive poverty" (Klein 1995a:192). Persistent poverty, that is, poverty that seems to recur generation after generation, can engender hopelessness and a structural situation that leads to fewer resources and attractions to conventional life pursuits. Tax bases decline, resulting in fewer services and less school funding. Manufacturing jobs and people with higher educations and incomes move out of the inner city to suburban locations. The inner cities become dominated by service-oriented jobs and racial and ethnic segregation. Gangs develop in part to fill the voids left by the economic and social declines from poverty (Klein 1995a:194–195). In effect, they become the avenue of upward mobility, or at least the perception of mobility, for young people living in this situation. As mentioned earlier, gang members are becoming older, and this explanation of gangs would predict that to happen, as legitimate opportunities for education and employment become harder to obtain.

Studies continue to document the importance of neighborhood characteristics in the explanation of crime and delinquency, including delinquent behavior not connected with gangs. The Moving to Opportunity (MTO) study reported in Kling and colleagues (2005) and discussed in chapter 7 demonstrates the impact of neighborhood characteristics on delinquency. The Project on Human Development in Chicago Neighborhoods (PHDCN) is a longitudinal study of over 6,000 youth and 9,000 adult residents living in 80 Chicago neighborhoods characterized by physical deterioration and social disorganization. These youth and their parents/caregivers were interviewed from 1995–2001. In addition, researchers observed social interaction and behavior patterns in these neighborhoods. Reports from these interviews have appeared from 1997 to the present. These analyses document the impact that neighborhood characteristics, including poverty and social disorganization, have on delinquency. One earlier analysis by Sampson and others (1997), for example, indicated that disorganized neighborhoods are characterized by a lack of *collective efficacy*. Collective efficacy refers to the expectation that neighbors share common values, goals, and concerns over the welfare of their youth and that these neighbors would intervene in a situation involving crime and delinquency among the youth in an area. Sampson et al. (1997) conclude that a lack of collective efficacy is associated with higher rates of crime and delinquency. Another study by Sampson et al. (2005) concluded that neighborhood characteristics were more important than ethnicity and marital status in the explanation of self-reported violence among youth. Other studies from the PHDCN series are discussed in Liberman (2007).

Related to the themes of social disorganization and urban underclass is the concept of *differential opportunity*. Differential opportunity occurs when a significant segment of the population, such as the lower class, are less able to take advantage of educational opportunities and legitimate avenues of employment (Cloward and Ohlin 1960). Crime and delinquency, therefore, become the accepted means of achieving success, at least economic success, for some lower- and working-class youth. Differential opportunity is similar to social disorganization and the urban underclass, but it does not focus on persistent poverty, and it describes societal conditions more generally, although the impact of less opportunity is magnified in low-income areas, especially in cities. This idea was introduced as an explanation of crime and deviance in general by Robert Merton and was associated with a societal condition of *anomie*, or structured normlessness in society (Merton 1957:chapters 4 and 5). The importance of anomie and differential opportunity as explanations of delinquency, gang related or not, is the assumption that poverty by itself is inadequate to explain criminality without considering the cultural values of a society. As Merton explains, crime becomes acceptable when the culture extols economic success but offers limited avenues for achieving it legitimately for a large number of people, again, such as those in the lower class (Merton 1957:146).

The notion of differential opportunity was used to explain gang development by Richard Cloward and Lloyd Ohlin in their analysis of gangs (1960). Cloward and Ohlin argue that gangs are specialized, similar to what Yablosnky maintains, but using a different conceptualization. According to Cloward and Ohlin, gang members come from lower- and working-class backgrounds, but the types of gangs that develop depend on the organization of the neighborhoods in which the gangs appear. Their contribution to an understanding of gang development is that *opportunities to commit crime are not evenly distributed* but depend on opportunities afforded by neighborhood structure and characteristics. They maintain that there are three types of gangs: *criminal, conflict,* and *retreatist* (Cloward and Ohlin 1960:chapters 6 and 7). A criminal gang is organized around crimes of theft. It tends to develop in neighborhoods in which criminal organization exists, exemplified by the presence of organized crime. Its members are not seriously disturbed psychologically, but they have limited opportunities, or at least perceived limits, for success and advancement through legitimate activities. Consequently, the members of the gang turn to illegitimate means of success, again exemplified by adult criminal figures living in the neighborhood.

A conflict gang emerges in neighborhoods where there is an absence of adult organization. In these areas, gang youth are left to express anger, resentment, and general youthful indulgences with no respected adult supervision. Thus, disagreements and conflicts are often settled through violent means.

In either type of neighborhood, members of former gangs sometimes merge to form another kind of gang, a retreatist gang. Retreatist gangs are focused on the use and sale of drugs. They have left or been dismissed from another gang, partially because of their drug use. In effect, they become social dropouts or, in the words of Cloward and Ohlin, "double failures," in that they have not only failed to develop a successful life through conformist means, such as education, but they have also failed as successful gang members (Cloward and Ohlin 1960:179–184).

Another structural explanation of gang development comes from Albert Cohen, who theorizes that working- and lower-class gangs develop from a collection of youth who find themselves in a position of wanting to achieve success by middle-class standards, but not being able to do so through legitimate means (Cohen 1955). According to Cohen, middle-class values emphasize such things as property ownership, punctuality, ability to communicate through writing and reading, planning ahead and being ambitious, and control of physical aggression. Furthermore, these values are not only learned at home but are also embodied in the school system, through teachers and school administrators (chapter 4). Since class values are taught at home and since middle-class values and standards are emphasized in school (and school attendance is compulsory in every state at least to the age of 16 or so), lower-class youth, especially male youth, are using a *middle-class measuring rod* by which to compare their progress and achievements, particularly within the school setting, and by doing so, they often come up short.

While virtually all lower-class youth are in this situation, some are able to work their way out of it and become successful despite their surroundings and background. These youth are referred to as "college boys," a term adapted from Whyte's study of gangs in Boston. College boys have adopted the middle-class standards by which all youth are measured, and they tend to do well at it. They may have superior intellect and/or good educational role models provided by parents, other relatives, or teachers. College boys aspire to succeed and become upwardly mobile within the middle-class system and are not good candidates for delinquency (Cohen 1955:104–119).

A more typical response of the working-class boy to the problem of adjusting to middle-class standards is to become the "corner boy," another term adopted from the work of Whyte. The corner-boy response is a type of accommodation to the situation. This person may or may not become criminal or a member of a gang, but he will likely remain conformist for the most part but not particularly upwardly mobile (Cohen 1955:104–119, 131).

The last response of the lower- or working-class youth to this situation is the "delinquent solution," or by implication, becoming the "delinquent boy" (chapter 5). The delinquent boy is characterized by "non-utilitarian, malicious, and negativistic" behavior (p. 25). This person and the gang with which he associates are full of anger and resentment toward middle-class society. It is as if the delinquent boy has developed a "reaction formation" in which he targets for hatred and spite the very things he may want but cannot achieve, that is, acceptance, achievement, and respect by middle-class standards as expressed through the school system (pp. 132–133). The rules of society not to be followed they are to be "flouted" (p. 28). School attendance and work are not to be respected but degraded (the practice of some delinquents to break into a school and defecate on a teacher's desk is an example of this attitude). Classmates are to be terrorized and harassed at playgrounds and in gymnasia. Stealing and vandalism are not done for profit but often "for the hell of it" (p. 26). In effect, the world of the middle-class value system is to be "turned on its head" (p. 28). Of course, violence and aggression are included in the delinquent boy's attitudes and behavior.

Cohen's argument is couched in terms of conflicts of class values, expressly highlighted within the school system. Another class-value-based explanation of gangs is offered by Walter Miller, who also maintains that gang life is dominated by a conflict between middle-class and lower-class values. However, Miller's argument is not that gang delinquents are full of hatred and resentment toward middle-class society. Rather, he suggests that gang youth, again especially boys, are merely acting according to the value system that surrounds their everyday life, the "lower-class value system" (Miller 1958). These values are expressed as "focal concerns." According to Miller, lower-class lifestyles are influenced by six focal concerns in particular: *trouble, toughness, smartness, excitement, fate,* and *autonomy.* Trouble refers to being involved with the police or courts and, for males, difficulties associated with drinking. Toughness is connected with the attitude that to be a man is to be physically tough and brave. Smartness refers to street smarts, not book learning. Excitement is associated with partying and the emotional highs generated from drinking and using drugs as well as sexual relationships. Fate means to believe one's future is out of one's hands. Things are left to fate or chance. Autonomy is opposite to fate in that it refers to the value of being independent, being "one's own man," and not having to take anything from anyone.

Collectively, these six focal concerns can lead one into a life of crime or contacts with the juvenile or criminal justice systems just by going along with what has been learned in growing up, not necessarily because of resentment or hatred of middle-class society. In effect, the lower-class lifestyle has in many ways become criminalized by middle-class-dominated laws and systems of justice. However, Miller contends that lower-class lifestyles are often characterized by the absence of the father in the home. Consequently, young males gravitate to the gang in part to seek male companionship and leadership, that is, masculine roles that are missing in their lives. According to Miller's observations of gang members, gang youth, including leaders, are often stable and characterized by leadership qualities, not hotheads or psychopaths as Yablonsky and Cohen would argue. That they have become involved with gang life is a part of their cultural value system, not internalized conflict with society.

Another cultural explanation of gangs posits that gangs tend to form because their members share common cultural conflicts created by language and cultural differences between their social environment and the background of their parents (Sellin 1938). In this case, the differences in culture between teens and their parents are augmented by definite cultural differences between the sending, or immigrant, country, and the host country (the United States). This explanation fits squarely with the immigrant background of many gang youth, as has already been discussed. However, research on this theory suggests that the real conflicts for immigrant youth tend to occur with second-generation immigrants, who experience conflicts between their parents' ways of living and that of their American classmates. These studies also indicate that delinquency, not necessarily gang delinquency, tends to increase with cultural assimilation of immigrants into American society, a finding consistent with the theory (Smith 1937; Young 1967; Sheu 1986:chapter 5; Wong 1997).

Structural explanations of gangs tend to come from the experiences of previous generations, prompting the concern that they are no longer relevant to today's gangs. However, some of these explanations, such as social disorganization theory, have modern counterparts, such as the urban underclass concept. In addition, many of the concepts in these explanations still have a ring of truth to them when analyzed in accordance with the characteristics of gangs and gang members from current research. Gangs still typically develop in urban areas and the interstitial areas of the city. Gangs are also still dominated by male youth who often come from minority backgrounds. Gang members still tend to have weakened social bonds with the family and school. Thus, in many ways, the traditional structural explanations of gangs have merit for understanding gangs in modern society.

However, despite the utility of structural explanations of gangs, some important shortcomings should be noted. For example, studies of gangs have not systematically followed the categories provided by theorists such as Cloward and Ohlin or Yablonsky. One study of gangs, for example, divided criminal gangs into "racket" and theft gangs, drawing attention to the more specific role of organized adult criminal activity on the shape and focus of youth gangs (Spergel 1964; see also Short and Strodtbeck 1965). In addition, studies of gangs have failed to identify a specific drug or retreatist gang as described by Cloward and Ohlin (Shoemaker 2005:124–138). While drug use is common in gangs and some gangs are heavily into selling drugs, a gang composed of double failures and dropouts whose lives are organized around using and selling drugs has been hard to locate. Thus, gang specialization does occur, but not always in predicted ways. While some, such as Cohen and Klein, contend that gang specialization is weak, it is likely the case that gangs do sometimes become specialized, such as with gangs that do deal in drugs, "entrepreneurial gangs" (Klein 1995a:131). Even here, there is controversy concerning exactly how entrepreneurial street gangs can be and whether differences between drug gangs and street gangs are too significant to put them into the same category. Drug gang members, for example, are thought to be older than typical street gang members. The gangs tend to be smaller in size and more cohesive than street gangs, as well as more into the business of selling drugs (Klein 1995a:132). While almost all street gangs engage in some type of violence, there are some gangs that have a stronger inclination toward violence, such as that associated with the MS-13 gangs.

A second difficulty with the structural explanations of gangs is the admitted fact that many, if not most, of youth living in structured situations of inequality or limited opportunity for legitimate advancement do not become involved with gangs (Klein 1995a:79). Shaw and McKay's data, for example, indicated that in the areas with high rates of delinquency, less than one-third of the juvenile residents had a court record of delinquency (Shoemaker 2005:91), and it can be assumed that fewer than this number were involved with gangs. In Miller's analysis of female gang and nongang members in St. Louis and Columbus, Ohio, there were clear indications that many of the girls living in conditions of poverty or economic stress or in areas where gangs existed chose not to join gangs as a way out of their difficulties (J. Miller 2001:38–62).

A third problem with structural explanations of gangs is their common assumption that structural conditions primarily, if not exclusively, affect those in lower- or working-class areas. This assumption seems based on the existence of official data at the times these explanations were developed, and as shown in chapter 3, official data on crime and delinquency often implicate the predominance of those from lower- and working-class backgrounds. However, since the 1950s, sociologists have been keenly aware of the existence of middle-class crime and delinquency. This point was also raised in chapter 3, and there have been several useful publications detailing the existence of *middle-class delinquency* since the 1960s (for example, Vaz 1967; Wooden and Blazak 2001). Some, such as Cohen (1955:157–159) and Bohlke (1967), attempt to explain the existence of middle-class delinquency by suggesting that middle-class delinquents come from homes where lower- and working-class values are still predominant, but this explanation has not been supported.

Information on middle-class *gangs* is even more limited than data on middle-class delinquency in general. We know that such gangs exist. The discussion of William Chambliss's (1973) research on a middle-class gang called the "Saints," in chapter 12, is one example of research on middle-class gangs. In that discussion, the motivation for the behavior of the Saints seemed to be boredom, but Chambliss did not provide much information on this topic. Wooden and Blazak (2001) also give an account of middle-class gangs, but not much detail is provided, and often their discussion blurs the distinction between social class and "youth culture." In those cases where middle-class gangs have clearly been identified, not much is provided in terms of why these kids join gangs. One former female member of a suburban high-school gang gives a clue to the kind of behavior committed by these youth: "They were like a nonviolent gang. They had a full initiation ceremony to become a Byrd, and the quest was for sex" (Wooden and Blazak 2001:59). A type of middle-class gang that specializes in graffiti and vandalism is called a "tagger" gang, crew, or posse. While some feel original taggers are not true street gangs (Klein 1995a:210), it is clear that some taggers have become "tag-bangers" and involved with crimes of theft and violence (Klein 1995a: 208–212; Wooden and Blazak 2001:117–128). Again, however, not much is known about these youth groups or the processes of changing from a tagging crew to a tag-banging street gang. Whatever the motivations or prevalence of middle-class gangs, their existence is real and must be accounted for in ways that do not focus on structured inequalities that characterize lower- and working-class lifestyles.

Psychological and Personal Reasons for Joining a Gang

While sociological factors play an important role in the explanation of why gangs exist, individual and personal factors seem to better explain why youth join the gangs that do exist. As discussed earlier, gang researchers have often referred to gang members in psychological terms, although these attributes have not been used to explain why a person joined a gang in the first place. Some have described gang members in terms of psychological pathology, such as sociopathic personality (Yablonsky), being negative, malicious, and hedonistic (Cohen), or being conflicted (Sellin), while others, such as Miller, have suggested that gang members are psychologically normal. Some prefer to identify particular *personal characteristics*, which are much like personalities, that tend to encourage membership and involvement in gangs. According to

Jankowski, for example, gang members can be described as having a "*defiant individualism*" characteristic. In addition, gang members are socially isolated, self-reliant, wary, and competitive (Jankowski 1991:23–28).

The personality characteristics attributed to gang members are often conflicting, a point made clear in Miller's analysis of focal concerns. Part of the differences in assumed personality characteristics of gang members may come from the often-reported existence of different types of "members," from core members, to fringe members, to "wannabes," as has been noted (Klein 1995a:57–62). Studies of gangs do not always clearly differentiate personality characteristics of fringe members, but core members are often described in terms of more psychological problems, such as noted by Yablonsky. Whatever the real personality profile of gang members may be, it is usually suggested that potential members think being in a gang can facilitate the personality and make a person comfortable, maybe a leader, in a group whereas before, he or she was not accepted in conventional group settings.

Comparisons of gang and nongang members in similar environmental circumstances suggest that gang members have different motivations for joining gangs, and these motivations may or may not coincide with specific personality patterns. In Miller's study of female gangs in Cleveland and St. Louis, gang members were more likely to have experienced violence, including family violence, than were nonmembers. In addition, gang members were more likely than nongang youth to have experienced drug use and abuse in their homes (J. Miller 2001:45–47). Given the violent context of many female gang members' lives, it is not surprising to learn that many of the gang members personally said they joined a gang for "protection," particularly from male violence (J. Miller 2001:155–159). Protection, or self-defense, is also mentioned by members of male gangs as a reason for joining a gang (Klein 1995a:79).

Others join a gang just to belong, as was suggested above. The need to be accepted and to belong "somewhere" is a powerful motivator for joining any group that will accept you, even a delinquent gang. As one gang member stated, "Why we join, see . . . is because we wanna belong to something. We can't belong to the school band, to the school council" (Klein 1995a:78).

Another reason for joining gangs is for the rewards membership can bring. The reward can be financial (albeit often illegal) profit, and money can bring, power, respect, and material possessions. Related to the prospect of making money illegally is the "thrill" of committing crimes and the possibility of getting caught coupled with the camaraderie associated with fights with other gangs or committing daring and/or illegal acts with others (Klein 1995a: 78–79).

Recent investigations identify factors connected with joining gangs that may separate females from males. For the most part, this research suggests that the reasons for joining gangs are much the same for both genders (Maxson and Whitlock 2002:25). However, some differences have been noted. For example, it has already been mentioned that females often join a gang because of abuse in the home. While abuse can be common among male gang members, the subject of sexual abuse is rarely mentioned in the backgrounds of male gang members. In addition, one study noted that female gang members predominantly join a gang because "family and friends were involved" or to "get a reputation." Often-cited reasons for joining gangs among males were "excitement," territoriality, "protection," and "belonging" (Maxson and Whitlock 2002:32). A study of youth gangs in Rochester, New York, an "emergent gang city," concludes that males are attracted to a gang if they are of a minority, a poor background, low parental education, and homes with the absence of both natural parents. For females, these factors are important but not significant. Females are predicted to be good candidates for gang involvement if they have parents who do not support education, especially the encouragement of a college degree, and if they have started dating at a relatively early age in life (Thornberry et al. 2003:65–69).

Why Do Gang Members Leave the Gang?

Another approach to understanding gang involvement is to look at why youth *leave* gangs. This topic has received little attention in the studies of gangs, but research that does exist suggests that some gang members may not wish to leave the gang because of the social and economic rewards of gang membership (and it seems the financial rewards become more important during times of economic downturns). Some gang members may die in violent conflicts or overdose or end up in prison, and prison is a common occurrence for gang youth who are involved with drug distribution (Moore 1978). Some gang members may move on to other criminal activities, either outside the original gang context and individually, or as part of smaller "crews." Others perhaps move on to organized crime, while others get legitimate jobs and leave the gang (Jankowski 1991:61–62). However, not much information exists on those gang members who simply decide to leave the gang.

One perception of gang life is that membership is so binding that members who wish to leave are either punished or sometimes killed for fear of their reporting the criminal activities of the gang. However, those who have examined this subject argue that while these retaliations do occur or are threatened, they are more myth than reality (Decker and Lauritsen 2002:60–61). One study of gang exits in St. Louis found that many gang members left the gang because they moved to another city, while others got married and started to raise a family and/or found a job and just "quit." As one former gang member put it, "I just quit. I stopped hanging out with them." Another ex-gang youth said, "Just stopped claiming" (Decker and Lauritsen 2002:59). However, the *major reason for leaving* a gang was the fear of getting hurt or killed by violence or getting tired of the worries associated with violence (Decker and Lauritsen 2002:58–66).

Although this line of inquiry is promising, not much is really known about why youth leave gangs. Part of the problem is determining whether a gang member has really left the gang. As one "ex-gang member" put it, "I never did quit. You can never get out of the gang" (Decker and Lauritsen 2002:60). Of course, some do entirely quit the gang, and even this informant said that can happen. However, for some, perhaps most, gang members, leaving the gang is not cut and dried. It can be accompanied by social and psychological impacts because of attachments to gang members and their lifestyle, as well as by financial setbacks (Decker and Lauritsen 2002:64–67). This situation is what John Hagedorn (1994) referred to in his study of gangs in Milwaukee. Hagedorn distinguished between "legits" and "homeboys" as types of ex-gang members. Legits were those who successfully exited the gang, while homeboys were those who tried to leave the gang but kept coming back, especially for economic reasons. However, the utility of Hagedorn's study is somewhat limited to the understanding of youth gangs because the gangs in his research were adults and involved in drug use and selling. While the topic of leaving a gang has not been well studied, continued research in this area should yield promising results for a clearer understanding of why youth join gangs.

While these individual characteristics and reasons for joining or leaving gangs have been identified in studies, remember that they reflect statistical probabilities and tendencies. Certainly, many youths who possess few or none of these factors may become members of a gang. In addition, the more of these characteristics possessed, the greater the likelihood that a young person will become a member of a gang if one exists in the neighborhood. As Thornberry and colleagues put it, "It does not appear that gang membership is associated with a single developmental domain; on the contrary, gang members have multiple disadvantages in multiple domains of their development" (2003:75). Gang youth have multiple difficulties, and in the theoretical terminology of researchers such as Thornberry and colleagues, as well as developmental theorists in general, they have developmental difficulties beyond those of other youth, and gangs serve as a major source of fulfilling those deficiencies in a gang youth's life. Consequently, it should not be expected that eliminating gangs, or even significantly reducing their presence in a community, will be a simple or easy task, and that is the next topic of discussion.

Attempts to Prevent or Control Gangs

In some ways, efforts to prevent gangs from occurring altogether or to reduce their activities reflect the reasons people think gangs form in the first place and why some youth are attracted to these gangs. However, in reality, most gang-prevention efforts are not based on specific theories. In addition, it should be emphasized that no matter what effort or program has been tried to prevent or reduce gang activity in a city, almost all efforts have come up short of hopes and expectations. In addition, according to some researchers, few gang-prevention programs have been carefully designed or analyzed, so the true impact of the programs is not clearly known (Thornberry, et al. 2003:201).

Gang Suppression

Efforts to suppress gangs usually involve increased police patrols and arrests along with stronger penalties for gang behavior. Although a clear theoretical basis for suppression is not always easy to identify, it seems better connected with the concept of deterrence; that is, crime must be stopped by making criminals "pay." At times, these efforts attempt to outlaw gang membership altogether, although this approach borders on unconstitutionality and is difficult to enforce. A more recent tactic is to enact "civil injunctions" against gangs or gang members, which focus not only on the gangs but also on the residents of neighborhoods. *Civil injunctions* involve surveillance of gang members and their movements but also focus on the cooperation of neighborhood residents in providing information about the gangs to the police. While these newer efforts may avoid the complications of outlawing a whole gang and have shown some degree of success, they also have potential constitutional issues and difficulties of enforcement (Maxson et al. 2005; Maxson et al. 2006).

Suppression is probably the most common and popular approach to the control of gangs. The popularity of suppression is undoubtedly associated with the common view that deterrence works (see chapter 4). In addition, its attraction may stem from the lack of societal interest in treating gang members, who typically come from poor minority backgrounds (Bjerregaard 2006:390–391).

As mentioned above, virtually no gang-prevention programs are evaluated, let alone properly evaluated, and this conclusion applies to suppression programs as well. As Klein observes, "Gang suppression is asserted to be the 'right' thing to do, and because it is 'right,' it requires little further justification and absolutely no research evaluation to assess its effects" (Klein 1995a:151).

Sometimes, suppression bleeds over into other areas of society, such as immigration. The earlier discussion of Virginia's new antigang laws supports this point. If gangs and gang violence are thought to be reflective of illegal immigration and lax efforts in enforcing immigration laws and policies, then the passage of "tougher" laws and restrictions on immigration as one way to control gangs would logically follow. However, these laws are often passed with little or no real information on gang membership or activity. Rather, as with the case of the MS-13 gangs in Virginia, information is provided by newspaper accounts and police estimates of gang memberships and motivations, rather than on detailed, time-consuming studies of gangs. Threats of gangs are perceived, sometimes correctly so, to be of immediate concern and needing immediate action. Given this scenario, the most logical approach to many is to enact stronger penalties for crimes involving gangs or gang recruitment, which is exactly how suppression efforts work. Often, this legislation, referred to as "STEP" legislation because of its original wording in California (Street Terrorism Enforcement and Prevention), attempts to create stronger penalties for gang-related crimes. Such laws are subject to the same kinds of problems that outlawing gangs can create, namely issues of constitutionality and difficulty of enforcement. Knowing who is a gang member at any one point in time, who actually committed a crime, and in whose name or organization a crime has been committed are not always easy questions to answer (Klein 1995a:178–182; Bjerregaard 2006). Even if short-term results can be noted, long-term changes may be harder to assess, and often, it seems, public attention focuses elsewhere so that follow-up studies or reports on gangs in a city or area may not develop unless new "gang-related" incidents occur.

Most suppression efforts are focused on police programs (Klein 1995a:161), and this seems logical, given that the police are the frontline units charged with enforcing laws and keeping the public safe. Police suppression programs include "sweeps," where members in gang areas are rounded up in a mass effort to arrest or disrupt as many gang members and activities as possible at a given time. Other suppressive techniques include "hot spot targeting," which involves intensive patrols and harassment or arrests of known or suspected gang members, even if these charges are dismissed. In addition, some departments may use what some call "caravanning," or using several patrol squads simultaneously, again, to create greater visibility and police presence in a gang area (Klein 1995a:161).

One of the difficulties with suppression programs is the lack of cooperation and communication among law enforcement agencies charged with controlling gangs. There are multiple law enforcement units—local, state, and federal—potentially involved with antigang efforts but also several governmental divisions, namely police, courts, and correctional agencies (Klein 1995a:chapter 6). *Local State Federal lack of commun.*

While it may be difficult to force cooperation among the police, courts, and correctional agencies, communication and cooperation among local police units is more achievable, at least to a degree. However, it has become increasingly clear that communication concerning gangs needs to be improved at the national level. The goal of creating a unified data system on gangs is behind the creation of a gang data collection and sharing system called GREAT, or Gang Reporting, Evaluation, and Tracking system. GREAT began in Los Angeles in the mid-1980s but has spread to over 150 other communities in several states, as well as to the Bureau of Alcohol, Tobacco, and Firearms (ATF). The GREAT system contains 150 lines of information on any individual gang member, many of which can easily be accessed through a computer (Klein 1995a:190–191). Other localities have developed similar tracking systems and with the common use of computers, this kind of tracking and surveillance system seems certain to gain popularity.

However, problems with sharing information among divergent law enforcement units as well as agreeing on common definitions of gangs and gang-related crimes has already created problems in the useful sharing of information through the GREAT system. In addition, ambiguities of gang and gang member identifications raise the prospect of constitutional issues and civil rights protections. In 1995, Malcolm Klein stated, "We now stand, it seems, on the threshold of a national gang roster system, based on GREAT, without anything approaching evaluation of its utility to law enforcement or its endangerment of civil liberties" (Klein 1995a:193). In the aftermath of 9/11 and increased government surveillance of immigrants and suspected terrorist groups and individuals, such problems may be expected to increase.

Community-Based Prevention Programs

Community-based programs have been around at least since the 1930s, when Shaw and McKay instituted the *Chicago Area Project (CAP)*. CAP was designed to work with community leaders and gang-prevention workers (detached street workers) in specifically targeted areas of Chicago that had high rates of crime and delinquency, including youth gangs. The project was designed to offer more recreational opportunities and neighborhood improvement programs, as these were identified as needs by local neighborhood leaders and organizers (Lundman 2001:102–108). While CAP addressed the prevention of delinquency in general, it also focused on gangs in the targeted neighborhoods.

Although Shaw and McKay did not formally evaluate the first CAP, there have been general analyses of these projects over the years (Kobrin 1959; Finestone 1976; V.I.P. Examiner 1992; Lundman 2001:108–112). These evaluations have concluded that the program generally results in improved perceptions of crime and delinquency reduction but provides little statistical data to support those conclusions. One indication of continued support for these projects is the extension of CAP to other communities in Illinois (V.I.P. Examiner 1992). However, there is little information to support the conclusion that CAPs actually reduce gangs and gang-related crime in a neighborhood or city.

A related community-based project was developed in Boston in the 1950s, the *Midcity Project*. The Midcity Project included the use of detached street workers assigned to seven specific gangs located in different inner-city neighborhoods in Boston, from 1954 to 1957. The purpose of the detached street workers was to intervene in gang feuds and help gang members with school and employment difficulties—in essence, to serve as a mediator between the gangs and the community in an effort to reduce the criminal behavior and negative attitudes of the gang members. The workers met with the gangs several times a week, for several hours per meeting, and also met with poor families and community agencies to work with the gangs in a broader community setting. The project was not carefully evaluated, but limited court data indicated that after three years, the efforts of the detached street workers did little to reduce the criminal behavior of the gang youth (Lundman 2001:112–116).

Community-based gang-prevention programs have continued to be used in different cities. One more recent example is the "*Neutral Zone*" project developed in the state of Washington in the 1990s (Thurman et al. 1996). The purpose of the program was to reduce the presence of youth ages 13–20 in the streets after dark on weekends, a curfew, as it were, as well as to provide more conformist recreational and job opportunities for "at-risk" youth. In one program, conducted near Seattle, a local elementary school was provided to offer basketball games, movies, music, free food, job counseling, and more to these youth in an effort to keep them away from gangs and criminal activities, especially on weekend nights. An evaluation of the Neutral Zone program in the metropolitan Seattle area concluded that the program did not lead to increased calls for police service during the hours when the program was in effect, and it did not cost much to operate the program (Thurman et al. 1996:288–292). Consequently, it was cost effective. However, data on gang activity in connection with this program were not provided.

In the past few years, the Boys & Girls Clubs of America (B&GCA) have become involved in several community-based gang-prevention activities. A major initiative is the Gang Prevention through Targeted Outreach program. This program provides educational, occupational, and recreational opportunities for "at-risk" youth living in areas where gangs are present or who are thought to be vulnerable to gang recruitment efforts. The focus is on youth who are not yet in gangs or are fringe members, and the goal is to encourage these youth to avoid gang contact and involvement in favor of following school and community programs, particularly those sponsored by B&GCA. Preliminary evaluations of the program indicate it is achieving some success in improving school attendance among targeted youth, but not much information on gang reduction has been provided (Esbensen 2000: 7–8; Boys & Girls Clubs of America 2002).

School-Based Gang Prevention

Some gang-prevention programs assume the school is a source of gang recruitment and involvement, and the literature suggests this is an accurate assumption. Consequently, the focus of attention should be on the school and school settings as the location of antigang efforts. One of the better-known of these school-based gang-prevention programs is G.R.E.A.T., or

Gang Resistance Education and Training. G.R.E.A.T. began in 1991 with pilot projects in Phoenix, Mesa, Tempe, and Glendale, Arizona, initiated by police officers and members of the Bureau of Alcohol, Tobacco, and Firearms. Now the program is national in scope and offers intensive gang-prevention information to middle-school students over a nine-week period. The training is offered by over 2,400 police officers in virtually every state in the country, and the officers themselves must first receive gang-prevention training before providing the courses to the students. Classroom instruction involves conflict-resolution skills and techniques, establishing goals and ways of achieving them, drug and gang information, and assuming personal responsibility for one's actions, highlighted by formal "graduation" ceremonies at the end of the instruction (Esbensen and Osgood 1997:1–2).

As a concept, G.R.E.A.T. has received strong support from the schools and the community. It is sponsored by police departments at the local and national levels and has been sanctioned by public schools and local communities virtually everywhere it has been offered. It is also one of the few gang-prevention programs that have received rigorous evaluation.

In one evaluation, 5,935 eighth-grade students who completed the training in 11 cities were contacted one year after the program to monitor their behavior and attitudes. The G.R.E.A.T. youth were compared with a group of 3,207 children who had not taken the program. The results of this survey concluded that those students who had completed G.R.E.A.T. had less criminal and delinquent behavior, including gang affiliations, and more positive attitudes toward the police and friends and less positive attitudes toward gangs than did the comparison group (Esbensen and Osgood 1997:2–5).

Another national evaluation of G.R.E.A.T., a longitudinal study, however, did not conclude that the program produced positive effects. This study examined a sample of 1,817 youth who completed G.R.E.A.T. in six cities during the 1995–1996 school year, compared with a control group of 1,697 students who did not complete the program, and contacted them one and two years after completing the program. The researchers concluded, "We found no systematic differences between G.R.E.A.T. students and the control group" (Esbensen 2006:379). For the moment, it is clear that *some* students completing G.R.E.A.T. demonstrate positive effects compared with control groups, but it is less clear that the program uniformly produces positive results. G.R.E.A.T. is still a promising gang-prevention effort, and its popularity suggests it will continue to be provided to school youth, but it needs to be evaluated in more depth before firmer conclusions about its effects can be made.

Comprehensive Gang-Prevention Efforts

In the past ten years or so, gang-prevention programs have begun to assume a multifaceted approach, particularly those funded or supported by federal agencies. Multipronged efforts make sense because it is known that the causes and contributors to gangs and gang-related crimes are numerous and diverse. Consequently, it is logical that truly effective gang-prevention programs should also be multifaceted.

In the 1980s, the Office of Juvenile Justice and Delinquency Prevention, OJJDP, initiated the National Youth Gang Suppression and Intervention Program. Gang-prevention programs were identified and supported across the country, based largely on what some call the "Spergel Model." The Spergel Model encourages partnerships and cooperation between and among police and community agencies and families to formulate a multipronged approach to the reduction of gangs in an area. The highlight of this model is that it encourages cooperation and mutual respect among all of the agencies utilized in any gang-prevention effort, rather than favoring a specific type of program, and such cooperation promises to achieve important results in the long run. A good discussion of this model and programs supported by OJJDP as well as other gang-prevention programs is provided by Fearn et al. (2006).

One example of these kinds of programs is the Gang Reduction Program, or GRP. The Gang Reduction Program has several important goals: identify and address the needs of individuals at risk or current gang youth and their families; catalog the financial needs of gang-prevention efforts and agencies and help to overcome them; utilize research findings in developing gang-prevention programs; and facilitate interagency and intergovernmental cooperation in developing gang-prevention projects. The projects combine suppression techniques with community-based prevention efforts and have been tested in four communities: Los Angeles; Miami; Milwaukee, Wisconsin; and Richmond, Virginia. No evaluations of the programs have yet been published (U.S. Department of Justice 2003; Shoemaker and Wolfe 2005:79–80).

Gang-prevention programs all share one thing in common, the goal of reducing gang activity in an area. In terms of successful results or even evaluations of such results, however, most gang-prevention programs are disappointing. However, most efforts have shown some positive results, some more so than others, but none has demonstrated overwhelmingly successful outcomes. Gang members can certainly be removed from the streets, but new members and new gangs seem to emerge in their place. Sometimes a program can produce the undesired effect of making a gang more cohesive by creating an image of "importance" among them because somebody is looking at them, and this can happen with suppression or prevention efforts (Klein 1995a:43–49), which can be very discouraging to gang workers. Even when one has identified a particular factor as an important contributor to leaving a gang, such as fear of violence, it is cautioned that concentrating on such fears to encourage gang members to leave a gang may actually have the reverse effect of augmenting a gang's attraction by highlighting a kind of "macho" violent image for the gang (Decker and Lauritsen 2002:66–67).

In addition, some gang researchers observed that gang development and gang behavior tend to run in "cycles." In some cities, such as Boston, Chicago, and New York, gang activity has traditionally peaked in the summer months, while in cities such as Los Angeles, gang activity is lowest in summer months. Gang activity can even be cyclical within the borders of cities. Gang membership also tends to be cyclical, or "epochal," as Klein puts it. That is, gang membership tends to swing in cycles involving as much as five or ten years (Klein 1995b:222–223). The point of considering gang cycles is that efforts to curb, reduce, or prevent gang activity may reflect cyclical patterns of gang membership and behavioral patterns as much as the efforts of the gang-prevention programs. As Klein says, "Gangs come and go; gang activity waxes and wanes, including the violence that so effectively draws our attention" (Klein 1995b:233). Given this view of gangs, nothing short of concentrated efforts to address the basic social and structural roots of gang development and growth can be expected to produce significant and long-term effects on gangs.

Summary

Juvenile gangs have existed for hundreds of years, although systematic studies of gangs in the United States did not appear until the 1920s. Gang violence seemed to become a problem in American cities after World War II, but gang violence today is commonplace. Gangs tend to reflect characteristics of their neighborhoods as well as contemporary immigration policies. In the 1920s, most gangs were composed of youth from European backgrounds, whereas contemporary youth gangs are largely composed of Hispanic and African American juveniles. Most gangs develop in the interstitial, or in-between, areas of cities, although some recent surveys suggest that rural and suburban areas are also experiencing growth in gangs. These kinds of gangs seem to be more the result of local conditions and individual motivations of local youth, as opposed to gang "migrations" from large metropolises to small towns. Gang members also tend to stay with gangs for longer periods of time when economic situations worsen, and this seems to be occurring more often today than in the past.

Many gangs have core members and fringe members, who participate with gang members on occasions. In some neighborhoods, younger juveniles form satellite gangs and take on names signifying their junior status to a "parent" gang, such as "midgets" or "pee-wees." In addition, many female gangs tend to identify with male gangs in an area, although some researchers contend that separate, independent female gangs are increasing in number.

Explanations of gangs involve sociological, structural factors, particularly social disorganization and economic decline, but also social and economic inequalities that can lead to a sense of frustration and discouragement with mainstream society and its accepted means of achieving success and recognition. In addition, most gang members lack strong social bonds with family and school, and the gang becomes a substitute for these bonds in society. Some join a gang for protection or because friends and relatives were gang members, and some research suggests these factors can differ for male and female gang members. Female gang members, for example, tend to suffer from sexual abuse in the home more than do male gang members.

Attempts to prevent gangs also focus on sociological and individual factors. Suppression, or the use of stronger laws and increased police activity, is the most popular means of preventing or controlling gangs. Some have developed preventive efforts that focus on societal contributions to gangs in the first place, again such as social disorganization and social and economic inequalities. However, no particular effort has produced dramatic or long-lasting results. Gangs are difficult to reduce. Putting gang members in prison will definitely get them off the street, but it does not eliminate the existence of gangs in a neighborhood or a city. Truly effective gang-prevention programs should integrate multiple factors, social as well as individual, along with suppression, and should acknowledge the diversity of gangs, their members, and the reasons for their existence.

References

Bjerregaard, Beth
    2006   Antigang Legislation and Its Potential Impact: The Promises and Pitfalls. *In* The Modern Gang Reader. 3rd edition. Arlen Egley, Jr., Cheryl L. Maxson, Jody Miller, and Malcolm W. Klein, eds. Pp. 381–393. Los Angeles: Roxbury.

Bohlke, Robert H.
    1967   Social Mobility, Status Inconsistency, and Middle-Class Delin-
            quency. *In* Middle-class Delinquency. Edmund W. Vaz, ed. Pp.
            222–232. New York: Harper & Row.
Boys & Girls Clubs of America
    2002   Annual Report: It's About Time. Atlanta: Boys & Girls Clubs of
            America.
Campbell, Anne
    1984   The Girls in the Gang. New York: Basil Blackwell.
Chambliss, William
    1973   The Saints and the Roughnecks. Society 11:24–31.
Chesney-Lind, Meda, and Lisa Pasko
    2004   The Female Offender: Girls, Women, and Crime. 2nd edition.
            Thousand Oaks, CA: Sage.
Chesney-Lind, Meda, and Randall G. Shelden
    2004   Girls, Delinquency, and Juvenile Justice. 3rd edition. Belmont, CA:
            Wadsworth.
Cloward, Richard A., and Lloyd E. Ohlin
    1960   Delinquency and Opportunity: A Theory of Delinquent Gangs.
            New York: Free Press.
Cohen Albert K.
    1955   Delinquent Boys: The Culture of the Gang. New York: Free Press
Curry, G. David, and Scott H. Decker
    2003   Confronting Gangs: Crime and Community. 2nd edition. Los Ange-
            les: Roxbury.
Decker, Scott H., and Janet L. Lauritsen
    2002   Leaving the Gang. *In* Gangs in America III. C. Ronald Huff, ed. Pp.
            51–67. Thousand Oaks, CA: Sage.
Delaney, Tim
    2006   American Street Gangs. Upper Saddle River, NJ: Pearson Prentice
            Hall.
Esbensen, Finn-Aage
    2000   Preventing Adolescent Gang Involvement. Juvenile Justice Bulletin,
            September. Washington, D.C.: U.S. Department of Justice, Office of
            Juvenile Justice and Delinquency Prevention.
    2006   The National Evaluation of the Gang Resistance Education and
            Training (G.R.E.A.T.) Program. *In* The Modern Gang Reader. 3rd
            edition. Arlen Egley, Jr., Cheryl L. Maxson, Jody Miller, and Mal-
            colm W. Klein, eds. Pp. 368–380. Los Angeles: Roxbury.

Esbensen, Finn-Aage, and D. Wayne Osgood

1997   National Evaluation of G.R.E.A.T. National Institute of Justice Research in Brief, November. Washington, DC: National Institute of Justice, Office of Justice Programs.

Fearn, Noelle E., Scott H. Decker, and G. David Curry

2006   Public Policy Responses to Gangs: Evaluating the Outcomes. *In* The Modern Gang Reader. 3rd edition. Arlen Egley, Jr., Cheryl L. Maxson, Jody Miller, and Malcolm W. Klein, eds. Pp. 312–324. Los Angeles: Roxbury.

Finestone, Harold

1976   Victims of Change. Westport, CT: Greenwood.

Hagedorn, John M.

1994   Homeboys, Dope Fiends, Legits, and New Jacks. Criminology 32:197–219.

Howell, James C., and Arlen Egley, Jr.

2005   Gangs in Small Towns and Rural Counties. NYGC Bulletin 1, June.

Jankowski, Martin Sanchez

1991   Islands in the Street: Gangs and American Urban Society. Berkeley: University of California Press.

Klein, Malcolm

1995a   The American Street Gang: Its Nature, Prevalence, and Control. New York: Oxford University Press.

1995b   Street Gang Cycles. *In* Crime. James Q. Wilson and Joan Petersilia, eds. Pp. 217–236. San Francisco: ICS Press.

Kling, Jeffrey R., Jens Ludwig, and Lawrence F. Katz

2005   Neighborhood Effects on Crime for Female and Male Youth: Evidence from a Randomized Housing Voucher Experiment. Quarterly Journal of Economics 120:87–130.

Kobrin, Solomon

1959   The Chicago Area Project—A 25 Year Assessment. Annals of the American Academy of Political and Social Science 322:20–29.

Liberman, Akiva

2007   Adolescents, Neighborhoods and Violence: Recent Findings from the Project on Human Development in Chicago Neighborhoods. NIJ Research in Brief, September. Washington, DC: U.S. Department of Justice, Office of Justice Programs.

Lundman, Richard J.

2001   Prevention and Control of Juvenile Delinquency. New York: Oxford University Press.

Maxson, Cheryl L.
    1998   Gang Members on the Move. Juvenile Justice Bulletin. Washington,
            DC: Office of Juvenile Justice and Delinquency Prevention.
Maxson, Cheryl L., Karen M. Hennigan, and David C. Sloane
    2005   It's Getting Crazy Out There: Can a Civil Gang Injunction Change
            a Community? Criminology and Public Policy 4:577–606.
    2006   For the Sake of the Neighborhood? Civil Gang Injunctions as a
            Gang Intervention Tool. In The Modern Gang Reader. 3rd edition.
            Arlen Egley, Jr., Cheryl L. Maxson, Jody Miller, and Malcolm W.
            Klein, eds. Pp. 394–406. Los Angeles: Roxbury.
Maxson, Cheryl, and Monica L. Whitlock
    2002   Joining the Gang: Gender Differences in Risk Factors for Gang
            Membership. In Gangs in America III. C. Ronald Huff, ed. Pp.
            19–35. Thousand Oaks, CA: Sage.
McGloin, Jean Marie
    2005   Policy and Intervention Considerations of a Network Analysis of
            Street Gangs. Criminology and Public Policy 4:607–636.
Merton, Robert K.
    1957   Social Theory and Social Structure. Rev. edition. New York: Free
            Press of Glencoe.
Miller, Jody
    2001   One of the Guys: Girls, Gangs, and Gender. New York: Oxford Uni-
            versity Press.
    2002   The Girls in the Gang: What We've Learned from Two Decades of
            Research. In Gangs in America III. C. Ronald Huff, ed. Pp. 175–197.
            Thousand Oaks, CA: Sage.
Miller, Walter B.
    1958   Lower-Class Culture as a Generating Milieu of Gang Delinquency.
            Journal of Social Issues 14: 5–19.
    1975   Violence by Youth Gangs and Youth Groups as a Crime Problem
            in Major American Cities. Washington, DC: U.S. Department of
            Justice.
    2001   The Growth of Youth Gang Problems in the United States:
            1970–1998. Washington, DC: Office of Juvenile Justice and Delin-
            quency Prevention.
Moore, Joan W.
    1978   Homeboys: Gangs, Drugs, and Prison in the Barrios of Los Ange-
            les. Philadelphia: Temple University Press.

1991 Going Down to the Barrio: Homeboys and Homegirls in Change. Philadelphia: Temple University Press.

Moore, Joan, and John Hagedorn

2001 Female Gangs: A Focus on Research. Juvenile Justice Bulletin. Washington, DC: Office of Juvenile Justice and Delinquency Prevention.

National Youth Gang Center

2000 1998 National Youth Gang Survey: Summary. Washington, DC: Office of Juvenile Justice and Delinquency Prevention.

2007 National Youth Gang Survey Analysis. Electronic document, http://www.iir.com/nygc/nygsa, accessed October 1, 2007.

New River Valley Community Services

2004 Gangs in Our Backyard: What to Watch for in Your School or Community. Workshop organized by the New River Valley (Virginia) Community Services and the Virginia State Police. Presented in Blacksburg, Virginia, November 20.

Roanoke Times

2005 Growing Gang Violence Across State Worries Virginia Officials. Roanoke Times, July 6.

Sampson, Robert J., Jeffrey Morenoff, and Stephen Raudenbush

2005 Social Anatomy of Racial and Ethnic Disparities in Violence. American Journal of Public Health 95:224–232.

Sampson, Robert J., Stephen W. Raudenbush, and Felton Earls

1997 Neighborhoods and Violent Crime: A Multilevel Study of Collective Efficacy. Science 277:918–924.

Sellin, Thorsten

1938 Culture Conflict and Crime. New York: Social Science Research Council.

Shaw, Clifford R., and Henry D. McKay

1942 Juvenile Delinquency and Urban Areas. Chicago: University of Chicago Press.

1969 Juvenile Delinquency and Urban Areas. Rev. edition. Chicago: University of Chicago Press.

Shelden, Randall G., Sharon K. Tracy, and William B. Brown

2004 Youth Gangs in American Society. 3rd edition. Belmont, CA: Wadsworth.

Sheu, Chuen-Jim

1986 Delinquency and Identity: Juvenile Delinquency in an American Chinatown. New York: Harrow and Heston.

Shoemaker, Donald J.
  2005   Theories of Delinquency: An Examination of Explanations of Delinquent Behavior. 5th edition. New York: Oxford University Press.
Shoemaker, Donald J., and Timothy W. Wolfe
  2005   Juvenile Justice: A Reference Handbook. Santa Barbara: ABC-CLIO.
Short, James F., Jr., and Fred L. Strodtbeck
  1965   Group Processes and Gang Delinquency. Chicago: University of Chicago Press.
Smith, William Carlson
  1937   Americans in Process. Ann Arbor, MI: Edwards Brothers.
Spergel, Irving
  1964   Racketville, Slumtown, and Haulberg. Chicago: University of Chicago Press.
Thornberry, Terence B., Marvin D. Krohn, Alan J. Lizotte, and Deborah Chard-Wierschem
  1993   The Role of Juvenile Gangs in Facilitating Delinquent Behavior. Journal of Research in Crime and Delinquency 30:555–87.
Thornberry, Terence P., Marvin D. Krohn, Alan J. Lizotte, Carolyn A. Smith, and Kimberly Tobin
  2003   Gangs and Delinquency in Developmental Perspective. Cambridge, England: Cambridge University Press.
Thrasher, Frederick M.
  1927   The Gang: A Study of 1,313 Gangs in Chicago. Chicago: University of Chicago Press.
Thurman, Quint C., Andrew L. Giacomazzi, Michael D. Reisig, and David G. Mueller
  1996   Community-Based Gang Prevention and Intervention: An Evaluation of the Neutral Zone. Crime & Delinquency 42:279–295.
U.S. Department of Justice
  2003   OJJDP News at a Glance, September/October, Vol. II, No. 5.
Vaz, Edmund W., ed.
  1967   Middle-Class Delinquency. New York: Harper & Row.
V.I.P. Examiner
  1992   Chicago Area Project: A Delinquency Prevention Project. V.I.P. Examiner, Summer:6–17.
Whyte, William Foote
  1955   Street Corner Society: The Social Structure of an Italian Slum.
  [1943] Chicago: University of Chicago Press.

Wilson, William Julius
>   1987   The Truly Disadvantaged: The Inner City, the Underclass, and Public Policy. Chicago: University of Chicago Press.

Wong, Siu Kwong
>   1997   Delinquency of Chinese-Canadian Youth: A Test of Opportunity, Control, and Intergeneration Conflict Theories. Youth and Society 29:112–133.

Wooden, Wayne S., and Randy Blazak
>   2001   Renegade Kids, Suburban Outlaws: From Youth Culture to Delinquency. 2nd edition. Belmont, CA: Wadsworth.

Yablonsky, Lewis
>   1970   The Violent Gang. Rev. edition. New York: Pelican Books.
>   [1962]

Young, Pauline V.
>   1967   The Pilgrims of Russian-Town. New York: Russell and Russell.
>   [1932]

Zimmerman, Nicolas
>   2004   MS-13s: Los Angeles' Unwelcome Export to Virginia. Electronic document, www.medill.northwestern.edu/~secure/docket/mt/archives/001409.php.

FEMALE DELINQUENCY

T
HROUGHOUT the 1980s and early 1990s violent crime rates for both juvenile males and females increased dramatically. The notion of the superpredator was characterized by both academics and the mass media as a new breed of juvenile offenders who were more ruthless than any previous generation (Mulvey et al. 2000). The concept of the superpredator never materialized as the number of juvenile violent crimes peaked in 1993 and has steadily declined since. However, what does remain with us is a genuine fear of juvenile offenders. This caused the juvenile system to move from its original intent of rehabilitating and treating young offenders to punishing juveniles through "get tough on crime" policies such as juvenile transfer and juvenile boot camps (Mulvey et al. 2000).

Girls have not been immune to this shift in the juvenile justice system and are often an afterthought within the system owing to their small numbers—girls are only 15 percent of all juveniles in residential placement (Snyder and Sickmund 2006:206). The ramifications of this have been that whatever is perceived as the problem and/or solution for male juvenile delinquents is then assumed to be the problem and/or solution for female juvenile delinquents. This has led to harsher policies dealing with delinquent acts such as assault and more girls being incarcerated than ever before. In this chapter, we will explore who female delinquents are, what their offenses are, and the theories that have been used to explain female delinquent behavior.

Who Are Female Delinquents?

Delinquent girls range from 13 to 18 years of age. In 2003, girl delinquents housed in detention centers tended to be 15 or 16 years old (51 percent) in comparison with boys, who were 16 or 17 years old (51 percent) (Snyder and Sickmund 2006:209). Therefore, girls in detention tend to be younger than boys in detention. There are also more boys in detention facilities at the age of 18 (16 percent) than girls (7 percent) (Snyder and Sickmund 2006:209). This suggests that girls enter into delinquent behavior and mature out of delinquent offending at a younger age than boys.

African American and Hispanic girls are the fastest-growing segment of female delinquents in detention centers and are 70–80 percent more likely to be referred to a detention facility than Caucasian girls (Bloom et al. 2003). In 2003, the girls detained were 45 percent Caucasian, 35 percent African American, 15 percent Hispanic, and 1 percent other (Snyder and Sickmund 2006:209). Compare these numbers to the percentage of Caucasians (68 percent), African Americans (12 percent), and Hispanics (13 percent) in the general population (U.S. Census Bureau 2000). In order for minority girls to not be considered overrepresented in detention centers, their percentages should be close to those of minorities in the general population. However, minority girls make up 55 percent of the total detained female juvenile population (Snyder and Sickmund 2006:209).

Class or socioeconomic status also affects girls in the juvenile justice system. Girls with few economic resources are more likely to end up being placed in a juvenile facility (Bloom et al. 2003). If one has money, her parents will be able to afford a private attorney, which often results in having charges dropped or reduced. Money also affects whether one has private insurance or not. Those who have private medical insurance are less likely to be placed in detention centers because they are generally allowed to remain in the community. In their communities, they can receive treatment that their insurance will cover, such as counseling and substance abuse treatment. Those who do not have private insurance are more likely to be placed in detention centers, where few resources are available to them. When examined together, race and class help to further explain the overreliance on detention centers for minority youth. White children are the least likely to be living in poverty, while 30 percent of all African American and 27 percent of all Hispanic children are living in poverty (Bloom et al. 2003). Therefore, fewer African American and Hispanic children will have the choice to hire a private attorney, and fewer will have private medical insurance.

Girls, Delinquency, and Status Offenses

In 2003, girls were 29 percent of all arrests, 29 percent of all cases processed through the juvenile system, and 15 percent of all residential placements (Snyder and Sickmund 2006:206). Girls consist of a small portion of all juvenile offenders, but the number of girls offending continues to rise. From 1985 to 2002, there was a 92 percent increase in the number of girls who entered the juvenile court system in comparison to a 29 percent increase for boys (Snyder and Sickmund 2006:206). During the same period, the number of girls placed in detention for a delinquent offense increased by 50 percent, while for boys there was a 4 percent increase (Harms 2003). The increase in the number of girls placed in detention is largely a result of the number of girls charged with person offenses, which increased by 202 percent from 1985 to 2002 (Snyder and Sickmund 2006:206). The majority of these person offenses are simple assaults, which have increased for both male and female delinquents (136 percent increase for girls and 80 percent increase for boys) (Stahl 2003).

Although there have been large increases in the number of girls arrested and placed in detention, girls still tend to be arrested for nonviolent offenses such as larceny-theft (21 percent) and running away from home (13 percent) (Collins 2002). In 2003, 27 percent of girls were in detention facilities for offenses against people, while 18 percent were detained for property offenses, 6 percent for drug offenses, 10 percent for public order offenses, and 10 percent for status offenses (Snyder and Sickmund 2006:209). Girls were also more likely than boys to be charged with and placed in detention for status offenses. Status offenses are acts that would not be considered criminal if one were an adult. However, because one is under the age of 18, these offenses are handled by the juvenile justice system. Status offenses include underage drinking, being incorrigible, truancy, and running away from home. In 2003, 4 percent of males and 10 percent of females were incarcerated for status offenses (Snyder and Sickmund 2006:209).

Girls who have been arrested for status offenses were typically arrested for curfew violations and running away from home (Chesney-Lind and Shelden 2004). Most girls, when asked why they ran away, stated that someone within their home was abusing them, and often the abuser was the girl's father or the mother's boyfriend. If the girl victim told a family member that she was being abused, she was often ignored, since the male who was abusing her was supporting the family financially. Therefore, the girl was left with two options: to allow the abuse to continue or to run away from home (Chesney-Lind and Shelden 2004).

When a girl runs away from home she is more likely to be arrested and placed in detention than a boy who runs away (Chesney-Lind and Shelden 2004). In 2003, 59 percent of all arrested runaways were female (Snyder and Sickmund 2006: 209). However, self-report surveys of juvenile delinquents have shown that girls and boys were equally likely to state that they have run away from home (Chesney-Lind and Shelden 2004).

The number of girls incarcerated for the status offense of running away, an offense that if they were 18 would not be a crime, has changed very little since the 1970s (Chesney-Lind and Shelden 2004). Girls are still arrested for running away because there is concern that a young girl alone on the streets could be further victimized. However, the juvenile justice system is not a replacement for a healthy home environment. In detention, there are few opportunities for treatment and counseling because of overcrowded facilities and the lack of funding. Therefore, girls who run away are being victimized not only at home but also by a juvenile justice system that is not prepared for the specific needs of girl delinquents.

Girls, Delinquency, and Theory

Since girls make up a small portion of all juvenile delinquents, most research and theory development have been conducted focusing on the characteristics and needs of male juvenile offenders. This has left a gap in our understanding of female delinquents, their characteristics, and their needs. To fill this void, theories that have been used to explain male juvenile delinquency are often applied to girls and their delinquent behavior without considering the differences between the two genders. This section of this chapter will focus on theories that have been used to explain girls' delinquent behavior while pointing out with current research why some theories work better with girls than others.

Biological Explanations

Cesare Lombroso (1835–1909), an Italian physician, was the first to study crime using a scientific approach (Lombroso and Ferrero 2004). Lombroso was heavily influenced by the work of Charles Darwin, the scientist who proposed that humans had evolved from a single-cell species into their current form over millions of years. Darwin believed that the strong survived and evolved because the traits that made them stronger were passed from parent to offspring, thereby increasing the offspring's chance for survival. Lombroso then applied this concept of evolution to his own theory of crime. He compared the cadavers of "normal" noncriminal men and women to those of criminal men and women and concluded that there were differences between criminal and noncriminal people's physical traits. Lombroso then stated that criminal men and women who possessed these physical traits were throwbacks to an earlier stage in the evolutionary scale, what he referred to as atavism. These atavistic men and women were not as developed as "normal" noncriminal men and women and were therefore born criminals (Lombroso and Ferrero 2004).

Lombroso (Lombroso and Ferrero 2004) was one of the first to attempt to explain female criminality. He did this by comparing the cadavers of criminal women, "normal" noncriminal women, and prostitutes to examine how these women differed physically. He found that criminal women tended to be short and have dark hair and moles. Lombroso did not find criminal women and prostitutes to be as marked physically as male criminals. This might suggest that women were less criminal than men because they possessed fewer atavistic traits. However, Lombroso explained this difference between criminal men and women by stating that women had to be more attractive than men to survive. Noncriminal women he concluded had to be attractive, passive, and maternal because these were characteristics that noncriminal men looked for when obtaining a mate. Lombroso believed that criminal women and prostitutes also had to be attractive because they would need to be able to seduce a man in order to have an accomplice. Lombroso explained that women committed less crime than men because men reproduced with only attractive women. Therefore, there were far fewer born-criminal women (Lombroso and Ferrero 2004).

Lombroso (Lombroso and Ferrero 2004) believed that normal men were the most advanced, followed by criminal men, then normal women, and criminal women. Lombroso believed that men, whether criminal or not, were superior to women physically and intellectually. He attributed this to men having to fight for mates, which as they evolved made them physically and intellectually superior to women. He believed that because women spent the majority of their time raising children this made them passive and did not allow them the time needed to advance their bodies physically or mentally. However, Lombroso predicted that women's crime rates would increase as women gained more education and advanced mentally (Lombroso and Ferrero 2004).

Lombroso produced two books regarding his findings, one pertaining to women and one about men. The book *Criminal Woman, the Prostitute and the Normal Woman* was published in 1893 in Italian and was translated into English in 1895 (Rafter and Gibson 2004). The book *Criminal Man* was not translated into English until 16 years after it was published. Its findings were disputed, and researchers proposed that environmental and social influences were more relevant than biological influences when examining criminal behavior. The same arguments were made regarding his book on women; however, this book had a much more lasting impression because there had been little research conducted on women and crime (Lombroso and Ferrero 2004).

Lombroso was not the first person to tie sexuality and criminality together, but he was the first one to support this assumption with scientific research. This influenced the work of psychologists and sociologists who continued to try and explain girls' delinquency through their sexuality. Sigmund Freud, for example, claimed that girls committed crime because they were envious that they did not have a penis and were rebelling against being female. In the 1950s, British researcher Katharina Dalton argued that premenstrual syndrome was tied to violent crimes by women, suggesting that women were more likely to commit violent crimes during this part of their menstrual cycle (O'Connor 2004). Dr. Dalton testified in the 1980s on behalf of women charged with violent crimes, asserting that it was related to their menstrual cycle. Even as recently as 1991, in Pittsburgh, Pennsylvania, a woman who worked in a nursing home who beat, choked, and stabbed to death an elderly patient argued in court that she committed her crime because she had been experiencing hysteria due to premenstrual syndrome (Cuddy 1991).

Social Role Theory

W. I. Thomas was a sociologist who studied delinquent girls in an attempt to explain and treat their behavior (Dummer 1923). Thomas was particularly concerned with prostitutes, as was the rest of the country, during the early 1920s. During World War I, it had been discovered that a large number of soldiers had contracted a venereal disease before they entered the service. This led to the government's placing women suspected of prostitution in jails and hospitals. Thomas used case studies of young prostitutes to examine and explain their criminality while also providing suggestions on how to treat these young women (Dummer 1923).

Thomas believed that women's criminality was directly tied to their sexuality (Thomas 1923). He suggested that women who came from middle-class and upper-class backgrounds had learned through their families, peers, community, and teachers that they were to remain chaste. By remaining chaste, these women were securing their role in society to become wives and mothers because a man would never marry a woman if she were not a virgin. Thomas suggested that this was why wealthier women did not commit crimes (Thomas 1923).

Thomas illustrated through his case studies that women from working-class families were also taught to remain chaste through their friends, families, communities, and teachers (Thomas 1923). Working-class women often worked in shops where they made enough money to support themselves, but not enough to indulge in the luxuries that married, wealthy women were able to purchase. These working women were often tricked into having sexual relations with men who enticed them by promising marriage. The promise of marriage always fell through, and the girl was left without her most prized possession—her virginity. Many of these women, upset with men and with their position in life, became prostitutes in order to purchase luxuries they otherwise could not afford. These women justified this behavior by stating that they had better use men before men attempted to use them (Thomas 1923).

Finally, Thomas discussed girls in poverty who became prostitutes (Thomas 1923). He illustrated through case studies how these girls came from not only extremely poor, but also dysfunctional families, which often faced problems of substance abuse and domestic violence. These girls also came from disorganized communities, where there was no social support. Therefore, they did not get the chance to learn from their parents, teachers, communities, and/or peers the proper role of a woman in society—to marry and have children. The only jobs available to these girls were hard labor in a factory or in a person's home as a servant, where they were treated as though they were inferior. These girls often left home at a young age looking for excitement, which led them to prostitution. They then were able to obtain their excitement through using men for sex and money (Thomas 1923).

The working-class prostitute confined her business to men of higher status who often were married (Thomas 1923). These business transactions took place indoors. However, the poorer prostitute often did her business on the streets with soldiers, which put her at risk to be arrested and placed in jail. There were also some programs that placed young girls in the home of a well-to-do family with the hopes that their values and morals would rub off on the girls. However, Thomas found that girls placed in these homes usually ran away. Instead of jail or the homes of the wealthy, Thomas suggested that these girls be placed in structured environments, where they could be educated and taught how to be good girls (Thomas 1923).

W. I. Thomas would have been considered very liberal in his time (Dummer 1923). He suggested that girls' delinquency originated with family problems, poverty, and a lack of community support. He argued that those who committed crimes were not biologically inferior and notes several female criminals who were considered intelligent. Thomas influenced the way we examine girls' delinquency and moved it toward social rather than biological factors (Dummer 1923). Thomas did, however, tie girls' sexuality and criminality together, suggesting that the solution to girls' delinquency is to teach girls how to better fill traditional roles. This way of thinking can still be seen in women's prisons and girl's detention centers, where vocational training often means training for stereotypical low-paying jobs such as hairstylist or secretary (Schramm 2002). It can also be seen in the way girls are treated when they arrive at a detention facility. Delinquent girls, for example, are often forced to undergo a gynecological exam because it is assumed that delinquent girls are also sexually active and possibly carrying diseases. Boys, however, are not examined for sexually transmitted diseases upon their arrival at detention (Schramm 2002).

Liberation Theory

During the 1960s and 1970s, women argued that they should be treated equally with men in the home and in the workplace. Many women during these years began to move from the traditional housewife role to one of workingwoman. This transition was made easier by advances in technology such as oral contraceptives and appliances that made housework less tedious (Adler 1975). Young girls were also now freed from time-consuming chores, allowing time for education and leisure. However, other changes for women and girls were also occurring, such as rising crime rates (Adler 1975).

Prior to these social changes, female crime had consisted primarily of prostitution or shoplifting, but now women could be found committing violent crimes as well (Adler 1975). There were instances of female bank robbers, for example, who pulled guns and got away with large amounts of cash, and those who worked in the criminal justice system began to express concern about the growing problem of female crime and delinquency (Adler 1975).

Criminologist Freda Adler in her 1975 book *Sisters in Crime: The Rise of the New Female Criminal* attempted to explain the increase in female crime through interviews with women offenders and those who worked with them in the criminal justice system. Adler discovered that handguns had evened the playing field for female criminals by allowing women who were once thought too weak the opportunity to commit a violent crime. Adler also concluded that these new female criminals believed that they could do anything men could do and seemed to enjoy the excitement of committing crimes (Adler 1975).

Adler (1975) concluded women's and girls' crime and delinquency rates would continue to rise and would one day be as high as men's and boys' rates. This increase would be caused by the newfound freedom women and girls had gained as a result of the women's movement. Women would enter the workforce enabled by new home appliances that considerably cut down the time needed to do household chores and a new sexual freedom because of technological advances in oral contraceptives. This meant women no longer had to define themselves through their virginity, which previously had been needed to attract a mate to support them. Women would then be out in public more often due to their new employment and freedom, which would also give them more opportunities to commit crimes at a rate comparable to that of men. Therefore, women's crime rates had been previously low because women were restricted in society, confined primarily to their homes and limiting their opportunities to offend (Adler 1975).

Adler (1975) also concluded that girls' rates of delinquency would increase and eventually be comparable to boys' rates. Adler believed that the changes in women's roles due to the women's movement would be a period of confusion for girls as they watched their older sisters and tried to understand what was expected of them. She noted that previous to the women's movement, girls were prosecuted for delinquent offenses that were tied to their sexuality, while boys were prosecuted for delinquent offenses associated with aggressive behavior. Adler predicted that as it became more socially acceptable for girls to be sexually active, they would be charged with delinquent offenses related to their sexual behavior less often. However, she hypothesized that girls would be prosecuted more often for delinquent offenses associated with aggressive behavior because girls were now expected to learn to be competitive and aggressive in order to compete in a man's world. Once this occurred, girls would have rates of delinquency that would approach the rates of boys (Adler 1975).

Women's rates of incarceration have increased at a rate higher than men's since the late 1980s. This has been primarily due to more women being brought into the criminal justice system for drug and/or property offenses, often related to their own drug addictions and/or partner's drug selling. One in four women incarcerated stated that she committed her crime in order to obtain money for her drug habit (Greenfeld and Snell 2000). These are probably not the women Adler had in mind because Adler had hypothesized that women would be committing more violent crimes similar to those of men. Adler (1975) does discuss drug addiction but states that women's drug addictions will increase as middle-class women face discrimination at their new jobs, while women from lower-class statuses will begin to experience divorce and poverty, leading to their drug abuse. However, Adler could never have predicted the war on drugs, which is responsible for the massive increase in the number of nonviolent women serving time.

Women's rates of white-collar crimes such as embezzlement did increase as women began to enter the workforce, and women's rates for embezzlement are now higher than men's. However, this may be more because of the type of job one holds than anything else (Britton 2000). Women, for example, are more likely to hold a lower-status job within a company, where there are many security checks. Therefore, women are more likely to be caught embezzling than men, who are more likely to hold management positions where there are fewer security checks.

Adler (1975) had predicted that girls' offenses would move from those tied to sexuality to violent offenses as girls gained more opportunities. In the 1970s, research studies showed there was a high percentage of both boys and girls in detention for status offenses (Schwartz et al. 1990). In 1971, for example, 21.5 percent of boys and 58.6 percent of girls were being detained for a status offense. In 1974, the Juvenile Justice and Delinquency Prevention Act was passed with the goal of decreasing the number of status offenders who were held in detention. This act did decrease the number of status offenders for both boys and girls who were held in detention; however, the act had a more direct impact on boys. In 1987, for example, 3.3 percent of all boys detained were held for a status offense, while 17.7 percent of all girls were being detained for a status offense. Often female status offenders were being abused in their homes and ran away to escape the abuse; however, running away is a status offense. This act was supposed to help these girls and provide alternatives for them other than detention, but due to the lack of alternatives, available status offenders are still placed in detention for their own protection (Schwartz et al. 1990).

The number of girls being arrested for simple assault has increased over the past ten years. This trend does appear to be related to society's not tolerating girls' aggressive behavior, as many of these girls would have been previously arrested for status offenses (Chesney-Lind 2001). Girls, for example, are now being arrested for simple assault for fighting with parents when previously they would have been charged with being incorrigible—a status offense (Chesney-Lind 2001).

It does appear that women have more opportunities to commit crimes, such as in the workplace, and that girls are arrested for delinquent offenses that do involve more aggressive behavior. However, girls' and women's delinquency and crime rates are nowhere near the rates of boys or men. Only one in 17 of all children in detention are girls, and women are only 6 percent of all adults incarcerated in state facilities (Bloom et al. 2003).

Power Control Theory

In 1985, Hagan and his colleagues (1985) developed the concept of power control theory. This theory was heavily influenced by the notion that as women began to enter the workforce, their role within their homes would change, directly affecting how they supervised their own children. It was hypothesized that as women gained more control in the workplace, this power would transfer into the home, and women would begin to take a more active role in supervising their sons. The changes in supervision, more intense for boys and less intense for girls than previously, would cause boys' delinquency rates to decline and girls' delinquency rates to increase (Hagan et al. 1985).

Prior to the women's movement, families in the United States tended to have a patriarchal structure. This structure occurred when the husband/ father went to work, supported the family financially, and made the majority of decisions regarding how the household was run, including how the children were disciplined and supervised (Hagan et al. 1985). Women in patriarchal families tended to be stay-at-home mothers who had the opportunity to closely monitor their daughters. Girls, through close contact with their mothers, learned how to rely on others for social support, a skill that would be valuable later as an adult. This focus on relationships then accounted for girls' lower rates of delinquency because girls did not want to damage their relationships and good reputations by behaving delinquently. However, boys in patriarchal families were not as closely monitored as girls and were encouraged to be independent and to take risks. This type of parental supervision would later in life help the boy to succeed in the workplace, where he would be expected to be independent and willing to take risks. Hagan et al. (1985) suggest that these differences in supervision explain why boys commit more delinquent acts than girls. First, boys have more opportunity because they are supervised less closely. Second, girls fear losing the close relationships that they have built with their mothers, while boys are encouraged to take risks, which often leads to delinquent behavior (Hagan et al. 1985).

After the women's movement, more women began to enter the workforce. Many women began to enter positions of power at their jobs, and some were even beginning to make more money than their husbands. Hagan et al. (1985) suggested that these changes in the workforce and in the home would directly affect how children were supervised and disciplined and would have a direct impact on delinquency rates.

Hagan et al. (1985) examined three major family types to explain changes in delinquency rates due to shifts in power and status in the workplace and home. In the *patriarchal family*, the father's job had more status and better pay than the mother's job. The father's power from work was then transferred to the home, allowing him to control most of the functions within the home. The sexist ideas that girls should be protected and boys need to be independent were then passed from father to family as the mother then implemented the supervision style advocated by the father.

The second type of family structure involved the *matriarchal family*. In this family structure, the mother's job had more status and higher pay than the father's job, which allowed her to transfer her power from the workplace to the home. Therefore, the mother controlled most of the functions within the home. The matriarchal mother tended to be less involved in the direct supervision of her daughter in comparison with the patriarchal family, while she may or may not have increased the direct supervision of her son.

The third family type was the *egalitarian family*. In this situation, both parents had jobs that were equivalent in status and pay, and both made decisions within the home equally. In this type of family structure, the daughter received less supervision than if she were in a patriarchal family, while the supervision of a son increased in comparison with the patriarchal family (Hagan et al. 1985).

Hagan et al. (1985) examined only two-parent families when exploring power control theory. They argued that families that have ended in divorce still fall into one of the three family types and that one can determine one's family type by examining the structure of the home before the divorce.

There were also many families headed by single parents that had never involved two parents. Hagan et al. (1985) argued that these families would fall into the matriarchal family type. However, the hypotheses regarding single parents and divorced parents have not been examined.

Hagan et al. (1985) hypothesized that as the family structure moves from patriarchal to egalitarian, boys' rates of delinquency will decrease, and girls' rates of delinquency will increase. In other words, as women begin to gain more power in the workforce and home, they will have more say in how their home functions, including how their children are supervised and disciplined. This will cause a shift in ideology within the home, where girls and boys will be treated more equally in regard to supervision. This shift in power will cause girls to be supervised less directly and boys to be supervised more intensely, changing the rates of delinquent offenses for the two genders (Hagan et al. 1985).

A study conducted by McCarthy and colleagues (1999) tested power control theory using high-school students in Toronto. A survey was distributed to determine their delinquency rates, family structure, and amount of supervision. There were few families that fell into the matriarchal family structure, so the researchers decided to examine families as either being more or less patriarchal. The researchers discovered that family structure did impact delinquency. As hypothesized, girls in patriarchal families were more heavily supervised, while boys received less direct supervision. Boys in patriarchal families then tended to have higher rates of delinquency because they believed that they would not get caught. Families that were categorized as being less patriarchal had mothers who did increase the direct supervision of their sons. In this family structure, boys tended to not be as delinquent because they feared getting caught. Girls' delinquency rates for the two family types did not change, but girls within the less patriarchal families did tend to hold more equitable views on family and work (McCarthy et al. 1999).

The results of the study conducted by McCarthy et al. (1999) suggest that that there have been changes within the family due to changes in women's roles within the workforce. However, this change seems to have had the largest impact on boys' rates of offending because boys were being monitored more by mothers who had a greater say in how their home functioned. The increase in supervision had directly affected boys' rates of offending because boys were noticing that they were being monitored and feared getting caught. The changes in the workforce and home seem to have had the least impact on girls' rate of delinquency. Girls' delinquency rates did not change due to the decrease in supervision, but girls in less patriarchal homes did have a more favorable view of women in the work-force and home (McCarthy et al. 1999).

Power control theory attempted to explain that girls had lower rates of delinquency than boys due to girls' being more heavily supervised. It was then hypothesized that girls' rates of delinquency would increase as girls received less supervision, while also being socialized to take risks. However, boys' rates of delinquency would decrease as boys received more supervision and consequently had fewer opportunities for risk taking. This hypothesis did hold true for boys, but girls' rates of delinquency did not change as they were less directly supervised. This suggests that there is something distinct about being male and female in our society that affects delinquency rates and that the amounts of supervision girls receive or one's parenting style is not enough to account for these differences.

Feminist Perspectives

Prior to the 1960s, criminology theories regarding women and girls had focused on sex or biological differences and gendered stereotypes (Holsinger 2000). These theories had been driven by the prevailing belief that women and girls were inferior to men and boys and focused on three themes: females as biologically inferior, female crime being motivated by sexual drive, and treatment that included teaching women and girls how to better fill the traditional female role (Holsinger 2000).

During the 1960s and 1970s, as the women's movement began to evolve, the way we viewed women and girls in society began to change as women demanded equal rights and opportunities. This movement also had an impact on criminology and the explanation of girls' and women's delinquency and crime, as feminists began to point out biases in criminology theory (Britton 2000). The majority of theories in criminology had been developed to explain males' criminal and delinquent behavior and then were later adapted to cover female criminal and delinquent behavior. Females were ignored in criminology theory because they were only a small percentage of all criminal and delinquent offenders. Feminists also emphasized the need to consider gender and not focus solely on one's sex when explaining female criminal and delinquent behavior. Previous theories had focused on biological differences, while not taking into consideration gender differences between males and females and their roles in society (Britton 2000).

Female criminologists then began to conduct research to explain female criminal behavior, and books such as Freda Adler's *Sisters in Crime* and Rita

James Simon's *Women and Crime* began to emerge (Britton 2000). During this period, research on rape and domestic violence also became more prevalent, which changed the way women were treated as victims of these crimes. Prior to the 1970s, rape was thought to be a struggle of lust and sexual desire; however, feminists were able to redefine rape as a power struggle between two people. This new definition had an impact on how women were treated in the courtroom as victims and the definition of rape as a criminal act. Feminists were also able to expose the problems of domestic violence by making people aware of the struggles these victims faced. This exposure led to changes in the way police and the courts handle this crime (Britton 2000).

During the 1960s and 1970s, feminists had primarily focused on white middle-class women, assuming that their experiences were universal (Daly 1997). However, during the 1980s, feminists began to become aware that some voices had been previously excluded. Feminists then began to explain how women from different classes and races have different life experiences. It is important to consider these differences when explaining female criminal and delinquent behavior and when trying to understand how laws and policies impact women differently (Daly 1997). Dr. Chesney-Lind, for example, is a scholar and advocate for girls and women in the criminal justice system who has dedicated her work to examining criminal justice policies and their implications for girls and women from different races and classes (www.chesneylind.com). Professor Chesney-Lind has been recognized numerous times for her work and has brought national attention to the problems experienced by girls and women in a juvenile and criminal justice system built for boys and men.

Chesney-Lind's work with girl delinquents began with her master's thesis, in the early 1970s, where she examined the records of girl delinquents and discovered that girls were receiving vaginal exams after being arrested (Belknap 2004). Chesney-Lind then applied the feminist perspective by showing how vaginal exams were being used to regulate sexual immorality in young girls. In the 1980s, Chesney-Lind worked with women inmates as a teacher at a prison in Hawaii. It was there that she began to hear the women's stories and to realize that many of these women had been abused as children. She then began to conduct research with women inmates to better understand their prior victimization. "Thus, through her scholarship, Chesney-Lind is not only responsible for identifying sexual abuse in the form of vaginal exams forced on girls apprehended for delinquency but also for documenting the sexually and physically abusive backgrounds of many delinquent girls and incarcerated women" (Belknap 2004:15).

In the late 1980s, Chesney-Lind began to focus on girls in gangs (Belknap 2004). She conducted many interviews with these girls to try and understand who they were and why they were involved in gangs. To her surprise, Chesney-Lind found that girls in gangs were not all that different from girl delinquents not involved in gangs. Chesney-Lind's research continues to focus on the plight of girl delinquents, but her focus has shifted toward understanding the experiences of girls' lives on the streets and in their homes (Belknap 2004).

The directions and suggestions that feminist criminologists have made and followed are referred to as the feminist perspective because this is not one theory, but rather a perspective that is still evolving (Britton 2000). This perspective asks criminologists, when studying females, to remember that most criminological theories have been developed to explain male criminal and delinquent behavior. Therefore, one should not directly apply these theories to females without taking into consideration the differences between males and females—both their biological differences and gender differences, or what it means to be male or female in our society (Holsinger 2000). When studying females it is also important to remember that inequalities in power between men and women are just as important as inequalities caused by race and class (Daly 1997).

Summary

Early theories that attempted to explain women's and girls' crime and delinquency rates tended to focus on sex and gendered stereotypes. Due to the women's movement and the increase in the number of feminist criminologists, the field of criminology became aware that its theories had been biased and were typically theories used to explain male behavior applied directly to female behavior. Criminologists are now beginning to understand that girls commit crimes for different reasons than boys and that girls' delinquency is often tied directly to their histories of victimization.

The delinquent offenses that girls tend to commit are nonviolent offenses, such as status and property offenses. The Juvenile Justice and Delinquency Prevention Act of 1974 attempted to decrease the number of status offenders held in detention. This act did decrease the number of boys held in detention for status offenses; however, for girls it was not quite as successful. The typical female status offender is a runaway who left home due to physical or sexual abuse. However, the reasons girls were committing status offenses were being overlooked, and these girls ended up in detention. Currently, we have a better understanding of why girls commit status offenses, but because of a lack of community programming, we don't have anywhere else to place these girls than detention. Status offenders then suffer, as they do not receive the help that they really need. There is a real need to implement programs in these girls' communities and detention facilities that specifically address their needs, such as nutrition and parenting classes for pregnant girls and counseling for those who have been victimized. Otherwise, we will continue to detain more and more young girls only to later release them to society unprepared and ready to reoffend.

References

Adler, Freda
  1975   Sisters in Crime: The Rise of the New Female Criminal. New York: McGraw-Hill.
Belknap, Joanne
  2004   Meda Chesney-Lind: The Mother of Feminist Criminology. Women and Criminal Justice 15:1–23.
Bloom, Barbara, Barbara Owens, Elizabeth P. Deschenes, and Jill Rosenbaum
  2003   Developing Gender-Specific Services for Delinquency Prevention: Understanding Risk and Resiliency. In It's a Crime: Women and Justice. Rosalyn Muraskin, ed. Pp. 517–543. Upper Saddle River, NJ: Prentice Hall.
Britton, Dana M.
  2000   Feminism in Criminology: Engendering the Outlaw. Annals of the American Academy of Political and Social Sciences 57:57–76.
Chesney-Lind, Meda
  2001   What About Girls? Delinquency Programming as if Gender Mattered. Corrections Today 63:38–45.
Chesney-Lind, Meda, and Randall G. Shelden
  2004   Girls, Delinquency, and Juvenile Justice. 3rd edition. Belmont, CA: Wadsworth.
Collins, Christopher
  2002   Girls and Juvenile Justice. Electronic document, www.girls-inc.org, accessed February 2, 2005.
Cuddy, Jim
  1991   Care-home Suspect Mentally Unstable, Doctor Says. Pittsburgh Post-Gazette, January 11:B1.

Daly, Kathleen
  1997   Different Ways of Conceptualizing Sex/Gender in Feminist Theory
          and Their Implications for Criminology. Theoretical Criminology
          1:25–51.
Dummer, Ethel S.
  1923   Foreword. *In* The Unadjusted Girl with Cases and Standpoint for
          Behavior Analysis. W. I. Thomas. Pp. v–xvii. Boston: Little, Brown.
Greenfeld, Lawrence, and Tracy L. Snell
  2000   Bureau of Justice Statistics Special Report: Women Offenders. Wash-
          ington, DC: U.S. Department of Justice.
Hagan, John, A. R. Gillis, and John Simpson
  1985   The Class Structure of Gender and Delinquency: Towards a Power
          Control Theory of Common Delinquency. American Journal of
          Sociology 90:1151–1178.
Harms, Paul
  2003   Detention in Delinquency Cases, 1990–1999. Electronic document,
          www.ncjrs.org/txtfiles1/ojjdp/fs200307.txt, accessed February 2,
          2005.
Holsinger, Kristi
  2000   Feminist Perspectives on Female Offending: Examining Real Girls'
          Lives. Women and Criminal Justice, 12:23–51.
Lombroso, Cesare, and G. Ferrero
  2004   Criminal Woman, the Prostitute, and the Normal Woman. N. H.
  [1893] Rafter and M. Gibson, trans. Durham, NC: Duke University Press.
McCarthy, Bill, John Hagan, and Todd S. Woodward
  1999   In the Company of Women: Structure and Agency in a Revised
          Power Control Theory of Gender and Delinquency. Criminology
          37:761–789.
Mulvey, Edward P., Melissa Sickmund, and Alfred Blumstein
  2000   Juvenile Crime Facts vs. Perceptions. Report 32, June. Pittsburgh:
          University of Pittsburgh Office of Child Development.
O'Connor, Anahad
  2004   Katharina Dalton, Expert on PMS, Dies at 87. New York Times, Sep-
          tember 28:A7.
Rafter, N. H., and Gibson, M.
  2004   Introduction. *In* Criminal Woman, the Prostitute, and the Normal
          Woman. Cesare Lombroso and G. Ferrero. Pp. 3–33. Durham, NC:
          Duke University Press.

Schramm, Pamela
   2002   Stereotypes and Vocational Programming for Women Prisoners. *In*
           The Incarcerated Woman: Rehabilitative Programming in Women's
           Prisons. Susan F. Sharp, ed. Pp. 17–28. Upper Saddle River, NJ: Pren-
           tice Hall.
Schwartz, Ira. M., Martha W. Steketee, and Victoria W. Schneider
   1990   Federal Juvenile Justice Policy and the Incarceration of Girls. Crime
           and Delinquency 36:503–520.
Snyder, Howard N., and Melissa Sickmund
   2006   Juvenile Offenders and Victims: 2006 National Report. Washington,
           DC: U.S. Department of Justice.
Stahl, Anne
   2003   Delinquency Cases in Juvenile Courts, 1999. Electronic document,
           www.ncjrs.org/txtfiles1/ojjdp/fs200302.txt, accessed February 2,
           2005.
Thomas, W. I.
   1923   The Unadjusted Girl with Cases and Standpoint for Behavior Analy-
           sis. Boston: Little, Brown.
U.S. Census Bureau
   2000   Census 2000. Electronic document, www.census.gov, accessed Feb-
           ruary 2, 2005.

LABELING AND CONFLICT THEORIES

L ABELING AND conflict explanations of delinquency focus on divergent social groups and alliances in society and the power these different groups exert on the passage and enforcement of laws. In general, these views of crime and delinquency identify offenders as more-or-less healthy and normal individuals who are responding to situations that are difficult to control. Juveniles, for example, may be labeled according to the groups or peers with whom they associate, and they have relatively little social power to change or alter these perceptions or legal actions based on the views of others.

A common assumption of labeling and conflict theories is that the enforcement of laws by the police and courts is neither uniform nor based strictly on legal issues. Minority suspects and, in general, people from politically and socially weak backgrounds are assumed to be disproportionately processed through the juvenile and criminal justice systems. Some of these issues have already been addressed, especially in chapter 3, and they will be discussed again in the chapters concerning the juvenile justice system. However, issues of discrimination are theoretically grounded in labeling and conflict theories.

In addition to the notion that more powerful groups in society seem to have the largest impact on laws and law enforcement, labeling theory also focuses on the result of having been identified as a criminal or delinquent by authorities such as the police and courts. In particular, labeling theory addresses the negative consequence in one's self-concept and ultimately behavior patterns as a result of having been labeled a delinquent or a criminal by official criminal and/or juvenile justice agents and organizations. For example, rather than desisting from criminal activity as a result of having been arrested or found delinquent in juvenile court, a juvenile might develop a hardened attitude toward the juvenile justice system and society in general, and become even more involved in delinquency. This emphasis on the reactions of suspects or offenders to the actions of official agents of social control and of members of society in general is used to name labeling theory a *societal reaction*, or *interactionist* explanation of crime and delinquency.

Key Concepts of Labeling Theory

Labeling theory is often identified with the works of Edwin Lemert and Howard Becker. However, many of its basic ideas can be found in the earlier writings of other scholars, such as C. H. Cooley, George Mead, and Frank Tannenbaum. Cooley, for example, coined the term *looking-glass self* (Cooley 1964). This concept argues that we obtain an image of ourselves by reacting to what we perceive others to be thinking of our behavior. As applied to labeling theory, the looking-glass self offers a basic understanding of how our self-concept may change because of the actions of the police or courts toward our behavior.

George Herbert Mead introduced the concept of "generalized other" as another term to describe the development of people in society (Strauss 1964). The generalized other is like our conscience, a view of what we should be doing according to what we think general society expects of us. As associated with labeling theory, the generalized other can be seen as a set of expectations and norms we pick up as we are socialized into society that can influence not only what we do but also how we react to the responses of others to our behavior. We may resist the label, try to change it, or accept it, depending in part on our notion of a generalized other.

Labeling theory is also evident in Thrasher's study of gangs in Chicago in the 1920s (Thrasher 1927), as discussed in chapter 10. However, Frank Tannenbaum, in a book titled *Crime and the Community* (1938) clearly identified labeling as one consequence of being processed through the juvenile justice system. Tannenbaum introduced the term *dramatization of evil*, through which he indicated a person can become the epitome of what he has been labeled. As Tannenbaum put it, "The process of making the criminal, therefore, is a process of tagging, defining, identifying, segregating, describing, emphasizing, making conscious and self-conscious; it becomes a way of stimulating, suggesting, emphasizing, and evoking the very traits that are complained of" (pp. 19–20).

The person who is generally credited with making labeling theory a contemporary perspective on crime and delinquency is Edwin Lemert, who discussed the theory and two of its more important terms in a book titled *Social Pathology*, published in 1951. In this volume, Lemert introduced the terms *primary* and *secondary deviance*. Primary deviance (or delinquency) is that which is committed *without a public label* being attached. The act may be noticed by one's family or close friends, or even by strangers in public. However, there is no formal processing of the individual in connection with primary deviance. The behavior is primary in the sense that it comes before an official label has been applied.

According to Lemert and many advocates of labeling theory, the causes of, or contributions to, primary deviance are several and varied. In effect, proponents of labeling theory downplay the importance of trying to understand the factors contributing to primary deviance *in favor* of emphasizing the consequences of tagging or labeling the act as criminal or delinquent and those who commit these acts as criminals or delinquents.

Secondary deviance is that which occurs after primary acts of crime and delinquency have been labeled. It is possible for a person to continue committing primary delinquency and never be caught or labeled as a delinquent. Strictly speaking, therefore, the continued commission of delinquency without formal labels having been applied represents primary deviance. Once the person has been caught and labeled as a delinquent, however, the process toward secondary deviance has begun.

Lemert envisioned secondary deviance as a process, involving several steps and potentially taking a long time to complete. The process includes committing the behavior, getting punished for it, reacting to the punishment or ignoring it altogether, continuing to commit acts of crime or delinquency and receiving punishment, and ultimately changing one's self-image to conform to the implications of the label (I am a "bad" kid) and continuing to commit deviant acts in accordance with a definition of deviant ("Everybody thinks I am a delinquent, so why not act that way?"). The exact place within this process wherein a person actually becomes a secondary delinquent is not clear, but the notion of changing one's self-concept to correspond to a label of delinquency and committing acts of criminality in connection with this definition are clear. That is the gist of secondary deviance.

Discussion of the Theory

Since the introduction of these concepts more than 50 years ago, there has been considerable discussion of these two terms and of labeling theory in general. Some, such as Akers (1968), suggest that the theory is too rigid in its depiction of how people come to accept a label placed on them by others. We may not easily accept condemning labels of who we are, and the acceptance of such pejorative terms thus becomes problematic and conditioned by a host of situations and variables. For example, some may look upon a label as a sign of importance, especially among those considered minorities when the label is applied by representatives of the dominant population, as mentioned in chapter 6, when self-concept was discussed in connection with containment theory.

In addition, there is the problem of how to deal with the seemingly contradictory existence of "hidden" crime and delinquency, that which goes unreported and undetected by officials. Is such behavior still criminal, or does it take an official label to make it criminal? Howard Becker (1973), for example, attempts to handle this issue by referring to hidden crime and deviance as "rule breaking," meaning behavior that is wrong but not technically labeled as criminal. It is still likely, however, that offenders realize their behavior is illegal, even though they have not been caught. Why go to lengths to conceal or justify criminal and delinquent behavior (see the discussion of neutralizations in chapter 6) if it is considered acceptable and normal?

It should also be remembered that, powerful as a label of crime and delinquency may be on one's self-concept and/or behavior, the reasons for committing delinquent acts in the first place may still exist. For example, if a child is involved with a delinquent peer group and begins to get into delinquent behavior, and if he or she is caught and labeled, continued involvement in crime might still be strongly influenced by the peer group—except that now there are additional problems of dealing with a label of delinquent, or perhaps a label of gang member, that were not there in the beginning. In some cases, simply being associated with a gang might be justification for the police to stop and perhaps arrest someone, regardless of what they have actually done. The distinctions between primary and secondary deviance and their connections to crime and delinquency are presented in figure 12.1.

Primary Deviance (caused by many possible factors and *not* labeled) → Possible Detection and labeling of the Behavior as Delinquent by Public Officials → Processing through the Juvenile Justice System → Public Identification as Delinquent → Acceptance of Delinquent Identification → Continued Delinquent Behavior (Secondary Deviance)

FIGURE 12.1 Labeling Theory and Delinquency

Labeling and Self-Concept

Self-concept was discussed earlier, in connection with containment theory. In that theory, self-concept is seen as a precursor to delinquency, a factor contributing to delinquency. With labeling theory, the self-concept is also important, but in a different way. Self-concept is thought to change in accordance with the label of one as a criminal or a delinquent. Presumably, the self-concept *before* the label was applied was normal, or at least not problematic. The evidence in support of this assumption is mixed. Some research tends to support the assumptions of labeling theory, but it seems more of the research refutes or questions these assumptions.

Case studies and qualitative analyses sometimes support the tenets of labeling theory. In a comparison of two gangs in a small midwestern town, for example, Chambliss concluded that labeling was a significant factor in the attitudes and behaviors of the two gangs, one lower class and one middle class. The lower-class gang (termed the "Roughnecks" by Chambliss) had a reputation for violence and crime in general, and their arrest records seemed to confirm that reputation. In contrast, the middle-class gang (the "Saints") were considered basically good kids by those in the community (in part because they tended to commit their delinquent acts in other towns) and had no arrest records, even though they were almost as involved in delinquent acts (based on Chambliss's observations) as were the Roughnecks. Furthermore, the boys' own attitudes seemed to agree with their reputation in the community (Chambliss 1973).

Other, more quantified research, however, does not systematically support the hypothesis that official labels create changes in self-concepts of delinquents. Some studies, for example, indicate that while delinquents tend to think of themselves as delinquent more so than do high-school students, this difference is not automatically caused by being arrested or sent to juvenile court (Gibbs 1974). In addition, official delinquents do not always view their lives or their reputations in the community as having been significantly affected or changed as a result of having been caught and labeled for their delinquent activity (Foster et al. 1972). Other studies conclude that the overall situation of a juvenile's life, such as social-class position and actual involvement in delinquency, have more to do with self-concept than does the existence of a formal label (Hepburn 1977).

Official labels may have more impact on middle-class youth and first offenders than on other youth (Jensen 1972, 1980; Mahoney 1974). Presumably, youth in these situations are more traumatized by the first time they are arrested or by the relatively low presence of police and court involvement in their neighborhoods. It may also be the case that being arrested by representatives of the dominant class (such as middle-class whites) can be seen as a kind of badge of courage and something to be proud of among minorities, particularly youth.

Labeling and Behavior

Does being labeled change one's behavior? Is labeling by official agents of social control the catalyst for a major change in one's behavior? Finding answers to these questions is not easy, in part because, as mentioned above, the behavior of delinquents is explained by many factors, and these contributors to behavior do not disappear just because one has been arrested or referred to court. Membership in gangs seems to lead to an increase in delinquency, as discussed in chapters 6 and 10, so we know that certain social circumstances can contribute to increased risk for committing delinquent acts.

Concluding that being labeled a delinquent actually leads to secondary deviance, however, is not always justified by available data. Qualitative studies, such as the Saints and the Roughnecks study mentioned above, provide some support for the continuation of delinquency based upon labels or reputations in the community. In addition, there is some evidence that being transferred to the criminal justice system may actually increase the risk for greater involvement in crime and delinquency, and this may be the result of labeling (Bishop et al. 1996). Also, the citation of negative labeling as an impetus to the development of techniques of neutralization is an important feature of neutralization theory, discussed in chapter 6.

However, there is also evidence that labeling does not increase delinquency. For example, the oft-noted "maturation effect," discussed in chapter 3, runs counter to the predictions of labeling theory. Instead of labeling's leading to more crime and delinquency, there is often a cessation of criminality with age, including among those who have been officially labeled as criminals or delinquents. Of course, there is the hard-core group of delinquents to be considered, the chronic offenders in the cohort studies. These offenders repeat their offenses and there is some evidence that the severity of their crimes increases somewhat as they repeatedly offend (Tracy et al. 1990:chapter 10). Chronic offenders are definitely labeled, since they have been contacted by the police at least five times during their juvenile years. However, the direct impact of labeling on the "careers" of these juveniles is difficult to assess within the reports of the cohort studies.

It is also the case that the behavior of the Saints and the Roughnecks, referred to above, was consistent with the labels and reputations each gang had in the community. All of the Roughnecks had been arrested, but none of the Saints had a police record, so labeling was definitely occurring in that study.

The effects of labeling are often difficult to determine because of the lack of longitudinal studies to test the theory. Some research suggests that labeling may increase delinquency. The aforementioned longitudinal study of over 2,700 juveniles referred to the adult court system in Florida, for example, concluded that waived youth were more delinquent than a matched sample of 2,700 juveniles who were not transferred to the adult system, and that this increase in criminality may have been attributed to labeling (Bishop et al. 1996). However, additional observations of these youth concluded that after a few years, the rate of crime among both samples of offenders was about the same (Winner et al. 1997), indicating that even if labeling had occurred previously, its effects were reduced over time, again somewhat contrary to the predictions of labeling theory.

Although Lemert and other labeling theorists concentrated on the effects of labeling within the criminal or juvenile justice systems, the impact of names and labels can also be felt when applied by other significant people in juveniles' lives, such as parents, teachers, or even peers. Some research suggests that these more informal sources of labeling can have strong impacts on delinquent behavior. In analyses of the National Youth Survey, for example, Ross Matsueda and colleagues conclude that negative labeling by parents (such as whether their child is well liked or is a troublemaker) is associated with lowered self-esteem and increased delinquency among children. In addition, these studies conclude that delinquency and labeling can be interactive, that is, delinquency can lead to labeling, which can then lead to more delinquency, and so on (Matsueda 1992). Negatively labeled youth may start to see themselves as what they have been labeled and act accordingly, that is, developing "reflected appraisals," especially among males (Heimer and Matsueda 1994; Bartusch and Matsueda 1996). The results of these analyses are only suggestive of a negative impact of labeling because they are based on conclusions and opinions of parents and children rather than on direct observations of parent–child interactions. Still, these results tend to support the basic ideas of labeling theory, except that the labeling is coming from parents as opposed to the police or court officials. Recent research, however, still maintains that labeling from agents of social control, such as the police, can have negative impacts on youth and thus contribute to delinquency (Hannon 2003).

The studies by Matsueda and associates also suggest that delinquency can weaken the social bond between parents and children (see chapter 6 and social control theory), which can lead to further involvement in delinquency and further alienation between parent and child (see also Triplett and Jarjoura 1994). This idea suggests that labeling may have an *indirect* impact on delinquency because it weakens bonds of youth to conventional adults in society such as parents and teachers. Howard Kaplan and his colleagues also suggest that the impact of labeling may indirectly lead to delinquency because labeling can lead to lowered self-esteem or self-rejection, which can then lead to more involvement with delinquent peers (see chapter 6 and differential association theory), which can then lead to delinquency (Kaplan and Johnson 1991; Kaplan and Fukurai 1992).

Connections with Juvenile Justice

Despite the uneven research support for labeling theory, it has been the theoretical basis for several juvenile justice concepts and practices over the past 20 years or so. For example, *diversion* is currently a popular method of handling young offenders, especially first offenders and those charged with minor criminal offenses or status offenses. Diversion will be discussed in more detail in the next chapter, on juvenile justice, but essentially it involves placing an offender in programs or agencies that are not directly within the formal juvenile justice system. One rationale behind this practice is that identifying juveniles as delinquent by processing them through the formal system of juvenile justice is potentially harmful to them by stigmatizing them and by placing restrictions on their successful return to conventional pursuits such as school and work. Some diversion programs operate at the police level, that is, youth are diverted from the system at the point of arrest or being taken into custody. Other diversion programs are introduced later in the system, such as after referral to the juvenile court.

Another feature of juvenile justice is *deinstitutionalization*, and this practice is also partially based on labeling theory. Deinstitutionalization means deemphasizing institutions as a response to delinquency. In its purest form, it is the total or near total removal of youngsters from juvenile correctional institutions, such as the "Massachusetts Experiment" initiated by Jerome Miller in the 1970s in Massachusetts (Miller 1991). Other examples of deinstitutionalization include significant reductions in inmate populations or the closing of a few institutions in a state. Deinstitutionalization will be discussed again in chapter 15, on juvenile institutions.

A third aspect of juvenile justice that is at least partially based on labeling theory is *restorative justice*. This concept essentially seeks to reconcile the differences between an offender and his or her victim(s), including members of the community who may also be affected by the crime or act of delinquency (Krisberg 2005:185–189). In part, restorative justice is based on the concept of *reintegrative shaming* (Braithwaite 1989). Reintegrative shaming maintains that attempts to reconcile, or reintegrate offenders back into the community, may help not only to produce more law-abiding behavior in offenders but also to promote order and conformity within the community. Thus, labeling offenders may produce more desired results in terms of reduced crime and delinquency *if* such labeling efforts are conducted with an eye toward *shaming* for the purpose of repentance on the part of offenders and acceptance of offenders back into the community. Reintegrative shaming and restorative justice will be discussed in more detail in chapter 15, in connection with prevention and treatment programs.

While diversion, deinstitutionalization, and restorative justice programs may not always significantly reduce delinquency, they are likely to remain a part of society's response to delinquency, and to that extent, the impact of labeling theory on juvenile justice practices is significant.

Conflict Theories

Conflict theories of crime and delinquency are similar to labeling theory in that they also identify differences between and among groups and components of society as having a major impact on the development and enforcement of laws and on criminal or delinquent behavior as well. However, conflict theories do not focus on the impact of labeling on one's self-concept, as is the case with labeling theory.

For this discussion, attention will focus on those conflict theories that attempt to explain delinquency. Conflict theories can be categorized by the type of conflict thought to contribute to delinquency. One kind of conflict theory, for example, looks at the conflict between cultures as an important explanation of delinquency. This is called *culture conflict* theory. As proposed by Thorsten Sellin, culture conflict theory argues that norms and laws in society are better interpreted as *conduct norms* (Sellin 1938). Conduct norms are prescriptions for behavior that are based on cultural values. They may be included in laws, but they can exist outside of laws as well.

Sellin argues that people immigrating to other cultures, especially countries that are economically and politically stronger than that of the immigrants, are at risk of becoming involved in criminal or delinquent behavior because of the confusion and misunderstandings derived from differences in conduct norms, or basic cultural values. Second-generation youth are especially vulnerable to such conflicts, primarily because they are exposed directly to at least two different, often conflicting, cultures, that of their parents and that of the new country. The values of the new country are expressed in the school system, which these youth are almost always forced to attend, at least for a while (Wirth 1931). The kids caught in these situations may have real problems handling the conflicts, frustrations, and confusions between what they are learning at school and what they hear and see at home, especially if different languages and values are involved. These confusions can become even more critical when compounded by the effects of peer interactions (see chapter 6). The desire to be accepted by one's peers can be much more difficult when major cultural and language differences are involved.

Culture conflict theory seems particularly appropriate as a partial explanation of gangs, discussed in chapter 10. It can also, however, be used to help understand the behaviors of many troubled and conflicted youth, especially immigrants, who are not necessarily involved with gangs but who may be engaged in other delinquent activity, such as status offending, using drugs, theft, and so on (Sheu 1986; Wong 1997).

Another conflict theory focused on youth is proposed by Austin Turk (1969). Turk argues that people act according to their values and that often these values come into conflict. This situation is particularly likely to occur when citizens are interacting with public officials, such as the police. Turk suggests that police–gang interactions are especially potentially conflicting situations because gangs represent gang values, such as sentiments of togetherness among gang members, while the police represent law and authority and the public's interest. The values expressed by the police also tend to label others as troublemakers or delinquents, and again, these are likely to be given to gang members. In this respect, Turk's conflict theory is similar to labeling theory except that his ideas are couched within a framework of value conflicts.

Perhaps the better-known conflict theory is that identified with the ideas of Karl Marx. Although Marx never explicitly posited a theory of crime or delinquency, many of his ideas have served as a basis for a conflict theory of criminality. In particular, theorists have argued that a prime or basic cause of crime is capitalism. Willem Bonger, a Dutch criminologist, was one of the first to offer a Marxian theory of crime in 1916 (Bonger 1969). However, Bonger did not separate the basic cause of crime by age, and his ideas tended to apply to adults or to the general population more than to juveniles. More contemporary Marxist, or better, neo-Marxist (Shoemaker 2005:231), theorists also fail to specify the relationship between capitalism as a basic cause of crime and its effects on juveniles (Chambliss 1975; Quinney 1980).

However, David Greenberg does try to connect neo-Marxist ideas with delinquency, although his explanation seems to combine other explanations along with neo-Marxist views. Greenberg (1977) argues that juveniles are economically disadvantaged by capitalist economic systems. However, even for juveniles, money and economic power are coveted and important for their social lives. Respect and friendship can sometimes be "bought," so the lack of money impedes these sources of satisfaction for many juveniles. Also, success at school is limited for some juveniles, especially those from working- and lower-class backgrounds, and this becomes another incentive for turning to crime. This scenario seems to stretch the connection between capitalism and the motivations for behavior among youth. Furthermore, to the extent that such a connection does exist, it makes more sense for the explanation of crime among lower-class youth and thus seems to be less useful as an explanation for middle-class delinquency, as others have noted (Klockars 1979).

In addition, as Greenberg's theory implies and as we have seen elsewhere in this book, it is not clear that juveniles are as influenced by money and jobs as they are by social status and peer acceptance, among other less economic measuring sticks. In that sense, the neo-Marxist approach seems less persuasive as an explanation of delinquency than other theories. The emphasis on capitalism or socialism as a basic cause of criminality also ignores or downplays the existence of delinquency in socialist nations such as Cuba, the People's Republic of China, and the former Soviet Union (Shoemaker 2005:235, 241).

The focus of attention in neo-Marxist criminology has also been on the effects of capitalism on the enactment and enforcement of laws. As indicated above, this topic will be addressed again in chapter 14. For the moment, however, note that while analyses of the child-saving movement and the development of juvenile justice in 19th- and early 20th-century America indicate the partial influence of social class (see chapter 2), several other studies of delinquency laws and juvenile courts do not support the neo-Marxist claim that delinquency laws are made and enforced on the basis of social-class privilege or influence. Rather, it seems that a combination of many factors, which sometimes may include social class, tend to collectively result in the passage of delinquency laws (Hagan and Leon 1977; Sutton 1985). In addition, the operations of the juvenile court are often individualized and may as much reflect the interactions among legalities, personalities, and interpersonal communications as the effect of structural and class-based considerations (Bortner 1984).

Largely because the suggested solution to crime lies in radically altering the socioeconomic systems of capitalist societies, this perspective has become known as the *radical perspective* or theory of crime and delinquency. However, even some earlier Marxist criminologists did not accept this point of view and opted for a less radical solution to the problem of crime and delinquency (Gordon 1973). More recently, many neo-Marxists have developed what has become known as the *left realist* position on crime control and prevention (Schwartz and DeKeseredy 1991; Young and Matthews 1992). Left realism focuses on more realistic goals for crime reduction, goals that seem more compatible with other explanations of crime such as social disorganization and social control perspectives (Groves and Sampson 1987). For some, the ultimate goal may be the eventual elimination of capitalism (Lynch and Groves 1989:126–130), but even then, the emphasis on more manageable problems and workable solutions seems favored over the radical restructuring of the socioeconomic system.

Summary

Labeling and conflict theories share a common interest in the understanding of how laws are made and enforced. In particular, these perspectives on crime and delinquency assume that laws reflect the interests of some, especially the more powerful in society, and that the enforcement of laws is also based on these influences. In addition, labeling theory addresses the important issues of the impact of being labeled a delinquent on one's self-concept and behavior. An important distinction within this theory is the difference between primary and secondary deviance. Primary deviance is deviance committed without an official label, while secondary deviance is based on the consequences of being labeled a deviant or delinquent, especially in terms of self-identification and subsequent involvement in crime or delinquency.

Attempts to examine these two theoretical perspectives on delinquency have not been uniformly positive. While there is ample evidence that many laws are enacted through the influences of interest groups, consistent with conflict theory, there is less evidence that delinquency laws have emerged through similar interests. The interests of middle-class women were particularly evident with the passage of the first delinquency laws in the 19th century. Even with these laws, however, there is evidence of some degree of consensus regarding the need for the protection of children from victimization by adults and other youth. In addition, anecdotal evidence is consistent with labeling theory's predictions that an official label of delinquency tends to change one's self-concept and self-identification and that repeated involvement in delinquency can develop in reaction to such labeling. However, more quantified data provide mixed evidence regarding this prediction. In particular, the often-noted maturation effect, in which most youth seem to move away from crime and delinquency around ages 16–18, suggests that while labeling may have some impact on youth, its effects are not long lasting.

Of course, the intent of labeling young people as delinquent is to correct their behavior, and in some, perhaps many, cases this happens. However, it is also true that labeling may have a reverse effect in that it may create more problems than existed in the first place and thus make it more likely that a juvenile would reoffend. Or it may be the case that labeling may have little direct effect on a child's attitudes and behavior apart from the many influences on behavior discussed in previous chapters.

Although the evidence concerning the predictions and assumptions of labeling and conflict theories is inconsistent, current practices in the juvenile justice system are sometimes based on these perspectives, especially labeling theory. Diversion, deinstitutionalization, and restorative justice programs, for example, are based in large part on the ideas of labeling theory. In addition, these views on crime and delinquency have the important value of sensitizing society to the potential for inequality and abuse in the operation of the juvenile justice system and other institutions designed to handle delinquent or troubled youth. In this sense, labeling and conflict theories provide invaluable knowledge and understanding, not only to the motivations for delinquency but also, perhaps more importantly, to the understanding of society and its institutions, especially the juvenile justice system.

References

Akers, Ronald L.
> 1968   Problems in the Sociology of Deviance: Social Definitions and Behavior. Social Forces 46:455–465.

Bartusch, Dawn Jeglum, and Ross L. Matsueda
> 1996   Gender, Reflected Appraisals and Labeling: A Cross Groups Test of an Interactionist Theory of Delinquency. Social Forces 75:145–177.

Becker, Howard
> 1973   Outsiders. New York: Free Press.
> [1963]

Bishop, Donna M., Charles E. Frazier, Lonn Lanza-Kaduce, and Lawrence Winner
> 1996   The Transfer of Juveniles to Criminal Court: Does It Make a Difference? Crime & Delinquency 42:171–191.

Bonger, Willem
> 1969   Criminality and Economic Conditions. Bloomington: Indiana
> [1916] University Press.

Bortner, M. A.
> 1984   Inside a Juvenile Court: The Tarnished Ideal of Individualized Justice. New York: New York University Press.

Braithwaite, John
> 1989   Crime, Shame, and Reintegration. Cambridge, England: Cambridge University Press.

Chambliss, William
> 1973   The Saints and the Roughnecks. Society 11:24–31.
> 1975   Toward a Political Economy of Crime. Theory and Society 2:149–170.

Cooley, Charles Horton
> 1964   Human Nature and the Social Order. New York: Schocken.
> [1902]

Foster, Jack D., Simon Dinitz, and Walter C. Reckless
> 1972   Perceptions of Stigma Following Public Intervention for Delinquent Behavior. Social Problems 20:202–209.

Gibbs, Leonard E.
> 1974   Effects of Juvenile Legal Procedures on Juvenile Offenders' Self-Attitudes. Journal of Research in Crime and Delinquency 11:51–55.

Gordon, David M.
    1973   Capitalism, Class, and Crime in America. Crime & Delinquency
            19:163–186.
Greenberg, David F.
    1977   Delinquency and the Age Structure of Society. Contemporary Cri-
            sis 1:189–223.
Groves, W. Byron, and Robert J. Sampson
    1987   Traditional Contributions to Radical Criminology. Journal of
            Research in Crime and Delinquency 24:181–214.
Hagan, John, and Jeffrey Leon
    1977   Rediscovering Delinquency, Social History, Political Ideology,
            and the Sociology of Law. American Sociological Review 42:
            587–598.
Hannon, Lance
    2003   Poverty, Delinquency, and Educational Attainment: Cumulative Dis-
            advantage or Disadvantage Saturation? Sociological Quarterly
            73:575–594.
Heimer, Karen, and Ross L. Matsueda
    1994   Role-Taking, Role Commitment, and Delinquency: A Theory of
            Differential Social Control. American Sociological Review
            59:365–390.
Hepburn, John R.
    1977   The Impact of Police Intervention upon Juvenile Delinquents.
            Criminology 15:235–262.
Jensen, Gary F.
    1972   Delinquents and Adolescent Self-Conceptions: A Study of the Per-
            sonal Relevance of Infraction. Social Problems 20:84–103.
    1980   Labeling and Identity: Toward a Reconciliation of Divergent Find-
            ings. Criminology 18:1212–129.
Kaplan, Howard B., and Hiroshi Fukurai
    1992   Negative Social Sanctions, Self-Rejection, and Drug Use. Youth &
            Society 23:275–298.
Kaplan, Howard B., and Robert J. Johnson
    1991   Negative Social Sanctions and Juvenile Delinquency: Effects of
            Labeling in a Model of Deviant Behavior. Social Science Quarterly
            72:98–122.
Klockars, Karl B.
    1979   The Contemporary Crises of Marxist Criminology. Criminology
            16:477–515.

Krisberg, Barry
    2005   Juvenile Justice: Redeeming Our Children. Thousand Oaks, CA: Sage.

Lemert, Edwin M.
    1951   Social Pathology. New York: McGraw-Hill.

Lynch, Michael J., and W. Byron Groves
    1989   A Primer in Radical Criminology. 2nd edition. New York: Harrow and Heston.

Mahoney, Anne R.
    1974   The Effect of Labeling upon Youths in the Juvenile Justice System: A Review of the Evidence. Law & Society Review 8:583–614.

Matsueda, Ross L.
    1992   Reflected Appraisals, Parental Labeling, and Delinquency: Specifying a Symbolic Interactionist Theory. American Journal of Sociology 97:1577–1611.

Miller, Jerome G.
    1991   Last One over the Wall: The Massachusetts Experiment in Closing Reform Schools. Columbus: Ohio State University Press.

Quinney, Richard
    1980   Class, State, and Crime. 2nd edition. New York: Longman.

Schwartz, Martin D., and Walter S. DeKeseredy
    1991   Left Realist Criminology: Strengths, Weaknesses, and the Feminist Critique. Crime, Law, and Social Change 15:51–72.

Sellin, Thorsten
    1938   Culture Conflict and Crime. New York: Social Science Research Council.

Sheu, Chuen-Jim
    1986   Delinquency and Identity: Juvenile Delinquency in an American Chinatown. New York: Harrow and Heston.

Shoemaker, Donald J.
    2005   Theories of Delinquency: An Examination of Explanations of Delinquent Behavior. 5th edition. New York: Oxford University Press.

Strauss, Anselm, ed.
    1964   George Herbert Mead on Social Psychology: Selected Papers. [1934] Chicago: University of Chicago Press.

Sutton, John R.
    1985   The Juvenile Court and Social Welfare: Dynamics of Progressive Reform. Law & Society Review 19:107–145.

Tannenbaum, Frank
    1938   Crime and the Community. New York: Ginn and Company.
Thrasher, Frederick
    1927   The Gang. Chicago: University of Chicago Press.
Tracy, Paul E., Marvin E. Wolfgang, and Robert M. Figlio
    1990   Delinquency in Two Birth Cohorts. New York: Plenum.
Triplett, Ruth A., and G. Roger Jarjoura
    1994   Theoretical and Empirical Specification of a Model of Informal
            Labeling. Journal of Quantitative Criminology 10:241–276.
Turk, Austin T.
    1968   Criminality and Legal Order. Chicago: Rand McNally.
Winner, Lawrence T., Lonn Lanza Kaduce, Donna M. Bishop, and Charles E.
Frazier
    1997   The Transfer of Juveniles to Criminal Court: Reexamining Recidi-
            vism over the Long Term. Crime & Delinquency 43:548–563.
Wirth, Louis
    1931   Culture Conflict and Misconduct. Social Forces 9:484–492.
Wong, Siu Kwong
    1997   Delinquency of Chinese-Canadian Youth: A Test of Opportunity,
            Control, and Intergenerational Conflict Theories. Youth & Society
            29:112–133.
Young, Jock, and Roger Matthews
    1992   Rethinking Criminology: The Realist Debate. Newbury Park, CA:
            Sage.

The Contemporary Juvenile Justice System

A S WAS DISCUSSED in chapter 2, the juvenile justice system is rooted in historical context that includes concepts and developments from Europe and the early years of American society. However, the contemporary form of juvenile justice in the United States is barely 100 years old and is based on the model created by the first juvenile delinquency laws passed in Chicago and Cook County, Illinois, in 1899.

From the legal inception of the first juvenile justice systems in various states until today, one of the cardinal features of justice for the young is the establishment of separate procedures and concepts designed to relate to the characteristics and situations of young people, including appropriate responses to their illegal actions. Central to these procedures and concepts is the notion that judgments and societal reactions should be based on the *best interests of the child,* often to include policies based on treatment and rehabilitation rather than societal punishment.

Within 30 years of the creation of the first juvenile court system in Illinois, virtually every state had developed some kind of juvenile court concept with attendant policies and programs. In 1912, the United States government created the Children's Bureau, which, in part, was given oversight responsibilities for all of the several juvenile courts in the country. For several decades, that agency was also responsible for collecting and reporting statistical data on juvenile courts and juvenile institutions. Today, that function rests with the National Center for Juvenile Justice (Krisberg 2005:12).

The modern system of juvenile justice is divided into three major units, or subsystems: the police, the courts, and correctional institutions. The purpose of this chapter is to present an overview of juvenile justice within this framework as well as to discuss basic terms, concepts, and procedures within the juvenile justice system. The chapters to follow will concentrate more specifically on the role of the police, juvenile courts, and correctional institutions as the major components of the overall system.

An Overview of the Modern
Juvenile Justice System

To describe juvenile justice as a "system" is, to some, a misnomer, in that the various parts and components of this system sometimes, perhaps often, do not mesh well and seem to be more fragmented than integrated (Bartollas and Miller 2005:28–30). That is, the various components or units of the juvenile justice system are often not interconnected such that information about a case or a juvenile flows evenly and smoothly from one unit to another. One common complaint heard from practitioners in the juvenile system is lack of communication between members or representatives of different units. This problem is often heard when referring to different organizations within one component of the system, such as the lack of communication between or among different police departments in one geographical area.

Regardless of the nature of the elements of juvenile justice, a major factor in the decision to handle a case in the juvenile or adult system of justice is the age of the accused. Usually, youth under the age of 18 are under the *original* jurisdiction of the juvenile courts. This age restriction is true for about 70 percent of the states. In some states, however, juvenile court jurisdiction ends for youth at the age of 17 or 16. In addition, in most states, once a juvenile has been sent to the juvenile court and handled within the juvenile system, the supervision of that juvenile may extend to the juvenile's 21st birthday, and this is true in the majority of the states. However, the upper age of juvenile justice *retention* of jurisdiction ranges from 18 in six states to 24 in California, Montana, Oregon, and Wisconsin. Three states—Colorado, Hawaii, and New Jersey—do not specify an upper age limit of jurisdiction. The original jurisdiction and retention of jurisdiction ages for each state are presented in table 13.1.

TABLE 13.1 Oldest Age for Original Juvenile Court Jurisdiction in Delinquency Matters, 2004

Age	State
15	Connecticut
	New York
	North Carolina
16	Georgia
	Illinois
	Louisiana
	Massachusetts
	Michigan
	Missouri
	New Hampshire
	South Carolina
	Texas
	Wisconsin
17	Alabama
	Alaska
	Arizona
	Arkansas
	California
	Colorado
	Delaware
	District of Columbia
	Florida
	Hawaii
	Idaho
	Indiana
	Iowa
	Kansas
	Kentucky
	Maine
	Maryland
	Minnesota
	Mississippi
	Montana
	Nebraska

(Continued)

TABLE 13.1 Oldest Age for Original Juvenile Court Jurisdiction in Delinquency Matters, 2004 (Continued)

Age	State
	Nevada
	New Jersey
	New Mexico
	North Dakota
	Ohio
	Oklahoma
	Oregon
	Pennsylvania
	Rhode Island
	South Dakota
	Tennessee
	Utah
	Vermont
	Virginia
	Washington
	West Virginia
	Wyoming

Oldest Age Over Which the Juvenile Court May Retain Jurisdiction for Disposition Purposes in Delinquency Matters, 2004.

Age	State
18	Alaska
	Iowa
	Kentucky
	Nebraska
	Okalahoma
	Tennessee
19	Mississippi
	North Dakota
20	Alabama
	Arizona*
	Arkansas
	Connecticut
	Delaware
	District of Columbia
	Georgia
	Idaho

	Illinois
	Indiana
	Louisiana
	Maine
	Maryland
	Massachusetts
	Michigan
	Minnesota
	Missouri
	Nevada**
	New Hampshire
	New Mexico
	New York
	North Carolina
	Ohio
	Pennsylvania
	Rhode Island
	South Carolina
	South Dakota
	Texas
	Utah
	Vermont
	Virginia
	Washington
	West Virginia
	Wyoming
21	
22	Florida
	Kansas
24	California
	Montana
	Oregon
	Wisconsin
	Colorado***
	Hawaii***
	New Jersey***

* Arizona statute extends jurisdiction through age 20, but a 1979 State Supreme Court decision held that juvenile court jurisdiction terminates at age 18.

** Until the full term of the disposition order for sex offenders.

*** Until the full term of the disposition order.

Note: Extended jurisdiction may be restricted to certain offenses or juveniles.

Source: Adapted from Snyder and Sickmund 2006:103.

Regardless of age restrictions, there is a process through which most *juveniles* are sent, from arrest to incarceration. A depiction of this process is presented in figure 13.1.

As the data in figure 13.1 indicate, the entry level for the juvenile justice system can either be through the police or some other source. Approximately 84 percent of the referrals to juvenile court come from the police. Other referral sources include parents or guardians, school authorities, victims, and probation officers (Snyder and Sickmund 2006:104). The police have several options when witnessing or being told of an offense by a juvenile. They can, for example, issue a warning, or citation, and let the juvenile go. They may take the youth to his or her parents as part of the warning. Or they may decide to arrest the child, that is, *take* him or her *into custody*. This procedure involves making a record of the event, entering it in the files of the department, and taking physical profiles of the juvenile, such as fingerprints or photographs (see Sanborn and Salerno 2005:123–412 for a more detailed discussion of the system described below).

Cases involving arrest usually are referred to the juvenile court system, not necessarily a juvenile court judge right away, but to the system. The first step in the juvenile court phase is *intake.* Intake involves information gathering by an officer of the court, usually a probation officer, concerning the specifics of the case. Typical attendees at intake are the officer of the court, perhaps the arresting police officer, the child and representatives of the child, such as parents or an attorney, and the victim, if one can be found, as well as representatives of the victim. The intake officer can dismiss the case, hold it for continued review, which usually means some type of informal probation, or refer the case to the juvenile court judge. Formal referrals to the court from the police or to the juvenile court judge by the intake officer are called *petitions.* A petition is a formal charge against the juvenile, one that lists the type of offense committed and the known particulars of the case, such as when and where the offense was committed, the victim, and other relevant information. Often the petition from the police is carried over, with possible modifications, as a petition to the juvenile court judge.

Once a case is petitioned to the juvenile court judge, a juvenile court hearing is established, which may be weeks or months removed. At this point, another kind of hearing is often scheduled, a *detention hearing*. The purpose of the detention hearing is to determine whether the juvenile should remain in custody pending the court hearing. This detention hearing is often presided over by the intake officer and may elicit information from a variety of caregivers of the youth as well as from representatives of the commu-

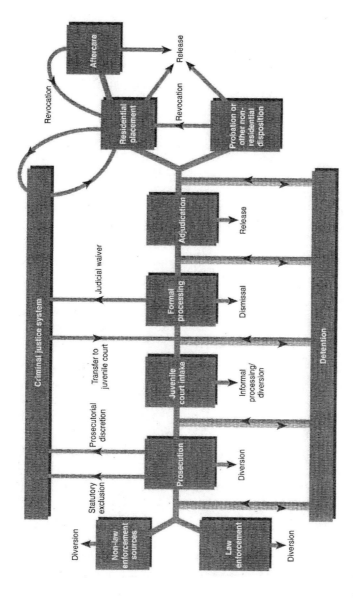

FIGURE 13.1 What are the stages of delinquency case processing in the juvenile justice system?

Note: This chart gives a simplified view of caseflow through the juvenile justice system. Procedures vary among jurisdictions.

Source: Snyder and Sickmund 2006:105.

nity and the juvenile justice system. Detention centers are similar to jails except that they hold only youth. In addition to those awaiting a hearing, however, detention centers may also hold youth awaiting transfer to the adult system or to a correctional institution or those awaiting placement in the community after having served time in a correctional institution.

The court hearing of a case is called an *adjudicatory hearing*, which is similar to a trial in the adult court system. The purpose of this hearing is to determine the merits of the case and whether the accused is likely to have committed the offense. The traditional nature of juvenile court hearings has been informal, with the goal of reaching a reasonable judgment concerning the best interest of the child, balanced with the interests of the community and the victim in the case. As such, then, adjudicatory hearings are not considered adversarial, as they are in the adult system, but, rather, informational. Thus, if the judge determines culpability in the case, the finding is considered a *finding of delinquency* rather than a finding of guilt. However, as will be discussed in the next chapter, several Supreme Court rulings have altered the nature of the juvenile court, collectively making contemporary juvenile court proceedings more formal and legalistic. Nonetheless, the basic assumption that juveniles in juvenile court are not being attacked by the state, but rather are being examined by court officials, is a central feature of juvenile courts and one that separates juvenile proceedings from adult ones.

The informal nature of the juvenile court operation is also exemplified by the options available to the judge upon a finding of delinquency. These options are often called *dispositions.* Dispositions include informal probation, or taking the case under advisement for a period of time to see whether the offender is able to change his or her behavior. The judge can also order the child to pay restitution to the victim, such as repairing damaged property or paying the victim monetary compensation for losses. The offender may also be ordered to pay a fine to the court or the community. All of these dispositions may be included as part of probation, formal or informal. Under formal probation, the offender is ordered to be supervised by a probation officer and to adhere to specific rules and regulations, such as attending counseling sessions, observing curfews, and attending school. At the end of a specified period of time, six months to a year, for example, the offender is brought back to court and his or her behavior is once again examined. At this point, however, the particulars of the original case are less relevant than the subsequent behavior of the offender, as attested by the supervising probation officer.

Besides restitution and probation, all of which occur in the community, juvenile court dispositions include placements outside the offender's home. One type of placement is an order to live with another relative or perhaps a referral the state's foster care system. The most restrictive disposition is commitment to the state system of juvenile correction. Almost always, this disposition is not to any particular institution, but to the system. Many states, such as Virginia, demand that committed juveniles first be examined in *diagnostic and reception centers* for careful evaluation before assignment to a particular type of institution. This process may last several weeks, but the point to remember is that the administrators of juvenile corrections, not the presiding judge, decide where the juvenile will ultimately be placed.

The length of confinement is usually determined by the administrators of the correctional system. Typically, commitments to state juvenile corrections are indeterminate, or open, and set by the administrators of the institutions. However, recent legislation has given juvenile court judges more authority over lengths of institutional confinements, allowing them in some cases, for example, to set specific periods of confinement. In almost all cases, juveniles cannot be held in confinement past the age of majority. However, some contemporary juvenile justice laws allow judges to sentence convicted defendants to specified terms in correctional institutions, subject to legislative maximum ages of confinement. Even in some of these cases, laws allow juveniles incarcerated in juvenile facilities to be transferred to adult prisons once they reach the age limit of juvenile justice jurisdiction. Often these sentencing options fall under the term *blended sentence* (Sanborn and Salerno 2005:373–383; Snyder and Sickmund 2006:103, 115–116).

A developing alternative sentence for juvenile court judges is the conviction and sentencing of parents of delinquents. Historically, courts have held parents of delinquent children civilly liable for their child's behavior, but increasingly, laws are being passed that allow judges to place criminal charges against parents and for judges to order criminal punishments for these parents upon conviction (Pollet 2004; Sanborn and Salerno 2005:383).

The final phase of the juvenile justice system is *aftercare*, called parole in the adult system. Aftercare is usually administered by the correctional component of the system and includes requirements for adhering to rules and regulations, similar to probation. One important difference with aftercare is that all of those assigned to this system have spent time in an institution, whereas probationers have avoided institutional confinement by being placed on probation in the first place. Aftercare is typically administered under the supervision of the correctional component of the system, but some jurisdictions assign aftercare cases to juvenile court judges, sometimes the same judge who committed the offender to juvenile corrections (for discussions and descriptions of these stages of the juvenile justice system, see Puzzanchera et al. 2004:25 and Sanborn and Salerno 2005:chapters 9–15).

A dominant philosophy of the juvenile justice system is treatment and prevention, as opposed to the philosophy of the adult criminal justice system, which is punishment. Thus, many of the terms and procedures associated with juvenile justice are focused on the interests of the juvenile rather than on the interests of the state. One reason why different terms, such as *take into custody* and *aftercare*, are used in the juvenile justice system is to reduce the stigma associated with arrest, trial, and imprisonment. This concern is also behind laws and regulations to protect the identity of juveniles in court as well as throughout the juvenile justice system (Snyder and Sickmund 1999:85–96). However, increasingly states are passing legislation that permits those with a "legitimate interest" to access the criminal records of juveniles. Most states allow one or more of the following "legitimate" individuals to gain access to juvenile records: police, prosecutors, social welfare workers, school officials, and victims of criminal offenses (Snyder and Sickmund 2006:108–109).

While the traditional concern of the juvenile justice system has been the interests of juveniles, current juvenile justice practitioners are expanding the focus of concern to include others affected by juvenile offending. For example, the American Prosecutors Research Institute has adopted a "balanced" approach to juvenile justice that includes three components: the juvenile, the victim, and the community. The balanced approach is in turn supported by the Balanced and Restorative Justice Model (BARJ). According to this model of juvenile justice, the state should be concerned with the *accountability of the offender* for his or her actions, the *protection of the community*, especially any victims of the offender's actions, and the *development of competencies* for the offender in an effort to prevent future criminal behavior (Harp 2002).

The Processing of Cases through the System

The flow of juvenile cases through the system is not uniform. For example, nationally, approximately 30 percent of arrests of juveniles are dismissed or diverted out of the system. About 70 percent of arrests are referred to the juvenile courts. These figures are significant because the majority of cases referred to the juvenile courts, approximately 84 percent, are sent by the police (Puzzanchera et al. 2004:24; Krisberg 2005:84; Snyder and Sickmund 2006:104). Furthermore, as the data in figure 13.2 indicate, in 2002, of the 1,615,400 delinquency cases presented to juvenile courts throughout the country, an estimated 940,300, or about 58 percent, were petitioned to a judge. Of those cases petitioned to a judge, 67 percent were adjudicated as delinquent. Among adjudicated delinquent cases, 2 percent were released, while the majority were placed on probation. Of the nonadjudicated cases, over two-thirds (71 percent) were released, but that means 29 percent of these cases were not released. Eight percent of these cases were placed on probation, which likely means informal probation.

Such discrepancies in the percentages of cases processed from one stage to another suggest that several factors are involved. Some, perhaps most, of the reasons for decision making in the juvenile justice system are not connected with the specific legal aspects of a case. Sociologically, statistical data indicate significant variations of processing by several social categories, such as age (which in some cases may reflect legal restrictions, but not always), gender, and race. Some of these factors have already been discussed in chapter 3. It is evident that there are disproportionate representations of minorities in the entire juvenile justice system (Snyder and Sickmund 2006:176). For example, arrest figures for juveniles indicate overrepresentation of minorities, particularly for index offenses (Krisberg 2005:85–86). Females are also disproportionately arrested for some offenses, particularly status offenses (Feld 1999:168; Chesney-Lind and Shelden 2004:9–11; Krisberg 2005:114; see also chapter 11).

Disproportionate representation of males and minorities also occurs throughout the rest of the juvenile justice system. In 2000, for example, 60 percent of all male delinquent cases were petitioned to the courts, while only 49 percent of female cases were petitioned. However, among male cases adjudicated as delinquent, 25 percent resulted in out-of-home placements, compared with 19 percent of female adjudications. In addition, 68 percent of female adjudicated cases resulted in probation, compared with 62 percent for males (Puzzanchera et al. 2004:57). Of juveniles committed to correctional institutions in 1999, 13 percent of females were committed for status offenses, compared with 3 percent of males (Sickmund 2004:14). In 2002, 63 percent of males charged with a violent offense were petitioned in juvenile court, compared with 54 percent of females charged with a violent crime. Eleven percent of males charged with a violent crime were placed in a correctional institution, compared with 6 percent of

In 2002, the most severe sanction ordered in 85,000 adjudicated delinquency cases (14%) was something other than residential placement or probation, such as restitution or community service

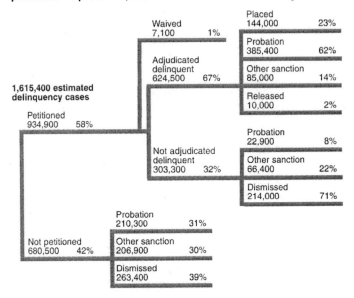

Adjudicated cases receiving sanctions other than residential placement or probation accounted for 53 out of 1,000 delinquency cases processed during the year

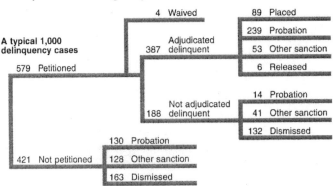

FIGURE 13.2 How were delinquency cases processed in juvenile courts in 2002?

Notes: Cases are categorized by their most severe or restrictive sanction. Detail may not add to totals because of rounding.

Source: Snyder and Sickmund 2006:177, from their adaptation of Stahl et al.'s Juvenile Court Statistics, 2001–2002.

females. Similar gender discrepancies existed for property, drug, and public order offenses (Snyder and Sickmund 2006:178–184).

With respect to race, in 2000, 64 percent of delinquency cases involving African American defendants were petitioned to the courts, compared with 55 percent of white cases. While percentages of delinquent adjudications and probation dispositions were nearly equal among white and African American defendants, the disposition of out-of-home placement was higher for African Americans, 27 percent, than for whites, 23 percent (Puzzanchera et al. 2004:58). In 2002, 57 percent of whites charged with a violent crime were petitioned to juvenile court for adjudication, compared with 66 percent of African American youth. This racial discrepancy existed for all other categories of offenses brought to the attention of juvenile courts in 2002, especially drug crimes, for which 56 percent of whites were petitioned versus 78 percent of African Americans (Snyder and Sickmund 2006:179–185).

Racial disparities also exist for juveniles committed to correctional institutions. In 1999, juvenile custody rates were 1,004 per 100,000 for African Americans, 485 for Hispanics, and 632 for American Indians, but only 235 for whites. Only Asians had lower custody rates than whites, at 182 per 100,000 youth (Sickmund 2004:11). According to the national survey of youth in corrections conducted in 1999, minorities were disproportionately represented in all aspects of detention and institutional placements in every state except Maine and Vermont, which had too few numbers for reliable calculations and comparisons (Sickmund 2004:10). In 2002, African American juveniles were ordered into correctional facilities proportionally more often than white youth for all crime categories (Snyder and Sickmund 2006:179–185).

Disproportionate representation does not always indicate prejudice or discrimination as underlying motivating factors in the processing of juveniles through the system. Bias can occur through other means, such as legal factors. Even if legal factors were accounted for and bias still existed, outright discrimination would not necessarily be involved (Snyder and Sickmund 2006:188). That being said, however, it is hard to imagine the absence of discriminatory bias in the juvenile justice system, as it would be hard to conclude that such discrimination does not exist throughout society. There is too much evidence from studies of the juvenile justice system to conclude otherwise (Feld 1999; Leiber 2003). As Barry Krisberg (2005:87) observes, "There is some reason to believe that the legacy of police violence against persons of color and the history of excessive use of force against minority citizens exert a profound influence on the ways in which minority youth and adults interact with the police." Such bias can be subtle and difficult to observe through analysis of collected data such as police and court records, or even through interviews with juvenile justice officials.

Lawmakers and decision makers in the field of juvenile justice are aware of minority misrepresentations in the system. Modifications of the Juvenile Justice and Delinquency Prevention Act, especially in 1988 and 2002, required states to examine minority representations in their juvenile justice systems and to take steps to reduce overrepresentations where they were found. This mandate from Congress exists today and is not expected to be removed for the foreseeable future (Feld 1999:268; Snyder and Sickmund 1999:192). Some impact of this legislation has already been seen in juvenile justice statistics. Between 1992 and 2002, racial discrepancies in the juvenile justice system declined. This decline was particularly evident at the points of arrest and waiver (Syder and Sickmund 2006:190; see also chapter 15). Despite these recent declines in minority overrepresentation in the juvenile justice system, the problem of minority misrepresentation in the juvenile justice remains a significant challenge for scholars, practitioners, and the public as a whole. Additional discussions of these issues will be presented in the next two chapters of this book.

Transferring Cases from Juvenile Court Jurisdiction to Adult Court Jurisdiction

In all juvenile court jurisdictions there exists the possibility of transferring, or waiving, a case from juvenile court to the adult court system. In most instances, the decision to transfer a case rests with the presiding juvenile court judge. This procedure is often referred to as *judicial waiver*. However, in recent years, states have modified this procedure to allow local prosecutors discretionary judgments concerning the transfer of cases. This method of waiver is called *concurrent jurisdiction*. In addition, some statutes provide for automatic transfer of cases to the adult system. This process is referred to as *statutory exclusion*. In 25 states, there exists a "reverse" waiver, which means that the case is first sent to adult court and then waived back to juvenile court (Kupchik 2006:154–159; Snyder and Sickmund 2006:110–116). Some research concludes that concurrent and statutory waivers are becoming more common, especially in urban areas (Rainville and Smith 2003).

In those situations where reverse waiver occurs, where the prosecutor has concurrent jurisdiction, or where there is a statutory provision for referring a case to the adult court, the original purpose of the juvenile court as the court of jurisdiction for all juvenile cases has been removed, suggesting some dissatisfaction with the philosophy of the juvenile court and/or a desire to expose certain crimes committed by juveniles to more severe punishments than can be administered in the juvenile justice system (Sanborn and Salerno 2005:277–278). However, juvenile courts have always reserved the right to transfer cases to the adult system, even before states began to remove that decision from the exclusive domain of the juvenile court judge (Sanborn and Salerno 2005:277–278; see also Sanborn and Salerno 2005:275–313 for an extended discussion of the waiver process and its consequences). In addition, as was discussed in chapter 2, the creation of juvenile courts and juvenile institutions was not without controversy and detractors. In reality, the modern juvenile justice system operates according to several models, but mostly according to principles of treatment and rehabilitation as well as punishment. In essence, there is a duality of justice, partly aimed at punishment and treatment and partly focused on the criminal justice system for adults (Shoemaker 1988). Furthermore, the emphasis on treatment or punishment seems to vacillate in what some describe as "cycles" (Bernard 1992).

Regardless of the specific procedure used or the stated or unstated objectives of transfer, in almost all cases the decision to waive a case is based on at least two criteria: the age of the accused at the time of the crime and the severity of the charge(s). In addition, judges or prosecutors may often consider the possibility of treatment and rehabilitation of the accused youth, the safety of the community, the social and personal characteristics of the juvenile, including offense history, and the availability of other options besides transfer to the adult system as factors in the final decision to waive a juvenile case to the adult system (Sanborn and Salerno 2005:282–285).

Age eligibility for transfer rests with each state. Twenty-three states set no minimum age for transfer, which suggests the minimum age would be seven, since that is the typical age at which a person can be prosecuted for a crime. In two states, Kansas and Vermont, the minimum age is ten. The highest minimum age is 15, in New Mexico. Most states that specify a specific minimum age for transfer set it at 14 (Snyder and Sickmund 2006:114).

In all states, the crime of murder is a transferable offense. Other offenses that might trigger a transfer include any capital offense, violent felonies or crimes involving the use of a firearm, burglary, and drug offenses such as drug selling (Sanborn and Salerno 2005:275–313, 519–526; Snyder and Sickmund 2006:110–114).

Legal changes permitting transfers from juvenile court to adult court began to occur in the 1970s. However, most of the changes occurred in the1990s. From 1992 to 1997, for example, most states modified transfer laws, and most of these provided for prosecutor discretion or mandatory waivers (Snyder and Sickmund 1999:103). Statistical data concerning juvenile court cases indicate that the use of waivers increased in the 1990s but peaked around 1994 and have decreased since. For example, in 1990, there were 8,300 transfer cases. In 1994, that number increased to 12,100 but decreased to 7,500 by 1999 (Sanborn and Salerno 2005:292). In 2002, there were approximately 7,000 cases waived to criminal court, about 0.8 percent of all petitioned cases of delinquency (Snyder and Sickmund 2006:186).

A developing concern over the use of waivers is the possibility of minority discrimination in decisions to transfer a juvenile to the adult court system, especially in situations where discretionary judgments and decision making are allowed. Studies of transfer cases indicate the existence of minority overrepresentation in the process (Kupchik 2006:146, 152). For example, one national survey of transfer cases found that minority youth represented 20 percent of the youth population, 34 percent of delinquency cases, and more than 50 percent of transferred cases (Bortner et al. 2000:288). In addition, an analysis of 16 published studies of transfers reported the existence of minority overrepresentation or racial discrepancies in ten of the studies. However, in several studies, the impact of race on the decision-making process was either statistically insignificant or explained by other factors, such as offense seriousness and offense history or the marital status of the defendant's parents (Bortner et al. 2000:282–288). Thus, while overrepresentation of minorities in transfer cases is well established, the demonstration of racial bias in such decisions is not clear (see also Sanborn and Salerno 2005:293–294).

Discrimination can be subtle or nuanced, however, and may be hidden by other factors. Much research concludes that race and ethnicity interact with offense severity in regard to decision making in the juvenile justice system. However, these kinds of interactions, where minority youth are more often involved with serious offenses than are other youth, can mask discriminatory reactions by the police and court officials based on offense stereotypes, such as stereotypes of minority drug users or gang members. In addition, evidence indicates that discretionary decision making still exists even after a transfer decision has been made, such as processing a case to the grand jury, or in sentencing convicted offenders. In addition, discrimination may be seen when considering the race of the victim of a crime. In cases where offenders are of a minority race and victims are white, sentences are often longer for the convicted offender than when the victim is nonwhite (Bortner et al. 2000:288–295).

Legal Guidelines for Waiver Decisions

Although transfer provisions have existed for several decades, the constitutionality of such procedures has been questioned. There have been several appellate court decisions concerning the constitutionality of waivers and, for the most part, the courts have ruled that such procedures are constitutional, provided certain safeguards and conditions are met. For example, in *Kent v. United States* (1966), a 16-year-old juvenile, Morris Kent, was arrested and charged with burglary, robbery, and rape in Washington, DC. The youth, Kent, requested a waiver hearing from the juvenile court, but none was granted. Nonetheless, his case was transferred to the adult court jurisdiction in Washington, DC, and Kent was subsequently convicted of the charges. Kent's attorney appealed the conviction, partly on the grounds that the waiver was invalid, and the case went to the U.S. Supreme Court. The Court ruled in favor of Kent, maintaining that juveniles are entitled to certain due process rights in decisions regarding waiver. Specifically, these rights include (1) a hearing on the transfer issue; (2) the presence of counsel at the hearing; (3) access to social histories and other records used by juvenile courts in reaching a decision; and (4) a written statement regarding the juvenile court judge's decision concerning waiver (Hemmens et al. 2004:61–63; Ahranjani et al. 2005:32–34).

While the Kent case was a significant one in the history of juvenile rights in the courts, its jurisdiction was limited to the federal system because it occurred in Washington, DC. However, since the 1960s several other cases regarding the constitutionality of transfer laws have been heard in state courts. One of the more significant of these cases was *Breed v. Jones* (1975). In this case, a 17-year-old juvenile was charged with armed robbery in California. His case was heard in juvenile court, where the presiding judge found him delinquent but not "amenable" to the treatment programs offered in the juvenile system. Consequently, the juvenile court judge ordered Jones's case transferred to the adult court system, over Jones's objections, where he was tried and found guilty of the same offense. Jones, through the assistance of his mother, appealed the case on the grounds that the trial in the adult court constituted double jeopardy since his case had previously been heard and adjudicated in the juvenile court. The appeal went to the U.S. Supreme Court, which ruled in Jones's favor. In its majority decision, the Court maintained that while transfer procedures are constitutional, hearing a case in juvenile court and then trying the same case in adult court is not constitutional, but, in fact, constitutes double jeopardy, a violation of basic rights established in the Fifth Amendment. In addition, the Court ruled that this decision be honored in all states (Hemmens et al. 2004:67–69).

Consequences of Transfers

A primary objective of waiving a case to the adult court is to punish the juvenile for his or her criminal acts. Punishment, in turn, is expected to reduce the future criminal behavior, or *recidivism*, of the juvenile. Research has produced conflicting results concerning the length of sentences transferred youth actually serve in prisons or other adult facilities. Some studies conclude that transferred juveniles serve longer sentences than do nontransferred youth, while other studies reach the opposite conclusion (Bartollas and Miller 2005:206–207; Sanborn and Salerno 2005:297–308). Regardless of the length of sentence, however, studies indicate that even if juveniles are required to be incarcerated separately from adults in adult prisons, the kind of treatment and services they receive in these prisons is often less age-specific and appropriate than if they had been handled within the juvenile system. Furthermore, some studies conclude that juveniles serving sentences in adult prisons are at higher risk of suicide and abuse than youth confined in juvenile facilities (Young and Gainsborough 2000:6–7; Bartollas and Miller 2005:209–211).

In addition, studies of the effects of transfers often conclude that juveniles who have been waived to the adult court system have *higher recidivism rates* than those youth whose cases have remained in the juvenile system (Redding and Howell 2000:150). One of the more detailed analyses of the effects of transfer cases comes from a series of studies conducted in Florida from the late 1980s to the late 1990s. In the first analysis, Donna Bishop and colleagues examined the records of more than 2,700 youth who had been transferred to the adult court system and compared them with more than 2,700 youth who had not been transferred. The two samples of juveniles were matched in terms of gender, age, and offense severity in order to obtain a clearer picture of the impact of transfers on subsequent behaviors of youth. The conclusion of this study was that the recidivism rates of those youth who had been transferred to the adult court system were *higher* than the recidivism rates of those youth who had not been transferred (Bishop et al. 1996).

Subsequent studies with these Florida samples indicated that recidivism rates between waived and nonwaived youth became more similar over time (Winner et al. 1997). In the late 1990s, the researchers located some of those youth who had been transferred to the adult system for their crimes and some who had remained in the juvenile system, a total of 144 males, 72 in each category. All respondents were interviewed in order to determine in more depth their reactions to their experiences (Lane et al. 2002). In many cases, the transferred youth had at one time also had experiences with the juvenile system. The results of these interviews indicated that those juveniles who had been sent to the adult prisons felt the experience benefited them to some extent but that they often felt prison left them with little hope for a better life. However, among both groups, it was felt that the *best impacts*, in terms of changing attitudes and behaviors, were derived from juvenile programs that involved not only incarceration but also life-skills or other educational training along with counseling that lasted from more than nine months to around three years ("deep-end" programs). Thus, transferring juveniles to adult courts may have some beneficial effects, but real changes in attitudes and behaviors would be better accomplished with programs that focus on juveniles and offer educational training and counseling over a number of months or years (see Bishop and Frazier 2000 for an extended discussion of the consequences of transfers).

Blended Sentences

Related to the use of transfer or waiver is the existence of blended sentencing, a concept that is growing in popularity in many states. Essentially, a blended sentence combines the use of both juvenile and adult correctional facilities and programs, as applied to juveniles. Blended sentences provide an opportunity for the juvenile justice system to retain jurisdiction and influence over a juvenile beyond the typical age of 18 or 21 and into young adulthood. In part, the concept is a reaction to the interests of those who wish to retain the purpose of juvenile justice, which is rehabilitation and individualized treatment, yet also utilize the punitive approach of the criminal justice system (Redding and Howell 2000:146–147).

The first blended sentence law was passed in Texas in 1987. From 1992 to 1997, blended sentence laws were passed in 20 states (Snyder and Sickmund 1999:108; Redding and Howell 2000:160–161). There are several models of blended sentences. One is called the *juvenile-exclusive model*, which allows a juvenile court judge to impose a sentence in either the juvenile or adult system of corrections. Another model is called the *juvenile-inclusive model*, in which a juvenile court judge imposes a sentence in juvenile court and a suspended sentence in adult court. A third model is the *juvenile-contiguous model*, wherein the juvenile court imposes a sentence in the juvenile system that is followed by the completion of the sentence in the adult system once the juvenile reaches the age of majority. Two other models originate with the criminal courts. One is the *criminal-exclusive model*, which allows the criminal court judge to impose a sentence in either juvenile or criminal corrections. The other is the *criminal-inclusive model*, which permits a criminal court judge to sentence a juvenile to both juvenile corrections and a suspended adult corrections sentence that can be used if the juvenile violates the conditions of the juvenile corrections sentence (Snyder and Sickmund 1999:108; 2006:115–116; Redding and Howell 2000:152–153).

In general, it is argued that such laws are constitutional and do not violate one's right to avoid double jeopardy. The constitutionality of blended sentences is protected because such laws focus on the disposition or sentencing of one who has already been convicted and not on the original conviction itself (Redding and Howell 2000:159–160).

Since blended sentence laws are relatively new, much about their actual use and effects needs to be learned, especially long-term consequences (Redding and Howell 2000:165–171). One suspected consequence is the possibility of increasing the numbers of juveniles being handled in the juvenile justice system because judges can order juveniles to be placed into programs operated by juvenile corrections agencies until a youth is past the age of 21. Proponents of blended sentences, however, argue that such occurrences are not only possible but also desired, since one of the purposes of such sentences is to avoid the exposure of juveniles to adult influences and prolonged sentences, often with little or inappropriate treatment for juveniles (Redding and Howell 2000:160–163). The previously discussed results of the research in Florida on longer-term consequences of transfers to adult corrections versus retention in the juvenile corrections system support this view.

Other Considerations

Diversion

While many issues concerning the contemporary juvenile justice system focus on processing juveniles through the system and transferring juveniles from the juvenile to the adult system, another consideration focuses on diverting youth from either system. *Diversion* refers to procedures whereby a juvenile is treated, or supervised, outside the formal procedures of juvenile courts or juvenile institutions. Diversion does not mean a youngster is not supervised at all or is free to go his or her own way. Rather, the concept means that the youth is handled by other agencies than the courts or correctional facilities. Diversion programs may themselves be formal, guided by fairly strict rules and procedures, or informal. Informal diversion is often used by the police (see the next chapter) and, as such, has been around for a long time. Formal diversion programs, sponsored by federal and state funds, began in the later 1960s and early 1970s, particularly with the JJDP Act of 1974, discussed earlier. Consequently, many diversion programs, especially earlier ones, have focused on juvenile status offenders. In addition, these programs are often characterized by the establishment of youth service bureaus (YSBs), which offer different types of programs for youth, programs not specifically controlled by juvenile courts (Bartollas and Miller 2005:271–272). A fuller discussion of diversion will be presented in the next chapter, which provides a more detailed discussion of the operations of juvenile courts.

Restorative Justice

Another program receiving a lot of attention within the juvenile justice system is *restorative justice*. Restorative justice involves mediation and conciliation between offender and victim, including relatives of victims, in an effort to create greater harmony among people living within a neighborhood or community. As with diversion, examples of restorative justice may be formal or informal. Many scholars argue, for example, that restorative justice has been a part of traditional society settlements for centuries, such as among the aboriginal people in Australia, and that other nations have used the principles of mediation and restoration as an integral part of their systems of justice (Morris and Maxwell 2001; Zehr and Toews 2004). In the Philippines, for example, disputes among neighbors and complaints against juveniles are most often settled in local governmental forums called *barangay* courts, and this system of justice is established in traditional Philippine society (Orendain 1978). Restorative justice is discussed again in the last chapter, when treatment and prevention programs are presented.

Summary

The contemporary system of juvenile justice has evolved from a collection of individual programs, concepts, and practices to a more coordinated effort involving agencies and organizations representing the police, the courts, and corrections. Many of the earlier programs and institutions developed to deal with juvenile offenders were established and operated by private individuals and organizations and often funded by private resources or combinations of private and public monies. Over time, however, especially since the beginning of the 20th century, the juvenile justice system has become more legalistic and structured, with standardized rules and procedures for processing juveniles through the system.

From its inception, the juvenile justice system has been based on the philosophy of treatment and rehabilitation of the individual. Traditionally, this philosophy has resulted in the development of informal procedures, focused more on the individual and social characteristics contributing to the behavior and attitudes of the juvenile, as opposed to legal rules and procedures. Over time, however, and particularly since the 1960s, the structure of the juvenile justice system has changed to reflect increasing judicial oversight of procedures and practices within the system and with special consideration of the constitutional rights of juveniles. This change has not come at the complete abandonment of the traditional philosophy and structure of the juvenile justice system, but instead has been created to exist alongside the traditional system. Consequently, some have suggested that the contemporary juvenile justice system is a kind of hybrid or dual system of justice, combining elements of traditional, informal procedures with formal, more legalistic rules and concepts.

Since 1974, with the passage of the Juvenile Justice and Delinquency Prevention Act, juveniles charged with status offenses have increasingly been handled outside the formal procedures and operations of the system and placed into diversion programs or otherwise handled informally. At the same time, however, juveniles charged with serious crimes are being handled by the formal procedures of the juvenile system, including case supervision of juveniles over the age of 18. Many of these cases are subject to transfer or waiver to the adult system of justice, especially young people who are 14 years of age or older. With the exception of the death penalty, juveniles who have been transferred to the adult system are subject to adult penalties and possible confinement with adult prisoners.

One important concern is the possibility of discrimination in the processing of cases through the juvenile justice system. Numerous studies of decision making in the system have been conducted, with mixed results concerning discrimination. On the one hand, most research indicates the existence of disproportionate representation of minority youth at virtually all stages of the system, including waiver or transfer decisions. On the other hand, racial or ethnic bias relative to minority overrepresentation is more difficult to demonstrate. Consequently, the issue of discrimination and minority overrepresentation in the juvenile justice system remains an important topic for continued research.

References

Ahranjani, Maryam, Andrew G. Ferguson, and Jamin B. Raskin
    2005   Youth Justice in America. Washington, DC: CQ Press.
Bartollas, Clemens, and Stuart J. Miller
    2005   Juvenile Justice in America. 4th edition. Upper Saddle River, NJ: Pearson Prentice Hall.
Bernard, Thomas J.
    1992   The Cycle of Juvenile Justice. New York: Oxford University Press.
Bishop, Donna, and Charles Frazier
    2000   Consequences of Transfer. *In* The Changing Borders of Juvenile Justice: Transfers of Adolescents to the Criminal Court. Jeffrey Fagan and Franklin E. Zimring, eds. Pp. 227–276. Chicago: University of Chicago Press.
Bishop, Donna M., Charles E. Frazier, Lonn Lanza-Kaduce, and Lawrence Winner
    1996   The Transfer of Juveniles to Criminal Court: Does It Make a Difference? Crime & Delinquency 423:171–191.
Bortner, M. A., Marjorie S. Zatz, and Darnell F. Hawkins
    2000   Race and Transfer: Empirical Research and Social Context. *In* The Changing Borders of Juvenile Justice: Transfers of Adolescents to the Criminal Court. Jeffrey Fagan and Franklin E. Zimring, eds. Pp. 277–320. Chicago: University of Chicago Press.
Chesney-Lind, Meda, and Randall G. Shelden
    2004   Girls, Delinquency, and Juvenile Justice. 3rd edition. Belmont, CA: Wadsworth.
Feld, Barry C.
    1999   Bad Kids: Race and the Transformation of the Juvenile Court. New York: Oxford University Press.
Harp, Caren
    2002   Bringing Balance to Juvenile Justice. Alexandria, VA: American Prosecutors Research Institute.

Hemmens, Craig, Benjamin Steiner, and David Mueller
  2004   Significant Cases in Juvenile Justice. Los Angeles: Roxbury.
Krisberg, Barry
  2005   Juvenile Justice: Redeeming Our Children. Thousand Oaks, CA:
          Sage.
Kupchik, Aaron
  2006   Judging Juveniles: Prosecuting Adolescents in Adult and Juvenile
          Courts. New York: New York University Press.
Lane, Jodi, Lonn Lanza-Kaduce, Charles E. Frazier, and Donna M. Bishop
  2002   Adult versus Juvenile Sanctions: Voices of Incarcerated Youth. Crime
          & Delinquency 48:431–455.
Leiber, Michael J.
  2003   The Contexts of Juvenile Justice Decision Making: When Race Mat-
          ters. Albany: State University of New York Press.
Morris, Allison, and Gabrielle Maxwell, eds.
  2001   Restorative Justice for Juveniles: Conferencing, Mediation, and Cir-
          cles. Portland, OR: Hart Publishing.
Orendain, Antonio
  1978   Barangay Justice: The Amicable Settlement of Disputes. Manila:
          Alpha Omega Publications.
Pollet, Susan L.
  2004   Responses to Juvenile Crime Consider the Extent of Parents'
          Responsibility for Children's Acts. Journal of the New York State Bar
          Association, July/August:26–29.
Puzzanchera, Charles, Anna L. Stahl, Terence A. Finnegan, Nancy Tierney, and
Howard N. Snyder
  2004   Juvenile Court Statistics 2000. Pittsburgh: National Center for Juve-
          nile Justice.
Rainville, Gerard A., and Steven K. Smith
  2003   Juvenile Felony Defendants in Criminal Courts: Survey of 40 Coun-
          ties, 1998. Bureau of Justice Statistics Special Report. Washington,
          DC: U.S. Department of Justice.
Redding, Richard E., and James C. Howell
  2000   Blended Sentencing in American Courts. In The Changing Borders
          of Juvenile Justice: Transfer of Adolescents to the Criminal Court.
          Jeffrey Fagan and Franklin E. Zimring, eds. Pp. 145–179. Chicago:
          University of Chicago Press.
Sanborn, Joseph B., Jr., and Anthony W. Salerno
  2005   The Juvenile Justice System: Law and Process. Los Angeles: Roxbury.

Shoemaker, Donald J.
    1988   The Duality of Juvenile Justice in the United States: History, Trends, and Prospects. Sociological Spectrum 8:1–17.
Sickmund, Melissa
    2004   Juveniles in Corrections. Washington, DC: Office of Juvenile Justice and Delinquency Prevention.
Snyder, Howard N., and Melissa Sickmund
    1999   Juvenile Offenders and Victims: 1999 National Report. Washington, DC: U.S. Department of Justice, Office of Justice Programs, Office of Juvenile Justice and Delinquency Prevention.
    2006   Juvenile Offenders and Victims: 2006 National Report. Washington, DC: U.S. Department of Justice, Office of Justice Programs, Office of Juvenile Justice and Delinquency Prevention.
Winner, Lawrence T., Lonn Lanza-Kaduce, Donna M. Bishop, and Charles E. Frazier
    1997   The Transfer of Juveniles to Criminal Court: Reexamining Recidivism over the Long Term. Crime & Delinquency 43:548–563.
Young, Malcolm C., and Jenni Gainsborough
    2000   Prosecuting Juveniles in Adult Court: An Assessment of Trends and Consequences. A Report of the Sentencing Project. Washington, DC: The Sentencing Project.
Zehr, Howard, and Barb Toews, eds.
    2002   Critical Issues in Restorative Justice. Monsey, NY: Criminal Justice Press.

POLICE AND COURTS

The Police

The police represent the most visible public sign of formal justice in society. Their physical presence signals society's concern for the enforcement of laws and the maintenance of public safety. At the same time, the police often depend on members of the public to perform their expected duties. Historically, however, juveniles were more often controlled by parents, relatives, and adults in the community rather than by police officers. Police forces were first established in response to social disorder and social changes associated with industrialization. The first police force was established in London in 1829 (Martin 2005:169). In the United States, police departments were first created in the 1830s and 1840s in large metropolises such as New York City, Boston, and Philadelphia. By the late 1800s, all large cities and many smaller ones had a police force (Bartollas and Miller 2005:113). Today, there are approximately 40,000 police departments throughout the United States, and these departments are found in large metropolitan areas as well as in rural areas and small towns.

While the early police departments were charged with controlling adult and juvenile crime, specialized juvenile units did not emerge until the 20th century. In cities such as Portland, Oregon, Washington, D.C., and New York, police officers were assigned details including juvenile crime prevention. Female officers were hired, and police were seen patrolling amusement parks and other places where juveniles congregated in efforts to prevent juvenile crimes from occurring. It has been estimated that by 1924, nearly 90 percent of police departments in the United States had some kind of juvenile crime prevention policies and programs (Bartollas and Miller 2005:113).

Historically, police departments in the United States have been divided into three eras: the political era, the reform era, and the community-strategy era. The political era lasted from the inception of police departments until the early 20th century. During this period, considerable discretion was used by the police to enforce laws and standards of behavior involving youth, and youngsters were often victimized by the police with little or no consequences. The reform era lasted from the early to the mid-20th century. This phase of police organization and behavior was characterized by concepts such as professionalism and prevention of crime as well as law enforcement. After World War II, specialized juvenile units or bureaus began to appear, particularly in large cities. The community-strategy era began after World War II and continues until today. This era is characterized by increased attempts to integrate the police into community activities, including the supervision and control of juveniles. Specialized juvenile units have become even more characteristic of police departments. An example of this philosophy is the creation of the International Juvenile Officers Association. Female officers continue to be hired, but they are no longer assigned primarily to juvenile bureaus (Martin 2005:169–170).

The Role of the Police in Juvenile Justice

As indicated earlier, historically, the police serve several functions in society. Some suggest that the police play three major roles in modern society: *law enforcement, order maintenance*, and *service.* Law enforcement is probably the most recognized and stereotypical role of the police. This function involves making investigations of criminal cases and arresting suspects. Order maintenance includes keeping the peace, maintaining orderly assemblies, and acting to prevent crimes from occurring. Service functions entail aiding those in difficult situations such as emergencies (Sanborn and Salerno 2005:125).

With respect to the law enforcement role, police actions are often referred to as *dispositions* or *interventions.* However, the police do not see all the criminal activity occurring in an area. Thus, they must rely on other members of the community to assist in their role of regulating juvenile behavior and guarding the law. These areas can be divided into three main categories: *family initiated, community initiated,* and *school initiated.* With family-initiated intervention, the police are asked to intervene in a situation by the child's family or the family of a crime victim. In community-initiated dispositions, the police are informed of a crime by neighbors, store owners or workers, or other community witnesses. In school-initiated dispositions, principals, guidance counselors, or teachers are the ones to report juvenile misconduct to the police (Martin 2005:170–171).

Processing Cases

Whenever the police become aware of a crime and a suspect, either through direct observation or through witnesses or other reports, there are several options, or dispositions, available. One option is to obtain basic information about the case and the suspect and to *release* the suspect. Studies show that arrests (taking into custody) of juveniles occur in less than 15 percent of the encounters. In addition, research indicates that the police take the child home to his or her parents in 16 percent of the cases. In addition to taking a child home, the police may decide to refer a child to some agency for help or even require that the child report to them on a regular but informal basis. These two decisions are examples of informal diversion, a topic to be discussed in more detail later in this chapter. Some also refer to release decisions as *station adjustments* (Sanborn and Salerno 2005:130–131).

Once a child has been taken into custody, or arrested, he or she is subject to other procedures. For example, those who have been arrested are typically *fingerprinted* and *photographed,* although these two procedures are somewhat controversial when applied to juveniles unless the case has already been transferred to the adult system. Both represent permanent records and can be used against juveniles for years after the arrest has occurred. Although the courts have ruled that the police may fingerprint a youth, the prints are often destroyed when the juvenile reaches age 18 and/or the prints are subject to judicial oversight. In addition, the U.S. Supreme Court has ruled that fingerprints of juveniles may not be used as evidence in courts. As indicated earlier, the public identification of juveniles is prohibited in most jurisdictions, so the exposure of a juvenile's photograph would be protected by such laws and regulations. However, photographs may be used by police and other authorities for aid in investigating criminal cases, and the concern is that such uses of photographs may unduly expose juveniles to the dangers of labeling and assumed guilt. Thus, states and courts have ruled that photographs, while legal, must be used with judicial oversight, should not be released to the newspapers or television stations, and must be destroyed when a juvenile reaches the age of majority, although such procedures are not always required or followed (Bartollas and Miller 2005:131–132). However, the trend now seems to be more in favor of expanding the use of fingerprints and photographs of juveniles in many states *requiring* such procedures, especially when felonies or serious crimes are involved (Sanborn and Salerno 2005:150–151).

While police departments have always been used to control juvenile offending, since the 20th century many departments have employed *specialized juvenile units*. These units or details often are found in large urban departments, which can afford to hire such officers and need their expertise. Officers in these units are educated in matters concerning child development and delinquency as well as juvenile laws and procedures. If a department has a specialized juvenile unit, consisting of several officers, they are often used to process a case involving juveniles, from taking into custody to court referral, and even serving as testifiers in a court hearing. These special units also handle cases involving gangs, although gang-related crimes may be referred to the adult system. In addition to conducting investigations of crimes involving youth, juvenile officers are also called upon to develop and implement crime prevention efforts in the community However, these crime prevention roles, unless they involve gang-related work, are often devalued within police departments, and juvenile officers often share the same low status as those handling juvenile delinquency cases in general (Bartollas and Miller 2005:134–136). In fact, the relatively low status of working with cases involving juveniles extends into other areas of juvenile justice, prompting some to refer to juvenile justice as the "stepchild" of the justice system in general (Grimes 2005:27).

If the decision is made to arrest or take into custody a juvenile suspect, eventually a decision has to be reached concerning the further processing of a case. Sometimes, the case may be waived to the adult court system, as was discussed in chapter 13. However, as we have already seen, very few juvenile cases become waived to the adult court. Sometimes the case is dismissed because the evidence is considered too weak for court review, or perhaps because the accused and/or his or her parents have expressed considerable remorse for the act. Studies show, however, that the percentage of cases of arrest that are eventually referred to the juvenile court has *increased* over the past few decades. In 1980, for example, 58 percent of the cases involving juveniles taken into custody were referred to the juvenile courts. But that figure had increased to 72 percent by 2001, and these percentages are consistent across communities of varying size (Sanborn and Salerno 2005:152). The role of the police in the juvenile justice system begins to wane after a referral decision has been made. Beyond completing required paperwork for cases of arrest, officers may be called to testify at juvenile court proceedings. If there are special juvenile units or bureaus in a department, those officers will often be asked to handle the paperwork and forms necessary for forwarding a case to the courts and to provide testimony in hearings. The role of the police in juvenile justice systems will be considered later in this chapter, when the topic of discretionary decision making is discussed.

The Court System

Although the police may not always refer cases to juvenile courts, statistics indicate that the large majority of cases *received* by juvenile courts are referred by the police. Research indicates that nearly 80 percent of juvenile court referrals have come from the police. Other referrals come from school authorities, parents, court officials, social service workers, and victims (Sanborn and Salerno 2005:152).

There are several juvenile court models. One type is the *independent juvenile court*, which is separated from other courts physically and by jurisdiction. These courts have different names, such as juvenile court or juvenile and domestic relations court, but their independent status remains. Another type of court is a *designated juvenile court*, which is a part of a larger court jurisdiction, such as a county or district court. A third model is the *coordinated juvenile court*, which coordinates duties with another court system, such as a family court. Regardless of the structure of a juvenile court, a basic purpose of the court is to establish justice within the framework of the best interests of the child. Since the inception of juvenile courts in 1899, courts have become more complex, employing people from different professional backgrounds and experiences (Martin 2005:203,195–201).

Important figures in juvenile courts include the judge, the intake officer or probation officer, the prosecutor (whose role has become increasingly important), and defense counsel. Certainly the most visible role in the courtroom is the judge. Juvenile court judges are elected to the position in some states and appointed in others. Standards for qualifications, selection methods, and length of office are not uniform across the 50 states. For example, although national standards suggest that juvenile court judges have law degrees, many states do not require a legal education in the list of qualifications for the position (Martin 2005:203–204).

Few cases are actually heard by a juvenile court judge directly from the police. Rather, in most situations, a complaint against a juvenile or a group of juveniles is first heard by an intake officer in a procedure called the *intake hearing*. The person in charge of this hearing is often a probation officer. Sometimes the courts use intake officers or assessment officers who are given the task of conducting intake procedures but not other roles of the probation officer. More recently, states have allowed social service agencies to conduct intake hearings. In a few states, such as South Dakota and Washington, prosecutors are allowed to conduct the intake (Sanborn and Salerno 2005:184).

Intake hearings are important to the traditional philosophy of juvenile courts. The purpose of the intake hearing is to determine the merits of the case, the accusations against the accused, and all relevant parties to the case. The intake officer may decide to dismiss the case or to handle it informally, sometimes in the form of *informal probation*. Informal probation includes continued monitoring of a juvenile but not strict supervision. The juvenile will be asked to reappear before the intake officer in some specified period of time, such as six months. If the officer is satisfied that significant progress is being made and that no further troubles will occur with the juvenile, especially with respect to the case at hand, then the juvenile is released. Another option for the intake officer is to *divert* the case to another agency with the provision that significant progress is made. If such progress is not made, then the case may be reviewed for further judicial action. A third option of the intake officer is to file a formal charge against the juvenile in the form of a *petition*. A petition is similar to an indictment or a bill of information in the adult system. Sometimes a petition is called a *complaint*. The petition goes to the juvenile court judge. Increasingly, states are allowing, sometimes requiring, prosecutors to file petitions in juvenile court, which is further demonstration of the trend toward criminalization in the juvenile court system (Sanborn and Salerno 2005:186–201).

In recent years, over half of intake cases have been dismissed, diverted, or handled informally. In 1997, 1998, and 1999, for example, 57 percent of intake cases resulted in formal charges or petitions. In 2000 and 2002, this percentage increased to 58 (Puzzanchera et al. 2004:53; Sanborn and Salerno 2005:201; Snyder and Sickmund 2006:177).

During intake proceedings and throughout the rest of the juvenile court process, a defense attorney is usually present. The attorney may be privately retained, court appointed, or part of a public defender system. Traditionally, defense attorneys have been present in juvenile court proceedings where issues of custody or child abuse or neglect have been present. In these situations, the role of the defense attorney has been that of *guardian ad litem.* However, the role of the defense attorney has become increasingly important in the juvenile justice system, particularly since a number of U.S. Supreme Court rulings in the past 40 years have collectively transformed the tenor of juvenile court proceedings from "kindly parent" in nature to more legalistic or adversarial in tone. Several of these cases will be discussed later in this chapter. While the presence of defense attorneys is part of the legal rights of juveniles in juvenile court, some judges may not welcome the appearance of defense attorneys, especially if the judge sees the role of the juvenile court in traditional terms. Thus, some juveniles may go unrepresented in juvenile court proceedings not because they do not have the right of counsel, but because some judges discourage the presence of defense attorneys in court proceedings (Martin 2005:206).

After a case has been referred or petitioned to the juvenile court judge or during the deliberation of this issue, the question of what to do with the youth until a hearing can be scheduled is considered. Specifically, should the juvenile be released to his or her home, or should the child be placed in confinement or detention? This question addresses the danger of the juvenile to the community or his or her risk of fleeing before any further court hearings may occur. The decision to detain or release the juvenile is usually made at the *detention hearing.* The detention hearing is conducted by the probation officer or intake officer in charge of the preliminary proceedings. Usually, a judge is the final authority in detention decisions, but sometimes detention home supervisors, the police, and/or prosecutors are allowed to make such decisions. In many states, detention policies have been created that remove discretionary detention decisions from probation officers. Juveniles charged with any of a list of crimes, such as using a firearm during a felony, homicide, rape, and robbery, are automatically presumed dangerous and must prove their harmlessness or trustworthiness in order not to be detained (Sanford and Salerno 2005:222). Detention homes will be discussed in more detail in the next chapter.

The actual hearing of a case is referred to as the *adjudicatory hearing.* In this stage, the purpose is to determine whether the accused actually committed the charge(s) (Bartollas and Miller 2005:182). In keeping with the traditional, informal nature of juvenile justice proceedings, the adjudicatory hearing is often closed to the public, and the information presented in such hearings is protected. In most cases, the deciding figure in the adjudicatory hearing is a juvenile court judge, but 24 states allow a "master" or "referee" to conduct the hearing. The decision of a master is not a true verdict but a recommendation to the juvenile court judge, which prevents the juvenile from being exposed to two "trials" and thus to double jeopardy (Sanford and Salerno 2005:328–335). An affirmative decision is often termed "found delinquent," or a "finding of fact," which is similar to a finding of guilt in a criminal court. The difference in these terms is somewhat semantic but is also reflective of the traditional philosophy of the juvenile court to work in the best interests of the child (while also considering the interests of society), not with punishing a guilty offender, as is the case in criminal court (Martin 2005:210–215).

If there has been a finding of fact in a case, another duty of the probation officer is to gather information on the juvenile, a *social history*. Social histories are also called predisposition or presentence reports or investigations. The details of a social history may vary, but most contain information on the juvenile's family situation, school progress, and criminal record. Family life includes the past and current status of family members, whether they are married or divorced, where they live, what they do for a living, and so on. School information includes the child's grades in school, attendance and behavioral records, and any other information available from the school. Criminal record often includes prior arrests and convictions as well as known associates in criminal behavior. Most reports also delve into a juvenile's personal information, such as attitudes and mental health. Sometimes probation officers seek information on the neighborhood where the juvenile lives and neighbors' opinions of the juvenile. These investigations are so important that cases of finding a youth delinquent in which presentence reports were not conducted have been overturned by appellate courts (Bartollas and Miller 2005:182–183, 231–232; Martin 2005:215; Sanborn and Salerno 2005:350–355).

The decision of what to do with a case of delinquency is usually called the *disposition hearing*. Almost always, this decision is rendered by a juvenile court judge. The hearing may sometimes be an extension of an adjudicatory hearing and occurs immediately following the adjudication. If this happens, the presentence report must be ready at the time of the adjudication in case the juvenile is found delinquent. More commonly, the disposition hearing is held at a later date than the adjudicatory hearing, maybe several weeks or months later. In this case, the presentence report is truly a postadjudicatory report (Bartollas and Miller 2005:183–185).

The disposition options available to the judge are numerous and include both informal and formal judgments. Informally, the judge can decide to take the case under advisement and review the case and the juvenile after a certain period of time. More commonly, the judge will order a formal, supervised disposition, ranging from performing community service and/or paying fines and restitution to commission to the state department of juvenile corrections. Another option is to remove the juvenile from her or his home and place the juvenile in the home of a relative or in foster care.

According to most studies of juvenile justice, the most common form of disposition is *probation*. Probation is the supervision of someone who has been adjudicated delinquent, but the supervision is conducted in the community. However, many jurisdictions combine some period of confinement with probation, usually beginning with confinement followed by probation. Not only is probation the most common disposition given to adjudicated juvenile offenders, but almost all juveniles processed through the system see a probation officer at some point, usually starting with intake. Thus, some refer to probation as the "workhorse" of juvenile justice (Torbet 1996). In addition, probation can either be a "front-end" or a "back-end" disposition. That is, probation may be given to offenders who are at the beginning stages of the system, perhaps first offenders considered to be low risks for reoffending. Or probation may be given to repeat or more serious offenders but whose next step in the system would be incarceration (Torbet 1996; Martin 2005:208–210).

The use of probation is thought to have begun in the 1840s with the work of a Boston shoemaker named John Augustus. Augustus worked with convicted offenders, adults and juveniles, to give them an opportunity to reform while under his supervision in place of going to jail or some other place of confinement. By the time of his death in 1859, Augustus had worked with 2,000 convicted criminals in Boston. Probation first became a legally recognized part of juvenile justice in 1869 in Massachusetts. The first probation officer was hired in that state in 1878. By the end of the 1920s, every state had enacted probation laws. In 1925, Congress passed the National Probation Act, which authorized the hiring of probation officers for convicted offenders in the federal system (Martin 2005:263; Shoemaker and Wolfe 2005:107–108). Today, probation functions are most often performed under the supervision of local juvenile court judges, but with restrictions and guidelines provided by state departments of juvenile corrections. Increasingly, states are turning to private contractors to provide the services of probation, especially for intensive counseling of clients (Bartollas and Miller 2005:229–230).

Sometimes young offenders are committed to correctional care or confinement. The topic of juvenile institutions will be discussed in chapter 15. Once youthful offenders have been released from incarceration, the next, and usually final, step is *aftercare*. Aftercare is similar to the adult concept of parole. In some ways, aftercare and probation are highly similar. For example, both utilize supervision of delinquents in the community. One major difference between the two, however, is that with the exception of blended sentences, probation occurs before incarceration, whereas aftercare *follows* incarceration (Martin 2005:chapter 9).

Decision-Making Factors

The preceding discussions and the discussions presented in chapter 13 clearly indicate that not all cases that come to the attention of the police and/or courts continue to be routed through the juvenile justice system. Some cases are dismissed, some are continued, or held for further observation and reflection, and some are processed to the next stage of the system. Theoretically, or perhaps ideally, all juvenile cases would be processed on the legal merits of the case, such as the nature of the charge and the extent of the criminal history of the defendant. In addition, since juvenile justice proceedings are supposed to operate according to the best interests of each child, one might expect to find individualized case processing, which would not yield statistical patterns of association with any one factor or set of factors, with the possible exception of legal considerations. Factors associated with decision making in the juvenile justice system were discussed in chapter 13. The next sections of this chapter present additional considerations of this issue.

The Police

One important factor to remember when discussing police decision making is that the police often use *visual cues* when determining the probability that a suspect has committed an offense. Even though the police often rely on witness or victim information about a suspect, much of the information they have to go on, especially in field situations, is based on visible signs. Thus a person's gender, age, or race/ethnicity can be determined or roughly guessed by visual appearance. In addition, a person's class status can be roughly determined by appearance, although in this matter, appearances can be deceiving. Besides the nature of the charge, the police often do not have much more information concerning legal factors when deciding what to do with a suspect when a decision is made in the field. In the modern age of computers, criminal histories might be readily available, but that is neither certain nor uniform across all police departments.

Given the nature of police work, it is not surprising that studies often single out what might be considered physical features as having an impact on the decision to arrest, release, or "adjust" a case. In chapter 13, it was pointed out that race and ethnic minority status are often significantly associated with police decisions. Gender also plays a role in such decisions. Studies indicate that police often treat females leniently except for status offenses. However, race and gender can interact to produce countertrends. When females behave contrary to "middle-class standards" of acceptable female behavior such as politeness and submissiveness, or when girls are suspects in violent crimes, then chivalrous behavior gives way to harsher treatment and higher arrests for girls (Visher 1983). Meda Chesney-Lind and Randall Shelden provide rich data on how race and gender interact to produce stereotypes and attitudes in the community, including the police and schoolteachers, for youth living in Hawaii (Chesney-Lind and Shelden 2004:chapter 10).

Overall, with respect to race and ethnicity, studies are not uniform in their conclusions. While numerous studies conclude that minorities are significantly overrepresented in police decisions to arrest juveniles, the results are not consistent (Sanford and Salerno 2005:135–136). In addition, some research concludes that the race of the officer and the suspect interact to affect arrest decisions. For example, in a study of police experiences with over 1,000 delinquent youth in Boston, Merry Morash (1984) concluded that white youth were more often arrested than black youth, in part because most police officers were white (p. 108). Overall, however, Morash concluded that male youth who associated with delinquent peers were most likely to be arrested, while girls who interacted with all-female groups were least likely to be arrested (p. 107).

Racial and Ethnic Profiling

Over the past few years, the topic of profiling has been discussed widely, particularly in connection with police behavior. *Criminal profiling* occurs when a person is selected for questioning about possible criminal activity because of certain traits, personal and behavioral, that the person possesses and that seem to fit a "profile" of characteristics believed to be associated with criminal behavior (Harris 2002:16). As such, profiling has been around for probably as long as police work has existed. In general, the right of the police to stop and search people and their possessions has been validated by several Supreme Court decisions. In a case decided in 1968, *Terry v. Ohio*, the Supreme Court ruled that the police have the right to detain and quickly search people who the police "reasonably" suspect of having committed a crime. Later, in *Florida v. Bostick* (1991), the Court concluded that police have the right to ask for one's consent to search his or her car or personal property. Of course, people can refuse such consent but then may find themselves being cited for any number of "violations," so often people in these situations provide their consent to have their vehicles or other personal possessions searched. A third recent case is *Whren v. United States* (1996), in which the Court ruled that police can pull one over for a traffic offense on the *pretext* that a crime has been committed. In other words, the police have the right to stop a vehicle and then look for incriminating evidence even if they had no reasonable grounds for suspecting that the occupant(s) of the vehicle were engaged in criminal behavior in the first place (Pampel 2004:9–10).

The long-standing practice of profiling and recent Supreme Court decisions permitting stop-and-search practices among the police have led to an increased concern for the potential of *racial and/or ethnic profiling*. The sole use of race or ethnicity in developing a profile is often considered racial profiling, and as such is illegal and in violation of the Fourteenth Amendment to the U.S. Constitution (Pampel 2004:7). Profiling can occur almost anywhere, such as on the highways ("driving while black"), in streets when looking for ethnic gang members, and along borders or in customs sections of airports for drug trafficking suspects and illegal immigrants (Harris 2002:chapters 2 and 6; Pampel 2004:12–23). President Clinton said of racial profiling that it is "morally indefensible. . . . It is wrong, it is destructive and it must stop." On the subject of racial profiling, President George W. Bush declared in his State of the Union address in January 2001 that "It's wrong, and we will end it in America" (Pampel 2004:31).

Racial profiling has existed throughout the history of the United States, including Jim Crow laws in the 19th and 20th centuries and the internment of Japanese Americans during World War II (Pampel 2004:10–11). In contemporary times, some may justify the use of racial profiling in counteracting terrorism, but even then, it can be argued that such tactics may be not only inefficient in identifying terrorists but also potentially harmful to the maintenance of cooperative relations and attitudes among the vast majority of loyal and law-abiding Arab Americans in the country (Pampel 2004:20–39).

The extent of racial profiling in American police work is virtually impossible to ascertain with certainty. Anecdotal (personal, subjective) data clearly indicate that minority populations have been the victims of profiling in recent years (Pampel 2004:39–42). Surveys of the American public reveal numerous instances of racial profiling among minorities, especially among *middle-class* African Americans (Weitzer and Tuch 2002). Perhaps this latter finding reflects greater sensitivity and awareness of racial profiling among the better-educated minorities, but that is not certain.

Studies have attempted to identify instances of racial and/or ethnic profiling by observing police behavior connected with traffic violations. These studies conclude that African American motorists are detained more than twice as often as white drivers. One study of the New Jersey State Police concluded that African American motorists constituted 13.5 percent of the motorists on the highways during the course of the study but 73.2 percent of those arrested for traffic violations (Harris 2002:55–68). Another study of racial profiling in North Carolina concluded that race was a significant variable in the decision to stop motorists by *local* police, but race was not significant in the decision to stop motorists by *state* police (Warren et al. 2006).

One drawback to observational studies concerning racial profiling is that police may be aware of such observations and modify their behavior during the course of the study. Findings such as the one noted above on the New Jersey State Police suggest that this does not always occur, but still, it is a valid criticism of observation-based studies. One attempt to correct for this effect is to analyze computer-based mobile data terminals (MDTs), which reflect police officer activity *before* a vehicle is pulled over. One such study concluded there is "systematic evidence of profiling," especially for African American drivers in white neighborhoods or "out of place" areas (Harris 2002:69–71). Thus, this study concluded that profiling can occur *before* the police confront a suspect or pull over a car to obtain information on the driver and/or occupants of the vehicle. Even if observers cannot detect evidence of racial profiling by observing police traffic pullovers, it can occur during earlier stages of the police–citizen interaction and observation process. Thus, more accurate measures of profiling and determining specific police officer motives are difficult to achieve.

Some research has shown that being the victim of profiling or even suspecting that it occurs has a detrimental effect on the perception of the police (Weitzler and Tuch 2002; Tyler and Wakslak 2004). So in addition to the possibility of identifying the wrong suspect in a case, profiling can cause citizens to lose respect for the legitimacy and authority of the police and the system of justice they represent. As some of the theoretical discussions presented earlier indicate, when respect for law and authority is eroded, it is easier to justify committing crimes. Studies indicate that only a small proportion of officers engage in racial profiling. The aforementioned study of MDTs, for example, indicated that only 10 percent of the officers most often used racial profiles. Nevertheless, among other deleterious consequences attributed to racial profiling, its existence can also contribute, at least indirectly, to increased levels of crime and delinquency.

Situational or Interpersonal Factors

Situational or interpersonal variables are unplanned, spur-of-the-moment factors. Such variables often occur at the point of contact between the police and citizens. Among the situational factors that have often been cited as having an influence on police decision making are the *demeanor* of the suspect and the *preference* of a victim for the police to arrest or release the suspect. Several studies have documented the influence of demeanor using research based on observational techniques (Piliavin and Briar 1964; Terry 1967; Werthman and Piliavin 1967; Black and Reiss 1970; Lundman et al. 1980). These studies suggest that suspects who display a *hostile* or *antagonistic* demeanor or attitude, as well as an *overly polite* demeanor, will more likely be arrested than will a civil demeanor. This relationship is stronger for minor crimes.

Donald Black and Albert Reiss (1970) conducted a study of police–citizen interactions during the summer months of 1966 in Boston, Chicago, and Washington, D.C. The observers were all trained and many came from legal and police backgrounds. They rode along with police officers during all shifts. The observations were all conducted in the inner cities. Among the conclusions of this study were that victim–suspect encounters were almost exclusively *intraracial* (victim and suspect were of the same race). In addition, in cases involving minor crimes, such as misdemeanors (which represented the majority of criminal cases observed in the study), African American victims more often expressed the desire to have the suspect arrested and less often to have him or her released or treated leniently, compared with whites. When there was no complainant in the case, the arrest differences between African American and white juvenile suspects was "negligible" (14 percent versus 10 percent, respectively, p. 70).

In addition to victim preference, Black and Reiss concluded that a suspect's demeanor also had an impact on the arrest decision of the police. Suspects who were openly defiant or hostile toward the police were more likely to be arrested than were suspects who were polite and civil toward the police. In addition, among nonwhites, suspects who were overly polite toward the police were also more likely to arrested than civil suspects. There were too few whites expressing an overpolite attitude to measure its impact on police action. Overall, however, demeanor had less impact on decision making than did victim preference, in part because so few suspects were unusually hostile or polite toward the police (Black and Reiss 1970:74–75).

The Black and Reiss study was replicated in a midwestern city some ten years later, using the same methodology. The results were essentially the same. Victim preference was strongly associated with police action, and African American victims (most of whom had been victimized by African American suspects) more often and more visibly pressed the police to arrest the suspect than did white victims. In addition, juveniles who displayed a hostile or uncooperative demeanor were more often arrested than were youth who acted in a civil manner with the police, although this factor was less important than victim preference. An "unusually respectful" attitude was also connected with an arrest, except in this study the relationship held for whites, largely because so few African American youth displayed an overly polite demeanor toward the police. Overall, however, demeanor played a relatively small role in police decision making, again partly because so few youth were either unusually hostile or polite toward the police (Lundman et al. 1980:136–148).

The impact of demeanor on police decision making has been debated in recent studies, in part because hostile attitudes in earlier studies did not clearly separate words and gestures from physical contact. A hostile attitude, for example, might include actual pushing or hitting by the suspect or associates of suspects. This possibility has led some to question the impact of demeanor, even a slight impact, on police action (Klinger 1994). However, continued studies of this issue maintain the modest impact of demeanor on arrest decisions, even when only hostile words are considered (Lundman 1994; Worden and Shepard 1996). In addition, David Klinger (1996) suggests that the relationship between demeanor and arrest may not be linear. Rather, there may be a threshold or breaking point involving hostile attitudes toward the police, and when that point has been reached, the decision to arrest occurs. Despite these issues, research still concludes that demeanor and victim preferences exert an important influence on police decisions to arrest juvenile suspects (Sanborn and Salerno 2005:136–137).

Organizational Factors

Some research has concluded that organizational characteristics of police departments have an influence on arrest rates (Wilson 1968). James Wilson (1968) studied arrest rate patterns in two cities, one on the East Coast and one on the West Coast. Both cities were of similar population size, and both had similar problems with delinquency. The East Coast police department was characterized by more centralized organization and a weak juvenile bureau. Juvenile officers were not well respected within the department, and they were not used to process juvenile cases, thus making arrests of juveniles more burdensome on other officers. In addition, the officers in the eastern city did not have much education beyond high school, and most of them were brought up in the city. This department was named a "fraternal" department by Wilson. The West Coast department was more centralized in organization than was the East Coast department. Furthermore, this department had a well-organized juvenile bureau, and juvenile work was more respected than in the East Coast department. In addition, the officers in the West Coast city were college educated and reared outside the city, especially those officers in the juvenile bureau. This department was dubbed a "professional" department.

Wilson concluded that *arrests of juveniles were higher in the professional department.* In that city, the police indicated that they believed in the juvenile justice system and felt that juveniles needed to be arrested if the system were to work. In the fraternal department, officers had developed a "pass system," whereby the first time or two a juvenile was caught or suspected of committing a crime, he or she was passed by and handled informally. In essence, these officers had developed an informal diversion system. This reaction was particularly likely to occur in neighborhoods familiar to the officer, similar to those in which he was reared or where he knew the kids and their parents. The pass system was not used in areas undergoing racial change, essentially in areas with which the officers were not familiar.

Wilson's study indicates the potential impact organizational arrangements can have on arrest rates. However, another organizational variable to consider is the basic notion that police departments are bureaucratic organizations in general. Moreover, all police departments are part of city governance and ultimately responsive to local political issues. As William

Chambliss and Robert Seidman suggest, "Law enforcement agencies depend for resources allocation on political organizations." In addition, "It may be expected that the law enforcement agencies will process a disproportionately high number of the politically weak and powerless, while ignoring the violations of those with power" (Chambliss and Seidman 1971:269). These views remove decision making solely from the discretion of individual decision makers into a larger, bureaucratic, organizational, and political arena. Organizational factors can assume an important influence on police decisions. However, these factors, especially when compared with many of the other variables discussed, have not been well researched (Sanborn and Salerno 2005:139).

The Courts

Decision making among juvenile court workers has also been the subject of research. One significant difference between police and court settings, however, is the fact that virtually all court decisions are made in office settings, and usually with considerable time for thought and reflection. In addition, court officials have access to much more information concerning the case than do the police. Probation officers and juvenile court judges do not need to rely on quick judgments or on information largely based on appearances when deciding what to do with a case. Consequently, court decision-making studies typically do not reflect the importance of "curbside" or spur-of-the-moment factors, such as visual appearance, demeanor, and victim preferences.

Traditional juvenile court philosophy is based on individualized justice and decisions made in the best interests of the child. However, numerous studies of courts throughout the country have cast doubt on the degree to which such ideals are truly followed in actual decisions made within the court system (Bortner 1982). While the *seriousness of the offense plays a major role* in the decisions of officers of the juvenile court, especially in the judge's decision (Feld 1999:266–267), several studies of juvenile court proceedings indicate the significant impact of individual factors on the outcome of cases, including race, social class, and gender, apart from or in addition to the nature of the offense. Data presented in chapter 13 clearly indicate statistical overrepresentation of minority youth in the juvenile justice system, including the courts. While some studies also document statistical associations between minority status and the processing of cases through the system, others fail to find such associations (Bortner 1982:149; Sanford and

Salerno 2005:chapter 14), or they find that race is less important than other factors or is more important in some communities than in others (Leiber 2003:chapters 2–6). One reason there is disagreement concerning the amount of overrepresentation of minority youth in the juvenile justice system is because there is some overrepresentation of minorities in each of the several stages of the system. Thus, a little overrepresentation at each stage seems insignificant, but toward the end of the system, the overrepresentation becomes significant or amplified (Leiber 2003:chapters 5 and 6). In Virginia, for example, in 2005, 45.5 percent of juveniles processed at intake were African American, and 47 percent were white. Among those admitted to detention homes or centers, 51.4 percent were African American, and 40.3 percent were white. However, among those juveniles committed to juvenile correctional facilities in the state, 66.7 percent were African American, and 27.1 percent were white (Virginia Department of Juvenile Justice 2005:20, 98, 156; see also Feld 1999:268–269).

However, connecting statistical overrepresentations with outright bias and discrimination is not an easy task. Often, these overrepresentations are explained in terms of legal factors. Thus, it is contended that minorities end up in the system because they more often commit serious offenses. However, some research indicates the presence of racial and ethnic influences on the outcome of cases regardless of offense type. In addition, decisions made at the beginning of the process can affect later decisions and can be taken as legal factors. Detention decisions, for example, may be affected by whether a juvenile was arrested, which becomes a legal factor. However, as we have already seen, the decision to make an arrest can be affected by race and social class. In addition, being detained can negatively affect a juvenile's case during the adjudicatory hearing or the disposition hearing, and it, too, can become another legal factor. Thus, what on the surface seem to be legal factors have in reality been influenced by race, class, or other extralegal factors (Bortner 1982:23–34).

Race may also become a factor in court decision making apart from individual characteristics. Sometimes the racial composition of a community can affect the outcome of individual cases in juvenile court. A community with a large young, minority, and/or poor component may elicit fearful attitudes among adult whites in the community, attitudes that may reflect in higher minority representation in court decision making (Tittle and Curran 1988). In a national study of juvenile court decisions, for example, Robert Sampson and John Laub (1993) found that measures of racial inequality and "underclass" poverty, including families living in poverty and ratios of African American to white levels of poverty, were significantly associated with the filing of formal petitions to the court, detention decisions, and out-of-home placements or dispositions for minority youth (see also Leiber 2003:66–71 and Snyder and Sickmund 2006:188).

Other Considerations

Ethnographic studies of juvenile courts suggest the relationship between offender characteristics and case outcomes is subtle and can occur for a variety of reasons. For example, in a study of the juvenile court in a midwestern county, Bortner (1982) notes that the *interaction* between a court official and a juvenile can determine the outcome of a case. Most of the court officials in this study were white, and often they indicated an inability to understand or appreciate the background of an African American juvenile with whom they were working (chapter 9; see also Leiber 2003:chapter 8). This lack of appreciation or understanding of minority youths' situations may lead to differential, often harsher, dispositions for minority offenders. However, Bortner's study also concluded that the parents of minority or poor youth more often pressed for their children's cases to be processed through the courts rather than through other agencies outside the court system, primarily because these parents could not afford private or alternative means of dealing with their children (pp. 150, 170–171). The issue of minority parents' access to resources to pay for the treatment of children in trouble with the law and courts continues to be an important factor in differential handling of juveniles in the juvenile justice system, including access to private psychiatric care for troubled youth (Feld 1999:179–188; Leiber 2003: 133–145, 158–159).

Other studies of juvenile courts emphasize the importance of the defendant's demeanor in the courtroom, similar to the impact of *demeanor* on police decision making. Juvenile defendants who are disrespectful, insolent, or outright defiant toward the judge or other courtroom figures may find themselves at odds with the judge and more likely to be given harsher treatment than those who are respectful and cooperative (Emerson 1969:192–201; Bortner 1982:chapter 12). Some analyses indicate that the attitudes and perceived cooperativeness of a juvenile's *family* can also affect the outcome of a case (Sanborn and Salerno 2005:353–354).

Just as limited resources may influence the range of options available to the parents and guardians of youth in trouble with the law, the availability of resources for a court or juvenile justice system may also influence the dispositions of juveniles in that system (Mahoney 1987:66–69; Sampson and Laub 1993: 307; Feld 1999:271). Anne Mahoney's analysis of a juvenile court also indicates the importance of *time*, or perceived time, available to the court and all of its participants in the decisions ultimately reached by a judge (1987:chapter 4). The lack of resources, facilities, or alternative programs for troubled youth in a given jurisdiction may mean that adjudicated delinquents are more often committed to correctional institutions for "treatment" than to alternative programs offered in the community, and this situation can especially negatively affect female delinquents in a community (Sanford and Salerno 2005:357). Sometimes, however, lack of resources may serve to reduce the disposition of offenders, perhaps resulting in a decision to handle a case less harshly. Studies suggest, for example, that in *urban areas*, courts may have access to *more community resources* than do rural juvenile courts, and judges are more inclined to deal with juveniles *more severely* in terms of dispositions (Feld 1999:26).

Some suggest that the relationships among all of the key players in the system, including the police, lawyers, probation officers, and judge, may affect the outcomes of cases (Bortner 1982; Sanborn and Salerno 2005:358). While the juvenile justice system may be a "loosely coupled" one (Sampson and Laub 1993:286), still its participants may interact, both on and off the job, and over time, there may develop mutual expectations of what kinds of cases should be processed in a given court. These expectations and attitudes may have an influence on the outcome of a juvenile's case (Cicourel 1968). Thus, it should be little surprise to learn that judges often follow the recommendations of probation officers and others working with the court, as expressed in the predisposition report, in deciding what to do with a case (Sanborn and Salerno 2005:350).

Summary

With all of the potential variables that *could* affect decision making in the juvenile justice system, both at the police and court levels, little consistent agreement has been reached on exactly which variables affect these decisions or the amount of influence they have on the outcomes of cases (Sanborn and Salerno 2005:140,198–199, 358–360). However, numerous studies have indicated the presence of individual and social factors as having some impact on the decisions of the police and court officials, apart from the nature of the offense, and these findings cannot be ignored. There is too much evidence to simply dismiss the impact of these variables as immeasurable or inconsistent to the point of irrelevance. Perhaps there should always be some degree of discretion in the handling of juvenile cases. The philosophy of rehabilitation and individualized justice supports that kind of system. However, the presence of discretion should always be under review and subject to control or alteration. If juvenile cases are to be handled according to the best interests of the child and public welfare, fairness and equitable treatment must always be important goals in the deliberations involving youth brought into the juvenile justice system. In part, the topics of the final two sections of this chapter, court cases and diversion, address the need both to supervise the processing of cases through the juvenile system and/or to provide alternative means of handling cases outside the system.

Supreme Court Cases Affecting the Rights of Juveniles Processed by the Police and Courts

As was discussed in chapter 2, judicial reviews of criminal cases involving juveniles were not very common during the 19th and early 20th centuries. While the United States Children's Bureau was established in 1912 in part to oversee the interests of juveniles brought into the juvenile justice system, virtually all juvenile courts in the United States have been state based. Despite the creation of children's agencies, until the middle of the 20th century the courts remained largely absent from the oversight of juveniles who had been arrested, sent to court, and committed to institutions. Since the 1960s, however, there have been dozens of appellate court cases, often involving the United States Supreme Court. The decisions in these cases have largely resulted in granting juveniles increased protection while in the hands of the police and courts. Many of theses cases are discussed and analyzed in a text written by Craig Hemmens and his colleagues (Hemmens et al. 2004; see also Parry 2005). Some of these cases have already been discussed in other chapters of this book. The purpose of this discussion is to present highlights of several cases that have had an impact on the arrest of juveniles and their subsequent processing through juvenile courts.

One important area of interest to the courts has been the protection of a suspect's rights during interrogation by the police, both during and after an arrest. One of the earliest cases involving interrogations of juveniles was *Haley v. Ohio* (1948). In this case, a 15-year-old boy was arrested and charged with robbery. He was questioned nonstop for several hours, from midnight until around 5 a.m., without the presence of an attorney or parent. Eventually, he was presented with a signed confession of two accomplices, whereupon he also confessed. Later, Haley argued that the confession was forced. The U.S. Supreme Court ruled in favor of Haley's complaint and maintained that coerced or fraudulent confessions of juveniles cannot be used in court and that juveniles were protected by the Fourteenth Amendment to the U.S. Constitution. This was a significant case in that it was the first time that the Supreme Court ruled that juveniles should be accorded the same rights of protection provided to adults in the Constitution and Bill of Rights. Although the specific rights to be protected were not outlined in this case, it set the stage for later decisions that did identify specific rights of protection for juveniles (Hemmens et al. 2004:17–18).

In 1966, the Supreme Court handed down a decision that has probably had the most influence on police interrogation procedures over the past 50 years, *Miranda v. Arizona*. Probably the most important right protected with this decision was the right to an attorney at the time of police questioning or interrogation, provided the suspect was under arrest. In addition, this decision provided that the suspect be notified of the right to an attorney, whether privately retained or publicly provided, and that anything said by the suspect during interrogation could be used in court. Since this case involved an adult, there has been some discussion concerning whether *Miranda* applied to juveniles. However, the conclusion of jurists on this issue is that juveniles are to be included in the rights provided in *Miranda*, even if the Supreme Court has not specifically included juveniles in this decision (Sanborn and Salerno 2005:146–148). Another issue related to this case is whether others can be substituted for lawyers as legal representatives of youth. In a case decided in 1979, *Fare v. Michael C.*, the Court ruled that probation officers do not constitute lawyers and cannot serve in the capacity of lawyers. Michael C. had asked to see his probation officer instead of an attorney and subsequently confessed to a charge of murder. His confession was upheld in juvenile court because probation officers do not represent legal counsel. This decision was supported by the U.S. Supreme Court. Other cases have granted permission for juveniles to ask for their parents, although again, the presence of parents does not necessarily guarantee that juveniles are getting the best legal advice (Hemmens et al. 2004: 23–25; Sanborn and Salerno 2005:148–149).

Perhaps the most significant case involving the rights of juveniles in *juvenile court* is one decided in 1967, *In re Gault.* This case involved a 15-year-old Arizona boy, Gerald Gault, who was charged with making an obscene phone call to a neighbor. Upon the neighbor's claim that it was Gault who had made the phone call, the police arrested him at home, without the presence of his parents, and took him to the local detention home. Before his parents learned of his whereabouts and came to see him, Gault had been referred to a juvenile court hearing by a probation officer. At that hearing, there was conflicting testimony about what Gault had said at the detention home. The probation officer indicated that Gault had confessed to making the call, but Gault maintained that he only dialed the number and that another boy had actually made the obscene comments. The judge scheduled another hearing and ultimately decided that Gault had committed a delinquent offense and committed him to the Arizona State Industrial School for an indefinite time, or until he reached the age of 21, a possible sentence of six years. At no time did Gault's accuser appear during court proceedings, even though his mother had specifically requested the accuser's presence, nor had Gault or his parents actually seen the formal charges being brought against him. The case was ultimately heard by the Supreme Court, which overturned Gault's "conviction." In reaching this decision, the Court noted that Gault was never represented by an attorney in the case and that the maximum penalty for his offense, if he were an adult, would have been a fine of $5 to $50 *or* incarceration of up to two months. The Court ruled that in all juvenile court cases involving possible confinement of youth, the following rights must be honored (Hemmens et al. 2004:79–80; Parry 2005: 87–101):

1. To be notified of the charges
2. To be represented by an attorney
3. To confront and challenge one's accuser
4. To remain silent during questioning

In the 1970s, the Supreme Court reached other decisions affecting the rights of juveniles in the courts. Again, discussions of cases affecting juveniles from juvenile to adult court jurisdiction have already been presented. However, the Court also handed down decisions that affected the procedures in juvenile court. One such case was *In re Winship* (1970). In this case, a 12-year-old boy was charged with going into a locker and stealing $112 from a woman's purse. A New York family court judge found the youth delinquent on the basis of a "preponderance of evidence" that the boy committed the offense. Subsequently, the boy was committed to the state training school for an indefinite period up to his 18th birthday, or a possible term of six years. On appeal the U.S. Supreme Court overturned the conviction, arguing that in cases involving criminal charges, youths in juvenile court must be found "guilty" on the basis of evidence deemed "beyond a reasonable doubt," or the same standards of evidence applied in adult criminal courts. Even though juvenile court proceedings are considered civil, the potential for having a record of delinquency and possibly being confined for extended periods of time make it essential that adjudicatory hearings be governed by the same rules of evidence used in adult criminal trials. Again, it should be noted that the Court did not specify that such standards of evidence be applied to all juvenile court decisions, only those that involved criminal charges (Hemmens et al. 2004:80; Parry 2005:102–105).

In 1984, the Supreme Court ruled that juveniles can be placed in detention as a preventive measure. In this case, *Schall v. Martin,* a 14-year-old male was arrested in New York and charged with several felonies, including robbery and second-degree assault. Martin was detained overnight after the arrest and subsequently ordered to be detained by a family court judge for several days until a hearing could be scheduled. The grounds for the detention were that Martin was deemed unsupervised and liable to commit additional crimes if not placed in detention. This decision amounted to *preventive detention,* that is, detaining someone on the basis of what crimes they might, or probably would, commit if released. The Court ruled in this case that preventive detention is constitutional and not punitive. The issue of bail per se was not addressed in this case, since bail is not a guaranteed right for juveniles. Juveniles do not have a presumed right to freedom or liberty, as they "are always in some form of custody." Once placed in detention, they are likely to stay there until their case is resolved. While some states do provide for bail for juveniles, in juvenile court jurisdictions (and some even apply this privilege to status offense charges), the automatic right to bail is not presumed for juveniles (Hemmens et al. 2004:58–59; Sanborn and Salerno 2005:219–227).

In summary, the thrust of the decisions cited in this overview has been to grant more rights to juveniles during police interrogations and while they are undergoing juvenile court proceedings, even though some decisions, such as *Schall v. Martin,* seem to go against that direction. However, another effect seems to have been the creation of a dual justice system, one that includes both legalistic and traditional, rehabilitative ideals and goals (Shoemaker 1988; Feld 1999:94–108). As Barry Feld argues, "Courts and legislatures choose between competing characterizations of young people as autonomous and self-determining or as immature and incompetent in order to maximize their social control" (1999:108). Feld contends that this dual nature of juvenile justice can sometimes lead to *less* protection of procedural safeguards for juveniles (Feld 1999:109–165). Legalistic procedures might protect the rights of juveniles, but they also allow authorities to treat juveniles more punitively than would occur in more traditional, rehabilitative settings. As he says, "Once states grant youths a semblance of procedural justice, however inadequate, it becomes easier for them to depart from a purely rehabilitative model of juvenile justice. Providing any procedural rights legitimates the imposition of punitive, as well as therapeutic, sanctions" (Feld 1999:165). Although the full protection of juveniles' rights may not have been realized by Supreme Court decisions, the right to legal representation is most significant. Without this legal protection, many of the other rights and protections might not be enforced or even known by juvenile defendants. Moreover, having defense counsel is another means of reversing, or at least checking, the negative impacts of discriminatory and/or whimsical practices within the system, from the police through the courts.

Diversion

Another way of trying to deal with discriminatory handling of juveniles in the system is to develop and promote programs that divert youth away from the system. As indicated earlier, the practice of diverting juveniles away from the formal system of juvenile justice has existed for as long as police and courts have existed. It has already been noted that the police, for example, often use "informal diversion" when deciding what to do with juveniles with whom they come into contact, and most often these diversionary tactics are used instead of arresting a youth. Some have suggested that the juvenile justice system is itself a form of diversion from the punitive aspects of the adult criminal justice system (Zimring 2005:33–48). However, the formal, state-sanctioned use of diversion in the United States began in the 1970s, after the passage of the Omnibus Crime Control and Safe Streets Act in 1968. This act was promoted by the conclusions of the President's Commission on Law Enforcement and the Administration of Justice, published in 1967 (President's Commission on Law Enforcement 1967). These sources of influence led to the creation of the Juvenile Justice and Delinquency Prevention Act of 1974, which sponsored many formal, government-sponsored diversion programs in the 1970s and 1980s (Lemert 1971:92–95; Sanborn and Salerno 2005:424–425). Many of these programs focused on diverting youth from the courts by using police officers as sources of referrals to diversion programs. Others focused on diversion from institutions as part of *deinstitutionalization* policies. No matter where the diversion takes place, however, most of these programs have been connected to the judicial system, thus making it unlikely that diversion can be a true deflector of bias and discriminatory behavior.

In many ways, diversion as a concept is supported by the tenets of labeling theory (see chapter 12). The idea is to remove juveniles from the potentially stigmatizing consequences of being labeled a delinquent. One of the more extreme positions advocated in this respect is Edwin Schur's call for "radical nonintervention," or the principle of not doing much of anything formally with all but serious and violent juvenile offenders, in the expectation that a change in behavior or attitudes will occur through some other means (Schur 1973). However, labeling theory is not the only reason for supporting diversion programs. Handling offenders within the community or home of a juvenile is another advantage for the potential rehabilitation or change of attitude and behavior for a young person. In addition, diverting youth away from the courts should lighten the caseload of probation officers and others working with juvenile courts and allow these workers to concentrate on the presumably more serious cases that come to the courts' attention. The practice of treating or supervising offenders in the community is also thought to be a cost-effective strategy, since the juvenile will not be placed in expensive confinement facilities (Roberts 1989:170–189; Champion 1992:340). The issue of costs associated with institutional confinement will be discussed in chapter 15.

Initially, government-sponsored diversion programs were assisted by the creation of local youth service bureaus, or YSBs. These agencies were established for the explicit purpose of helping juveniles in trouble without resorting to the formal system of juvenile justice. By 1973, there were approximately 150 YSBs in the country. They offered assistance to youth in the form of runaway centers, crisis hotlines, pregnancy counseling, school resource services, employment assistance, and many other services. Today, however, while the concept of diversion remains alive and well, YSBs are virtually nonexistent (Bartollas and Miller 2005:272).

Although initially, diversion programs focused on status offenders, some branched out to include more serious juvenile offenders. Over the years, these programs have demonstrated cost savings, compared with traditional institutional confinement costs, as well as reductions in recidivism, again compared with institutionalized youth (Roberts 1989:170–189; Champion 1992:337–346). Despite these advantages, one of the common occurrences associated with diversion programs is a concept known as *net widening*. Net widening occurs when more juveniles are brought into the system than would have been the case without a diversion program (Roberts 1989:183–184; Sanborn and Salerno 2005:425–426). This situation runs counter to the expectations and benefits of diversion. Diversion is supposed to *reduce* the numbers of juveniles in the system, not increase their numbers. Some have suggested that net widening may actually be beneficial to the welfare of juveniles, since they would be exposed to possible benefits of treatment or rehabilitative services that they otherwise might not have received (Roberts 1989:183–184). This result may well be true, but if so, then the value of diversion is questioned.

Others have questioned the utility of diversion on the basis of selectivity of those youth placed into diversion programs. Specifically, some research has suggested that diversion programs have tended to serve white, middle-class youth more so than minority youth (Roberts 1989:183). This issue has not been well researched, but its possibility raises concerns about the fairness of diversion as an alternative to the processing of cases through the juvenile justice system. Still others suggest that even if diversion programs have been class specific, minority youth will still be better served by being placed in the juvenile justice system, compared with the adult criminal justice system (Zimring 2005:172–174).

As a concept, diversion has been, and remains, an important component of the juvenile justice system. As a system of specific programs sponsored by governmental funds, however, diversion has lessened in scope since the1990s. It has already been observed that YSBs have virtually disappeared. Part of this decline is related to an increased atmosphere of "accountability" and punitiveness directed toward youth since the 1990s (Zimring 2005:44). While transfers of juvenile cases to adult courts are definitely a component of modern juvenile justice procedures, the practice of transfers has actually decreased over the past ten years or so, as has already been discussed in this book. Besides a trend toward more juvenile accountability, however, juvenile justice policies have shifted to more specific types of diversionary practices. In particular, there has been an increased reliance on drug courts, teen courts, mediation, mentoring, and other procedures during the past few years. Drug courts for juveniles were discussed in chapter 9. Mediation and mentoring programs will be discussed in the next chapter. The topic of youth courts will be discussed next.

Youth Courts

Youth courts are an alternative to the traditional juvenile court setting in which youth play important roles in the hearing of a complaint against another youth. Youth courts, also known as peer juries, teen courts, and student courts, have been in existence for several years. The constitutionality of these courts was verified in 1975, in a case known as *McKeiver v. Pennsylvania.* In that case, the U.S. Supreme Court ruled that youth or peer juries may be substituted for juvenile courts (where juries do not exist). Such alternatives were *not required* by the Supreme Court in that case but were *allowed* (Hemmens et al. 2004:81). After that ruling, peer juries began to appear throughout the country. By 1979, 12 states had authorized the use of peer juries (Reichel and Seyfrit 1984). In the 1990s, the popularity of peers handling cases of juveniles grew rapidly (Pearson 2004). According to the fall 2005 Newsletter of the National Youth Court Center, for example, in 1994, there were an estimated 78 youth courts in the United States. By October 2005, that number had grown to 1,050 (National Youth Court Center 2005:1). They exist in 49 states (Connecticut does not yet have one) and the District of Columbia. These courts exist in all regions of the country and in small towns as well as in metropolises. Youth courts are estimated to handle between 110,000 and 125,000 juvenile offenders and involve more than 100,000 youth volunteers every year. In addition, approximately 9 percent of juveniles arrested are diverted from juvenile courts to youth courts (Pearson and Jurich 2005:5, 9).

All youth courts operate under the supervision of adults. Roughly 44 percent are supervised by an agency within the juvenile justice system, mostly either the police or probation office of a jurisdiction. The majority of such courts are operated by private, local government or school agencies (Pearson and Jurich 2005:14). All participants are volunteers and receive training in juvenile justice concepts and procedures before hearing cases. Juvenile volunteers are between age 13 and 18. In addition, offenders voluntarily enter youth court procedures. Youth courts, however, are usually restricted to minor cases of delinquency, such as truancy and other status offenses, alcohol and minor drug offenses, larceny and minor crimes of theft, vandalism, and school-related infractions, including bullying, and they typically handle only first-time offenders. Studies suggest that about one-fifth of youth court volunteers are youth whose cases have previously been handled in youth court. Sometimes, these offenders are required to participate in a youth court proceeding as part of their sentencing, but some do this voluntarily (Pearson 2004:2; Pearson and Jurich 2005:10–12).

Most courts retain the structure of juvenile courts, and teen volunteers assume the role of intake officer, jury members, and judge, as well as other support roles in the court system, such as clerks and bailiffs. There are four basic types of youth courts: (1) the *adult judge* model, which is the most popular model, where the adult supervisor is a judge or lawyer and often serves as the judge in the case; (2) the *youth judge* model, where a juvenile volunteer serves as the judge and the adult supervisor serves only as a monitor; (3) the *youth tribunal*, which consists of three youth judges serving as a panel with no jury, and (4) the *peer jury*, which has a youth jury but an adult judge (Pearson and Jurich 2005:13). Most often, juveniles who accept being processed in a youth court plead guilty to the charge, and the court serves primarily as a dispositional court rather than as an adjudicatory court. Most dispositions focus on accountability and youth development and include apologies to victims, community service, attendance of workshops addressing crime and drug issues, tutoring, counseling, and other personal awareness and development programs (Pearson and Jurich 2005:8–9).

Youth courts or peer juries have been studied and evaluated for several decades. For the most part, these evaluations have concluded that youth courts are successful in terms of reducing further involvement in crime and delinquency, reduced costs of operation, and acceptance among youthful offenders (Reichel and Seyfrit 1984; Pearson and Jurich 2005). One analysis, for example, concluded that among youthful offenders who agreed to appear before a youth court, only around 10 percent reoffended within one year of their youth court appearance. In addition, nearly 90 percent of young offenders successfully complete the disposition assigned by the youth court (Pearson and Jurich 2005:15). The costs of operating youth courts are considerably less than the costs of traditional court operations. Using 2002 dollars, for example, the average annual budget for youth courts across the country was $49,000, or approximately $430–$480 per juvenile. In contrast, in 2001, the estimated annual cost of juvenile probation was $1,635 per juvenile (Pearson and Jurich 2005:16).

Overall, it seems that youth courts are becoming more popular throughout the country. They are less costly to run than traditional juvenile court programs, and the recidivism rates of those processed by youth courts is only around 10 percent per year. As an alternative to traditional courts, youth courts seem a viable option.

Summary

The formal juvenile justice system as we know it in the United States is now over 100 years old. From the beginnings of a single court in Chicago, the "system" has grown to hundreds of police juvenile units, juvenile or family or domestic relations courts, and court service units throughout the country.

While an important feature of the juvenile justice system has been individualized justice served for the best interests of the child and the community, current practices and procedures reflect diverse goals and interests, not always individualized and not always in the "best" interests of the child. Current court procedures involve several figures, each with specialized roles to perform and each having significant contact with juveniles. Some argue that these diverse units between and among police and court operations result in the existence of a collection of units rather than a true "system."

In addition to the topic of diversification and specialization within juvenile justice, an important issue is fairness and true individualized handling within the system. Specifically, there has been much discussion and research over the past few decades regarding the equal treatment of youth from diverse backgrounds within the system, from the police through the courts. While much of this research has established the existence of overrepresentation of youth from minority backgrounds in the official records of juvenile justice agencies, the actual documentation of bias and discriminatory attitudes among juvenile justice workers is more difficult to establish.

While discrimination in juvenile justice system operations may be difficult to establish accurately, since the 1970s two major trends have occurred that together serve to supervise the handling of juvenile cases or to bypass the formal operations of juvenile justice altogether. U.S. Supreme Court decisions have given numerous rights to juveniles, similar to the constitutional rights given to defendants in criminal court proceedings. Perhaps the most significant constitutional protection now applied to juvenile defendants in the juvenile justice system is the right to an attorney, from the point of arrest through the juvenile court adjudicatory hearing. While several other rights are now provided to juveniles, the right to an attorney helps to further ensure that other protections are honored. In addition, attorney representation helps to further provide legal supervision of operations, which can help prevent discriminatory and capricious decision making within the system, including the practice of racial and ethnic profiling.

A second trend in juvenile justice is the increasing use of procedures that provide an alternative to the formal operations of the juvenile justice system. In the 1970s, the government established formal diversion programs, often initially funded by government monies. Since the 1980s, these formal diversion programs have waned, but in their place, myriad programs have been established that help to continue the practice of providing diversionary alternatives to the formal operations of the juvenile justice system. One example of such alternatives is the youth court or peer court. There are now

over 1,000 youth courts operating in the United States, involving hundreds of thousands of juvenile defendants and volunteer court workers. Positive evaluations of these courts suggest that their presence will continue to grow. At the same time, the formal operations of juvenile courts will also likely continue, perhaps concentrating on the more serious cases, at least those that have not been transferred to the adult system. The continued monitoring of the handling and processing of cases as a means of reducing discriminatory practices will also likely continue for all aspects of juvenile justice, including diversion programs.

References

Bartollas, Clemens, and Stuart J. Miller
    2005   Juvenile Justice in America. 4th edition. Upper Saddle River, NJ: Pearson Prentice Hall.
Black, Donald J., and Albert J. Reiss, Jr.
    1970   Police Control of Juveniles. American Sociological Review 35:63–77.
Bortner, M. A.
    1982   Inside a Juvenile Court: The Tarnished Ideal of Individualized Justice. New York: New York University Press.
Chambliss, William J., and Robert B. Seidman
    1971   Law, Order, and Power. Reading, MA: Addison-Wesley.
Champion, Dean J.
    1992   The Juvenile Justice System: Delinquency, Processing, and the Law. New York: Macmillan.
Chesney-Lind, Meda, and Randall G. Shelden
    2004   Girls, Delinquency, and Juvenile Justice. 3rd edition. Belmont, CA: Wadsworth.
Cicourel, Aaron V.
    1968   The Social Organization of Juvenile Justice. New York: Wiley.
Emerson, Robert
    1969   Judging Delinquents: Context and Process in Juvenile Court. New York: Aldine.
Feld, Barry C.
    1999   Bad Kids: Race and the Transformation of the Juvenile Court. New York: Oxford University Press.
Grimes, Michael D.
    2005   Patching Up the Cracks: A Case Study of Juvenile Court Reform. New York: Lexington Books.

Harris, David A.
    2002   Profiles in Injustice: Why Racial Profiling Cannot Work. New York: New Press.
Hemmens, Craig, Benjamin Steiner, and David Mueller
    2004   Significant Cases in Juvenile Justice. Los Angeles: Roxbury.
Klinger, David A.
    1994   Demeanor or Crime? Why "Hostile" Citizens Are More Likely to Be Arrested. Criminology 32:475–493.
    1996   Demeanor, Crime, and Police Behavior: A Reexamination of the Police Services Study Data. Criminology 34:61–82.
Leiber, Michael J.
    2003   The Contexts of Juvenile Justice Decision Making: When Race Matters. Albany: State University of New York Press.
Lemert, Edwin M.
    1971   Instead of Court: Diversion in Juvenile Justice. Chevy Chase, MD: National Institute of Mental Health, Center for Studies of Crime and Delinquency.
Lundman, Richard J.
    1994   Demeanor or Crime? The Midwest City Police–Citizen Encounters Study. Criminology 32:631–656.
Lundman, Richard J., Richard E. Sykes, and John P. Clark
    1980   Police Control of Juveniles: A Replication. In Police Behavior: A Sociological Perspective. Richard J. Lundman, ed. Pp. 130–151. New York: Oxford University Press.
Mahoney, Anne Rankin
    1987   Juvenile Justice in Context. Boston: Northeastern University Press.
Martin, Gus
    2005   Juvenile Justice: Process and Systems. Thousand Oaks, CA: Sage.
Morash, Merry
    1984   Establishment of a Juvenile Police Record: The Influence of Individual and Peer Group Characteristics. Criminology 22:97–111.
National Youth Court Center
    2005   Youth Courts Pass the 1,000 Mark!! In Session 5(1):1.
Pampel, Fred C.
    2004   Racial Profiling. New York: Facts on File.
Parry, David L.
    2005   Essential Readings in Juvenile Justice. Upper Saddle River, NJ: Pearson Prentice Hall.

Pearson, Sarah S.
    2004   Policymakers Support Youth Court Growth: Voices and Recommen-
            dations from the Field. National Youth Court Center Policy Brief,
            September:1–9.
Pearson, Sarah S., and Sonia Jurich
    2005   National Update: Communities Embracing Youth Courts for At-
            Risk Youth. Washington, DC: American Youth Policy Forum.
Piliavin, Irving, and Scott Briar
    1964   Police Encounters with Juveniles. American Journal of Sociology
            70:206–214.
President's Commission on Law Enforcement and Administration of Justice
    1967   Task Force Report: Juvenile Delinquency and Youth Crime. Wash-
            ington, DC: U.S. Department of Justice.
Puzzanchera, Charles, Anna L. Stahl, Terence A. Finnegan, Nancy Tierney, and
Howard N. Snyder
    2004   Juvenile Court Statistics 2000. Pittsburgh: National Center for Juve-
            nile Justice.
Reichel, Philip, and Carole Seyfrit
    1984   A Peer Jury in the Juvenile Court. Crime and Delinquency 84:423–438.
Roberts, Albert R.
    1989   Juvenile Justice: Policies, Programs, and Services. Chicago: Dorsey.
Sanborn, Joseph B., Jr., and Anthony W. Salerno
    2005   The Juvenile Justice System: Law and Process. Los Angeles: Roxbury.
Sampson, Robert J., and John H. Laub
    1993   Structural Variations in Juvenile Court Processing: Inequality, the
            Underclass, and Social Control. Law and Society Review 27:285–312.
Schur, Edwin M.
    1973   Radical Nonintervention: Rethinking the Delinquency Problem.
            Englewood Cliffs, NJ: Prentice-Hall.
Shoemaker, Donald J.
    1988   The Duality of Juvenile Justice in the United States: History, Trends,
            and Prospects. Sociological Spectrum 8:1–17.
Shoemaker, Donald J., and Timothy W. Wolfe
    2005   Juvenile Justice: A Reference Handbook. Santa Barbara: ABC-CLIO.
Snyder, Howard N., and Melissa Sickmund
    2006   Juvenile Offenders and Victims: 2006 National Report. Washington,
            DC: U.S. Department of Justice, Office of Justice Programs, Office
            of Juvenile Justice and Delinquency Prevention.

Terry, Robert M.
  1967   The Screening of Juvenile Offenders. Journal of Criminal Law,
          Criminology, and Police Science 58:173–181.
Tittle, Charles R., and Debra A. Curran
  1988   Contingencies for Dispositional Disparities in Juvenile Justice. Social
          Forces 67:23–58.
Torbet, Patricia McFall
  1996   Juvenile Probation: The Workhorse of the Juvenile Justice System.
          Juvenile Justice Bulletin, March. Washington, DC: Office of Juvenile
          Justice and Delinquency Prevention.
Tyler, Tom R., and Cheryl J. Wakslak
  2004   Profiling and Police Legitimacy: Procedural Justice, Attributions of
          Motive, and Acceptance of Police Authority. Criminology 42:253–281.
Virginia Department of Juvenile Justice
  2005   Data Resources Guide, Fiscal Year 2005. Richmond: Virginia Depart-
          ment of Juvenile Justice.
Visher, Christy A.
  1983   Gender, Police Arrest Decisions, and Notions of Chivalry. Crimi-
          nology 21:5–28.
Warren, Patricia, Donald Tomaskovic-Devey, William Smith, Matthew Zingraff,
and Marcinda Mason
  2006   Driving While Black: Bias Processes and Racial Disparity in Police
          Stops. Criminology 44:709–738.
Weitzer, Ronald, and Steven A. Tuch
  2002   Perceptions of Racial Profiling: Race, Class, and Personal Experi-
          ence. Criminology 40:435–456.
Werthman, Carl, and Irving Piliavin
  1967   Gang Members and the Police. In The Police: Six Sociological
          Essays. David J. Bordua, ed. Pp. 56–98. New York: Wiley.
Wilson, James Q.
  1968   Varieties of Police Behavior: The Management of Law and Order in
          Eight Communities. Cambridge, MA: Harvard University Press.
Worden, Robert E., and Robin L. Shepard
  1996   Demeanor, Crime, and Police Behavior: A Reexamination of the
          Police Services Study Data. Criminology 34:83–105.
Zimring, Franklin E.
  2005   American Juvenile Justice. New York: Oxford University Press.

JUVENILE INSTITUTIONS AND THE TREATMENT AND PREVENTION OF DELINQUENCY

AS DISCUSSED in chapter 2, juvenile correctional institutions in the United States were developed in the early to mid-19th century. These facilities were established and supported by both private and public funds. Most of them were considered long term in that they were designed to house residents, or inmates, for several years. In addition, most of these institutions were designed to retain custody of their charges, which meant they were built with walls and fences and with a purpose to supervise and control the juveniles in their custody. A common model for earlier examples of correctional facilities was the *cottage system*, in which the notion of two-parent family heads was established. Even within this system, however, institutional administrators were able to maintain an atmosphere of supervision and custody.

Today, correctional institutions can be designed for short-term or long-term accommodations. Short-term facilities are often called *detention centers* or *homes*. They typically serve populations of juveniles who are awaiting a juvenile court hearing or a transfer to the state correctional system. Long-term institutions are designed to house and care for juveniles who have been committed to the state juvenile correctional system by a juvenile court judge.

The length of time served by juvenile residents in these places is often undetermined, but it is always restricted by a juvenile's age, usually age 21. They are referred to by many names but more commonly are called *training schools, reformatories,* or *juvenile correctional institutions.*

The purpose of this chapter is to discuss the characteristics of juvenile institutions, both short term and long term, as well as the characteristics of their residents. In addition, this chapter will discuss some of the treatment programs provided in these institutions, especially the long-term facilities. Because the historical development of correctional institutions was presented in chapter 2, the discussion in this chapter will focus on contemporary institutions.

The chapter will also contain a discussion of some prevention programs that have been developed for juveniles in the community, particularly for youth who have already been identified as delinquent or who are considered "at risk" of being labeled delinquent by the courts. Many treatment and prevention programs have already been discussed in this book in connection with specific topics, such as family- and school-based or drug prevention programs. Thus, the community-based prevention programs to be discussed in this chapter will focus on general populations of youth.

Juvenile Correctional Institutions

Juvenile correctional facilities can generally be divided into two categories: short-term, or local, and long-term, or state. In addition, most local facilities are publicly operated, while state facilities can be operated by public or private funds. Overall, in 2003, the *number of institutions* for juveniles was 2,861, and this number was about the same as in 1997. In that same year, the *number of youth* confined in residential facilities was 109,225, and this figure represented a drop from 116,701 in 1997 (see table 15.1). Overall, in 2003, 307 youthful offenders were in custody per 100,000 juveniles in the United States (Snyder and Sickmund 2006:201).

Detention Centers or Homes

Juvenile detention centers or homes are comparable to juvenile jails and are most often considered local institutions. These kinds of facilities have been developed for the purpose of housing juveniles who are waiting for a court appearance, as opposed to having been committed to the facility by a juvenile court judge (Snyder and Sickmund 2006:200, 202). However, in the past

TABLE 15.1 Juvenile Residential Facilities

Residential Placement Facilities

	Number				Percentage of Total	
Type of Facility	*1997*	*1999*	*2001*	*2003*	*1997*	*2003*
All	2,842	2,938	2,980	2,861	100	100
Public	1,106	1,134	1,197	1,170	39	
State	508	533	533	501	18	18
Local	598	601	664	669	21	23
Private	1,736	1,795	1,774	1,682	61	59
Tribal		9	9	9	0	0

Juvenile Offenders in Residential Placement

	Number				Percentage of Total	
Population Held	*1997*	*1999*	*2001*	*2003*	*1997*	*2003*
All facilities						
All residents	116,701	120,996	118,008	109,225	100	100
Juvenile offenders	105,055	107,856	104,413	96,655	90	88
Other residents	11,646	13,140	13,595	12,570	10	12
Public facilities						
All residents	77,798	78,519	75,461	67,917	67	62
Juvenile offenders	75,600	76,379	73,328	66,210	65	61
Other residents	9,354	11,082	11,509	10,862	8	10
State facilities						
All residents	48,185	49,011	45,224	38,470	41	35
Juvenile offenders	46,516	47,504	43,669	37,335	40	34
Other residents	2,586	2,293	2,376	1,855	2	2
Local facilities						

(Continued)

TABLE 15.1 Juvenile Residential Facilities (Continued)

All residents	29,613	29,508	30,237	29,447	25	27
Juvenile offenders	29,084	28,875	29,659	28,875	25	26
Other residents	9,354	10,908	11,315	10,738	8	10
Private facilities						
All residents	38,903	42,298	42,353	41,177	33	38
Juvenile offenders	29,455	31,303	30,891	30,321	25	28
Other residents	1,669	1,507	1,555	1,135	1	1
Tribal facilities	179	194	131	0	0	
Juvenile offenders	174	194	124	0	0	
Other residents	5	0	7	0	0	

Notes: Six in ten juvenile facilities holding offenders were private; public facilities held more than six in ten juvenile offenders. Other residents include youth age 21 or older and those held in the facility but not charged with or adjudicated for an offense. Detail may not total 100 percent because of rounding.

Source: Snyder and Sickmund 2006:197, from their analysis of OJJDP's Census of Juveniles in Residential Placement for 1997, 1999, 2001, and 2003 (machine-readable data files).

few years, detention center populations have included many residents who are awaiting transfer to juvenile correctional institutions or placement in community programs after having spent time in a correctional institution. The average length of stay in a detention home is about two to three weeks. In Virginia, for example, in 2005, the average length of stay in detention homes was 23 days (Virginia Department of Juvenile Justice 2005:20).

Since juvenile detention centers are supposed to keep the residents in custody until their release date, their design is characterized by single-cell construction, with a common dining area and recreational facilities, as permitted by space and location. Detention centers are often required (or at least expected) to provide their residents with some kind of education while in confinement. Consequently, they are also characterized by some type of classroom facility.

Detainees may be temporarily housed in a detention home because of the presumed emergency of the situation, such as a youngster suspected of being high on drugs or in a dangerous state of mind. In addition, a child may be placed in a detention home because of the time of day at which the child is apprehended, such as at midnight or on a weekend, when other facilities such as shelters may not be available. In these cases, the detention usually can last no longer than one or two days. After that time, a detention hearing is scheduled, and a final decision of detention is ordered by a juvenile court judge. In addition, many states have passed legislation that restricts the ages and types of offenses eligible for juvenile detention. For example, most states now restrict detention to those juveniles who are ten years of age or older and who have been charged with a criminal offense. Status offenders may be placed in a detention home, but again, for a limited period of time, such as one or two days.

One issue with detention homes and correctional facilities in general is the mental state of many detainees. For instance, an analysis of 1,829 youth detained in the Cook County (Chicago) Detention Center from 1995 to 1998 concluded that *66.3 percent of the males* and *73.8 percent of the females* in the study exhibited one or more psychiatric symptoms within six months of the study, and females were more likely to exhibit two or more psychiatric symptoms. When conduct disorders, many of which included status offenses, were excluded, the results were similar (Teplin et al. 2006). If these data were extrapolated to the entire country, the authors of this study suggest that on any given day, as many as 72,000 youth in detention in the United States would have at least one psychiatric disorder and 12,000 juveniles would have both a serious psychiatric disorder and a substance abuse disorder. This situation is sometimes described as "dual diagnosis" or "comorbidity," that is, a combination of behavioral and psychiatric problems.

In the study of Cook County detainees, the most common psychiatric diagnoses found among the detainees were *substance use disorder* and *disruptive behavior*, and this was true for both males and females. Additional studies of juveniles in custody reveal significant incidences of psychiatric disorders, although the estimated prevalence of these disorders ranges from 5 percent to 88 percent of juveniles in custody. The psychiatric disorders exhibited by juvenile detainees present additional responsibilities for administrators and staff workers at detention homes because these workers *must* attend to the disorders of those in their custody (Teplin et al. 2006). According to congressional studies, what makes the situation more difficult for custodial staff and their detainees is that many youth are held in detention centers because there is no other place for them to go. That is, there are no community mental health facilities in their area to which they can go for assistance (Pear 2004).

Correctional Facilities

Juveniles who have been found delinquent by a juvenile court judge face the risk of being committed to a correctional facility. As indicated in chapter 2, the history of these institutions dates back to the middle of the 19th century in the United States. Historically, the purpose of correctional institutions for youth has been to rehabilitate or treat residential inmates sent there, as well as to retain custody of these youth while they are in the facility. Also historically, judges have committed youth to these institutions for an indefinite period of time or until they reach the age of majority. In the past, this age was 21, and even today, many states allow juvenile facilities to retain custody of juvenile offenders until the age of 21. Because of the possibility of retaining an inmate for several years, these institutions are sometimes referred to as "long-term" institutions, while detention centers are called "short-term facilities."

Types of Correctional Institutions

Traditionally, long-term juvenile institutions were known as industrial schools, training schools, or reform schools. Today these kinds of institutions still exist, but there have also developed other kinds of juvenile facilities. For example, in several states, there are *forestry camps, wilderness programs, ranches,* or other *challenge* facilities (Sanborn and Salerno 2005: 468–469). These facilities can be either privately operated or part of the public correctional system in a state. Often, the facilities are open or minimally secured, meaning no fencing or constant surveillance. The programs focus on teaching youth to be more self-reliant and aware of their need to depend on others for successful completion of projects. For example, in a 2002 survey of juvenile institutions, 19 percent of administrators of wilderness facilities reported the use of locked doors or gates for custody purposes, compared with a figure of 87 percent for training schools and 91 percent for detention centers (Sickmund 2006:6). However, these kinds of residential facilities are relatively rare compared with the total number of facilities in the country. In 2002, approximately 5 percent of the 2,964 facilities surveyed were ranch or wilderness camps.

One example of a wilderness program that has existed for several decades is Vision Quest, or VQ. VQ was established in 1973. It emphasizes emotional balance and greater self-control as objectives for effective rehabilitation. Although VQ offers several types of treatment opportunities, such as group homes, sea experiences, and alternative schools, one traditional element is a wagon-train trek across many western states and into Canada. This experience is expected to teach juveniles self-reliance skills but also the need to work with others in some situations. However, some contend that the wagon train and other VQ programs operate more like boot camps and expose youth to harsh, sometimes degrading conditions. Although general evaluations of wilderness types of programs have not concluded that such experiences have a major impact on recidivism, VQ claims to have a one-year postprogram recidivism rate between 14 and 31 percent (Sanborn and Salerno 2005: 468–469; Martin 2005:300–301; also, on the web at www.vq.com).

Another wilderness or challenge experience is Outward Bound. Outward Bound began in Colorado in 1962 and emphasizes character development and self-confidence improvement through a number of challenging exercises, including rock climbing, hiking, and similar outdoor activities. In addition, Outward Bound emphasizes education and stresses that outdoor experiences should be combined with school-related settings, including exams concerning what was learned from the challenges. A variation of Outward Bound is Homeward Bound, which combines daytime and nighttime experiences similar to those offered in Outward Bound, but over a period of six weeks (Martin 2005:299–300).

Other kinds of juvenile correctional institutions include *group homes* and *halfway houses*, which serve as a community-based alternative to confinement in long-term institutions. In addition, these facilities serve to help integrate the juvenile into the community or serve as a location for treatment and rehabilitation services outside the home and neighborhood where the child previously lived. They also serve as an alternative to home-based probation or house arrest dispositions. Group homes are becoming popular alternatives to reformatories and other correctional kinds of facilities for juveniles. In 2002, about 38 percent of all institutional facilities surveyed were group homes, compared with a figure of 13 percent for training schools (Sickmund 2006:5).

Characteristics of Correctional Institution Residents

Most residents or inmates of correctional institutions are juveniles who have been found delinquent of a criminal offense, such as robbery or burglary.

The data in table 15.2 display the most serious offense categories for institutionalized juvenile offenders, by public and private facilities, and from 1997 to 2003. As the figures in this table indicate, in 2003, 4,824 correctional residents, or approximately 5 percent of the total population of residents, were found delinquent of a status offense, primarily ungovernability. In addition, the number of juveniles confined for status offenses is significantly larger for private institutions, compared with public facilities. Over two-thirds of juveniles sent to an institution for a status offense were confined in private institutions. However, this number is decreasing, in part because of the Juvenile Justice and Delinquency Prevention Act, which restricts the use of incarceration for status offenders. Between 1997 and 2003, for example, the number of juveniles confined in all residential facilities for status offenses declined by 29 percent. Note, though, that not only are status offenders decreasing in institutional populations, but the total number of juveniles confined is decreasing as well (see table 15.1).

Other figures in table 15.2 reveal that the *most common offense* (again, in terms of the most serious offense for confined juveniles) for youth in either public or private institutions is a *person offense,* usually some kind of assault or robbery. In this context, it is important to note that the number of offenses involving *sexual assault is increasing,* by 34 percent for all institutions from 1997 to 2003, contrary to the general trend for decreasing numbers of institutional residents.

It has been noted that the majority of juvenile offenders are male, and this difference holds for official as well as self-report measures of delinquency. The data in figure 15.1 clearly show that the total number of institutional residents, for all types of facilities, is greater for males than for females. In addition, these figures indicate that the percentage of female residents

TABLE 15.2 Offenses of Residents

| Most Serious Offense | Juvenile Offenders in Residential Placement, 2003 | | | Percentage Change, 1997–2003 | | |
| | Type of Facility | | | Type of Facility | | |
	All	Public	Private	All	Public	Private
Total Offenders	96,655	66,210	30,321	−8	−12	3
Delinquency	91,831	64,662	27,059	−7	−12	11
Person	33,197	23,499	9,671	−6	−13	21

Criminal homicide	878	803	73	−54	−56	−28
Sexual assault	7,452	4,749	2,698	34	20	68
Robbery	6,230	5,157	1,073	−33	−35	−22
Aggravated assault	7,495	5,745	1,741	−21	−24	−7
Simple assault	8,106	4,984	3,113	22	21	25
Other person	3,036	2,061	973	38	22	87
Property	26,843	18,740	8,073	−16	−18	−10
Burglary	10,399	7,481	2,904	−17	−21	−7
Theft	5,650	3,793	1,848	−22	−26	−12
Auto theft	5,572	3,756	1,812	−15	−14	−16
Arson	735	514	220	−19	−25	0
Other property	4,487	3,196	1,289	−4	−4	−6
Drug	8,002	4,851	3,137	−12	−23	15
Drug trafficking	1,810	1,284	522	−37	−41	−24
Other drug	6,192	3,567	2,615	0	−14	28
Public order	9,654	6,782	2,866	0	−5	11
Weapons	3,013	2,346	665	−28	−29	−24
Other public order	6,641	4,436	2,201	20	16	29
Technical violation	14,135	10,790	3,312	14	5	56
Status Offense	4,824	1,548	3,262	−29	−11	−36
Ungovernability	1,825	253	1,570	−36	−45	−34
Running away	997	417	577	−33	−14	−43
Truancy	841	207	634	−37	−49	−32
Curfew violation	203	65	138	5	−18*	21
Underage drinking	405	210	186	27	86	−10
Other status offense	553	396	157	−14	98	−64

*Percentage change is based on a denominator less than 100.

Notes: Total includes juvenile offenders held in tribal facilities. In 2003, public facilities held 64,662 delinquents and private facilities held 27,059 delinquents on the 2003 census date. For most offenses, fewer juveniles were held in 2003 than in 1997. For some offenses (e.g., drug offenses other than trafficking), the public facility population decreased, but the private facility population increased. For several offenses (e.g., simple assault), both public and private populations increased.

Source: Snyder and Sickmund, 2006:198, from their analysis of OJJDP's Census of Juveniles in Residential Placement for 2003 (machine-readable data files).

confined for status offenses is greater than the percentage of males confined for status offenses, 13 percent versus 6 percent in 2003. However, the percentage of females confined for status offenses dropped significantly from 1991 to 2003, from 33 percent to 13 percent, while the percentage of males sent to institutions for a status offense increased slightly, from 3 percent to 6 percent. Still, while females represent 15 percent of the total number of residents in juvenile facilities, they constitute 40 percent of all juveniles confined for status offenses (Snyder and Sickmund 2006:206).

The racial and ethnic composition of institutions is now of predominantly minority status. The overrepresentation of minority youth in different stages of the juvenile justice has been discussed in previous chapters (see also Penn 2006). The information in table 15.3 shows the disproportional representation of black or African American youth in all stages of the juvenile justice system, including juveniles in residential placement. The overrepresentation of minorities in juvenile institutions is also evident from institutional data. According to the figures in table 15.4, in 2003 the majority (61 percent) of residents in juvenile institutions were of minority racial and ethnic backgrounds. Most of the minority residents were African American (see also Leiber 2006).

The overrepresentation of minorities varies by type of institution. For example, in 2003 among minority youth, 36 percent were found in detention homes and 34 percent were housed in long-term facilities, compared with 32 percent each among white juveniles. In addition, in 2003 minority youth represented over half of all residents in all but one type of residential facility, shelters. For all other types of institutions, minorities represented well over half of all residents, including 76 percent of ranch and wilderness residents, 69 percent of boot camp inmates, and 63 percent of youth in long-term institutions. However, racial and ethnic statuses do not vary much among the offenses committed by youth in institutions. In 2003, for example, 95 percent of white inmates and 96 percent of minority inmates were incarcerated for delinquent offenses, while 5 percent of whites and 6 percent of minorities were placed into institutional confinement for a status offense (Snyder and Sickmund 2006:212).

While minority overrepresentation in the juvenile justice system is an important issue to address, recent statistics indicate that the proportion of minority youth *in custody* is declining relative to white inmates. Between 1997 and 2003, the proportion of minority offenders in custody declined by 10 percent, compared to a drop of 5 percent for white residents. The largest relative decline in minority juvenile institutional residents was among Asians, whose population declined by 39 percent between 1997 and 2003

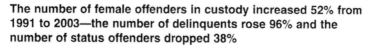

The number of female offenders in custody increased 52% from 1991 to 2003—the number of delinquents rose 96% and the number of status offenders dropped 38%

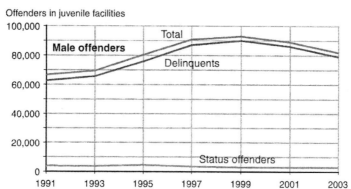

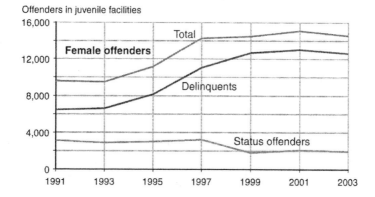

- Among males in juvenile facilities, the number of delinquents increased 26% and the number of status offenders decreased 26% from 1991 to 2003, for an overall increase in male offenders of 23%.

- Status offenders accounted for a greater share of female offenders in custody than of male offenders. However, the status offender proportion of female offenders in custody dropped from 33% in 1991 to 13% in 2003. For males, the status offender proportion held steady between 3% and 6%.

FIGURE 15.1 Institutional Residents by Gender

Note: Because data were not collected from tribal facilities prior to 1999, tribal facility data are excluded from this presentation.

Source: Snyder and Sickmund 2006:206, from their analysis of OJJDP's Census of Juveniles in Residential Placement for 1997, 1999, 2001, and 2003 (machine-readable data files) and Children in Custody Census of Public and Private Juvenile Detention, Correctional, and Shelter Facilities for 1991, 1993, and 1995 (machine-readable data files).

TABLE 15.3 Racial Profile, 2002 (in percentages)

Stage/Offense	White	African American	Other Races	Total
Referred				
Delinquency	67	29	3	100
Person	60	37	3	100
Property	68	28	4	100
Drugs	76	21	3	100
Public order	68	29	3	100
Detained				
Delinquency	61	36	3	100
Person	56	41	3	100
Property	60	36	4	100
Drugs	61	36	2	100
Public order	66	31	4	100
Petitioned				
Delinquency	64	33	3	100
Person	57	40	3	100
Property	65	31	4	100
Drugs	70	28	3	100
Public order	66	31	3	100
Waived to Criminal Court				
Delinquency	62	35	3	100
Person	55	41	4	100
Property	71	26	3	100
Drugs	58	39	2	100
Public order	65	32	4	100
Adjudicated				
Delinquency	67	29	4	100
Person	61	36	4	100
Property	68	27	4	100
Drugs	74	23	3	100
Public order	69	27	4	100
Ordered to Residential Placement				
Delinquency	63	33	4	100
Person	58	37	4	100

Property	65	30	5	100
Drugs	59	38	3	100
Public order	65	31	4	100
Ordered to				
Formal Probation				
Delinquency	67	29	3	100
Person	61	36	3	100
Property	68	28	4	100
Drugs	75	22	3	100
Public order	69	28	3	100
Juvenile Population				
Ages 10 to upper age	78	16	6	100

Note: Detail may not total 100 percent because of rounding.
Source: Snyder and Sickmund 2006:176.

(Snyder and Sickmund 2006:211). In part, these reductions in minority representations in juvenile institutions reflect state and federal efforts to reduce minority overrepresentation in the juvenile justice system. In particular, the modifications of the 1974 Juvenile Justice and Delinquency Prevention Act and the efforts of the Office of Juvenile Justice and Delinquency Prevention (OJJDP) have contributed to more awareness of minority overrepresentations in all areas of juvenile justice (Snyder and Sickmund 2006:188). However, it is recognized that political issues are still important in the allocation of funds and resources to address this issue, and there are still efforts to resist significant alterations in the ways in which minority youth are handled in the juvenile justice system (Leiber 2006; Feld 2006).

Characteristics of Long-Term Institutions

The purpose of all long-term correctional facilities is to retain custody of residents or inmates and to provide some type of treatment or rehabilitation services. Long-term facilities are expected to offer programs and services that require several months or perhaps even years of placement or confinement. Government surveys often classify these kinds of institutions as group homes, boot camps, ranch or wilderness camps, and training

TABLE 15.4 Race and Ethnicity of Residents (in percentages)

Most Serious Offense	Total	White	Total Minority	Black	Hispanic	Minority American Indian	Asian
						Race/Ethnic Profile of Juvenile Offenders in Custody, 2003	
Total	100	39	61	38	19	2	2
Delinquency	100	38	62	38	19	2	2
Homicide	100	27	73	40	26	2	4
Sexual assault	100	57	43	26	13	2	1
Robbery	100	15	85	60	22	1	2
Aggravated assault	100	28	72	41	26	2	3
Simple assault	100	40	60	40	15	2	1
Burglary	100	44	56	33	19	2	1
Theft	100	43	57	40	13	2	2
Auto theft	100	33	67	39	23	2	3
Arson	100	57	43	27	11	3	1
Drug trafficking	100	21	79	60	16	1	2
Other drug	100	38	62	36	22	2	1
Weapons	100	21	79	45	30	1	2
Technical violations	100	39	61	36	21	2	1
Status offenses	100	48	52	34	12	3	1

Notes: Totals include a small number of youth for whom race/ethnicity was not reported or was reported as "other" or "mixed." Detail may not total 100 percent because of rounding. In 2003, white youths' share of juveniles held in custody was greatest for the offenses of sexual assault and arson; black youths' share was greatest for robbery and drug trafficking.

Source: Snyder and Sickmund, 2006:211, from their analysis of OJJDP's Census of Juveniles in Residential Placement for 2003 (machine-readable data files).

schools. Group homes and wilderness camps are considered community based, while the others are more restrictive in their philosophies and schedules of operation (Sickmund 2006).

Even community placements can be categorized according to their philosophies concerning custody or treatment. According to one typology, community-based facilities can be divided into three categories. One type is referred to as *restrictive community placement.* This kind of facility is characterized by restrictions in movement and definite property boundaries, although not necessarily fences. Group homes are an example of these kinds of institutions. A second type of facility is called a *benign community placement.* This kind of community placement is characterized by greater flexibility of movement than the restrictive facility, almost to the point of total freedom of movement. Of course, since the resident is confined to this place, total freedom of movement is not to be expected, but the flexibility of the resident's schedule reflects the philosophy that the resident is to be trusted to remain in the placement for as long as an agreement maintains. A good example of this type of placement is a foster home. A third category is *experiential community placement.* This type of facility is often located in rural or sparsely populated areas with the expectation that the resident participates in character-building exercises, such as are offered in wilderness programs. Each of these placements is geared to long-term stays, meaning at least several months and possibly more than one year. In addition, the length of stay is open, or variable, except for wilderness programs, which may have fixed lengths of placement (Martin 2005:296–301).

Structural Organization

Traditionally, reformatories or training schools have been organized according to the *cottage system* (Polsky 1962). A cottage is a residential facility located on the grounds of the institution. It serves as a general meeting place for the residents as well as a place for recreation and sleeping. A cottage is often headed by a team of cottage parents, who are in charge of the daily supervision of the youth. They live in the cottage, often in a separate efficiency apartment, separated from the living quarters of the residents by a common room. In essence, then, the cottage becomes a kind of home to the resident. Of course, it is difficult for any institutional setting to truly replace the atmosphere and structure of a child's home, but this system attempts to approximate such an atmosphere.

Total Institutions

In many ways, correctional institutions are *total institutions* (Goffman 1961:xiii–124). A total institution is a physical place, such as a prison or reformatory, that must meet the total needs of its residents. These needs are mostly physical and can include health and nutrition, clothing, shelter, and so on. In addition, juvenile institutions must meet the educational and treatment needs of youth. The totality of the care provided in institutions is also reflected in the 24-hour, around the clock confinement of the residents, including weekends. Residents are to be supervised and accounted for virtually every hour of the day and night, either individually or in terms of block schedules, such as sleeping (Bortner and Williams, 1997:19–21).

Inmate Social System

Those who have studied institutions and their characteristics often cite the tight schedule and total supervision of residents as one reason inmates tend to develop accommodative responses to the deprivation of freedom such routines create. A typical accommodative response is called an *inmate social system* or *subculture*. The inmate social system, or subculture, is a set of rules and codes that influences the lives of almost every resident in a long-term institution (Barker and Adams 1959; Giallombardo 1974; Bartollas et al. 1976; Feld 1977; Propper 1981; Bortner and Williams 1997).

The inmate code contains proscriptions for talking with cottage parents or other institutional staff members. It also prohibits inmates from informing on others. Specific examples of the inmate code include "Exploit whomever you can," "Be cool," "Don't rat on your peers," "Don't kiss ass," and "Don't buy the mind-f***" (Bartollas et al. 1976:62–64). It is easy to see that adhering to these codes will undermine treatment efforts developed by the staff. Specific efforts to establish treatment-oriented cottages and subcultures, especially group treatment strategies, can offset the negative influences of the inmate social system, but these effects can be fragile and quickly reversed if the staff does not monitor and closely manage the treatment culture (Polsky 1962; Street 1965; Street et al. 1966; Feld 1977:167–169, 200).

The inmate social system sometimes reflects gender differences. Among *male residents*, for example, the system often revolves around concepts related to physical force and intimidation. It is used to bolster the power and influence one inmate, or more likely, a group of inmates, may have over others. In recent years, the male inmate system has taken on racial overtones.

Some researchers have argued that nonwhite inmates often control and manipulate white inmates because nonwhites are more organized and are more powerful than whites inside the institution (Bartollas et al. 1976:chapters 4–7; Feld 1977:180–185).

Among *females*, however, the inmate social system typically includes roles and relationships related to the family system, including parents, children, and more distant relatives (Propper 1981:chapter 7). Within some institutions, authorities have discovered marriage contracts and divorce settlements among inmates. Marriage among inmates is highly prized and can serve to confirm one's higher status among inmates. According to Giallombardo (1974), "The inmates who marry are those who have been successful in their respective roles. The major goal for the Eastern inmates is marriage; hence, to attract an individual and to marry—in the face of considerable competition on campus—is an achievement of sorts. For this reason, inmates sometimes make it a special point to invite rivals to the wedding" (p. 172). Despite alliances with pseudofamilies, females tend to adapt to institutional life differently from males, with females following more conformist attitudes and institutional adjustment lifestyles than males (Sieverdes and Bartollas 1980).

There are two views concerning the existence of the inmate system. Some argue that it is *imported* into the institution by inmates, who have learned this system in the streets, in gangs, and elsewhere in the community. Other scholars maintain that the inmate social system is caused by the *deprivation* of freedom and other human needs that occurs within an institution. Thus, the system develops as a means of survival and coping among inmates confined in a restrictive and exploitative social setting (Sykes 1958; Grosser 1968; Giallombardo 1974:chapter 1; Bartollas et al. 1976:68–69; Feld 1977:171–181; Propper 1981:11–20, 179–181). Studies have documented the influence of both models or interpretations of the inmate social system, so it is not easy to say that one or the other is the true cause of the social system. It would seem safe to argue, however, that regardless of the sources of inmate social systems, the existence of such a subculture within a correctional institution necessitates strategies for dealing with this system if effective treatment goals are to be realized. Bortner and Williams (1997) remind us that the attributes of race, social class, and gender often interact within the restrictive environments of institutions to produce strong effects on the identities and behavior of inmates, whether in the context of coping with a closed and sometimes violent setting or in the context of responding to treatment programs. As they put it, "The racial, class, and gender dimensions of youths' identities are related intricately to their delinquent behavior. They all affect how the youths make sense of the social world and their places in it, including how they see themselves and how others see them. . . . Minority youths are especially aware of the racialized context of their existences" (p. 46).

Effectiveness of Correctional Institutions

An important concern about juvenile institutions is what happens to those released from the custody of such facilities. In other words, does the experience of living in a correctional institution change a young person's attitudes and behavior? For the most part, this question is answered in terms of the future behavior of the individual. The behavior of concern is typically continued delinquency or criminality, and this concept is often measured in terms of *recidivism* figures. Recidivism means a return to crime or delinquency. When applied to the postrelease behavior of former residents, recidivism has been measured in a variety of ways: re-arrest, referral to court, reconviction, and/or re-incarceration (Snyder and Sickmund 2006:234). According to one report, the average re-arrest rate within one year of release for juveniles released from institutions was 55 percent. The average recidivism rate for referral to court was 45 percent; for reconviction, the rate was 33 percent, and for re-incarceration, around 25 percent (Snyder and Sickmund 2006:234). Another survey of recidivism in Virginia found similar rates in 2003 and 2004. In that survey, 52.1 percent of those released from juvenile correctional institutions were arrested within one year of release; 37.6 percent were reconvicted; and 21.2 percent were re-incarcerated (Virginia Department of Juvenile Justice 2005:183). Arrest recidivism figures are higher than the numbers for the other measures because many of those arrested are never convicted or incarcerated. In addition, some may argue that arrests are not proof of guilt and that truer indications of criminal behavior are found in conviction or incarceration rates.

While the recidivism rates for those released from institutions may seem high to some, it should be noted that experiences within institutions may not be the only factors involved in the recidivism of former residents. The conditions that contributed to their delinquency *before* they were incarcerated may still be affecting their behavior upon release. In addition, these pre-incarceration factors may now be interacting with postrelease variables in the community to further compound the delinquency-producing forces in a child's life. One of these postrelease variables may well be the stigmatizing effects of being labeled an ex-offender or an ex-inmate (see chapter 12).

Another way to gauge the effectiveness of institutions is to look at their costs. National data suggest that the per-resident annual costs of institutions are very high. In the late 1980s, for example, the average cost per resident in public institutions was $29,600 per year. The range of annual costs was from $17,600 in South Dakota to $78,800 in Rhode Island (Allen-Hagen 1991:9). Although these figures are nearly 20 years old, estimates of institutional costs continue to climb. For example, an analysis of secure institutional confinement for youth in Pennsylvania concluded that in 2004 the cost *per resident was $306 per diem, or $111,000 annually* (Nagin et al. 2006:640).

Others point to abuses of authority within institutions, numerous accounts of violence and assaults on residents by other inmates as well as by staff, and instances of neglect by institutional authorities as evidence that institutions do not always protect or rehabilitate residents. Exposés and government reports of abuse and neglect within institutions as well as in other parts of the juvenile justice system have appeared for decades (Murphy 1974; Wooden 1976; Ahranjani et al. 2005:282–288). Scholarly studies of institutions and institutional life continue to document abuse and neglect within the walls and on the grounds of juvenile facilities (Bartollas et al. 1976; Feld 1977; Bortner and Williams 1997). Whether these incidents of violence, assault, abuse, and neglect are intentional, and sometimes they are, or the result of oversight or carelessness, their impact on the quality of life for the residents is negative. In addition to the countervailing influence of the inmate social system on the rehabilitation of residents, the stressful, intimidating, and often violent atmosphere of many institutions also contributes to the difficulty in achieving meaningful change in their behavior and attitudes.

The Massachusetts Experiment

While many suggest that juvenile institutions do not do an adequate job of rehabilitating residents, few have gone so far as to advocate the elimination or closing of institutions. However, this is what was done in the 1970s by Jerome Miller, then director of juvenile corrections in Massachusetts. Miller was hired by the governor to develop changes in the juvenile correctional system. Changes were thought to be needed because the system was characterized by political patronage and charges of abuse and neglect of residents (Miller 1991:48–49, 170).

Miller's first actions were to reform the system. For instance, he advocated relaxing some of the strict rules for the residents, such as requirements for clothing and hair length. Over two or three years, however, these reform efforts were resisted by those in the system, including cottage parents. Consequently, the decision to close the reformatories in the state was made as a kind of last resort (Miller 1991; Lundman 2001:226–227).

Analyses of the results of the Massachusetts Experiment have concluded that recidivism rates have remained about the same as they were before the decision to close the institutions. In those areas characterized by the presence of community-based treatment programs, the recidivism rates have been lower than before 1970 (Miller 1991:chapter 17). In addition, the system of juvenile corrections became based on community-treatment models, with private provision of services. Youth are still wards of the state, but their care and custody is being provided by private agencies with state oversight (Ohlin et al. 1977:12–18; Miller 1991:chapter 13). Studies also estimated that the state was making considerable economic savings by moving to the community-centered, private system of services One early analysis of Harvard researchers concluded that by the mid-1970s, the cost of community care and treatment was about $50 per week per youth, compared with an estimated $145–$290 per week for intensive residential care (Ohlin et al. 1977:16).

Despite these favorable results, the Massachusetts Experiment remains as the title suggests, an experiment. Miller recounted continuous efforts by politicians and others in the state to undermine his efforts and to introduce legislation designed to continue the existence and funding of institutions (Miller 1991:chapter 16). Despite the conclusions of the Harvard study that the experiment was replicable in other states (Ohlin et al. 1977:113), the virtual elimination of institutions has been tried in only one other state, Maryland, but without the documented success of Massachusetts (Lundman 2001:233). Over time, the number of commitments to institutional facilities in Massachusetts has increased, but the rate has been far below the national average. In the late 1990s, for example, the rate of institutionalization, private and public, per 100,000 youth was 110, compared with a national average of 265, and nearly 64 percent of its commitments were to private facilities (Lundman 2001:232).

Positive Views of Institutional Confinement

Despite these unfavorable comments and views regarding the effectiveness of juvenile institutions, some suggest that institutions do result in positive outcomes for youth, at least for some juvenile offenders. The results of the cohort studies discussed in chapter 3, for example, concluded that institutionalization of some offenders, particularly chronic offenders, might reduce some crime and delinquency (Wolfgang et al. 1972; Lundman 2001:260–272). For example, one analysis of these data concluded that confining all the 982 chronic offenders in the first (1958) cohort would have eliminated 72 percent of their contacts with the police (Lundman 2001:267). Other longitudinal studies have also concluded that institutionalization can be good for some offenders. Laub and Sampson's follow-up analyses of the youth studied by the Gluecks in Boston (Glueck and Glueck 1950) concluded that confinement could sometimes be considered a positive "turning point" (see chapter 5) in the lives of some youthful offenders (2003:129–130).

Some point to a relative reduction in recidivism as a result of incarceration. This reduction is referred to as a "suppression effect" (Murray and Cox 1979:31; Lundman 2001:280–281). Researchers recognizing the suppression effect argue that the complete elimination of delinquency is impossible, so studies should concentrate on the relative decline, if any, in delinquency after release. In essence, this approach focuses on the positive rather than the negative impact of incarceration (Snyder and Sickmund 2006:235). For example, in one longitudinal study of institutionalized offenders in Illinois, researchers noted that among a sample of 317 youthful offenders confined to institutions in the state, there was a drop of average arrests rates from 6.2 in the year preceding incarceration to 2.3 in the year following incarceration (Murray and Cox 1979:118; Lundman 2001: 280–283). Of course, this analysis is flawed in that part of the decline in arrests was due to the restrictions *of* confinement, as opposed to the results *after* confinement. Nonetheless, the idea of a suppression effect is a useful concept with which to evaluate the impact of any program, whether it is focused on custody or treatment.

Treatment and Prevention Programs

Programs focused on the treatment or prevention of delinquency have been addressed in previous chapters, such as those focusing on the family, schools, drugs, and youth gangs. In the following discussions, the emphasis is on more general examples of treating youth already involved in the juvenile justice system, as well as a few programs focused on general delinquency prevention. There is also a discussion of the effectiveness of treatment and/or prevention efforts, and issues that should be considered in the evaluation of delinquency prevention programs.

Treatment Programs within Institutions

As discussed in chapter 2 of this book, the development of juvenile justice and the creation of juvenile courts were historically based on a medical model of behavior. This model presumes that delinquent behavior is symptomatic of underlying conditions that will likely worsen over time and lead to increased criminal behavior and increased severity unless the individual is treated or rehabilitated. Although historically, juvenile institutions and other juvenile justice agencies have incorporated the treatment model into their programs and policies, the *right to treatment* for juveniles in confinement has been confirmed by various court decisions since the 1960s. That is, juveniles who have been placed in the custody of juvenile correctional systems must be provided some sort of treatment and rehabilitation while they are in the care of the correctional institutions (Hemmens et al. 2004:104–108).

Consistent with the medical model of delinquency, efforts to change the behaviors and/or attitudes of juveniles confined in institutions have tended to focus on individual change. Many programs have tried to accomplish such changes by focusing on the *individual* resident, that is, his or her personality, behavioral patterns, social skills, education, or other person-centered attributes. Other programs have attempted to effect significant changes among residents by developing *group-centered* efforts. The focus in these programs is still ultimately on the individual, but the approach to changing individual attitudes and/or behavior is through social pressure or example, that is, the group-centered approach.

Individual Treatment

Individual treatment programs for institutional residents have focused on counseling techniques, which may differ according to the theoretical basis of the program or the presumed causes of delinquency. For example, some individual treatment efforts have focused on techniques and strategies informed by psychoanalysis (chapter 4). One example of such therapeutic techniques is *transactional analysis*. Transactional analysis, or TA, is based on the idea that the "patient," adult or child, should be able to understand the bases of his or her attitudes or behavior from a realistic vantage. In this approach, it is important for the treated individual to be aware of the underlying reasons for his or her choices and behaviors. It is not absolutely necessary for the individual to actually confront and resolve internal conflicts that may shape behaviors, but only to be aware of these conflicts and to develop methods to manage them in everyday life and decision making. Often, transactional analysis is practiced through group therapy, but it may be used in individual treatment as well. In addition, TA is used in the treatment of noncriminal or delinquent people, and, according to some advocates, it has been useful in the treatment of individuals thought difficult to reach, such as psychopaths (Berne 1961).

A related individual-based treatment strategy is known as *reality therapy*. Reality therapy was developed in the 1960s by William Glasser (1965). It rejects the medical assumption often seen in psychiatric treatment programs that the delinquent child suffers from some kind of psychopathology. Rather, reality therapy assumes that behavioral problems commonly result from two conditions: the person lacks love in his or her life, and the person lacks self-esteem or a sense of self-worth (Glasser 1965:9; Rachin 1974:49). Reality therapy focuses on the need to recognize the reality of our world and the basic needs underlying our behavior. It stresses the importance of confronting the reality of a situation and the strengths and weaknesses of each person, as well as the need to respect the needs of others. In addition, reality therapy stresses the importance of people taking responsibility for their actions and their situations as well as recognizing the need to address the underlying causes of their behavior. Supporters of reality therapy argue that this form of treatment is more effective for juveniles and others who have not benefited from traditional psychiatric therapies, although factual support for these claims is lacking (Rachin 1974:49–53).

Another individual method of treating delinquency is focused on treating the delinquent behavior. This method is popularly known as *behaviorism* or *behavior modification*. Behaviorism is based on the psychological principles of learning and can be traced to the learning experiments of psychologists such as Pavlov, John B. Watson, and B. F. Skinner (Bandura 1969: chapters 1 and 3; Milkman and Wanberg 2005:205; Sanborn and Salerno 2005:478–479). In this connection, behavior modification is similar to the ideas of differential association theory (see chapter 6). One difference between these two perspectives is that behavior modification focuses on the individual, while differential association focuses on the group context in which behavior is learned. Consistent with the idea that behavior is learned is the notion that it can be relearned, especially through the use of *positive and negative reinforcement*. A positive reinforcement includes the introduction of a consequence *after* a behavior has occurred. A negative reinforcement involves the removal or withholding of something (Sparzo 1999:18–20). For example, a situation in which a person learns that drinking milk is pleasant and so decides to continue drinking milk exemplifies positive reinforcement. However, a person who covers his ears in order to block unwanted noise exhibits negative reinforcement. Both illustrate principles of learning and behavior modification, but in different ways. In the first case, one learns from what has happened and seeks to continue doing the things associated with the consequences of the behavior. In the second situation, the person has learned that loud noises are obnoxious and that covering the ears (removing sound) can reduce obnoxious noise.

Behavior modification programs tend to focus on the behavior rather than on personality or attitudinal characteristics that may underlie the behavior. As such, behavioral programs are attractive to administrators and supervisors of institutional facilities, especially ones that emphasize custody and control functions. Often, these programs use what is known as a "token economy," which replaces monetary exchanges with increased privileges or rewards for conformist behavior. Thus, a resident may expect to receive extra hours of free time or extra meal privileges in exchange for "good" behavior (Sanborn and Salerno 2005:478–479). Thus, behavioral programs can help maintain order and discipline within an institution by continuing to reward those who obey institutional rules. Some argue that this method of control can also be used to help increase the effectiveness of other treatment programs by focusing the attention of residents on the efforts of treatment administrators (Sanborn and Salerno 2005:479).

Behavioral programs have existed since the 1950s and 1960s, and some contend that their use in modifying behavior is successful (McQuire and Priestly 1995:16–19). Others contend that behavioral methods are effective with youth when combined with other, more inclusive methods, such as multisystemic or multifamily strategies (Milkman and Wanberg 2005: 249–257). Although behavioral programs may reduce unwanted behaviors in the short term, their long-term effectiveness is questionable. The issue of retention of desired behaviors is particularly problematic when the resident returns to his or her home or community. Unless the underlying or environmental sources of the behavioral problem are addressed, the chances of long-term successful behavioral change are reduced when the individual returns to the setting that has contributed significantly to the behavior (Mace et al. 1993:94; Sanborn and Salerno 2005:479–480). If a child is influenced by his or her peers in a community or is having trouble with parents and/or siblings at home, returning to these settings might easily trigger delinquent behaviors, even if acceptable behavior has been "learned" in an institutional setting.

Increasingly, individual institutional treatment programs are being focused on generic problems, such as substance abuse, violent tendencies, sexual deviance, and life skills and decision making difficulties. In Virginia, for example, common treatment programs are *anger management, substance abuse treatment,* and *life skills training,* which are offered in virtually all of the correctional institutions in the state (Virginia Department of Juvenile Justice 2005:162–177).

Group Treatment Programs

Individual treatment programs are still predominant in juvenile corrections (Bazemore 2001:204). Sometimes treatment is conducted in group settings. In these situations, the focus of attention is still on the individual, and the treatment effect is expected to occur *in* the group rather than *through* it (Empey and Lubeck 1971:77). Some programs, however, focus more on the dynamics of the group context and the utility of using groups to affect change or rehabilitation in the individual. This is known as the *group-centered* approach. In the group-centered method of treatment, the group becomes a *change agent,* not just a setting in which change may occur. This approach recognizes that most adolescents are influenced by their peers and that much delinquent behavior occurs in a group context (Empey and Lubeck 1971:74–77).

One example of using a group-centered approach in the treatment of delinquency is guided group interaction, or GGI. GGI emphasizes changing behavioral and attitudinal patterns within a group context. In this method, residents are scheduled to meet regularly, often for one hour a week, in groups of ten or fewer, to discuss and work through important issues in their lives. The youth are expected to interact with one another in these sessions and to point out inconsistencies and mistakes in the attitudes and justifications of their fellow group members. The youth are expected to help reform others in these group settings and are encouraged to seek meanings and motivations for their own behaviors in the process. The sessions are led by a trained and skilled adult leader, one who *guides the interactions* among the youth (Weeks 1958:160–161; Empey and Lubeck 1971:16–17). The presence of the adult leader in these sessions is important for directing the focus of the discussions to meaningful dialogue among the youthful participants. In addition, this leader can help to prevent potentially harmful consequences resulting from defamatory or denigrating comments made by members of the group toward one another.

Evaluations of the early use of GGI were generally positive. One comparative assessment gauged behavioral and attitudinal changes of youth in a project called *Highfields*, which was the former estate of Charles Lindbergh in New Jersey. The authors of this assessment concluded that the Highfields youth (all male) exhibited lower recidivism rates upon release from the program than a control group of juvenile offenders who had been committed to the state institution at Annandale. Lowered recidivism rates were particularly noticeable among the nonwhite youth at Highfields. However, this study did not find significant changes in the attitudes of the youth who had been exposed to GGI at Highfields (Weeks 1958).

The use of GGI has expanded to community settings, but evaluations of these efforts have not produced uniformly positive results. One of the more detailed comparative assessments of GGI conducted in a community setting occurred in a program called Silverlake, a suburb of Los Angeles. The Silverlake Experiment introduced GGI to 140 adjudicated delinquents who lived at a former orphanage for Japanese-American children in Los Angeles County. These 140 youth were also enrolled in a nearby high school and lived in the community, with the exception of being allowed to go to their own homes on the weekend. The treatment program lasted three years, with a one-year follow-up. The resultant behavior and attitudes of the Silverlake youth were compared with a control sample of 121 delinquent youth committed to a state institution called Boys Republic. The results of this experiment did not confirm the effectiveness of GGI in reducing recidivism or creating significant changes in attitudes among the Silverlake youth. The authors of the study concluded that part of the reason for the ineffectiveness of the treatment was the harsh reception by the community, particularly school officials, of the Silverlake youth, who were identified by school administrators as "outsiders" and potential troublemakers who should not have been placed in their school (Empey and Lubeck 1971:14–276; Lundman 2001:220–224).

In the 1970s and 1980s, a similar treatment strategy to GGI emerged. This new version of GGI is called positive peer culture, or PPC (Vorrath and Brendtro 1985). Positive peer culture is particularly useful in an institutional setting becomes it attempts to defuse the negative influences of the inmate culture (see the discussion earlier in this chapter). At the same time, PPC tries to instill a greater sense of positive self-worth, or a stronger self-concept, in the residents. Evaluations of PPC are no more positive or encouraging than those of GGI. These programs can have some positive effect on residents, but overall, their impact is moderate. Some behaviors, such as aggression and running away, are reduced in connection with PPC, but others, such as violating institutional rules and breaking and entering, are not Results do suggest that PPC can have a significant positive impact on academic achievement, which can lead to reduced delinquency in the long term (Vorrath and Brendtro 1985:151–159).

Overall, programs such as GGI and PPC can be useful intervention treatments for delinquents. However, these programs do have several potential drawbacks, including the possibility of abusive confrontations among residents, confrontations that can damage self-esteem or result in physical attacks. This possibility is increased if the adult leaders are not properly trained or if they adopt an uncaring attitude toward the programs or the residents involved in the treatments (Vorrath and Brendtro 1985:164–166).

Boot Camps

In 1983, the concept of boot camps for correctional treatment of adults emerged in the United States. By the early 1990s, the concept had spread to include correctional treatment for juveniles (Lundman 2001:238). Boot camps are generally considered "tough" alternatives to traditional rehabilitation programs based on changing attitudes and behaviors of youth and adults. They usually, though not always, incorporate the stereotypic military style of basic training for new recruits and attempt to instill discipline and toughness in those exposed to this "treatment." Many of these programs are confrontational and employ adult leaders who exemplify a hard, no-nonsense stance toward offenders. Some defend this style of treatment for juveniles on the idea that boot camps help prepare youthful offenders for more extensive treatment later in their correctional experience. In addition, these supporters argue that boot camps foster a more secure environment for juveniles than they might experience in other juvenile facilities or in their home communities. Others suggest that boot camps present a threatening atmosphere for juveniles and one that might serve to shake already weakened self-concepts or social ties to adults and authority figures in their lives. Some supporters of boot camps argue that they must "break down" a youthful offender before they can build him or her back up again. However, detractors suggest that females and juveniles who have been abused are particularly more likely to react negatively to a stressful boot camp experience (Lundman 2001:238; MacKenzie et al. 2001:281–283).

There have been several evaluations of boot camp effectiveness for juveniles, many of which are comparative in format. One detailed evaluation occurred with three pilot boot camps for youth, initiated in the early to mid-1990s. Three cities were chosen for the locations of these boot camps: Cleveland, Ohio; Denver, Colorado; and Mobile, Alabama. The youth sent to these camps were 13- to 17-year-old males, most of whom were minority youth and most of whom had been adjudicated on property or drug-related offenses and were headed for institutional confinement. However, all three camps also accepted juveniles adjudicated on violent offenses. The camp in Mobile also accepted more youth on probation than those bound for correctional incarceration (Borque et al. 1996; Lundman 2001:239–248).

All three boot camps were designed to use the tough military-style approach to handling offenders, and all three camps were designed to last three to four months. However, two of the camps, Cleveland and Mobile, incorporated education and life-skills training into their program. In addition, the program in Cleveland used guided group interaction as an important component of the total treatment experience (Lundman 2001:239–248).

Follow-up evaluations of each boot camp program concluded that the youth sent to the boot camps fared worse than those incarcerated in traditional youth correctional facilities. In terms of postrelease recidivism, for example, boot camp graduates from all three programs exhibited *higher rates of convictions or adjudications* for new offenses upon release and *shorter periods of time from release until adjudication,* compared with juveniles released from traditional juvenile correctional institutions. For example, 72 percent of the youth released from the Cleveland project were adjudicated of a new offense within 32 months of release, compared with a rate of 50 percent for juveniles released from the control facility. In Denver, which used the most extreme harsh and negative components of boot camps, the figures were more comparable, but still in favor of juveniles released from the control institution; 36 percent adjudication rate for controls versus 39 percent for boot camp graduates. The overall conclusion from these evaluations and others, such as in California and Texas, is that boot camp experiences do not result in lower rates of recidivism upon release when compared with rates for juveniles released from traditional correctional facilities (Lundman 2001: 239–256). What is more troubling for supporters of boot camps is that in all three pilot programs, aftercare placements and programs were made available to those youth who had been through the boot camp phase of treatment. Despite these aftercare services, the youth still had higher recidivism rates than those released from traditional institutions (Bourque et al. 1996:7).

Additional evaluations of these three boot camps concluded that their per-person costs were lower than comparable costs for traditional confinement. The average daily cost for the Cleveland boot camp was $75, compared with an estimated cost of $99 for youth confined in Ohio state correctional facilities in the early 1990s. In Denver, the average daily cost was $71, compared with a figure of $138 for youth confined to secure custodial institutions in Colorado (Bourque et al. 1996:7–8).

Other analyses of boot camps address the effects of these experiences on the attitudes and social adjustments of the youth exposed to these programs. In the evaluations of the programs in Cleveland, Denver, and Mobile, for example, the majority of the youth surveyed indicated that they felt better able to control their behavior and emotions as a result of the boot camp experience. In addition, they expressed more positive sentiments about their levels of responsibility, honesty, ability to get along with others, and themselves in general as a result of boot camp (Borque et al. 1996:6).

Additional analyses of these attitudinal and social impacts of boot camps were examined in a national study of boot camps in the late 1990s (MacKenzie et al. 2001). This study surveyed participants in 26 juvenile boot camps, public and private, in the United States, except Alaska and Hawaii, as of 1997. The responses of these youth were compared to those housed in 22 comparative traditional correctional institutions throughout the country. This methodology yielded a sample of 2,668 boot camp youth and 1,848 institutionalized youth. All of the youths were surveyed twice, once just after the boot camp youth entered the program, and another time just before their intended release.

The results of these surveys indicated that the *boot camp youth* saw the boot camps as *more restrictive* than did the institutional youth. However, the boot camp residents also viewed the camps as *more therapeutic and less threatening* than did the control group. However, the authors noted that the boot camp youth were more often selected because of their less violent and "troubled" backgrounds, so the results may have, in part, been affected by these personal characteristics as opposed to the characteristics of the institutions and their programs. This study also found that youth from abusive families or backgrounds did not do as well as other youth in boot camps (MacKenzie et al. 2001:294–305). According to this study, boot camps do not create unusual stress and tension in the youth exposed to the military style and strict discipline offered in boot camps, but young people who have been abused are sometimes further damaged by these kinds of "treatment" methods.

Despite the conclusion of research that boot camps do not increase stress and anxieties in youth, instances of abuse and tragic outcomes from boot camp experiences have been documented. In January 2006, a 14-year-old male died in a boot camp in Florida. Investigations into his death led to criminal charges of aggravated manslaughter filed in November 2006 against six guards who were caught on video beating the youngster before his death, as well as a nurse who worked at the camp (Central Florida News 13 2006). While the death of an inmate is rare, the likelihood that cruel and unusual punishments may be given to inmates in boot camps is not uncommon. Some have examined the types of punishments doled out in boot camps and found them demeaning, humiliating, abusive, and very close to violations of the Eighth Amendment to the U.S. Constitution, which protects inmates from being subjected to cruel and unusual punishment while incarcerated (Lutz and Brody 1999). While this constitutional issue has not been resolved in the courts, deaths such as the one reported in Florida in 2006 may well prompt a more careful judicial examination of the methods of punishment and handling of those sent to boot camps, especially youthful offenders.

Despite evidence that boot camps do not reduce or prevent delinquency, sometimes border on violations of constitutional rights, may cause physical and emotional harm, and occasionally lead to a juvenile's death, they remain a popular intervention strategy in the country. Limited evaluations claim that boot camps are less expensive to operate than traditional reformatories or similar correctional institutions for juveniles, and this is a positive feature of boot camps. However, cost-saving advantages may be claimed by many other treatment and intervention strategies, especially ones focused on community or nonresidential living. It is these kinds of prevention efforts that are discussed next.

Delinquency Prevention Programs

Scared Straight

Scared Straight is a name given to prevention programs that utilize prison settings in an effort to change or "scare" delinquents or youths thought to be at risk of becoming delinquent. These programs are based on the philosophy of deterrence and are often associated with a "get-tough" attitude toward delinquency prevention. In this respect, Scared Straight programs and boot camps share similar philosophies and approaches to the prevention of delinquency. They also share what some call a "panacea" approach to delinquency prevention, that is, a program thought to offer a quick and wide-ranging solution to the problem of delinquency (Finckenauer and Gavin 1999:1–16; Petrosino et al. 2003:41–44).

Scared Straight began in the mid-1970s, in the Rahway State Prison in New Jersey. A group of inmates in prison for life formed a group called the Lifer's Group. This group of men decided that one way for them to give something back to society was to develop a delinquency prevention program, one that would attempt to make budding delinquents aware of the possible consequences of their behavior and of the dangers and difficulties facing youngsters in prison. In essence, the goal was for the inmates to confront these youth in group settings and literally to scare them straight (Finckenauer and Gavin 1999:19–29).

Initial reports of the impact of Scared Straight were positive. A film was produced concerning the history and goals of Scared Straight, showing some of the confrontation sessions between inmates and juveniles. This film received numerous film awards and further served to validate the success of the project. In the late 1970s, James Finckenauer received a grant to study the impact of Scared Straight by examining the postconfrontation behavior of 46 juveniles who had been through the program and comparing these youth to the delinquent behavior of 35 juveniles who were used as a control group. The results of Finckenauer's study indicated that the program did not result in a reduction of delinquency, but rather was associated with an *increase* in delinquency among the Scared Straight youth (Finckenauer and Gavin 1999:45–106). For example, among the 46 Scared Straight youth, 41.3 percent had at least one recorded act of delinquency six months after the confrontation experience. The comparable rate of delinquency for the controls was 11.4 percent. In addition, the recorded delinquent acts of the Scared Straight group were significantly more serious than those of the control group (Finckenauer and Gavin 1999:86–89).

Although research was beginning to cast doubt on the effectiveness of Scared Straight programs, their popularity and presumed successes had resulted in the establishment of similar programs in other states. One such program in Virginia was called the Insiders Program, and it lasted from 1978 to 1984. Evaluations of the Insiders Program concluded that the court appearance rates for the experimental group (those exposed to Scared Straight tactics) were about the same as those for a group of controls. Longer periods of evaluation, from nine to 12 months, suggested that the experimental youth were faring better than the controls, but some have questioned the validity of these longer follow-up estimates of recidivism (Lundman 2001:196–198).

Despite the popularity of Scared Straight programs, some began to express concerns about possible injuries to youth during confrontations early on. Reports of inmates manhandling or touching youth were surfacing, and questions about the ethics of the film and the emotional impact of the confrontations on the youth and their families were being raised (Finckenauer and Gavin 1999:53–54; Lundman 2001:192). Many states, however, continued to develop these programs, sometimes with the confrontation model and sometimes without. In California, for example, officials introduced the "Squires" program, which de-emphasized the confrontation method in favor of less threatening but still informative sessions. This program was also evaluated and found to be unsuccessful in reducing delinquency, compared with control groups (Finckenauer and Gavin 1999:130–131). In the 1990s, other countries such as Norway began to experiment with the Scared Straight model, but these, too, have not demonstrated any measurable impact on reducing delinquency. Although many of the youth who experienced the program in Norway said their experiences were "positive," interviews with these youth indicated they were not measurably affected by the experience. In addition, although most of the youth expressed positive reactions to the way they were treated by the inmates, there were reports of physical confrontations between the inmates and the youth (Finckenauer and Gavin 1999:143–199; Lundman 2001:201).

Continued surveys of Scared Straight programs have consistently concluded that they do not deter delinquency (Finckenauer and Gavin 1999:136–139; Lundman 2001:202; Petrosino et al. 2003). In fact, the results sometimes show that such programs are associated with an *increase* in delinquency. The authors of one survey of Scared Straight programs offer the following conclusion: "These randomized trials, conducted over a quarter of a century in eight different jurisdictions and involving nearly one thousand participants, provide evidence that Scared Straight and other 'juvenile awareness' programs are not effective as a stand-alone crime prevention strategy. More important, they provide empirical evidence—under experimental conditions— that these programs likely increase the odds that children exposed to them will commit another delinquent offense" (Petrosino et al. 2003:55, 58).

Despite these negative conclusions concerning Scared Straight programs, they remain popular in the public eye and among corrections officials across the country (Finckenauer and Gavin 1999:136–137, 215–219; Petrosino et al. 2003:59–60). In part, this popularity is associated with the appeal to get tough with juvenile offenders. As Finckenauer and Gavin note (1999:218–219), Scared Straight programs continue to develop along with boot camps and other get-tough programs, such as D.A.R.E. (see chapter 9). Perhaps, they suggest, such programs speak to the need for the public to locate a simple solution to delinquency, one that offers a panacea for the problem. Perhaps one day these kinds of programs will result in true crime-reducing effects on juveniles. However, according to available research on the topic, such a measurable impact has not been found.

Restorative Justice

Some treatment programs are conducted primarily in the community setting and often include the goal of prevention as well. This situation seems to apply to two popular programs today, *restorative justice* and *mentoring.* Restorative justice involves face-to-face meetings or conferences between offenders and their victims, including the families of victims. In addition, such conferences are usually accompanied by a mediator or juvenile justice professional, who attempts to reconcile feelings and interests of both parties but with the benefit of the community also in mind. Thus, restorative justice programs attempt to integrate the interests of three parties to juvenile delinquency, the *offender,* the *victim,* and the *community* (Bazemore 1998:771–772; Kurki 1999; Bazemore 2001:199–206; McGarrell 2001:1–2; Sullivan and Tifft 2001:25–49).

Historically, restorative justice became popular in the United States in the 1990s, particularly after the publication of books and articles by John Braithwaite on shaming and reintegration (Braithwaite 1989, 1993; McGarrell 2001:2), but also in conjunction with developing interest in restitution programs in general (Bazemore 2001:204). However, examples of restorative justice can be found in practices going back to the 1970s and 1980s, especially with the emergence of restitution and victim's rights issues and concerns (Sullivan and Tifft 2001:16–17). Others argue that restitution programs have existed for centuries and can even be found in the ancient Babylonian Code of Hammurabi in 1700 B.C. (Bazemore 1998:772).

Braithwaite (1989) discusses restorative justice in terms of reintegration into the community, facilitated by processes of formal "shaming" of the offender. This type of restorative program often uses a *family group conference* model, which includes face-to-face meetings between offender and victim, accompanied by a trained mediator. The offender is expected to speak in these conferences, and the focus of attention historically has been on the offender's admission of guilt and shame for the act. This type of restorative justice model began in New Zealand in the late 1980s and early 1990s, but it is now found in parts of the United States, such as Minnesota and Pennsylvania. These programs often include juveniles accused of any kind of offense except murder and manslaughter (see also Bazemore and Umbreit 2001:8–10). The use of conferences and the incorporation of shaming the offender in the process suggest this method of handling offenders may have a much longer history than is usually thought to be the case. For example, the mediation "conference" model is also a traditional method of settling disputes among neighbors and dealing with juvenile offenses in the Philippines that focuses on "amicable settlements" facilitated by elected officials known as *Barangay* captains, who serve as mediators, and which incorporates the use of shaming the offender into asking for forgiveness from the victim (Orendain 1978; Shoemaker 2006).

Restorative justice is often considered an alternative to formal juvenile justice processing in Western societies, a kind of diversion program (Bazemore and Umbreit 2001). In some ways, restorative justice is similar to youth courts, which were discussed in chapter 14. Both use some kind of community-based intervention to deal with offenders. Both serve as identifiable alternatives to traditional juvenile courts. However, restorative justice programs tend to involve victims and community values in the process of determining dispositions of offenders, more so than do youth courts. Often restorative justice includes face-to-face meetings between victim and offender, and this does not usually happen in youth courts. In addition, restorative justice programs usually include some type of mediation, involving a trained counselor or mediator, a role not often found in youth courts.

Although restorative justice programs all share many commonalities, such as those described above, there are several examples of restorative justice that tend to differ more in terms of historical use, point of diversion origination, where the program is used, and the nature of the charges against the offender. In addition to the family-conference model described earlier, there are several other types or models of restorative justice programs. One example is the *victim–offender mediation* model. This type of program is one of the oldest types of restorative justice, tracing its beginning to the mid 1970s, and is found throughout the United States. Often these programs are used as alternatives to juvenile courts and use probation in connection with dispositions. Sometimes they may also be sued in correctional settings. They typically handle nonviolent offenders but may also include violent offenders if the victim requests this type of procedure. *Reparative boards* started around 1995 and are found primarily in Vermont. They also serve the function of diversion from juvenile court, utilize probation, and usually accept nonviolent offenders into the process. In contrast to other restorative justice models, reparative boards seem to focus more on community concerns and less on victim involvement. *Circle sentencing* has been used since 1992 and is primarily found in Canada, Minnesota, Colorado, and Massachusetts. This program is usually a juvenile court diversion program but may sometimes be used in correctional settings. Usually, circle sentencing includes all types of offenders, especially repeat offenders, but it expects an admission of guilt and some sense of contrition on the part of the accused (Bazemore and Umbreit 2001:2–9).

All four models of restorative justice rely on the members of the juvenile justice system for referrals, oversight, and decision making. However, it is also understood that mediators and members of boards, conferences, and circles are also to be heard and respected when making decisions about what to do with accused youth. Although it may be said that even traditional juvenile court procedures always have been concerned about the interests of the accused *and* the community, restorative justice programs seem to emphasize the role of the victim and the overall interests of the community more than juvenile courts do. In this way, restorative justice seeks to restore some sense of holistic balance to the community, as well as between victim and offender. The offender is expected to receive some sort of punishment as a consequence of his or her criminal behavior, but this "punishment" must also be seen as just and acceptable in the eyes of the victim and the community (Bazemore 2001; Bazemore and Umbreit 2001). Restorative justice programs are good examples of the developing interests of juvenile justice programs and procedures to achieve a sense of balance among offenders, victims, and the community (Harp 2002; see also chapter 13).

Along with the continuing popularity of restorative justice programs, some have sought to assess or evaluate their impact on offenders, victims, and members of the community. One such study was an evaluation of a family-conference program developed in Indianapolis in 1997. The program involved young people 14 years old and younger who were first offenders charged with nonviolent crimes and who took responsibility for their crimes (McGarrell 2001). This was a juvenile court diversion program. The analysis covered the two-year period from 1997 to 1999 and included 232 youths who participated in the restorative justice program, compared with the experiences of 226 youths who were comparable to the restorative group but who did not participate in restorative justice and thus became a control group.

A common result of restorative justice was for the offender to offer the victim an apology for the crime. Other reparative consequences included financial restitution and community service. The results of the experiment suggested that the victims of the offenders in the experimental group were significantly more satisfied with the outcome of the case than were the victims of the control group of offenders. In addition, family-conference participants, such as offenders and victims, were more likely to support continuation of the conferencing program than were control group participants. Follow-up analyses concluded that the experimental group offenders were significantly less likely than control group offenders to be rearrested six and 12 months after leaving their respective programs (McGarrell 2001:3–9).

Bazemore and Umbreit (2001) compared the results of the four types of restorative justice models described earlier. Their comparison concluded that each model has strengths and weaknesses, but overall, the programs seemed to be effective in enforcing the agreements reached among conference participants with the process of restorative justice. Other studies have also concluded that restorative justice programs result in reduced recidivism for offenders who participate in them. In addition, some studies show that victims of violent crimes are less likely to want to harm their attackers if they go through a restorative justice program (Braithwaite 2007:692).

Despite the generally positive conclusions of restorative justice evaluations, some have expressed concerns and cautionary attitudes toward the future development of these kinds of interventions. For instance, there is concern that the power of the law may be reduced in favor of individual influence in restorative conferences. Less powerful people may lose their rights and influence in conferences to those who are powerful and/or persuasive in the community. Some are concerned that the formal reach of the juvenile justice system may be extended in connection with restorative justice because these programs rely heavily on judges and court personnel for referrals. Thus, "net widening" may occur, a consequence also possible with other diversion programs, a point raised in chapter 14 (Bazemore and Umbreit 2001:15–17; see Zehr and Toews 2004 for additional critiques of restorative justice programs).

Another concern about restorative justice programs is that they may not work as well as planned, in part because they seem to place more emphasis on balancing the needs and concerns of victims, community members, and offenders instead of ensuring that the offender receives due punishment for his or her offense. In some ways, this argument stems from the notion that shame and community reintegration are consistent with the values of some Asian societies and developing countries (Braithwaite 1989). However, Braithwaite (1993) suggests that the goals and methods associated with reintegrative shaming (an element of many restorative justice programs) not only are consistent with developing the values of societies but also can be effectively used in modern, developed countries. The key is to involve people who matter to the offender in the shaming, or restorative, process (p. 12). As Braithwaite (1993) puts it, "There is no structural inevitability about the impotence of shaming in an urbanized industrial society. Tokyo is a testimony to that. And so are Japanese, Chinese and Jewish communities within the most violent of American cities" (p. 15). This view is consistent with the positive evaluations of restorative justice programs in the United States discussed earlier (see also Hay 2001) as well as other considerations of such programs in New Zealand and Australia (Braithwaite and Mugford 1994).

Additional conceptualization on the themes of shaming and reintegration suggests that shaming is a more complex process than some may think, wherever it occurs. In essence, offending is usually considered wrong, and some sense of shame will always accompany reintegrative efforts. Even if a person has accepted responsibility for wrongful acts and been accepted back into the community, or reintegrated, there will always be some stigma and shame associated with the offender, especially if he or she chooses to live in the same community where the offense occurred. Thus, the goal should be to *manage* the shaming process included in restorative justice programs (Harris and Maruna 2006).

With continued funding and experimentation with conferences and other models of restorative justice, perhaps truly independent programs will emerge that will reduce the problems seen with many of the existing programs. In this case, restorative justice may become an innovative method of dealing with youthful offenders outside the formal parameters of the traditional juvenile justice system. Those wishing to learn more about restorative justice programs and/or participate in discussions about restorative justice may go to the Restorative Practices eForum at www.restorativepracitves.org. In addition, a good resource for current practices and thinking about issues concerning restorative justice is Dennis Sullivan and Larry Tifft's *Handbook of Restorative Justice* (2006).

Mentoring: A National Movement?

A popular method of preventing delinquency is the use of *volunteers*, some younger, some older, who agree to work with and *mentor* young people. As it is commonly understood, mentoring is not a new phenomenon. Historians cite examples of adults tutoring youth as far back as 800 B.C. According to Homer's epic saga *The Odyssey*, Mentor was a friend of Odysseus, the king of Ithaca. Mentor agreed to look after Telemachus, the son of Odysseus, while Odysseus was away fighting the Trojan War. Over time, the word *mentor* has become synonymous with the voluntary tutelage of young people (Baker and Maguire 2005:14).

In the United States, the use of mentors for youthful offenders or at-risk youth is often connected with the development of an organization called Big Brothers, which later became known as Big Brothers Big Sisters of America, or BBBSA. The idea of adults volunteering their time and effort to help troubled youth is traced to 1902 in New York City. In that year, the Ladies of Charity of New York City formed a program based on the work of volunteer women to provide support for children appearing before the juvenile court in New York. That program later came to be known as the Catholic Big Sisters of New York. Also in 1902, the juvenile court judge of New York City, Julius Mayer, called for 90 adult male volunteers to help youth who had been sent to the court. This call was noted by a journalist named Ernest Coulter, who later became employed as a clerk of the juvenile court and who promoted the idea throughout the city. Initially, only 40 men volunteered, but the idea was becoming popular. Coulter referred to the male volunteers in New York as "big brothers" and is credited with forming the first Big Brothers organization in New York. Around the same time, an influential businessman in Cincinnati, Irvin Westheimer, also became interested in developing an organization of adult men to help troubled boys and led the way for the formation of the Big Brothers group in that city in 1910 (McGill et al. 2001:7; Baker and Maguire 2005:18–19).

While Big Brothers programs were rapidly developing in the country, adult women were also promoting similar programs for girls coming before juvenile courts. In addition to the Catholic Big Sisters in New York City, there also appeared the New York Jesuit Big Sisters and the Protestant Big Sisters. Around the same time, the Chicago Women's Club and administrators of the Hull House in Chicago (see chapter 2) were recruiting volunteers to work with troubled girls in that city. By 1917, it is estimated that there were Big Brothers or Big Sisters organizations in 98 cities in America. In 1978, the two organizations merged to form the BBBSA (Baker and Maguire 2005:19).

By the 21st century, BBBSA had grown to more than 500 clubs, serving over 100,000 youth (Baker and Maguire 2005:18). The youth served by these organizations are 6–18 years old, but most often 14–18. Many of the youth selected for participation in BBBSA are from single-parent homes, and they meet with their volunteer three times a month for three to five hours (McGill et al. 2001:xxviii).

In addition, mentoring as a juvenile justice treatment and prevention program has grown considerably since the mid-1990s. From 1996 to the early 2000s, the U.S. Office of Juvenile Justice and Delinquency Prevention spent over $40 million on mentoring programs. In 2004, the U.S. Congress authorized $100 million to be spent on mentoring programs, a fourfold increase from 2003, when the budget for mentoring was $27.4 million (Blechman and Bopp 2005:454).

In 2005, a national organization focusing on mentoring, named Mentor, conducted a national survey of mentoring (Mentor 2006). One conclusion of this study was that over 3,000,000 adults were involved in one-to-one mentoring relationships with youngsters, and this number is increasing. In addition, this survey found that the average mentoring relationship lasted nine months, but 38 percent lasted more than one year. (Mentor 2006:ii). One concern with mentoring relationships is the potential for child abuse or inappropriate relationships between adult and child. Some formal programs, such as BBBSA, take preventive measures to detect and screen out potential abusers from their programs (McGill et al. 2001:24–25). However, it cannot be assumed that all mentoring efforts take these precautionary steps in identifying and assigning volunteers to work with youth, and this issue remains a concern regarding mentoring programs.

The 2005 Mentor survey also concluded that most mentoring was conducted informally. Formal mentors were most often associated with Big Brothers/Big Sisters, Boy and Girl Scouts, school programs, faith-based organizations, and work-related associations. In addition, mentoring was more common among middle-aged and young, nonwhite adult males. Nonwhites were more likely to be informal mentors. A little more than one-half (51 percent) of the mentoring relationships occurred in group settings. Also, the most common mentee was a child in need of special education services (38 percent). Only 16 percent of the mentees were involved in the juvenile justice system, but 67 percent of the mentors said they would consider mentoring a child in the juvenile justice system (Mentor 2006:2–6).

Some, such as the group Mentor, argue that mentoring relationships are associated with positive results for youth involved in these relationships (Mentor 2006:1). In 1992 and 1993, a controlled study of the impact of BBBSA on a sample of approximately 1,000 children of age 10–16 concluded from an 18-month follow-up study that those youth involved in mentoring exhibited reduced instances of drug use and hitting others, increased school attendance and better grades in school, and improved relationships between youth and their parents, as well as with other youth (McGill et al. 2001:10).

However, other evaluations of mentoring programs do not reach such positive conclusions (Coyne et al. 2005:546–547; Taylor et al. 2005:290–293).

Developing research on this topic suggests that structured, or more formal, mentoring is associated with more positive outcomes among at-risk youth than is unstructured mentoring. However, research is also showing that other programs, such as skills training, are more effective in preventing or reducing delinquency than is mentoring (Blechman and Bopp 2005:458–460). Some have attempted to analyze the cost and benefit of mentoring, but again, the results are inconsistent. Some studies maintain than mentoring saves thousands of dollars per youth, but others argue that such savings are offset by higher recidivism rates among youth exposed to mentoring. Most of the cost savings are in comparison to formal juvenile justice system processes. However, when compared to other diversion or community-based programs, mentoring does not seem to produce significant savings to the community (Taylor et al. 2005:458–460; Yates 2005: 433–441).

Overall, detailed evaluations of the impact of mentoring, especially with respect to delinquency, are sparse. One reason for this lack of information on the impact of mentoring may be because so much of it is informal and relatively undocumented and unsupervised. While it may seem obvious to some that volunteer mentoring will produce positive results for juvenile mentees, the lack of research on this topic makes it difficult to reach that conclusion with confidence at this time.

A Note on Treatment and Prevention Program Evaluation

In 1974, Robert Martinson published a review of evaluations and studies of treatment and prevention programs for adult and juvenile offenders and essentially concluded that "Nothing works." While that judgment might seem a little harsh and overreaching, the conclusion seemed to stick, and it led to critical assessments of efforts to treat and/or prevent delinquency throughout the country for the next several years. Continued research and investigation regarding the impact of treatment and prevention programs has led to the conclusion that some programs do, indeed, "work," but that the matter is not as simple and direct as earlier conclusions might suggest (Losel 1995). As one reviewer of numerous treatment and prevention programs for juveniles concluded, "As a generality, treatment clearly works. We must get on with the business of developing and identifying the treatment models that will be most effective and providing them to the juveniles that they will benefit" (Lipsey 1995:78). Descriptions and assessments of countless treatment and prevention programs now exist, all published well after the Martinson article (McGuire 1995; Giacobbe et al. 1999; Klopovic et al. 2003; Milkman and Wanberg 2005).

Meta-analyses of hundreds of published records of treatment programs for juveniles conclude that psychological programs and programs emphasizing deterrence or punishment have less effect on posttreatment behavior (recidivism) than do school-participation programs or programs that focus on job-related or social skills. In addition, these assessments conclude that specific characteristics of juveniles seem to have less impact on outcome measures than do the characteristics of the treatment programs themselves. Specifically, programs that allow for at least 100 hours of treatment and are more carefully monitored by the treatment specialist or researchers involved have the highest levels of success (Lipsey 1995).

However, another assessment of treatment programs for serious juvenile offenders suggests that individual counseling, along with training in interpersonal skills and behavior modification programs, offer the best outcomes for noninstitutionalized youth. In addition, this analysis suggests that interpersonal skill training and community-based group treatment programs that use behavior modification have experienced positive outcomes for institutionalized youth. Programs that have resulted in little or no treatment effect include deterrence programs, wilderness or challenge programs, and vocational programs (Lipsey et al. 2000).

Although some specific treatment strategies seem to be more effective than others, continued research into the effect(s) of treatment and/or prevention programs suggests that individualized treatment and multiple treatment approaches offer more promising results than traditional "one-size-fits-all" strategies. This approach was demonstrated in the discussion of drug courts for substance abusers (chapter 9), in discussions of treatment and prevention programs for juvenile gangs (chapter 10), and in strategies focused on families and schools (chapters 7 and 8). One multiple treatment strategy that seems to be gaining popularity is *multisystemic therapy*, or MST (Milkman and Wanberg 2005:254). The goal of the therapist using MST is to locate specific behavioral problems and associated treatment strategies for all of a juvenile's environment, including families, schools, and peers (McGill et al. 2001:xxix; Milkman and Wanberg 2005:254–259). Although MST is often used in family-based counseling programs for juvenile offenders and at-risk youth, the principle of incorporating multiple levels and strategies of intervention for treatment and prevention programs is potentially applicable to a variety of settings.

Another important issue to consider in the evaluation of a treatment program's impact is the degree of *dedication* to the treatment process. If the treatment, whatever it may be, is to be successful, it must be accepted by the receiver as well as the giver (Milkman and Wanberg 2005:249–252). While there is debate in the field of counseling concerning the utility of treatment when the receiver does not want to be treated (Satel 2000), it is difficult to force a person to change against his or her will. Likewise, if the treatment giver does not really believe in a treatment program but is pushed into administering treatment as part of his or her job, such as a counselor working in a correctional facility, it is hard to imagine that the outcome of the program will be positive for the receiver.

In addition to dedication to treatment on the part of the receiver and the giver, there is the issue of *trust*. That is, if the receiver does not trust that the giver is working for the receiver's best interests, it is again unlikely that the results will be successful. This concern is recognized by treatment counselors, especially with respect to racial and/or ethnic differences between treatment giver and receiver (Pope-Davis and Liu 1998). Although this concern is often addressed to cases of individualized treatment, the issue also applies to any kind of intervention effort, including community-based prevention programs. If the receivers do not trust the motives or dedication of the treatment or prevention specialists or givers, then it would seem a successful outcome is less likely to happen.

Overall, research has established that treatment and prevention programs do have positive effects on receivers as well as on the community in general. Progress is being made in further determining which kinds of treatments or combinations of treatment/prevention programs are more beneficial for different offenders or at-risk youth, and what costs to the public are required for offering these interventions. However, it is wise to heed Lipsey's comments made at the beginning of this section supporting the need to continue searching for more effective and efficient treatment and prevention strategies.

Summary

Juvenile institutions can be divided into two primary types; long term and short term. Long-term institutions are often called reformatories, training schools, or correctional facilities. Short-term institutions are often referred to as detention homes or detention centers. Recent data indicate that minorities represent a majority of residents in public facilities, within long-term institutions. In addition, almost 85 percent of institutional residents are male. However, females are more often confined for status offenses than are males.

Both long-term and short-term facilities must maintain security and custody of residents, but long-term institutions must also demonstrate some type of treatment of residents in their care. Short-term facilities are primarily concerned with securing the custody of their inmates, but most offer minimal rehabilitation services such as educational assistance.

Long-term facilities are also known as total institutions. They have the task of caring for virtually all of their residents' needs, 24 hours a day. The stress of living in such facilities around the clock, plus the attitudes and behavioral patterns transported into institutions by residents, lead to an inmate social system. This system exerts considerable influence on the residents and tends to psychologically separate inmates from staff and others charged with the supervision and control of residents. Within institutions for females, the inmate system often conforms to family-like structures and roles. Many researchers contend the influence of the inmate social system works against receptivity toward treatment programs.

Most treatment programs for institutionalized youth are individually oriented and are often based on psychotherapeutic efforts. However, many programs also utilize group treatment techniques, such as guided group interaction or positive peer culture.

Recent community-based prevention programs are exemplified by such programs as restorative justice and mentoring. Both have historical precedents that can be traced back hundreds of years to other cultures. However, in the United States, these prevention strategies began to appear in the 1970s and 1980s. Evaluations of these programs show some promise as delinquency prevention measures, but more research is needed for firmer conclusions to be reached.

In the mid-1970s, critiques of treatment and prevention programs argued that such efforts did not work. However, in the past few decades, numerous assessments and meta-evaluations of treatment and prevention programs have concluded that these programs do work but that there should be more specificity and connection between the needs of delinquent and at-risk youth and treatment or prevention techniques available to them. In addition, current thinking on the impact of treatment and prevention suggests that multistrategy approaches are more effective than single-focus efforts. One such approach that is gaining acceptance is MST, or multisystemic therapy.

References

Ahranjani, Maryam, Andrew G. Ferguson, and Jamin B. Raskin
    2005   Youth Justice in America. Washington, DC: CQ Press.

Allen-Hagen, Barbara
    1991   Public Juvenile Facilities: Children in Custody, 1989. Washington, DC: Office of Juvenile Justice and Delinquency Prevention.

Baker, David B., and Colleen Maguire
    2005   Mentoring in Historical Perspective. *In* Handbook of Youth Mentoring. David L. DuBois and Michael J. Karcher, eds. Pp. 14–29. Thousand Oaks, CA: Sage.

Bandura, Albert
    1969   Principles of Behavior Modification. New York: Holt, Rinehart & Winston.

Barker, Gordon H., and W. Thomas Adams
    1959   The Social Structure of a Correctional Institution. Journal of Criminal Law, Criminology, and Police Science 49:417–422.

Bartollas, Clemens, Stuart J. Miller, and Simon Dinitz
    1976   Juvenile Victimization: The Institutional Paradox. New York: Sage.

Bazemore, Gordon
    1998   Restorative Justice and Earned Redemption: Communities, Victims, and Offender Reintegration. American Behavioral Scientist 41:768–813.
    2001   Young People, Trouble, and Crime: Restorative Justice as a Normative Theory of Informal Social Control and Social Support. Youth & Society 33:199–226.

Bazemore, Gordon, and Mark Umbreit
    2001   A Comparison of Four Restorative Conferencing Models. Washington, D.C.: U.S. Department of Justice, Office of Juvenile Justice and Delinquency Prevention.

Berne, Eric
    1961   Transactional Analysis in Psychotherapy: A Systematic Individual and Social Psychiatry. New York: Grove Press.

Blechman, Elaine A., and Jedediah M. Bopp
    2005   Juvenile Offenders. *In* Handbook of Juvenile Mentoring. David L. DuBois and Michael J. Karcher, eds. Pp. 454–466. Thousand Oaks, CA: Sage.

Bortner, M. A., and Linda M. Williams

    1997   Youth in Prison: We the People of Unit Four. New York: Routledge.

Bourque, Blair B., Roberta C. Cronin, Daniel B. Felker, Frank R. Pearson, Mei Han, and Sarah M. Hill

    1996   Boot Camps for Juvenile Offenders: An Implementation Evaluation of Three Demonstration Programs, Research in Brief. Washington, DC: U.S. Department of Justice, National Institute of Justice.

Braithwaite, John

    1989   Crime, Shame, and Reintegration. Melbourne, Australia: Oxford University Press.

    1993   Shame and Modernity. British Journal of Criminology 33:1–16.

    2007   Encourage Restorative Justice. Criminology & Public Policy 6: 689–696.

Braithwaite, John, and S. Mugford

    1994   Conditions of Successful Reintegration Ceremonies: Dealing with Juvenile Offenders. British Journal of Criminology 34:139–171.

Central Florida News 13

    2006   Charges Filed in Boot Camp Death. Electronic document, www.nospank.net/n-q51r.htm.

Coyne, Shawn M., Jennifer L. Duffy, and Abraham Wandersman

    2005   Mentoring for Results: Accountability at the Individual, Community, and Policy Levels. In Handbook of Youth Mentoring. David L. Dubois and Michael J. Karcher, eds. Pp. 546–560. Thousand Oaks, CA: Sage.

Empey, Lamar T., and Steven G. Lubeck

    1971   The Silverlake Experiment: Testing Delinquency Theory and Community Intervention. Chicago: Aldine.

Feld, Barry C.

    1977   Neutralizing Violence: Juvenile Offenders in Institutions. Cambridge, MA: Ballinger.

    2006   The Politics of Race and Juvenile Justice: The "Due Process Revolution" and the Conservative Reaction. In Race and Juvenile Justice. Everette B. Penn, Helen Taylor Greene, and Shaun L. Gabbidon, eds. Pp. 187–222. Durham, NC: Carolina Academic Press.

Finckenauer, James O., and Patricia W. Gavin

    1999   Scared Straight: The Panacea Phenomenon Revisited. Prospect Heights, IL: Waveland.

Giacobbe, George A., Elaine Traynelis-Yurek, and Erik K. Laursen

    1999   Strengths Based Strategies for Children & Youth: An Annotated Bibliography. Richmond, VA: G & T Publishing.

Giallombardo, Rose
  1974   The Social World of Imprisoned Girls: A Comparative Study of
          Institutions for Juvenile Delinquents. New York: John Wiley &
          Sons.
Glasser, William M.
  1965   Reality Therapy: A New Approach to Psychiatry. New York: Harper
          and Row.
Glueck, Sheldon, and Eleanor Glueck
  1950   Unraveling Juvenile Delinquency. New York: Commonwealth Fund.
Goffman, Irving
  1961   Asylums: Essays on the Social Situations of Mental Patients and
          Other Inmates. Chicago: Aldine.
Grosser, George H.
  1968   External Setting and Internal Relations of the Prison. *In* Prison
          Within Society: A Reader in Penology. Lawrence E. Hazelrigg, ed.
          Pp. 9–26. New York: Doubleday.
Harp, Caren
  2002   Bringing Balance to Juvenile Justice. Alexandria, VA: American Pros-
          ecutors Research Institute.
Harris, Nathan, and Shadd Maruna
  2006   Shame, Shaming, and Restorative Justice: A Critical Appraisal. *In*
          Handbook of Restorative Justice: A Global Perspective. Dennis Sul-
          livan and Larry Tifft, eds. Pp. 452–462. New York: Routledge.
Hay, Carter
  2001   An Exploratory Test of Braithwaite's Reintegrative Shaming Theory.
          Journal of Research in Crime and Delinquency 38:132–153.
Hemmens, Craig, Benjamin Steiner, and David Mueller
  2004   Significant Cases in Juvenile Justice. Los Angeles: Roxbury.
Klopovic, James, Michael L. Vasu, and Douglas L. Yearwood
  2003   Effective Program Practices for At-Risk Youth: A Continuum of
          Community-Based Programs. Kingston, NJ: Civic Research Institute.
Kurki, Leena
  1999   Incorporating Restorative and Community Justice into American
          Sentencing and Corrections. Washington, DC: U.S. Department of
          Justice, Office of Justice Programs.
Laub, John H., and Robert J. Sampson
  2003   Shared Beginnings, Divergent Lives: Delinquent Boys to Age 70.
          Cambridge, MA: Harvard University Press.

Leiber, Michael J.
    2006   Disproportionate Minority Confinement (DMC) of Youth: An Analysis of State and Federal Efforts to Address the Issue. *In* Race and Juvenile Justice. Everette B. Penn, Helen Taylor Greene, and Shaun L. Gabbidon, eds. Pp. 141–185. Durham, NC: Carolina Academic Press.

Lipsey, Mark W.
    1995   What Do We Learn from 400 Studies on the Effectiveness of Treatment with Juvenile Delinquents? *In* What Works? Reducing Reoffending: Guidelines from Research and Practice. James McGuire, ed. Pp. 63–78. New York: Wiley.

Lipsey, Mark W., David B. Wilson, and Lynn Cothern
    2000   Effective Intervention for Serious Juvenile Offenders. Washington, DC: U.S. Department of Justice, Office of Juvenile Justice and Delinquency Prevention.

Losel, Friedrich
    1995   The Efficacy of Correctional Treatment: A Review and Synthesis of Meta-Evaluations. *In* What Works? Reducing Reoffending: Guidelines from Research and Practice. James McGuire, ed. Pp. 79–111. New York: Wiley.

Lundman, Richard J.
    2001   Prevention and Control of Juvenile Delinquency. 3rd edition. New York: Oxford University Press.

Lutz, Faith E., and David C. Brody
    1999   Mental Abuse as Cruel and Unusual Punishment: Do Boot Camp Prisons Violate the Eighth Amendment? Crime & Delinquency 45:242–255.

Mace, F. Charles, Joseph S. Lalli, Elizabeth Pinter Lalli, and Michael C. Shea
    1993   Functional Analysis and Treatment of Aberrant Behavior. *In* Behavior Analysis and Treatment. Ron Van Houten and Saul Axelrod, eds. Pp. 75–99. New York: Plenum.

MacKenzie, Doris Layton, David B. Wilson, Gaylene Styve Armstrong, and Angela R. Glover
    2001   The Impact of Boot Camps and Traditional Institutions on Juvenile Residents' Perceptions, Adjustment, and Change. Journal of Research in Crime and Delinquency 38:279–313.

Martin, Gus
    2005   Juvenile Justice: Process and Systems. Thousand Oaks, CA: Sage.

Martinson, Robert
 1974 What Works? Questions and Answers about Prison Reform. Public Interest 35:22–54.

McGarrell, Edmund F.
 2001 Restorative Justice Conferences as an Early Response to Young Offenders. Washington, DC: U.S. Department of Justice, Office of Juvenile Justice and Delinquency Prevention.

McGill, Dagmar E., Sharon F. Mihalic, and Jennifer K. Grotpeter
 2001 Blueprints for Violence Prevention, Book Two: Big Brothers Big Sisters of America. Boulder, CO: Institute for Behavioral Science, University of Colorado.

McGuire, James
 1995 What Works? Reducing Reoffending: Guidelines from Research and Practice. New York: Wiley.

McGuire, James, and Phillip Priestley
 1995 Reviewing "What Works": Past, Present, and Future. In What Works? Reducing Reoffending: Guidelines from Research and Practice. James McQuire, ed. Pp. 3–34. New York: Wiley.

Mentor
 2006 Mentoring in America 2005: A Snapshot of the Current State of Mentoring. Electronic document, http://www.mentoring.org/downloads/mentoring_333.pdf.

Milkman, Harvey B., and Kenneth W. Wanberg
 2005 Criminal Conduct and Substance Abuse Treatment for Adolescents: Pathways to Self-Discovery and Change. Thousand Oaks, CA: Sage.

Miller, Jerome G.
 1991 Last One over the Wall: The Massachusetts Experiment in Closing Reform Schools. Columbus: Ohio State University Press.

Murphy, Patrick T.
 1974 Our Kindly Parent—The State: The Juvenile Justice System and How It Works. New York: Viking.

Murray, Charles A., and Louis A. Cox, Jr.
 1979 Beyond Probation: Juvenile Corrections and the Chronic Delinquent. Beverly Hills, CA: Sage.

Nagin, Daniel S., Alex R. Piquero, Elizabeth S. Scott, and Laurence Steinberg
 2006 Public Preferences for Rehabilitation versus Incarceration of Juvenile Offenders: Evidence from a Contingent Valuation Survey. Criminology & Public Policy 5:627–652.

Ohlin, Lloyd E., Alden H. Miller, and Robert D. Coates
    1977   Juvenile Correctional Reform in Massachusetts: A Preliminary
            Report of the Center for Criminal Justice of the Harvard Law
            School. Washington, DC: U.S. Department of Justice, National Insti-
            tute for Juvenile Justice.
Orendain, Antonio
    1978   Barangay Justice: The Amicable Settlement of Disputes. Manila:
            Alpha Omega Publications.
Palmer, Ted
    1975   Martinson Revisited. Journal of Research in Crime and Delinquency
            12:133–152.
Payne, Pedro R.
    2005   Youth Violence Prevention through Asset-Based Community Devel-
            opment. New York: LFB Scholarly Publishing.
Pear, Robert
    2004   Many Youths Reported Held Awaiting Mental Help. New York
            Times, July 8.
Penn, Everette B.
    2006   Black Youth: Disproportionality and Delinquency. In Race and Juve-
            nile Justice. Everette B. Penn, Helen Taylor Greene, and Shaun L.
            Gabbidon, eds. Pp. 47–64. Durham, NC: Carolina Academic Press.
Petrosino, Anthony, Carolyn Turpin-Petrosino, and John Buehler
    2003   Scared Straight and Other Juvenile Awareness Programs for Prevent-
            ing Juvenile Delinquency: A Systematic Review of the Randomized
            Experimental Evidence. Annals of the American Academy of Polit-
            ical and Social Sciences 589:41–62.
Polsky, Howard W.
    1962   Cottage Six: The Social System of Delinquent Boys in Residential
            Treatment. New York: Russell Sage Foundation.
Pope-Davis, Donald B., and William M. Liu
    1998   The Social Construction of Race: Implications for Counselling Psy-
            chology. Counselling Psychology Quarterly 11:151–162.
Propper, Alice M.
    1981   Prison Homosexuality: Myth and Reality. Lexington, MA: D. C.
            Heath.
Rachin, Richard
    1974   Reality Therapy: Helping People Help Themselves. Crime and
            Delinquency 20:45–53.

Sanborn, Joseph B., Jr., and Anthony W. Salerno
   2005   The Juvenile Justice System: Law and Process. Los Angeles: Roxbury.

Satel, Sally
   2000   Drug Treatment: The Case for Coercion. National Drug Court Institute Review 3:1–56.

Shoemaker, Donald J.
   2006   Juvenile Justice in the Philippines: An Overview. In Delinquency and Juvenile Justice Systems in the Non-Western World. Paul C. Friday and Xin Ren, eds. Pp. 83–97. Monsey, NY: Criminal Justice Press.

Sickmund, Melissa
   2006   Residential Facility Census, 2002: Selected Findings. Washington, DC: Department of Justice, Office of Justice Programs, Office of Juvenile Justice and Delinquency Prevention.

Sieverdes, Christopher M., and Clemens Bartollas
   1980   Institutional Adjustment among Female Delinquents. In Improving Management in Criminal Justice. Alvin W. Cohn and Benjamin Ward, eds. Pp. 91–103. Beverly Hills: Sage.

Snyder, Howard N., and Melissa Sickmund
   2006   Juvenile Offenders and Victims: 2006 National Report. Washington, DC: U.S. Department of Justice, Office of Justice Programs, Office of Juvenile Justice and Delinquency Prevention.

Sparzo, Frank J.
   1999   The ABC's of Behavior Change. Bloomington, IN: Phi Delta Kappa Educational Foundation.

Street, David
   1965   The Inmate Group in Custodial and Treatment Settings. American Sociological Review 30:40–55.

Street, David, Robert D. Vinter, and Charles Perrow
   1966   Organization for Treatment: A Comparative Study of Institutions for Delinquents. New York: Free Press.

Sullivan, Dennis, and Larry Tifft
   2001   Restorative Justice: Healing the Foundations of Our Everyday Lives. Monsey, NY: Willow Tree Press.

Sullivan, Dennis, and Larry Tifft, eds.
   2006   Handbook of Restorative Justice: A Global Perspective. New York: Routledge.

Sykes, Gresham
   1958   Society of Captives. Princeton, NJ: Princeton University Press.

Taylor, Andrea S., Leonard LoSciuto, and Lorraine Porcellini
2005   Intergenerational Mentoring. *In* Handbook of Youth Mentoring. David L. DuBois and Michael J. Karcher, eds. Pp. 286–299. Thousand Oaks, CA: Sage.

Teplin, Linda A., Karen M. Abram, Gary M. McClelland, Amy A. Mericle, Mina K. Dulcan, and Jason J. Washburn
2006   Psychiatric Disorders of Youth in Detention. Washington, DC: U.S. Department of Juvenile Justice, Office of Justice Programs, Office of Juvenile Justice and Delinquency Prevention.

Virginia Department of Juvenile Justice
2005   Data Resources Guide, Fiscal Year 2005. Richmond: Virginia Department of Juvenile Justice.

Vorrath, Harry H., and Larry K. Brendtro
1985   Positive Peer Culture. 2nd edition. New York: Aldine.

Weeks, H. Ashley
1958   Youthful Offenders at Highfields: An Evaluation of the Effects of the Short-Term Treatment of Delinquent Boys. Ann Arbor: University of Michigan Press.

Wolfgang, Marvin E., Robert M. Figlio, and Thorsten Sellin
1972   Delinquency in a Birth Cohort. Chicago: University of Chicago Press.

Wooden, Kenneth
1976   Weeping in the Playtime of Others: America's Incarcerated Children. New York: McGraw-Hill.

Yates, Brian T.
2005   Cost-Benefit and Cost-Effectiveness Analysis. *In* Handbook of Youth Mentoring. David L. Dubois and Michael J. Karcher, eds. Pp. 525–545. Thousand Oaks, CA: Sage.

Zehr, Howard, and Barb Toews, eds.
2004   Critical Issues in Restorative Justice. Monsey, NY: Criminal Justice Press.

Epilogue

SOCIETIES HAVE been concerned with the deviance of their youth for centuries. As Wiley Sanders indicates, youthful offending has been a concern of societies for at least a thousand years (1970). Despite this age-old concern of adults for misbehaving youth, separate courts and institutions for correcting juvenile offenders did not appear until the 19th century. Until that time, juveniles were often handled the same as adults.

However, the development of separate institutional procedures for youth compared to those for adults did not happen suddenly, but took decades to appear. In addition, public acceptance of these changes was not always consistent, and many youthful offenders were still being treated as adults. As Sanders's research indicates, for example, youthful offenders in England and America were executed for crimes as late as the 17th and 18th centuries. In 17th-century England, for example, children as young as eight could be executed (by hanging) for committing acts of homicide. In addition, young children could be executed for "pettie treason," which included an indentured child's killing a master or mistress or a child's killing his or her parent. Convicted offenders of this offense were to be executed according to their gender; men were to be drawn and hanged, while women were to be burned alive. Also in England, in 1716, a woman and her 11-year-old daughter were both executed for witchcraft (Sanders 1970:10–13, 37–38). Throughout the 17th, 18th, and 19th centuries in England, children, especially poor children, as young as eight years old were burned on the hand, whipped, put on ships at sea (sometimes warships), or eventually trans-ported to prison colonies in Australia for crimes of theft or assault (Sanders 1970:21–70).

In addition, in 17th-century New England colonies, which based their laws on interpretations of the Old Testament, youth ages 16 or older could be executed for hitting or cursing their mother or father unless they were suffering abuse from their parents. Interestingly, these same laws permitted the execution of a rebellious or stubborn *son*, age 16 years or older, but not a stubborn daughter. In 1786, a 12-year-old Pequot Indian girl, Hannah Ocuish, was executed in Connecticut for killing a six-year-old white girl (Sanders 1970:317–323).

Toward the end of the 18th century and the beginning of the 19th century, the conceptualization of juveniles began to change, and societal reaction to juvenile offenders started to focus on specific needs and interests of *juveniles.* While juveniles were still being subjected to harsh penalties, including the death penalty, for their crimes, increasingly they were being handled with different penalties and treatment strategies than those given to adults. Institutions housing juveniles or youthful offenders were constructed in the early to mid-1800s. Later, special court proceedings were established for juvenile cases. Ultimately, by the end of the 19th century, separate laws involving the handling of juvenile offenders were passed, and these laws became known as delinquency laws. By the first third of the 20th century, most states had passed delinquency legislation. A common feature of these new laws was the inclusion of a term called the "status offense," or an act of illegality that applies only to juveniles. These status offense laws permitted police to arrest juveniles for wide-ranging acts, almost all of which were not criminal, and for judges to confine youth for these behaviors.

As with any significant social change, the new legislation and court system developed to implement these new laws were not always well received. Several court cases challenged the rights of police and court officials to take children out of their homes and place them in institutions without parental permission. For the most part, the outcomes of these court cases were favorable to the new system of handling youthful offenders. However, the specialized treatment of juvenile offenders was not always accepted as the best reaction to juvenile crime. Some felt that youthful offenders should be treated as adults, not "coddled" as special people.

For the first several decades of the 20th century, the concept of a juvenile court and juvenile justice in general seemed to receive wide acceptance.

At the least, critics and doubters might have been taking a "wait-and-see" attitude toward this innovative idea. However, around the middle of the century, especially in the 1960s, criticisms began to emerge again. However, at this time, the criticisms of the juvenile justice system often ended in court cases. In particular, issues concerning the constitutional rights of juveniles began to occupy the attention of appellate courts, including the U.S. Supreme Court.

Although juveniles have been granted several constitutional rights, the right to a trial by jury has not been afforded. States may allow hearings in juvenile court to include juvenile jurors, but such juries are not mandated. Since the 1970s, however, the use of youth courts or youth panels has steadily increased. By 2006, youth courts had appeared in nearly every state. Usually youth courts are supervised by judges or prosecutors, and they are often used in cases involving less serious offenses, such as status offenses or minor criminal offenses.

The trend to use alternative structures, such as youth courts, for hearing cases involving status offenses is consistent with a larger movement to remove status offenders from the juvenile justice system through legislation. Since 1974, with the passage of the Juvenile Justice and Delinquency Prevention Act, states have developed legislation to either remove status offenses from delinquency codes altogether or to specify when status offending becomes a matter of concern for the courts, such as when the behavior is repeated or becomes habitual.

Since the 1960s, it seems there have developed two kinds of juvenile court approaches, although both may exist in the same court. One approach retains many of the features and philosophies of the original, traditional kinds of juvenile courts. This approach to juvenile justice is based on the idea that treatment and prevention, particularly early intervention, are the best ways to curb delinquency. The other approach to juvenile justice is based on providing more legal protection to juvenile defendants. This type of approach is more similar to the adult criminal justice system (Shoemaker 1988). This legalistic approach to juvenile justice does not always translate into more punitive responses to delinquency, but it provides the basis for such responses because juvenile defendants are offered more legal rights, especially the right to legal representation. Offering legal rights and protections can lead to an adversarial and confrontational atmosphere in the court and throughout the entire system, which then undermines the "kindly parent" approach of the traditional juvenile justice system.

At the same time that status offenders are being legislated out of the juvenile justice system and youth courts are developing to take over the tasks of deciding dispositions for these offenses, other legislation is allowing for the transfer of juvenile cases to adult court jurisdiction. These kinds of transfers are typically restricted to serious offenses, such as murder, rape, and robbery, and they usually focus on adolescents age 14 or older. While traditionally, the decision to transfer a case from juvenile to adult court rested with the juvenile court judge, today such decisions are also made by prosecutors or by legislative direction. Sometimes such cases are "split" or "blended," in that a case is decided in adult court but the punishment involves confinement in a juvenile correctional institution or supervision by those in the juvenile justice system (Snyder and Sickmund 2006:115–116).

During the early to middle part of the 19th century, social reformers believed the significant causes of delinquency were to be found in social factors, particularly the negative influences of weak families and bad parenting, plus the crime-inducing effects of urban life. By the end of that century, the influence of biological and psychological views of human behavior had become more powerful. The notion that delinquency was something of a "disease," the causes of which needed to be addressed early in a child's life, became associated with the establishment of the first juvenile courts as well as other parts of the juvenile justice system. Later, social scientists turned to sociological explanations of delinquency, but the dominant perspective of the juvenile justice system remained focused on individual explanations of delinquent behavior and corresponding methods of treating or rehabilitating delinquents. Today, the examination of the contributions to delinquency incorporate explanations from several disciplines, including biology, psychology, and sociology.

Historically, the emphasis of treatment or rehabilitation versus punishment for juvenile offenders has been cyclical (Bernard 1992). While historically, societies have gradually changed from a punitive to a more treatment-oriented approach to the handling of delinquency, within societies there are cyclical shifts in terms of the emphasis placed on one approach or the other, or on some combination of the two approaches. Transferring cases from juvenile court to the adult criminal justice system is one example of an approach that seems to favor punishment over treatment for juvenile offenders. While transfers of cases are still a big part of current discussions regarding juvenile justice, historically, the popularity of transferring peaked in the mid-1990s.

Whither Juvenile Justice?

Although juvenile institutions were established in the early to mid-19th century, the beginnings of the juvenile justice *system* occurred in 1899, when the first juvenile delinquency law and corresponding juvenile court were established in Chicago. During the first several decades of the 20th century, there were few critics of this new system and few court challenges to its existence and scope. However, since the 1960s, there have been several court cases concerned with the operations of juvenile courts and juvenile institutions as well as other institutions that deal primarily with youth, such as schools. In addition to the operation of institutions and other components of the juvenile justice system, court cases have addressed the *rights* of juveniles in the system as well as in society in general. These cases have significantly altered the manner in which juvenile courts have operated and made them more legalistic, similar to the operation of the adult criminal justice system. The use of transfers, or waivers, continues, and blended sentences, that is, combining dispositions to include both juvenile and adult correctional placements and services, have become increasingly popular in the juvenile justice system in the United States. All of these innovations in the juvenile justice system and continued court monitoring of juvenile justice practices suggest that societies are coming closer to managing juvenile offending. Some argue that the problem of delinquency will never be "solved," but that some day it will simply "end" (Bernard 1992:188). It is not clear exactly what is meant by this conclusion, but the notion that the current system of juvenile justice is not going to eradicate delinquency is likely a correct observation. Others go as far as to suggest that the juvenile *court*, though not necessarily the juvenile justice system, should be abolished, especially for young "criminal" offenders (Feld 1999:chapter 8). As mentioned earlier, this suggestion has become a part of the current juvenile justice policy, especially with respect to waivers and blended sentences. In addition, and also as mentioned earlier, the presence of youth courts signals the dissatisfaction of the public with the ability of the juvenile court to deal with less serious cases of juvenile offending. However, the 100-year history of the juvenile court and the longer existence of juvenile correctional institutions suggest that neither is going to be eliminated any time in the near future, if ever (Kupchik 2006:161–164; Mears et al. 2007:245).

The current understanding of delinquent behavior and the corresponding attempts of the entire juvenile justice system, public as well as private, to correct, treat, or otherwise handle delinquency have clearly evolved over the past 200–300 years to become more systematic and evidence and performance based. However, as many observers of the juvenile justice system have noted (Bernard 1992; Feld 1999; Mears et al. 2007:249–250), there are too many gaps between knowledge and practice for us to be assured that the policies employed within the system are the products of careful study and reasoning. However, while societies will likely always have juvenile offenders, efforts to understand youthful offending are becoming increasingly clearer, and corresponding efforts to manage delinquency are becoming increasingly more rational and productive.

References

Bernard, Thomas J.
    1992   The Cycle of Juvenile Justice. New York: Oxford University Press.
Feld, Barry C.
    1999   Bad Kids: Race and the Transformation of the Juvenile Court. New York: Oxford University Press.
Kupchik, Aaron
    2006   Judging Juveniles: Prosecuting Adolescents in Adult and Juvenile Courts. New York: New York University Press.
Mears, Daniel P., Carter Hay, Marc Gertz, and Christina Mancini
    2007   Public Opinion and the Foundation of the Juvenile Court. Criminology 45:223–257.
Sanders, Wiley B., ed.
    1970   Juvenile Offenders for a Thousand Years: Selected Readings from Anglo-Saxon Times to 1900. Chapel Hill: University of North Carolina Press.
Shoemaker, Donald J.
    1988   The Duality of Juvenile Justice in the United States: History, Trends, and Prospects. Sociological Spectrum 8:1–17.
Snyder, Howard N., and Melissa Sickmund
    2006   Juvenile Offenders and Victims: 2006 National Report. Washington, DC: U.S. Department of Justice, Office of Justice Programs, Office of Juvenile Justice and Delinquency Prevention.

Index

abuse: in adult prisons, 324; in correctional institutions, 385, 393, 395–96; emotional, 149, 151, 203; female delinquents and, 271–72, 278, 283, 284; physical, 149, 151–52, 203; sexual, 149, 151, 203, 239–41, 251. *See also* child abuse

academic performance, 100–101, 162–64, *165*, 166, 168–69, 183–84

accountability, 316, 359, 361

achieved *v.* ascribed statuses, 201

"An Act for the Treatment and Control of Dependent, Neglected and Delinquent Children," 6–7, 24

ADD. *See* attention deficit disorder

Addams, Jane, 21

ADD Health Study, 55

addiction, drugs and, 65, 192, 206

adjudicatory hearing, 314, 317, 339–40

Adler, Freda, 277–78, 282

adolescence, 13

adolescence-limited (AL) offenders, 98–99, 104, 106

adoptions, 72

adult(s): arrest data for juveniles *v.,* 33; children treated as, 2, 5–6, 11–12, 63, 66, 419–20; judges, 360–61; prisons,

abuse in, 324; youth courts and, 360–61

adult criminal justice system: suspended sentence in, 326; waiver or transfer to, 1, 3–4, 39, 295, 314–15, 320–26, 328–29, 336, 359, 422–23

adulthood, 3

African Americans: arrests of, 35, 43, 346–47; in correctional institutions, 376, *378–79*; decision making and, 346–47, 350–51; drugs and, 200, 211; families, 140, 143; female delinquents, 270; gangs, 231, 232, 234, 237; GTC and, 100–101; hate crimes and, 57; houses of refuge and, 14; in juvenile justice system, 41, 319; preschool program for, 178–81; probation and, 26; profiling of, 345; religion and, 129; victimization of, 56, 170

after care, 315–16, 342

age: arrests and, 33–34, 36, *37,* 38, 59; cohort studies and, 53–54; correctional institutions and, 368, 371, 372; crime decline with, 101; drugs and, 199–200; gangs and, 222, 224, 229, 230, 232, 234, 235; juvenile justice

Voss, Harwin L., 168
VQ. *See* Vision Quest

wagon-train trek, 373
waiver or transfer, to adult court system,
    1, 3–4, 39, 295, 314–15, 320–26,
    328–29, 336, 359, 422–23; age and,
    4, 321; consequences of, 324–25,
    326; laws regarding, 321–24; race
    and, 322–23, 329. *See also* blended
    sentences
wannabes, 231, 250
Warr, Mark, 115
Watson, John B., 389
Wells, L. Edward, 142
Westheimer, Irvin, 404
Whren v. United States, 344
Whyte, William Foote, 225–26, 245
wilderness programs, 372–73, 379, 381,
    407
Wilkinson, Karen, 141
Williams, Linda, 383–84
Wilson, James, 348

Wilson, Mary Ellen, 150
witchcraft, 419
Women and Crime (Simon), 282–83
women's movement, 277, 279–80, 282,
    284
Wooden, Wayne S., 249
work: females and, 277–82; schools and,
    166–67, 168, 178, 180; turning points
    and, 102–3, 106
World War I, 80, 274
World War II, 80, 226, 260, 334, 344
Wright, Kevin N. and Karen E., 154–55

Yablonsky, Lewis, 226–28, 246, 247,
    250
youth courts, 359–61, 362–63, 400
youth service bureaus (YSBs), 327, 358,
    359
youth tribunal, 361
YSBs. *See* youth service bureaus

zero tolerance, for bullying, 176
Zingraff, Matthew T., 154

ABOUT THE AUTHOR

DONALD J. SHOEMAKER is professor of sociology at Virginia Polytechnic Institute and Stage University. He received the PhD in sociology from the University of Georgia in 1970. His research interests include national and international topics. Most of his international work has been conducted in the Philippines, but current interests include other countries, such as Turkey. Recent publications in the field of crime and delinquency include an article in *Youth and Society* on self-report delinquency, gender, and social class in Metro Manila, Philippines, coauthored with Filomin Gutierrez. In addition, he is working on a sixth edition of *Theories of Delinquency: An Examination of Explanations of Delinquent Behavior.*